ATTITUDE EQUALS ALTITUDE

MASTERING THE ART OF GOAL SETTING, VISUALIZATION AND SELF-EMPOWERMENT

RAE A. STONEHOUSE

LIVE FOR EXCELLENCE PRODUCTIONS

INTRODUCTION: THE ALTITUDE OF YOUR ATTITUDE

WELCOME to a transformative journey that will empower you to soar to new heights of personal growth and achievement. As you start this path of self-discovery and empowerment, the key to unlocking your full potential lies within your attitude. Your mindset, the lens through which you perceive and interact with the world, has the power to shape your reality and determine the altitude of your success.

In the pages that follow, we will dive deep into the art of goal setting, visualization, and self-empowerment, exploring how these powerful tools can help you cultivate a positive, growth-oriented attitude and overcome the negative beliefs and self-imposed limitations holding you back. By mastering these techniques and integrating them into your daily life, you'll learn to harness the power of your mind to create the life you desire.

Throughout this book, you'll discover practical strategies and proven methods for setting clear, compelling goals that align with your values and passions. You'll learn how to break these goals down into manageable steps and create personalized action plans that keep you motivated and on track. You'll also explore the transformative power of visualization, using mental imagery and positive affirmations to reprogram your subconscious mind for success and build unshakable self-confidence.

But this journey is about more than just meeting your goals. It's about developing a deep sense of self-awareness, self-acceptance, and self-love. By learning to embrace your unique strengths, talents, and experiences, you'll cultivate an unwavering belief in yourself and your ability to overcome any challenge that comes your way. You'll discover how to reframe setbacks and failures as opportunities for growth and learning, and how to use your experiences to fuel your determination and resilience.

As you progress through these pages, you'll also learn the importance of surrounding yourself with positive influences and building a strong support system. Whether it's through connecting with like-minded individuals, seeking guidance from mentors and coaches, or immersing yourself in uplifting books and resources, you'll discover the power of community in helping you stay motivated, accountable, and inspired on your journey of personal growth.

But perhaps most importantly, this book will challenge you to embrace the discomfort and uncertainty that comes with stepping outside your comfort zone. It's only by pushing yourself beyond your perceived limitations and taking bold, courageous action that you can unlock your full potential and achieve the extraordinary. By learning to view discomfort as a sign of growth and progress, you'll develop the mental toughness and resilience needed to overcome any obstacle and reach new heights of success and fulfillment.

In "Attitude Equals Altitude: Mastering the Art of Goal Setting, Visualization and Self-Empowerment," I'll be sharing strategies for elevating your mindset and helping you achieve meaningful goals. This book invites you to focus on what matters, find balance, and live a life aligned with your true self. It's about embracing the journey, not just the destination, and discovering joy along the way.

We'll explore these topics in depth, sometimes revisiting them to gain new perspectives. My advice? Read through the entire book once, then come back to specific chapters when you need some extra guidance or a fresh outlook.

Note: I have provided case studies throughout this book. Unless they are stated as being true, they are based on fictional stories for illustrative and inspirational purposes.

So, as you start this transformative journey, remember that your *attitude* is the key to your *altitude*. By cultivating a mindset of positivity, possibility, and unwavering self-belief, you'll unlock the power to create a life of passion, purpose, and boundless potential. Get ready to soar to new heights of personal and professional achievement and discover the incredible power of your own limitless potential.

Let's begin.

Rae A. Stonehouse

Author

May 2024

COPYRIGHT

PART ONE
THE POWER OF ATTITUDE: UNVEILING THE LENS THROUGH WHICH WE PERCEIVE AND NAVIGATE LIFE

INTRODUCTION: THE ESSENCE AND SIGNIFICANCE OF ATTITUDE

IN THE GRAND tapestry of human experience, attitude emerges as a fundamental thread, weaving together the complexities of our thoughts, emotions, and behaviors. It is the lens through which we perceive the world, coloring our interactions, shaping our decisions, and ultimately defining the trajectory of our lives. Attitude, in essence, is the intangible yet potent force that permeates every aspect of our being, acting as a compass that guides us through the ever-changing landscape of existence.

At its core, attitude encompasses the intricate interplay of our beliefs, values, judgments, and feelings. It is the subjective filter through which we process and interpret the myriad stimuli that bombard our senses, assigning meaning and significance to the people, objects, and ideas that populate our reality. Like a pair of tinted glasses, our attitude casts a unique hue upon the world, influencing how we perceive and respond to the challenges and opportunities that life presents.

The power of attitude lies in its pervasive influence on the fabric of our being. It is the unseen hand that molds our thoughts, sculpting the contours of our mental landscape. When we adopt a positive attitude toward a particular part of life, such as health and well-being, our minds naturally gravitate toward information and experiences that align with this perspective. We become attuned to the nuances of nutrition, the benefits of physical activity, and the wisdom of self-care, as our attitude acts as a beacon, illuminating the path toward a healthier and more vibrant existence.

Attitude is intimately intertwined with our emotional state, acting as a catalyst that shapes the quality and intensity of our feelings. When we approach the world with an attitude of compassion and empathy, we open ourselves up to the profound joy and fulfillment that comes from nurturing deep connections with others. An attitude of love and appreciation for animals, for example, can transform a simple encounter with a furry companion into a moment of pure bliss, filling our hearts with warmth and igniting a desire to protect and cherish these precious creatures.

Beyond the realm of thoughts and emotions, attitude exerts a powerful influence on our actions, guiding the choices we make and the paths we pursue. When our attitude is aligned with a cause or purpose that resonates deeply within us, such as environmental conservation, we are compelled to act in ways that reflect this commitment. We may naturally gravitate toward eco-friendly practices, such as recycling, reducing waste, and advocating for sustainable living, as our attitude becomes a driving force that propels us toward meaningful change.

Perhaps most remarkably, attitude has an infectious quality, capable of spreading its influence to those around us. When we embody an attitude of collaboration and teamwork, our positive energy has the power to transform the dynamics of a group, fostering a sense of unity and shared purpose. As our attitude radiates outward, it touches the lives of others, inspiring them to adopt a similar mindset and creating a ripple effect of positivity that extends far beyond our immediate circle.

Attitude is the invisible architect of our lives, shaping the contours of our reality and guiding us through the complexities of the human experience. It is the prism through which we refract the light of the world, casting a unique spectrum of colors upon our thoughts, emotions, and actions. By cultivating an awareness of our attitudes and nurturing those that align with our highest aspirations, we harness the power to transform not only our own lives but also the lives of those around us.

As we start this exploration of the power of attitude, let us approach the journey with open minds and hearts, ready to uncover the profound impact that our attitudes have upon the canvas of our existence. By understanding the essence and significance of attitude, we arm ourselves with the knowledge and tools necessary to navigate the intricacies of life with greater clarity, purpose, and joy. So let us embrace the transformative potential of attitude, and in doing so, unlock the boundless possibilities that await us on the horizon of personal growth and self-discovery.

~

THE RIPPLE EFFECT OF ATTITUDE IN LIFE AND WORK - HOW ATTITUDE SHAPES OUR WORLD

In the grand scheme of human existence, attitude emerges as a powerful force that permeates every aspect of our lives, from the most mundane interactions to the loftiest aspirations. It is the unseen thread that weaves through the fabric of our daily experiences, coloring our perceptions, shaping our relationships, and ultimately defining the trajectory of our personal and professional journeys. Attitude is not merely a superficial veneer that we present to the world; rather, it is the lens through which we interpret and navigate the complexities of life.

The impact of attitude extends far beyond the limits of our own minds, creating a ripple effect that touches the lives of those around us. In relationships, a positive attitude acts as a beacon of light, drawing others into its warm embrace. When we approach interactions with a smile and an open heart, we radiate an energy that is both inviting and infectious. Our optimism and kindness become a magnet for like-minded individuals, fostering deep connections and nurturing a sense of belonging. But a persistent negative outlook can cast a shadow over our interactions, erecting invisible barriers that hinder the formation of meaningful bonds.

In the professional arena, attitude plays a pivotal role in shaping the trajectory of our careers. A can-do spirit, fueled by positivity and resilience, becomes a catalyst for success, propelling us toward our goals with unwavering determination. When we approach challenges with optimism and a growth mindset, we unlock our full potential, inspiring those around us to rise to the occasion. Employers and colleagues are naturally drawn to individuals who exude confidence and enthusiasm, recognizing the value of a positive attitude in fostering innovation, collaboration, and a thriving work environment. This infectious positivity extends beyond the limits of the workplace, leaving an indelible mark on clients and customers, opening doors to new opportunities and fostering long-lasting partnerships.

The power of attitude is perhaps clearest in the pursuit of our dreams and aspirations. When we cultivate an inner cheerleader, armed with self-belief and unwavering optimism, we transform even the most daunting goals into achievable milestones. It is the fire within us, fueled by a positive outlook, that propels us forward, even in the face of adversity. Resilience becomes our ally, enabling us to weather the storms of setbacks and disappointments, while maintaining a steadfast commitment to our vision. But when doubt and negativity take hold, they act as invisible weights, dragging us down and hindering our progress. By nurturing a positive attitude, we unlock the full potential of our abilities, empowering ourselves to overcome obstacles and achieve the extraordinary.

Beyond the realms of relationships and professional success, attitude plays an important role in our overall well-being and happiness. The power of positive thinking extends far beyond mere platitudes; it has real effects on our mental and physical health. When we embrace joy, gratitude, and optimism, we create an internal environment conducive to healing and growth. A sunny disposition acts as a buffer against the stresses and challenges of daily life, fortifying our resilience and enabling us to maintain a sense of equilibrium.

Research has shown that a positive attitude can have profound physio-logical benefits, from boosting our immune system to promoting cardiovascular health. By cultivating a mindset of positivity, we not only enhance our own well-being but also contribute to the collective happiness of those around us.

Attitude is the cornerstone on which we build the edifice of our lives. It is the invisible hand that shapes our experiences, molds our relationships, and guides us toward personal and professional fulfillment. By recognizing the transformative power of attitude and nurturing a positive outlook, we become the architects of our own destiny. We harness the ability to create ripples of positivity that extend far beyond our immediate sphere, touching the lives of others and contributing to a more compassionate and harmonious world.

As we navigate the complexities of life and work, let us remember that our attitude is a choice – a powerful tool we can wield to shape our reality. By embracing optimism, resilience, and kindness, we not only enhance our own journey but also become a force for good in the lives of those around us. So let us approach each day with a heart full of positivity, knowing that our attitude has the power to transform not only our own existence but also the tapestry of the world we inhabit.

EXPLORING THE ORIGINS OF OUR ATTITUDES: A JOURNEY THROUGH UPBRINGING, EXPERIENCES, AND BELIEFS

Attitudes are not merely random or superficial; they are deeply rooted in the complex tapestry of our lives, shaped by a confluence of factors that include our background, life experiences, and personal values. By digging into the origins of our attitudes, we can gain a profound understanding of how these influential forces mold our perceptions and guide our interactions with the world.

The Role of Upbringing:

Our early years serve as the bedrock on which our attitudes are built. Just as the strength and stability of a building depend on its foundation, our childhood experiences lay the groundwork for the development of our attitudes. The family environment and the influence of our primary caregivers play an important role in shaping our worldview, imparting values, beliefs, and cultural norms that become deeply ingrained within us. A nurturing and supportive upbringing can foster open-mindedness, empathy, and acceptance, while exposure to negative or prejudiced attitudes may lead to the internalization of biases and limiting beliefs.

Life's Experiences:

As we navigate through life, our experiences serve as brushstrokes that add depth and complexity to the canvas of our attitudes. Each encounter, whether positive or negative, contributes to the tapestry of our perceptions, shaping how we view and respond to the world around us. A traumatic experience, such as a dog bite, can instill a deep-seated fear or aversion toward dogs, coloring future interactions with apprehension. But exposure to diverse cultures and perspectives can broaden our horizons, cultivating a spirit of acceptance, empathy, and understanding. These experiences, both big and small, continuously mold and refine our attitudes, adding nuance and depth to our worldview.

Beliefs and Values:

At the core of our attitudes lie our fundamental beliefs and values, which serve as the guiding principles that shape our perceptions and actions. These beliefs may be rooted in religious or spiritual convictions, political ideologies, or personal philosophies that define our sense of right and wrong, justice and injustice, and the nature of our place in the world. An individual who holds a deep commitment to fairness and equality may naturally gravitate toward supporting social justice causes, as their attitudes are informed by a strong belief in the inherent worth and dignity of all humans. Similarly, religious or spiritual beliefs can profoundly influence attitudes toward significant life issues, such as the sanctity of life, the nature of morality, and the purpose of existence.

The Fluidity of Attitudes:

While our attitudes are deeply influenced by our upbringing, experiences, and beliefs, they are not fixed or immutable. As we journey through life, we are presented with countless opportunities for growth, learning, and transformation. Exposure to new ideas, perspectives, and information can challenge our preconceived notions and invite us to reexamine our attitudes. Education, both formal and informal, plays an important role in broadening our understanding and fostering a more inclusive and open-minded outlook. By engaging with diverse viewpoints, seeking out new experiences, and cultivating a spirit of curiosity and self-reflection, we can consciously shape and evolve our attitudes, aligning them with our highest values and aspirations.

The Importance of Understanding:

Recognizing the complex interplay of factors that shape our attitudes is an important step toward fostering a more empathetic, compassionate, and inclusive society. By acknowledging the role of our upbringing, experiences, and beliefs in molding our perceptions, we can develop a deeper understanding of ourselves and others. This self-awareness empowers us to examine our biases, challenge our assumptions, and actively work toward cultivating attitudes that promote unity, respect, and understanding. It is through this process of introspection and growth we can contribute to building a world where diverse perspectives are valued, and where individuals are judged not by the color of their skin, their background, or their beliefs, but by the content of their character.

Our attitudes are not merely superficial or arbitrary; they are deeply rooted in the rich tapestry of our lives, shaped by the complex interplay of our upbringing, experiences, and core beliefs. By exploring the origins of our attitudes, we gain a profound understanding of the forces that mold our perceptions and guide our interactions with the world. Through self-reflection, education, and a willingness to embrace new perspectives, we can consciously shape our attitudes, aligning them with our highest values and aspirations. It is through this process of growth and understanding we can work toward fostering a more inclusive, compassionate, and united society, where every individual is valued for their unique contributions and perspective.

~

NAVIGATING LIFE'S STORMS: THE TRANSFORMATIVE POWER OF A POSITIVE MINDSET

Life's journey is rarely a smooth, uninterrupted path; it is often punctuated by unexpected obstacles, setbacks, and challenges that can test our mettle and shake our resolve. Whether we grapple with professional disappointments, health concerns, financial strain, or the profound grief of personal loss, these trials can leave us feeling depleted and disoriented. However, during these moments of adversity, the true strength of our attitude reveals itself, serving as a beacon of hope and resilience in the face of life's storms.

Embracing a positive outlook during trying times is not an act of naiveté or denial; rather, it is a conscious choice to approach challenges with a spirit of resilience, adaptability, and determination. This mindset empowers us to perceive obstacles not as insurmountable barriers, but as opportunities for growth, learning, and transformation. By focusing on the potential for positive change, even in the darkest of circumstances, we unlock our capacity to find meaning, purpose, and even unexpected blessings in hardship.

Spotting Opportunities in Challenges:

When confronted with a seemingly devastating setback, such as losing a job, it is tempting to succumb to feelings of despair and helplessness.

However, by shifting our perspective and embracing a positive attitude, we can reframe this challenge as a catalyst for personal and professional growth. Maybe this unexpected detour is the impetus needed to pursue a long-held passion, acquire new skills, or start an entirely new career path. By viewing setbacks as steppingstones rather than dead ends, we open ourselves up to a world of possibilities and opportunities for reinvention.

Creative Problem-Solving:

A positive attitude is not merely a superficial veneer of optimism; it is a powerful tool for igniting our creativity and resourcefulness in the face of adversity. When confronted with a complex problem, a positive mindset encourages us to approach the situation with curiosity, open-mindedness, and a willingness to explore unconventional solutions. Rather than succumbing to frustration or resignation, we are inspired to think laterally, challenge assumptions, and seek innovative approaches that may have seemed impossible. By cultivating a positive outlook, we tap into our innate problem-solving abilities, enabling us to navigate even the most challenging circumstances with ingenuity and grace.

The Ripple Effect:

The impact of our attitude extends far beyond our personal experiences; it has the power to shape the emotional landscape of those around us. Positivity is infectious, radiating outward and touching the lives of others in profound ways. When we approach challenges with optimism and resilience, we become a source of inspiration and motivation for our loved ones, colleagues, and communities. Our positive energy creates a ripple effect, fostering a supportive and empowering environment that encourages collective problem-solving, collaboration, and mutual upliftment. By embodying a positive attitude, we not only enhance our own capacity to overcome adversity but also contribute to the resilience and well-being of those around us.

Cultivating Positivity: A Practice, Not Just a Trait:

Maintaining a positive outlook in the face of life's challenges is not always an effortless endeavor; it requires conscious effort, self-reflection, and a willingness to persevere in the face of adversity. Cultivating positivity is a practice, a daily commitment to choosing hope over despair, resilience over resignation, and growth over stagnation. Through consistent effort and mindful attention, we can strengthen our capacity to maintain a positive mindset, even in the most trying of circumstances. As we integrate this practice into the fabric of our lives, it becomes a fundamental part of our identity, a reservoir of strength and resilience we can draw on whenever life's storms threaten to overwhelm us.

Our attitude is the thread that connects the various experiences, challenges, and triumphs in our lives. It is the compass that guides us through the tempests of uncertainty, the alchemist that transforms obstacles into opportunities, and the catalyst that inspires others to rise above their own challenges. By cultivating a positive mindset, we not only enhance our own resilience and well-being but also contribute to the collective strength and unity of those around us.

As we navigate the inevitable ups and downs of life's journey, let us embrace the transformative power of a positive attitude. Let us approach each challenge with a spirit of resilience, creativity, and unwavering belief in our ability to overcome and thrive. For in the crucible of adversity, we forge the strength of our character, discover the depths of our potential, and emerge as more compassionate, resourceful, and inspiring individuals, ready to weather any storm that life may bring.

~

SELF-EFFICACY: UNLEASHING THE POWER OF BELIEVING IN YOURSELF

THE ESSENCE OF SELF-EFFICACY:

Faced with life's challenges and setbacks, some individuals seem to have an innate ability to rebound, emerging stronger and more resilient than ever before. At the heart of this remarkable capacity lies self-efficacy, a concept pioneered by renowned psychologist Albert Bandura. Self-efficacy refers to an individual's unwavering belief in their ability to succeed in specific situations or accomplish tasks, despite the obstacles they may encounter. It is the internal driving force that fuels self-confidence, resilience, and the determination to persevere in the pursuit of one's goals.

The Role of Attitude:

Attitude serves as the lens through which we perceive and interpret the world around us, including our own capabilities and potential. It is a complex interplay of beliefs, values, and emotions that shape our approach to life and the challenges we face. A positive attitude ignites a sense of optimism and a "can-do" spirit, bolstering our belief in our ability to overcome obstacles and achieve our aspirations. But a negative attitude can cast a shadow of self-doubt, eroding our confidence and hindering our ability to bounce back from setbacks.

Nurturing Confidence and Resilience:

The power of a positive attitude extends far beyond mere feelings of positivity; it has a profound impact on our self-efficacy, confidence, and resilience. When we approach challenges with a positive outlook, we are more likely to perceive them as opportunities for growth and learning, rather than insurmountable obstacles. This mindset fosters a deep-seated belief in our abilities, providing the motivation and determination to persevere in the face of adversity. By embracing a positive attitude, we cultivate a reservoir of inner strength that enables us to navigate life's challenges with grace and resilience.

On the other hand, succumbing to the pitfalls of negativity can harm our self-efficacy and overall well-being. When we constantly doubt our abilities or expect failure, we risk creating a self-fulfilling prophecy. This negative mindset can lead us to shy away from challenges, abandon our goals at the first sign of difficulty, or fail to recognize and capitalize on opportunities for growth. By letting negativity take hold, we limit our potential and hinder the development of the resilience necessary to overcome life's obstacles.

Cultivating a Positive Mindset:

While shifting from a negative to a positive attitude may not happen overnight, it is a transformative journey well within reach. The first step in this process is to engage in self-reflection and acknowledge our strengths, accomplishments, and the progress we have made. By focusing on our successes and the obstacles we have overcome, we begin to shift our perspective from one of self-doubt to one of self-assurance. Celebrating our achievements, no matter how small, rein-forces our belief in our abilities and lays the foundation for continued growth and success.

Surrounding ourselves with a supportive network of individuals who believe in us and uplift us can also play a pivotal role in fostering a positive attitude. The encouragement and affirmation we receive from others can serve as a powerful source of motivation, especially during challenging times. By seeking and nurturing relationships with those who inspire and empower us, we create a positive feedback loop that reinforces our self-efficacy and resilience.

Setting and achieving realistic goals is another effective strategy for boosting self-efficacy and cultivating a positive attitude. By breaking down larger aspirations into smaller, manageable steps, we create a roadmap for success that lets us build momentum and confidence along the way. Each goal achieved, no matter how modest, serves as a building block, reinforcing our belief in our abilities and propelling us forward toward even greater accomplishments.

Chapter Summary

Self-efficacy is not merely a psychological construct; it is a powerful testament to the transformative potential of believing in oneself. Our attitude plays an important role in shaping this belief, influencing our ability to face challenges head-on, persevere in the face of adversity, and ultimately meet our goals. By cultivating a positive outlook, acknowledging our strengths and achievements, seeking the support of others, and setting realistic goals, we can enhance our self-efficacy, boost our confidence, and develop the resilience necessary to navigate life's ups and downs.

Ultimately, the power to believe in ourselves lies within each of us. By harnessing the force of a positive attitude and nurturing our self-efficacy, we unlock our full potential and empower ourselves to tackle any challenge that comes our way. Remember, the journey toward self-belief is an ongoing process, but each step we take brings us closer to realizing our dreams and living a life of purpose, fulfillment, and resilience.

∽

THE CATALYST FOR SUCCESS: HARNESSING THE POWER OF A POSITIVE ATTITUDE

UNLEASHING POTENTIAL AND SEIZING OPPORTUNITIES:

The impact of attitude on succeeding cannot be overstated; it serves as both a key that unlocks hidden potential and a lens through which we perceive and interact with the world. While skills and experience are undoubtedly important, it is often a positive mindset that distinguishes those who seize opportunities and realize their dreams from those who remain trapped in a cycle of missed chances and unfulfilled aspirations. Embracing a positive attitude is not merely advantageous; it is a fundamental prerequisite for success in all parts of life.

A positive mindset is a catalyst for resilience and adaptability, two essential qualities for navigating the complex tapestry of life's challenges and opportunities. When faced with obstacles or setbacks, a "can-do" spirit enables individuals to approach these challenges as manageable hurdles rather than insurmountable barriers. By viewing failures and disappointments as valuable learning experiences, those with a positive attitude can extract wisdom and growth from even the most difficult circumstances. This approach not only helps with personal growth and development but also positions individuals as attractive collaborators and team members, opening doors to new opportunities and networks of support that might otherwise remain inaccessible.

A positive attitude acts as a powerful magnet, attracting opportunities and possibilities that may be invisible to those mired in negativity. By maintaining an optimistic outlook, individuals are more likely to identify potential avenues for growth and success, even in situations that others might dismiss as dead ends. This mindset encourages individuals to step outside their comfort zones, embracing calculated risks and pursuing innovative solutions, secure in the belief that bold actions can yield significant rewards. By cultivating a positive attitude, individuals increase their chances of being in the right place at the right time, poised to seize opportunities as they arise.

Beyond its impact on resilience and opportunity recognition, a positive attitude directly influences an individual's ability to perform and excel in their chosen pursuits. When approaching tasks and challenges with a firm belief in the possibility of success, individuals are more likely to exhibit heightened levels of commitment, motivation, and openness to learning from mistakes. This growth mindset is essential for overcoming obstacles, adapting strategies in the face of adversity, and persisting in the pursuit of goals, even when others might succumb to frustration or despair. The result is a virtuous cycle of enhanced productivity, increased resilience, and, ultimately, superior outcomes across personal and professional domains.

Cultivating a Positive Attitude:

Developing and maintaining a positive attitude is an active and ongoing process that requires conscious effort and self-reflection. It involves recognizing and celebrating one's strengths, extracting valuable lessons from setbacks and failures, and approaching challenges as opportunities for growth and self-discovery. By fostering an environment of optimism and positivity, individuals not only enhance their own prospects for success but also inspire and motivate those around them to strive for excellence and reach for their highest potential.

To cultivate a positive attitude, individuals must engage in practices that promote self-awareness, gratitude, and a focus on solutions rather than problems. This may involve regular self-reflection, setting and celebrating achievable goals, surrounding oneself with supportive and uplifting influences, and seeking out opportunities for personal and professional development. By consistently nurturing a positive mindset, individuals can transform their attitude into a powerful tool for navigating life's challenges and seizing opportunities for growth and success.

Chapter Summary

The connection between attitude and success is undeniable, with positivity serving as an important catalyst for unlocking potential, seizing opportunities, and achieving goals. A positive attitude opens doors to new possibilities, attracts opportunities by changing our perception of the world, and significantly enhances performance and resilience in the face of challenges. Adopting and cultivating a positive mindset is one of the most transformative steps an individual can take on their journey toward personal and professional fulfillment.

As you navigate the winding path of success, remember that your attitude is not merely a passive companion but an active guide, illuminating the way forward and revealing hidden reserves of strength and potential within yourself. By harnessing the power of a positive attitude, you equip yourself with tools to overcome obstacles, seize opportunities, and realize your most ambitious aspirations. Embrace positivity as your catalyst for success, and watch as the world opens up before you, revealing a landscape of limitless possibility and achievement.

∼

SOWING THE SEEDS OF POSITIVITY AND EMPOWERMENT

As the first rays of the sun gently caress the tranquil streets of a sleepy town, we find ourselves at the threshold of a transformative journey. This expedition is not merely a passive turning of pages but an invitation to start a profound personal metamorphosis. In the following chapters, we will unravel the essence of cultivating an attitude that not only perceives the glass as half full but also actively seeks to replenish it. Welcome to the path of nurturing a more positive and empowering outlook that will serve as your guiding light through the intricate tapestry of life's joys and challenges.

Picture yourself standing before a mirror, looking at a reflection that transcends mere physical appearance. The image staring back at you is a kaleidoscope of your experiences, aspirations, and the lingering shadows of past struggles. The perception of this reflection may vary— a visage etched with the scars of life's trials or a face illuminated by the radiant spark of hope and the promise of change. This book is your compass, guiding you on the journey from introspection to realization, from the depths of self-doubt to the heights of empowerment.

The Transformative Power of Gratitude:

Our first step on this path is the wholehearted embrace of gratitude. In life's relentless pursuits and perplexing quandaries, it is all too easy to overlook the small miracles that surround us. Yet, by acknowledging the beauty that lives in everyday moments, the strength we glean from our past battles, and the warmth of the connections we forge, we shift the foundation beneath our feet from one of instability to a bedrock of optimism and resilience.

Cultivating Mindfulness:

The frenetic pace of modern life often blurs the lines between reality and our reactions to it. Through the practice of mindfulness, we seek clarity amidst the chaos. This is not a call to empty our minds but an invitation to observe our thoughts and emotions as they are—transient guests in the inn of our consciousness. By cultivating this understanding, we empower ourselves to consciously choose our responses and weave a narrative of positivity and purpose.

Affirming Your Inherent Worth:

The words we whisper to ourselves have the power to erect castles or construct cages. Affirmations serve as our tools of creation, laying brick by brick the fortress of our self-esteem and the lens through which we view the world. With each positive declaration, we challenge the outdated narratives of doubt and replace them with tales of strength, resilience, and unwavering self-belief.

Fostering Resilience:

The journey through life is punctuated by both storms and sanctuaries. Resilience is our capacity to weather these tempests and emerge not merely unscathed but enriched by the experience. It teaches us that every setback is a lesson in disguise, each failure a cornerstone on which we build our next triumph. Cultivating resilience means transmuting adversities into advantages, shaping a life imbued with purpose and positivity.

As we draw this introduction to a close, take a moment to envision the vibrant energy of possibility that lies ahead. This book is a garden where the seeds of positivity and empowerment lie dormant, waiting to be nurtured into full bloom. Each chapter, each carefully crafted strategy, is a step toward not merely facing life but wholeheartedly embracing and shaping it with a positive and empowering attitude. The narrative of your existence is yours to author—let these pages serve as your guide, illuminating the path toward a story of growth, strength, and boundless potential.

Together, let us start this transformative journey, our eyes fixed on a horizon suffused with light and limitless possibilities. May the seeds we sow throughout these chapters take root in the fertile soil of your mind, blossoming into a life marked by positivity, resilience, and the unwavering belief in your own extraordinary potential. The time has come to step forward, to embrace the power within, and to rewrite the script of your life—a tale of transformation, empowerment, and the triumph of the indomitable human spirit.

Case Study:

Alice had always been a high achiever, excelling in her studies and landing a prestigious job at a top consulting firm right out of college. She approached her work with dedication and enthusiasm, pouring herself into every project. However, after several years, Alice felt burned out and unfulfilled. The long hours and high-pressure environment were taking a toll, and she began to question whether this was the right path for her.

One day, a colleague mentioned a motivational speaker they had seen at a conference who spoke about the power of attitude in shaping one's life and career. Intrigued, Alice looked up the speaker and came across their book on cultivating a positive and empowering mindset. As she dug into the pages, Alice felt a spark of recognition - the principles resonated deeply with her own experiences and struggles.

The book emphasized the main role that attitude plays in coloring our perceptions and guiding our choices. Alice reflected on how her own attitude had shifted over time, from the bright-eyed optimism of her early career to the jaded weariness she now felt. She realized that by focusing only on external markers of success, she had lost sight of her own values and aspirations.

Inspired by the strategies outlined in the book, Alice resolved to make a change. She started by practicing gratitude, taking time each day to appreciate the small joys and accomplishments in her life. This shift in perspective helped to reframe her challenges as opportunities for growth rather than insurmountable obstacles. Alice also began to pay closer attention to her self-talk, catching herself in moments of negativity and consciously replacing those thoughts with affirmations of her strengths and capabilities.

As she continued to implement these principles, Alice noticed a profound transformation in her outlook and energy levels. She approached her work with renewed enthusiasm, focusing not just on outcomes but on the inherent value of the process itself. Her positive attitude was infectious, inspiring her team members and catching the attention of the leadership.

When an opportunity arose to lead a new initiative within the company, Alice stepped forward with confidence, secure in her abilities and excited by the chance to make a meaningful impact. She brought a spirit of creativity and collaboration to the project, fostering an environment where every team member felt empowered to contribute their unique skills and perspectives.

The initiative was a resounding success, exceeding all expectations and garnering accolades from clients and colleagues. For Alice, however, the true reward was the personal growth she had undergone. By cultivating a positive and empowering attitude, she had not only achieved external success but also discovered a deep sense of purpose and fulfillment in her work.

Alice's story serves as a powerful reminder of the transformative potential that lies within each of us. By consciously choosing the lens through which we view ourselves and the world, we open up limitless possibilities for growth, resilience, and achievement. In harnessing the power of a positive attitude, we become the architects of our own lives, equipped to navigate challenges with grace and seize opportunities with confidence. Alice's journey is a testament to the truth that when we change our mindset, we change our reality, unleashing the full force of our potential to create a life of purpose, joy, and boundless success.

～

PART ONE WRAP-UP:

Key Points:

• Attitude is the lens through which we perceive and navigate life, shaping our thoughts, emotions, and behaviors.

• Our attitude influences our relationships, professional success, personal growth, and overall well-being.

• Attitude creates a ripple effect, affecting not only our own lives but also the lives of those around us.

• Our attitudes are deeply rooted in our upbringing, life experiences, and beliefs.

• Attitudes are not fixed; they can evolve through self-reflection, education, and embracing new perspectives.

• A positive attitude is a powerful tool for navigating life's challenges, fostering resilience, creativity, and problem-solving skills.

• Self-efficacy, the belief in one's ability to succeed, is closely tied to our attitude and plays an important role in meeting our goals.

• A positive attitude serves as a catalyst for success by unlocking potential, attracting opportunities, and enhancing performance and resilience.

Action Items:

• Engage in self-reflection to identify the origins of your attitudes and assess how they impact your life and relationships.

• Actively seek diverse perspectives and experiences to broaden your understanding and challenge limiting beliefs.

• Practice gratitude by acknowledging the positive aspects of your life and celebrating your accomplishments, no matter how small.

• Cultivate mindfulness by observing your thoughts and emotions without judgment, letting you consciously choose your responses.

• Use affirmations to replace negative self-talk with positive declarations that reinforce your self-worth and capabilities.

• Set achievable goals and break them down into manageable steps to build momentum and boost self-efficacy.

• Surround yourself with supportive individuals who uplift and inspire you, fostering a positive environment for growth.

• Embrace challenges as opportunities for learning and personal development, viewing setbacks as temporary and valuable lessons.

• Regularly assess your progress and adjust your strategies as needed, maintaining a flexible and adaptable mindset.

• Share your journey and insights with others, inspiring them to cultivate a positive attitude and harness their own potential for success.

In our next part...

... we'll dive into the transformative power of positivity and explore how nurturing a positive mindset can lead to profound personal growth and resilience. We'll uncover the secrets to cultivating posi-tivity in various parts of life, from the professional realm to personal relationships and inner development. Get ready to discover practical strategies and insights that will help you sow the seeds of optimism, joy, and unwavering belief in yourself and your abilities.

As we start this journey, you'll learn how to become the master gardener of your own mindset, tending to your thoughts, beliefs, and emotions with loving care and attention. We'll explore the art of setting goals with intention and grace, finding the hidden lessons in moments of adversity, and focusing on self-care as a powerful affirmation of your worth. By integrating these practices into your daily life, you'll unlock a world of boundless potential and discover the radiant essence of joy, love, and purpose that has always lived within you.

PART TWO
CULTIVATING THE GARDEN OF POSITIVITY: NURTURING PERSONAL GROWTH AND RESILIENCE

UNVEILING THE TRANSFORMATIVE POWER OF ATTITUDE

LIKE A VIBRANT THREAD, our attitude is interwoven into every part of our existence, forming an intricate tapestry of life. It is the silent architect of our perceptions, actions, and reactions, shaping the lens through which we view and interact with the world. This chapter serves as an invitation to peel back the layers and dig into the profound influence that attitude wields over our lives, guiding us toward a richer, more fulfilling journey of self-discovery and personal growth.

Cultivating Personal Evolution:

At the core of personal development lies the transformative power of attitude. It is the catalyst that fuels our insatiable quest for knowledge, self-improvement, and the relentless pursuit of our highest potential. When we consciously nurture a mindset rooted in growth and positivity, we not only unlock the doorway to endless possibilities but also arm ourselves with the resilience necessary to embrace change and adapt to life's inevitable challenges. This proactive approach to life fosters a continuous evolution of the self, enriching our personal and professional lives, and empowering us to become the best versions of ourselves.

Nurturing Richer Relationships:

The quality and depth of our relationships often serve as a reflection of our attitude toward others. A positive outlook, grounded in empathy, trust, and genuine connection, lays the foundation for meaningful interactions and the cultivation of strong, supportive bonds. A negative or cynical stance can cast a shadow over our interpersonal connections, breeding misunderstandings, conflict, and emotional distance. By recognizing the pivotal role our attitude plays in shaping our relationships, we can intentionally foster connections that are both enriching and mutually uplifting, creating a network of support and positivity that extends far beyond ourselves.

Elevating Mental Well-being:

The landscape of our mental well-being is intricately intertwined with the fabric of our attitude. Positivity acts as a guiding light, illuminating the path to enhanced resilience, emotional balance, and the ability to navigate life's inevitable stressors with grace and fortitude. It is a powerful ally in the quest for psychological well-being, providing a buffer against the storms of adversity and enabling us to maintain a sense of perspective and inner peace. By recognizing the profound connection between attitude and mental health, we empower ourselves to consciously shift our focus toward optimism, cultivating a mindset that not only promotes emotional stability but also lets us thrive in the face of life's challenges.

Charting the Course to Success:

In the pursuit of our dreams and aspirations, attitude serves as the compass that guides our journey. It is the driving force behind our determination, resilience, and the unwavering belief in our ability to overcome obstacles and transform challenges into opportunities for growth and achievement. With a mindset firmly rooted in positivity and a steadfast commitment to personal development, the path to success becomes clearer, and our goals, once seemingly distant, begin to feel within reach. By understanding the intricate relationship between attitude and achievement, we are empowered to cultivate a mindset that not only confronts challenges head-on but also embraces them as steppingstones to greatness, propelling us forward on our journey to realizing our full potential.

The Transformative Power of Attitude: A Call to Action

At its core, attitude is the bedrock on which we construct the edifice of our lives. It is a potent tool that, when harnessed effectively, holds the power to catalyze personal transformation, enrich our relationships, fortify our mental well-being, and pave the way to enduring success. The journey to cultivating a positive and empowering attitude is one of introspection, self-discovery, and unwavering commitment to personal growth. It is a path that offers unparalleled rewards, guiding us toward a life imbued with purpose, fulfillment, and boundless joy.

As we conclude this chapter, let it serve as a clarion call to start a transformative exploration of the art and science of attitude cultivation. May the insights and strategies presented ignite a spark within you, illuminating the untapped potential that lies dormant, waiting to be unleashed. By embracing the transformative power of attitude and making a conscious choice to nurture positivity in every part of your life, you hold the key to shaping your own destiny, turning dreams into reality, and creating a life that is nothing short of extraordinary. The journey begins now, and the possibilities are limitless.

$\sim$

UNRAVELING THE INTRICACIES OF ATTITUDE: A TRIAD OF THOUGHTS, FEELINGS, AND ACTIONS

DIGGING into the Depths of Attitude:

Attitude, a force that permeates every part of our lives, emerges as a complex tapestry woven from the threads of our beliefs, emotions, and behaviors. It is the invisible hand that shapes our interactions with the world, guiding our perceptions, reactions, and the trajectory of our existence. Like the rudder of a ship navigating the vast ocean of life, attitude steers the course of our thoughts, feelings, and actions, ultimately becoming the architect of our experiences. In this chapter, we will start a journey to dissect the intricate parts of attitude, unraveling the mysteries that lie at the heart of this powerful psychological construct.

The Three Pillars of Attitude: A Framework for Understanding

The Cognitive Realm: The Foundation of Our Attitudes

At the core of our attitudes lies the cognitive part, a complex network of beliefs, thoughts, and perceptions we hold about the people, situations, and objects that populate our world. This mental framework serves as the lens through which we interpret and make sense of our experiences, shaping our judgments and evaluations of the reality that surrounds us. Whether we embrace an optimistic outlook, viewing challenges as opportunities for growth, or succumb to the shadows of pessimism, perceiving obstacles as insurmountable barriers, our cognitive processes play a pivotal role in defining the contours of our attitudes. It is through this cognitive filter we assign meaning to the events of our lives, laying the foundation for the emotional and behavioral responses that follow.

The Affective Domain: The Emotional Heart of Attitude

Intertwined with our cognitive perceptions lies the affective part of attitude, a vibrant tapestry of emotions that color our experiences and imbue them with personal significance. From the warmth of love and the radiance of joy to the chill of fear and the ache of sorrow, our emotions serve as the barometer of our attitudes, reflecting the deep-seated feelings we harbor toward the various aspects of our lives. This emotional charge infuses our attitudes with a powerful energy, driving the intensity of our reactions and shaping the way we navigate the complexities of our relationships, pursuits, and aspirations. The affective dimension breathes life into our attitudes, transforming them from mere mental constructs into dynamic forces that shape the fabric of our existence.

The Behavioral Manifestation: Attitude in Action

The behavioral part of attitude represents the visible manifestation of our inner beliefs and emotions, the real expression of our psychological states in the world. It is through our actions, decisions, and interactions that our attitudes transcend the realm of the abstract and become a living, breathing reality. From the words we speak and the choices we make to the body language we exhibit and the initiatives we undertake, our behaviors serve as the ambassadors of our attitudes, communicating our values, beliefs, and emotional states to those around us. This behavioral dimension is where attitude transforms from a private, internal experience into a public, observable phenomenon, shaping the course of our lives and leaving an indelible mark on the tapestry of our relationships and experiences.

The Interplay of Thoughts, Feelings, and Actions: A Dynamic Dance

While the cognitive, affective, and behavioral parts of attitude can be examined independently, their intricate interplay truly defines the essence of this psychological construct. Our thoughts, emotions, and actions engage in a continuous, dynamic dance, each element influencing and being influenced by the others in a complex web of reciprocal interactions. Our beliefs and perceptions shape the emotional landscape of our attitudes, while our feelings, in turn, color the lens through which we interpret the world. This emotional charge then fuels the behavioral manifestations of our attitudes, guiding our actions and shaping the course of our lives. It is through this intricate interplay that attitude emerges as a holistic, multifaceted force, a symphony of thoughts, feelings, and actions that defines our unique approach to life.

Unraveling the Mysteries of Attitude: A Path to Personal Growth

As we delve into the intricacies of attitude, we start a transformative journey of self-discovery and personal growth. By understanding the cognitive roots of our attitudes, we gain the power to challenge limiting beliefs, reframe our perceptions, and cultivate a mindset of resilience and possibility. Through exploring the emotional depths of our attitudes, we develop a greater awareness of our inner landscape, learning to navigate the tides of our feelings with grace and emotional intelligence. And by examining the behavioral expressions of our attitudes, we unlock the potential to align our actions with our values, making conscious choices that shape the trajectory of our lives.

In unraveling the mysteries of attitude, we uncover a path to personal transformation, a journey that invites us to embrace the power of our thoughts, harness the wisdom of our emotions, and channel the energy of our actions toward creating a life of purpose, fulfillment, and authentic self-expression. As we navigate the complexities of attitude, let us remember that within this triad of thoughts, feelings, and actions lies the key to unlocking our highest potential and shaping a reality that reflects the best of who we are and who we aspire to become.

∾

THE PROFOUND
SIGNIFICANCE OF
ATTITUDE: WHY IT MATTERS

ATTITUDE: A Dynamic Force Shaping Our Lives

Attitude, far from being a mere mental state, emerges as a dynamic and influential force that permeates every part of our existence. Its impact extends beyond the limits of our inner world, shaping the contours of our daily experiences and holding profound implications for our long-term well-being and success. By understanding the true significance of attitude and cultivating a mindset that aligns with our highest aspirations, we harness the power to transform our lives and create a reality that reflects our deepest values and dreams. Let us explore the multifaceted ways attitude shapes our journey through life.

Attitude as the Lens of Perception: Shaping Our Worldview

At its core, attitude serves as the lens through which we perceive and interpret the world. It is the filter that colors our experiences, imbuing them with meaning and shaping our responses to the challenges and opportunities that life presents. A positive outlook, rooted in optimism and resilience, illuminates the path ahead, revealing possibilities and fostering a mindset of growth and adaptability. A negative attitude casts shadows of doubt and fear, obscuring the potential for progress and limiting our capacity to embrace change and overcome adversity. By recognizing the power of our attitudes to shape our worldview, we gain the agency to consciously craft a perspective that empowers us to navigate life's complexities with clarity, courage, and unwavering determination.

The Ripple Effect of Attitude: Influencing Interpersonal Dynamics

The impact of our attitudes extends far beyond the boundaries of our individual experiences, radiating outward to influence the quality and depth of our interpersonal relationships. The energy we emanate through our attitudes has the power to attract or repel, to build bridges of connection or erect walls of misunderstanding. A positive attitude, grounded in empathy, compassion, and a genuine desire for collaboration, fosters an environment of trust, respect, and mutual support. It invites others to engage with us openly and authentically, creating a tapestry of meaningful relationships that enrich our lives and contribute to our personal and professional growth. But a negative attitude, characterized by cynicism, judgment, or indifference, can strain our connections, breeding conflict, misunderstandings, and a sense of isolation. By cultivating an attitude that radiates positivity and encourages understanding, we become architects of harmonious and fulfilling interpersonal dynamics.

Attitude as the Fuel of Achievement: Propelling Us Toward Our Goals

In the pursuit of our aspirations and the realization of our full potential, attitude emerges as the driving force that propels us forward. It is the wind in the sails of our dreams, providing the motivation, resilience, and unwavering belief to overcome obstacles and persist in the face of adversity. A positive attitude, infused with determination and an unwavering commitment to personal growth, empowers us to approach challenges as opportunities for learning and transformation. It fuels our passion, ignites our creativity, and sustains our efforts, even in the face of setbacks and disappointments. A negative attitude can act as an anchor, weighing us down with self-doubt, fear, and a sense of limitation. By nurturing an attitude that aligns with our highest aspirations, we harness the power to break free from the chains of negativity and chart a course toward the realization of our most cherished goals.

Cultivating a Positive Attitude: The Path to Personal Transformation

Armed with a deep understanding of the cognitive, affective, and behavioral parts that shape our attitudes, we have the tools to actively cultivate a mindset that serves as a catalyst for personal growth, happiness, and success. By consciously nurturing positive thoughts, embracing constructive emotions, and aligning our actions with our values and aspirations, we start a transformative journey of attitude engineering. This process involves challenging limiting beliefs, reframing our perceptions, and developing a resilient and adaptable outlook in the face of life's challenges. It requires a commitment to self-awareness, a willingness to confront our inner shadows, and a dedication to personal development. As we navigate this path of attitude cultivation, we unlock the doors to a life of profound fulfillment, authentic self-expression, and the realization of our highest potential.

The Essence of Attitude: A Catalyst for Transformation

Attitude emerges as a powerful catalyst for personal transformation, a force that shapes our perceptions, emotions, and actions, and holds the key to unlocking the full potential of our lives. By digging into the intricacies of its cognitive, affective, and behavioral parts, we gain invaluable insights into how attitude influences every facet of our existence. As we start the subsequent chapters of this transformative journey, we will explore practical strategies and techniques to harness the positive power of attitude, cultivating a mindset that empowers us to navigate life's challenges with grace, resilience, and an unwavering commitment to personal growth.

Let this chapter serve as the foundation of our quest to understand and master the art of attitude cultivation, igniting within us a passion for self-discovery and a deep appreciation for the transformative potential that lies within. As we integrate these insights into our daily lives, we open ourselves to a world of boundless possibilities, where our attitudes become the guiding light that illuminates the path to a life of purpose, fulfillment, and authentic happiness. May our exploration of attitude's profound significance inspire us to embrace the power within and create a reality that reflects the best of who we are and who we aspire to become.

THE TRANSFORMATIVE POWER OF POSITIVITY: EMBRACING THE LIGHT WITHIN

POSITIVITY: A Beacon of Transformation

Positivity is the light that leads us to fulfillment and growth in life's tapestry. Like a beacon piercing through the fog of uncertainty and doubt, a positive attitude illuminates the path to unlocking our true potential and enriching every facet of our existence. From the intimate realm of our relationships to the ambitious heights of our professional aspirations, the transformative impact of positivity knows no bounds. In this chapter, we start a journey to explore the profound influence of maintaining a positive mindset, uncovering the keys to cultivating an attitude that not only elevates our own lives but also radiates outward, touching the lives of those around us.

The alchemy of positivity lies in its ability to transform the ordinary into the extraordinary, to infuse even the most challenging circumstances with a sense of hope, resilience, and possibility. By consciously choosing to embrace a positive outlook, we open ourselves to a world where obstacles become opportunities for growth, where setbacks serve as steppingstones to greater wisdom and understanding. Through this lens of positivity, we see the inherent beauty and potential in ourselves and others, fostering a mindset conducive to personal and interpersonal flourishing.

Nurturing the Gardens of Relationship: Positivity as a Catalyst for Connection

In relationships, positivity emerges as a powerful catalyst for nurturing deep, meaningful connections with others. By approaching our interactions with an attitude of openness, empathy, and genuine appreciation, we create an atmosphere where relationships can blossom and thrive. Positivity enables us to see beyond surface-level differences and to recognize the inherent worth and potential in every individual we encounter. It equips us with the emotional intelligence to navigate the complexities of human interaction with grace and understanding, to approach conflicts with a solution-oriented mindset, and to listen with the intent to comprehend and connect. Through the lens of positivity, we cultivate relationships characterized by trust, respect, and mutual support. We become attuned to the needs and emotions of others, fostering a sense of empathy and compassion that lets us build bridges of understanding and forge unbreakable bonds. By radiating positivity in our interactions, we attract like-minded individuals who share our values and aspirations, creating a network of support and collaboration that enriches our lives in countless ways. Positivity becomes the language of connection, the key to unlocking the doors to meaningful, lasting relationships that serve as a source of strength, inspiration, and personal growth.

The Alchemy of Achievement: Positivity as a Catalyst for Professional Success

In the competitive landscape of professional life, positivity emerges as a secret weapon, a powerful catalyst for accelerating career success and achieving our most ambitious goals. By approaching our work with an attitude of optimism, resilience, and unwavering determination, we cultivate a mindset conducive to innovation, collaboration, and continuous growth. Positivity enables us to see beyond the immediate challenges and setbacks, to maintain a clear vision of our long-term goals, and to persist in the face of adversity with unshakable resolve.

When we radiate positivity in the workplace, we become a source of inspiration and motivation for those around us. Our enthusiasm and optimism become contagious, fostering a culture of collaboration, creativity, and shared purpose. By focusing on solutions rather than problems, by celebrating the successes of others, and by maintaining a growth-oriented mindset, we position ourselves as valuable contributors and leaders within our organizations. Positivity, in this sense, becomes a magnet for opportunity, attracting the support, resources, and recognition necessary to propel our careers to new heights.

A positive attitude serves as a powerful antidote to the stresses and pressures of professional life. By maintaining a sense of perspective and gratitude, by finding joy and meaning in our work, and by cultivating a resilient spirit, we develop the emotional fortitude necessary to navigate the challenges and uncertainties of the modern workplace. Positivity becomes the fuel that sustains our passion, drives our performance, and enables us to find fulfillment and purpose in our professional endeavors.

The Keystone of Happiness: Positivity as a Path to Personal Fulfillment

Perhaps the most profound impact of positivity lies in its ability to unlock the gates to personal happiness and fulfillment. By cultivating a positive mindset, we develop the capacity to find joy and meaning in the present moment, to appreciate the beauty and richness of life in all its forms. Positivity enables us to reframe our experiences, to see challenges as opportunities for growth and learning, and to approach life with a sense of curiosity, wonder, and gratitude.

When we embrace positivity as a way of being, we become architects of our own happiness. We develop the resilience to bounce back from setbacks, the adaptability to navigate change and uncertainty, and the inner peace that comes from knowing we have the strength and resources to overcome any obstacle. Positivity becomes a wellspring of contentment, a source of joy and fulfillment that is not dependent on external circumstances but emanates from within.

The impact of our positivity extends far beyond the boundaries of our own lives. By radiating positivity, we become a beacon of hope and inspiration for others, a catalyst for positive change in the world. Our optimism, kindness, and compassion ripple outward, touching the lives of those we encounter and contributing to a greater sense of connection, unity, and shared purpose. In this way, positivity becomes not just a personal choice but a powerful force for social transformation, a means of creating a world that is more just, compassionate, and filled with possibility.

Cultivating the Garden of Positivity: A Lifelong Journey

Embracing positivity as a way of life is not a destination but a lifelong journey of growth, self-discovery, and conscious choice. It requires a commitment to self-awareness, a willingness to confront and transform limiting beliefs and patterns of thought, and a dedication to cultivating habits and practices that support a positive mindset.

This journey begins with a simple yet profound shift in perspective, a recognition that our thoughts, beliefs, and attitudes shape the reality we experience. By becoming mindful of our inner dialogue, by challenging negative self-talk and replacing it with empowering, affirming language, we begin to rewire our minds for positivity and resilience. We learn to focus our attention on the good in ourselves, others, and the world, cultivating a sense of gratitude and appreciation that enriches our lives in countless ways.

The path of positivity also requires a willingness to embrace vulnerability, to confront our fears and insecurities with courage and compassion. By acknowledging and accepting the full range of our emotions, by learning to respond to challenges with patience, understanding, and self-compassion, we develop the emotional intelligence necessary to navigate life's ups and downs with grace and resilience.

Ultimately, cultivating positivity is a choice we make in each moment, a commitment to bringing our best selves to every interaction and experience. It is a practice of aligning our thoughts, words, and actions with our highest values and aspirations, of living in integrity with our deepest truths. By making positivity a conscious, intentional part of our daily lives, we open ourselves to a world of infinite possibility, a life filled with purpose, meaning, and enduring happiness.

The Enduring Power of Positivity: A Call to Embrace the Light

As we come to the end of this exploration of the transformative power of positivity, let us reflect on the profound impact that a positive attitude can have on every part of our lives. From the depths of our relationships to the heights of our professional achievements, from the inner landscape of our emotions to the outer world of our actions and contributions, positivity emerges as a guiding light, a catalyst for personal and collective transformation.

By choosing to embrace positivity as a way of being, we open ourselves to a life of endless possibility, a journey of growth, connection, and fulfillment. We become architects of our own reality, creators of a world that is more just, compassionate, and filled with love and understanding. We discover within ourselves a reservoir of strength, resilience, and boundless potential, a source of light that can illuminate even the darkest of moments.

Let this chapter function as a motivating force, an opportunity to begin the lifelong journey of fostering positivity in all that we do. May we commit ourselves to the practice of self-awareness, to the cultivation of empowering beliefs and habits, and to pursuing a life aligned with our highest values and aspirations. May we radiate positivity in every interaction, every decision, and every moment, realizing that by doing this, we not only shape our own lives but also contribute to the healing and advancement of the world.

As we step forward into the unfolding story of our lives, let us carry the flame of optimism within us, allowing it to lead our way, clarify our mission, and motivate us to become the finest versions of ourselves. For in embracing positivity, we discover the key to unlocking our true potential and creating a life filled with meaning, joy, and fulfillment.

With each passing day, we have the opportunity to choose how we perceive and interact with the world. By consciously cultivating a positive mindset, we open ourselves up to a realm of endless possibilities and opportunities. Positivity acts as a catalyst, transforming challenges into growth, setbacks into lessons, and dreams into realities.

When we radiate positivity, we not only elevate our own lives but also uplift those around us. Our optimism and enthusiasm become contagious, creating a ripple effect of goodness that touches the lives of others. By being a beacon of positivity, we inspire others to embrace their own light and pursue their aspirations with renewed vigor and determination.

Positivity is a powerful tool for resilience and perseverance. Faced with adversity, a positive outlook enables us to find the silver lining, to see the opportunity within the obstacle. It grants us the strength to push through difficult times, knowing that every challenge is a chance to learn, grow, and emerge stronger than before.

So, let us embrace positivity as our guiding principle, our north star in the journey of life. May we greet each day with a smile, a grateful heart, and an unwavering belief in the goodness that surrounds us. For when we live with positivity, we not only transform our own lives but also contribute to bettering the world.

Positivity is the golden thread that connects the moments of joy, growth, and triumph in our lives. By embracing its power, we unlock the door to a life of boundless potential, where dreams become reality, and where happiness and success are not just aspirations but everyday companions on our journey.

~

THE SHADOW OF NEGATIVITY: NAVIGATING THE PITFALLS OF A PESSIMISTIC MINDSET

The Shroud of Negativity: A Barrier to Growth and Fulfillment

Like a dark thread, negativity emerges in the fabric of our experiences, casting shadows that obstruct meaningful connection and personal growth. Like a dense fog that envelops the landscape of our minds, a negative attitude can distort our perceptions, cloud our judgment, and erect barriers that hinder our ability to navigate the challenges and uncertainties that inevitably arise on the journey of life.

This chapter serves as a beacon of awareness, illuminating the insidious ways negativity can infiltrate our thoughts, emotions, and actions, and the profound impact it can have on every part of our lives. By digging into the pitfalls of a pessimistic mindset, we arm ourselves with the knowledge and tools necessary to break free from the chains of negativity and embrace a more positive, empowering outlook that enables us to thrive in the face of adversity and unlock our full potential.

The Shadows of Stagnation: How Negativity Stunts Personal Growth

At the core of personal growth and evolution lies the willingness to embrace change, to step outside of our comfort zones and confront the unknown with courage and curiosity. It is in these moments of discomfort and uncertainty that we discover hidden strengths, acquire new skills, and expand our understanding of ourselves and the world. However, when negativity takes hold, it acts as a powerful force of resistance, erecting walls of self-doubt, fear, and limiting beliefs that limit us to a narrow existence, devoid of the richness and fulfillment that comes from continuous learning and self-discovery.

A negative attitude fosters a mindset of scarcity and limitation, where challenges are seen as insurmountable obstacles rather than opportunities for growth and transformation. It whispers messages of inadequacy and failure, eroding our self-confidence and causing us to shrink from the experiences that hold the key to our personal and professional development. By succumbing to the shadows of negativity, we risk becoming stagnant, trapped in a cycle of complacency and unfulfilled potential, forever haunted by the specter of what might have been.

The Fog of Frustration: Negativity's Impact on Problem-Solving

Faced with challenges and setbacks, a negative attitude can act as a distorting lens, obscuring our ability to perceive solutions and possibilities. When viewed through the fog of negativity, problems take on an exaggerated sense of complexity and hopelessness, causing us to become overwhelmed and paralyzed by a sense of helplessness and despair. This defeatist mindset narrows our focus, fixating on the obstacles and limitations rather than the opportunities and resources available to us.

Negativity breeds a reactive, problem-focused approach to life, where energy is wasted on complaining, blaming, and ruminating on the difficulties we face. It robs us of the clarity, creativity, and resourcefulness necessary to generate effective solutions and take proactive steps toward resolution. By surrendering to the fog of frustration, we become trapped in a self-perpetuating cycle of negativity, where each unresolved problem further erodes our confidence and reinforces a sense of powerlessness and futility.

The Corrosive Nature of Negativity: Its Impact on Relationships

Just as negativity can cast shadows on our personal growth and problem-solving abilities, it can also act as a corrosive force in our relationships, eroding the bonds of trust, empathy, and connection that form the foundation of healthy interpersonal dynamics. When we approach interactions with a negative mindset, we become prone to criticism, judgment, and a focus on the flaws and shortcomings of others. This toxic energy radiates outward, creating an atmosphere of tension, conflict, and emotional distance that slowly poisons the well of goodwill and understanding.

Negativity breeds a cycle of reactivity and defensiveness, where even the most innocent remarks or actions can be perceived as attacks or slights. It fosters a culture of blame and resentment, where the focus shifts from finding common ground and nurturing connection to keeping score and nursing grudges. Over time, the cumulative weight of negativity can strain even the most resilient of relationships, leading to a sense of isolation, loneliness, and a profound disconnect from the people who matter most in our lives.

Charting a Course Toward Positivity: The Journey of Transformation

Recognizing the insidious impact of negativity on our lives is an important first step in breaking free from its shadows and charting a course toward a more positive, empowering mindset. This journey of transformation requires a willingness to confront and challenge the deeply ingrained patterns of thought and behavior that perpetuate negativity, and to cultivate new habits and perspectives that support personal growth, resilience, and connection.

The path to positivity begins with self-awareness, a commitment to mindfully observing our thoughts, emotions, and reactions, and acknowledging how negativity manifests in our lives. It involves developing the courage to step outside of our comfort zones, to embrace challenges as opportunities for learning and growth, and to reframe setbacks as temporary obstacles rather than definitive failures. By seeking out the lessons and silver linings in even the most difficult of circumstances, we begin to shift our focus from the problems we face to the solutions and possibilities that lie within our reach.

Cultivating positivity also requires a willingness to let go of the past, to release the grudges, resentments, and limiting beliefs that keep us trapped in a cycle of negativity. It involves practicing forgiveness, both for ourselves and others, and recognizing that holding onto anger and bitterness only poisons our own well-being and relationships. By choosing to focus on the present moment, to express gratitude for the blessings in our lives, and to approach others with empathy, compassion, and understanding, we create the conditions for positive, nurturing connections to thrive.

The journey toward positivity is not a one-time event, but a lifelong process of growth, self-discovery, and conscious choice. It requires a commitment to ongoing self-reflection, a willingness to learn from our mistakes and setbacks, and a dedication to surrounding ourselves with people, experiences, and environments that uplift and inspire us. By making positivity a daily practice, a way of being in the world, we gradually rewire our minds and hearts for resilience, optimism, and a deep sense of purpose and fulfillment.

Emerging from the Shadows: A Call to Embrace the Light

As we come to the end of this exploration of the pitfalls of negativity, let us reflect on the profound impact that our mindset and attitude have on every part of our lives. Whether we choose to dwell in the shadows of negativity or step into the light of positivity, our perspective shapes the reality we experience and the quality of our relationships, our personal growth, and our ability to navigate the challenges and opportunities that life presents.

By recognizing the corrosive nature of negativity and making a conscious choice to embrace a more positive, empowering outlook, we open ourselves to a world of limitless possibility and potential. We become the architects of our own reality, the creators of a life rich in meaning, purpose, and authentic connection. We discover within ourselves a reservoir of strength, resilience, and boundless creativity, a source of light that can illuminate even the darkest of moments and guide us toward fulfilling our deepest aspirations.

Let this chapter serve as a call to action, an invitation to start the life-long journey of cultivating positivity in all that we do. May we find the courage to confront and transform the shadows of negativity that have held us back, and to embrace the light of optimism, hope, and endless possibility. May we radiate positivity in every interaction, every decision, and every moment, knowing that by doing so, we not only transform our own lives but also contribute to the healing and elevation of the world.

As we step forward into the unfolding story of our lives, let us carry the light of positivity with us, letting it guide our path, illuminate our purpose, and inspire us to become the best versions of ourselves. For in embracing positivity, we discover the key to unlocking the fullness of our potential and creating a life that is extraordinary.

THE POWER OF SELF-BELIEF

Self-belief, also known as self-efficacy, is an individual's confidence in their ability to succeed in specific situations, overcome challenges, and meet their goals. It is a powerful psychological construct that greatly influences a person's motivation, resilience, and overall performance in various parts of life.

The Impact of Self-Belief on Performance:

Research has consistently shown that self-belief plays a significant role in determining an individual's success and achievement. People with high levels of self-belief tend to:

1. Set challenging goals for themselves and remain committed to achieving them.

2. View obstacles and setbacks as opportunities for growth and learning.

3. Put forth greater effort and persist longer in the face of difficulties.

4. Approach tasks with confidence and a positive mindset.

5. Recover quickly from failures and maintain motivation despite adversity.

Individuals with low self-belief often doubt their abilities, shy away from challenges, and are more likely to give up when faced with obstacles. This lack of confidence can limit their potential and hinder their progress in various domains of life.

Developing and Strengthening Self-Belief:

While some individuals may naturally have high levels of self-belief, this quality can be cultivated and strengthened. Some strategies for enhancing self-belief include:

- Setting and achieving small, incremental goals to build confidence and momentum.
- Focusing on personal strengths and past successes as evidence of capability.
- Reframing failures and setbacks as learning experiences and opportunities for growth.
- Seeking positive role models and mentors who provide guidance and encouragement.
- Engaging in positive self-talk and affirmations to combat negative self-doubts.
- Embracing challenges as opportunities to expand skills and knowledge.
- Celebrating achievements, both big and small, to reinforce a sense of accomplishment.

The Relationship Between Self-Belief and Attitude:

Self-belief and attitude are closely intertwined, as an individual's attitude toward themselves and their abilities can greatly influence their level of self-belief. A positive attitude characterized by optimism, resilience, and a growth mindset can foster a strong sense of self-belief. But a negative attitude marked by pessimism, self-doubt, and a fixed mindset can undermine self-belief and limit personal growth.

By cultivating a positive attitude and working to strengthen self-belief, individuals can unlock their full potential, overcome obstacles, and meet their goals across various domains of life. Whether in academics, career, relationships, or personal pursuits, a strong sense of self-belief is a powerful catalyst for success and fulfillment.

The Relationship Between Attitude and Self-Belief

Attitude and self-belief are closely intertwined and have a profound impact on an individual's life experiences and outcomes. The way we perceive and evaluate ourselves, others, and the world shapes our self-belief, which influences our attitudes and behaviors.

The Impact of Attitude on Self-Belief:

Our attitudes, whether positive or negative, can significantly influence our self-belief. When we hold positive attitudes, we are more likely to:

- Approach challenges with confidence and optimism.
- Believe in our ability to overcome obstacles and meet our goals.
- Maintain a growth mindset, viewing failures as opportunities for learning and improvement.
- Encourage and support ourselves through positive self-talk and affirmations.

On the other hand, negative attitudes can undermine our self-belief by:

- Fostering self-doubt and limiting beliefs about our capabilities.
- Magnifying obstacles and challenges, making them seem insurmountable.
- Encouraging a fixed mindset, where failures are seen as reflections of personal inadequacy.
- Perpetuating negative self-talk and self-criticism, eroding confidence and motivation.

The Impact of Self-Belief on Attitude:

Just as attitudes influence self-belief, our level of self-belief can shape our attitudes toward ourselves, others, and life experiences. When we have a strong sense of self-belief, we are more likely to:

- Cultivate positive attitudes toward challenges and opportunities.
- Approach life with a sense of optimism and resilience.
- Maintain a positive self-image and self-esteem.
- Engage in behaviors and actions that align with our goals and values.

Conversely, low self-belief can contribute to negative attitudes by:

- Fostering pessimism and a defeatist outlook on life.
- Encouraging avoidance behaviors and self-sabotage.
- Perpetuating negative self-perception and low self-esteem.
- Limiting our willingness to take risks and pursue growth opportunities.

Cultivating Positive Attitudes and Self-Belief:

Given the interconnected nature of attitude and self-belief, it is essential to actively cultivate both to promote personal growth, well-being, and success. Some strategies for fostering positive attitudes and self-belief include:

Practicing self-awareness and identifying negative thought patterns and beliefs.

- Challenging and reframing negative self-talk with positive affirmations and self-encouragement.
- Setting realistic goals and celebrating achievements, no matter how small.
- Surrounding oneself with positive and supportive individuals who encourage growth and belief in oneself.
- Engaging in activities and pursuits that align with personal values and passions.
- Practicing self-compassion and treating oneself with kindness and understanding.
- Continuously learning and embracing opportunities for personal and professional development.

By cultivating positive attitudes and nurturing self-belief, individuals can create a powerful synergy that propels them toward greater success, fulfillment, and personal growth. Recognizing the interplay between attitude and self-belief empowers us to take control of our mindset and shape our life experiences positively and meaningfully.

The Power of a Positive Attitude:

Self-belief is a powerful force that can transform our lives in profound ways. When we have faith in ourselves and our abilities, we are more likely to take on challenges, pursue our dreams, and meet our goals. This inner conviction serves as a driving force, propelling us forward and giving us the courage to overcome obstacles and setbacks.

One of the most significant impacts of self-belief is its ability to enhance our performance and productivity. When we believe in ourselves, we are more likely to set high standards and work hard to meet them. We approach tasks with confidence and determination, knowing we have the skills and knowledge to succeed. This self-assurance enables us to push past our limits, take risks, and strive for excellence in all that we do.

Self-belief plays an important role in shaping our relationships and interactions with others. When we have a strong sense of self, we are more likely to communicate effectively, assert ourselves when necessary, and establish healthy boundaries. We are less likely to seek validation from others or let external opinions dictate our self-worth. Instead, we trust in our own judgment and make decisions that align with our values and goals.

Self-belief also has a profound impact on our mental and emotional well-being. When we believe in ourselves, we are more likely to maintain a positive outlook, even in the face of adversity. We are better equipped to manage stress, cope with setbacks, and bounce back from failures. This resilience and adaptability let us navigate life's challenges with greater ease and grace, ultimately leading to a more fulfilling and satisfying existence.

Self-belief is the foundation on which we build our lives. It is the key to unlocking our full potential and achieving our dreams. By cultivating a strong sense of self-belief, we empower ourselves to take control of our lives, pursue our passions, and create the reality we desire. When we believe in ourselves, there are no limits to what we can achieve.

Overcoming Negative Attitudes and Cultivating Self-Belief

Given the destructive impact of negative attitudes on self-belief, it is important to develop strategies for overcoming these limiting thought patterns and cultivating a positive mindset. While challenging negative attitudes and building self-belief requires time and effort, it is a journey worth undertaking for the sake of personal growth and well-being.

One of the first steps in overcoming negative attitudes is to learn of our thought patterns and the impact they have on our self-belief. By practicing mindfulness and self-reflection, we can identify the negative self-talk and limiting beliefs that undermine our confidence and hold us back. Once we recognize these patterns, we can actively challenge and reframe them with more positive and empowering thoughts.

Another powerful tool for cultivating self-belief is to focus on our strengths and accomplishments. Often, when we are caught in a cycle of negative thinking, we usually overlook our own capabilities and successes. By intentionally redirecting our attention to the times when we have overcome challenges, met our goals, or made a positive impact, we can build a more accurate and affirming self-image.

Setting realistic goals and celebrating small victories along the way can also help to boost self-belief. When we break down our aspirations into manageable steps and acknowledge our progress, we create a sense of momentum and accomplishment that reinforces our confidence in our abilities. By consistently setting and achieving goals, we build a track record of success that serves as evidence of our potential and capabilities.

Surrounding ourselves with supportive and positive influences is another key strategy for overcoming negative attitudes and cultivating self-belief. When we engage with individuals who believe in us, encourage our growth, and provide constructive feedback, we are more likely to internalize their positive perceptions and develop a stronger sense of self-worth. Seeking mentors, joining supportive communities, and engaging in activities that align with our values and passions can all contribute to a more affirming and empowering social environment.

Ultimately, overcoming negative attitudes and cultivating self-belief is an ongoing process that requires patience, persistence, and self-compassion. It involves challenging our limiting beliefs, focusing on our strengths, setting achievable goals, and surrounding ourselves with positive influences. By consistently engaging in these practices, we can gradually shift our mindset from one of self-doubt and negativity to one of confidence, resilience, and self-belief. As we embrace this transformative journey, we open ourselves up to a world of possibilities and unlock our full potential for personal growth and success.

Practicing Gratitude and Positive Self-Talk

Cultivating a positive attitude is greatly enhanced by practicing gratitude and engaging in positive self-talk. These practices help to shift our focus from negative thoughts and limiting beliefs to a more optimistic and empowering mindset.

The Power of Gratitude:

Gratitude is the practice of acknowledging and appreciating the good things in our lives. By regularly focusing on what we are thankful for, we train our minds to seek the positive aspects of our experiences, even in challenging times. Some ways to practice gratitude include:

• **Keeping a Gratitude Journal:** Set aside time each day to write down three to five things you are grateful for. This habit helps to reinforce a positive outlook and reminds us of the blessings in our lives.

• **Expressing Appreciation:** Make a conscious effort to express gratitude to others for their kindness, support, or positive impact on your life. Acknowledging the good in others can also help to foster a more positive self-image.

• **Savoring Positive Experiences:** Take the time to fully engage in and appreciate positive moments, no matter how small. By savoring these experiences, we create lasting positive impressions that contribute to a more optimistic mindset.

The Impact of Positive Self-Talk:

Positive self-talk involves the conscious effort to reframe our internal dialogue in a more supportive and encouraging manner. By replacing negative self-talk with positive affirmations, we can boost our self-belief and cultivate a more confident and resilient attitude. Some strategies for practicing positive self-talk include:

• **Using Affirmations:** Develop a set of positive affirmations that resonate with you and align with your goals. Repeat these affirmations regularly, especially when faced with challenges or self-doubt.

• **Reframing Negative Thoughts:** When you catch yourself engaging in negative self-talk, actively challenge and reframe those thoughts into more positive and constructive statements.

• **Celebrating Your Successes:** Acknowledge and celebrate your accomplishments, no matter how small. Recognizing your own progress and achievements reinforces a sense of competence and self-worth.

By incorporating gratitude and positive self-talk into your daily life, you can cultivate a more optimistic and self-affirming attitude. This shift in mindset will not only enhance your self-belief but also contribute to greater resilience, motivation, and overall well-being.

Cultivating Resilience and a Growth Mindset

Developing resilience and a growth mindset is essential for maintaining a positive attitude and strong self-belief in the face of challenges and setbacks. Resilience refers to the ability to bounce back from adversity, adapt to change, and persevere through difficult times. A growth mindset is the belief that one's abilities and intelligence can be developed and improved through dedication and hard work.

Strategies for Building Resilience:

Reframe Challenges as Opportunities: View obstacles and setbacks as chances to learn, grow, and become stronger. Embracing challenges with a positive outlook can help you develop resilience and adaptability.

Focus on What You Can Control: In difficult situations, direct your energy toward the parts that are within your control, such as your attitude, effort, and response. Accepting what you cannot change and focusing on what you can influence fosters a sense of empowerment and resilience.

Practice Self-Care: Prioritize self-care activities that promote physical, mental, and emotional well-being. Engaging in regular exercise, getting enough sleep, practicing mindfulness, and pursuing hobbies can help you build resilience and manage stress effectively.

Build a Support Network: Surround yourself with positive and supportive people who encourage and uplift you. A strong support system can provide a sense of belonging, validation, and encouragement during challenging times.

Learn from Setbacks: Treat Failures and Setbacks As Valuable Learning Experiences. Reflect on What You Can Learn from Each Challenge and Use That Knowledge to Grow and Improve in the Future.

Cultivating a Growth Mindset:

Embrace Challenges: Approach challenges with enthusiasm and view them as opportunities to stretch your abilities and expand your knowledge. Embracing challenges with a growth mindset can lead to greater personal and professional development.

Believe in Your Potential: Recognize that your abilities and intelligence are not fixed traits but can be developed and enhanced through effort and learning. Believing in your own potential can motivate you to pursue growth and improvement.

Focus on the Process: Shift your focus from outcomes and results to learning and development. Celebrate the effort, progress, and lessons learned along the way, rather than only fixating on the end goal.

Learn from Criticism: View constructive criticism as valuable feedback that can help you identify areas for improvement. Embrace feedback with an open mind and use it to refine your skills and strategies.

Cultivate a Love for Learning: Develop a genuine curiosity and passion for learning. Seek new experiences, knowledge, and skills that can broaden your horizons and contribute to your personal growth.

By cultivating resilience and a growth mindset, you can navigate challenges with greater confidence, adaptability, and self-belief. These qualities will not only help you overcome obstacles but also foster a positive attitude that propels you toward personal and professional success.

The Power of Positive Influences in Your Life

Have you ever noticed how the people around you can significantly affect your thoughts, feelings, and overall well-being? It's true! The individuals we choose to surround ourselves with play an important role in shaping our attitudes, beliefs, and personal growth. When we're with positive influences, they can lift our spirits, encourage us to pursue our goals, and help us navigate life's ups and downs with resilience and optimism. But negative influences can weigh us down, erode our self-confidence, and hinder our progress.

That's why building a strong network of positive influences is so important for our mental, emotional, and even physical health. Let's explore compelling reasons why surrounding yourself with positivity is essential:

Attitude and Mindset: When you're around positive people, their optimistic outlook can rub off on you. They can help you maintain a constructive attitude and mindset, even when times get tough. Their encouragement, motivation, and unwavering belief in your abilities can be the fuel you need to stay focused on your goals and overcome obstacles with determination.

Self-Belief and Confidence: There's nothing like being surrounded by people who genuinely believe in you and your potential. When your support system uplifts and encourages you, it can work wonders for your self-belief and confidence. Positive influences help you recognize your strengths, embrace your unique qualities, and dare to take on new challenges. They inspire you to stretch beyond your comfort zone and strive for personal growth.

Emotional Well-Being: The relationships we nurture have a profound impact on our emotional well-being. When you're with supportive and caring individuals, it can alleviate feelings of loneliness, anxiety, and stress. Instead, you'll experience a greater sense of happiness, security, and fulfillment. Positive influences create a safe space where you can express yourself, share your joys and sorrows, and find comfort in knowing you have people who genuinely care about your well-being.

Energy and Motivation: Have you ever been around someone who radiates positivity and enthusiasm? It's contagious! Positive influences have a way of energizing and motivating us to pursue our passions and dreams. When you surround yourself with individuals passionate about their own goals and genuinely excited about yours, it can ignite a spark within you. Their encouragement and support can be the driving force that propels you forward, even when the path ahead seems challenging.

So, how can you intentionally surround yourself with positive influences? Here are practical tips to consider:

· **Evaluate Your Current Circle**: Take a moment to reflect on the people you spend the most time with. Do they uplift and support you, or do they usually drain your energy and bring negativity into your life? If you find that certain relationships are consistently weighing you down, it may be time to gradually distance yourself and make space for more positive connections.

· **Seek Out Like-Minded Individuals**: Surround yourself with people who share your values, goals, and interests. Engage in activities and communities where you can connect with individuals who inspire and motivate you. Whether it's joining a club, attending workshops, or participating in online forums, actively seek environments where you can meet like-minded people who will support and encourage your growth.

· **Cultivate Healthy Relationships**: Investing time and effort into nurturing positive relationships is important. Whether it's with friends, family members, or mentors, focus on connections that bring out the best in you. Foster open communication, be empathetic, and actively listen to others. When you create an atmosphere of mutual support and understanding, positive relationships thrive.

· **Practice Gratitude**: Don't forget to express your appreciation for the positive influences in your life. Thank those who have supported you, uplifted you, and believed in you. Acknowledging their impact reinforces the importance of positive relationships and encourages them to continue being a source of light in your life.

Remember, the power to shape your environment lies within you. By intentionally surrounding yourself with positive influences, you create a supportive ecosystem that nourishes your personal growth, fosters resilience, and enhances your overall happiness. Be mindful of the company you keep, and actively cultivate relationships that empower and inspire you to be your best self. Embrace the transformative power of positive influences and watch as your life flourishes in ways you never imagined possible.

Unleashing the Power of Self-Belief to Achieve Your Goals

Crafting Attainable Goals

When achieving success and staying motivated, setting realistic goals is paramount. By aligning your goals with your personal values and beliefs, you create a strong foundation for commitment and focus. It's all about finding that sweet spot between goals that stretch you beyond your comfort zone and those that are within your reach.

Imagine the boost in self-belief you'll experience when you set goals that are achievable. It's like giving yourself a high-five every time you cross a milestone. On the flip side, setting unrealistic goals can be a motivation killer. It's like trying to climb a mountain without the right gear - you'll likely feel discouraged and defeated.

That's why it's important to approach goal setting with a clear understanding of your own capabilities and limitations. Take a honest look at where you are now and where you want to be. Break down your big goals into smaller, manageable steps. Celebrate each victory along the way, no matter how small.

When you set realistic goals that align with your values and beliefs, you tap into a deep sense of purpose and motivation. It's like having a personal compass guiding you toward your desired destination. You'll wake up each day with a renewed sense of determination and drive.

So, embrace the power of realistic goal setting. Let it be the catalyst that ignites your self-belief and propels you toward success. Remember, it's not about reaching perfection; it's about making progress and becoming the best version of yourself. With each goal you achieve, you'll build momentum and confidence, paving the way for even greater accomplishments.

Fueling Your Journey with Self-Belief and Perseverance

When it comes to achieving your goals, self-belief is the secret sauce that keeps you even when the road gets bumpy. Unwavering faith in yourself that whispers, "You've got this!" when obstacles try to stand in your way. But how do you cultivate that unshakable self-belief and maintain motivation when the going gets tough? Let's dive in and explore powerful strategies.

It's important to set clear goals for yourself. Take the time to define your goals with precision and break them down into bite-sized, manageable steps. By doing so, you transform your goals from daunting mountains into achievable milestones. Each small victory along the way will fuel your self-belief and keep you motivated to keep pushing forward.

Next, harness the power of visualization. Close your eyes and imagine yourself conquering your goals, basking in the glow of success. Picture the positive outcomes and feel the sense of accomplishment coursing through your veins. By regularly engaging in this mental rehearsal, you reinforce your self-belief and create a magnetic pull toward your desired destination.

But what about those pesky doubts that try to sabotage your progress? That's where positive self-talk comes in. Become your own cheerleader and replace self-doubt with empowering affirmations. Remind yourself of your unique strengths, capabilities, and past triumphs. When negative thoughts try to creep in, challenge them head-on and reframe them into opportunities for growth and learning.

Remember, you need not navigate this journey alone. Surround yourself with a supportive tribe—people who believe in you and have your back through thick and thin. These cheerleaders will be there to lift you up when you stumble and celebrate your victories along the way. Their encouragement and unwavering support can work wonders in boosting your self-belief and keeping you motivated.

Now, let's talk about the inevitable setbacks and failures that may cross your path. Instead of letting them deflate your self-belief, embrace them as valuable lessons. Every challenge you face is an opportunity to learn, grow, and come back stronger. Use these experiences as steppingstones, extracting the wisdom they offer and applying it to your future endeavors.

Above all, remember that perseverance is the key that unlocks the doors to success. Stay committed to your vision, even when the path becomes rocky. Keep putting one foot in front of the other, no matter how small the steps may seem. And most important, never give up on yourself. Your self-belief is the compass that will guide you through the toughest of times and lead you to fulfilling your dreams.

So, as you start this transformative journey, fuel yourself with an unwavering belief in your own abilities. Embrace the power of perseverance and let it propel you forward, even when the road ahead seems uncertain. With self-belief as your anchor and motivation as your engine, there's no limit to what you can achieve. Believe in yourself, act, and watch as your goals become a reality, one courageous step at a time.

Embracing the Transformative Power of Self-Belief

As we conclude this exploration of self-belief and its profound impact on our lives, let's reflect on the incredible journey we've started. We've delved into the intricate relationship between attitude and self-belief, uncovering how our mindset shapes our confidence, motivation, and resilience.

It's become clear that cultivating a positive attitude is not merely a nice-to-have; it's a fundamental necessity for overcoming self-doubt and unlocking our true potential. When we adopt an optimistic outlook, we ignite a powerful force within ourselves—a force that propels us forward, even in the face of adversity.

But how do we nurture this transformative self-belief? It starts with challenging the limiting beliefs that hold us back. By questioning the narratives that no longer serve us and replacing them with empowering truths, we break free from the shackles of self-doubt and embrace a newfound sense of confidence.

Resilience, too, plays an important role in fortifying our self-belief. As we navigate the ups and downs of life, it's essential to develop the ability to bounce back from setbacks and view challenges as opportunities for growth. By cultivating a resilient spirit, we equip ourselves with the strength to persevere, even when the path ahead seems daunting.

The company we keep has a profound influence on our self-belief. Surrounding ourselves with positive, supportive individuals who believe in our potential can work wonders for our confidence and motivation. These uplifting influences serve as a reminder of our inherent worth and encourage us to reach for the stars.

As we step forward with a renewed sense of self-belief, we unlock a world of possibilities. No longer held back by self-doubt or fear, we can tackle challenges head-on, embracing the opportunities that come our way. With a strong foundation of self-belief, we have the power to shape our lives in accordance with our deepest aspirations and create a future that resonates with our authentic selves.

So, let us embrace the transformative power of self-belief. Let us cultivate a positive attitude, challenge limiting beliefs, develop resilience, and surround ourselves with uplifting influences. As we do so, we'll see a remarkable shift within ourselves—a shift toward greater confidence, motivation, and the unwavering belief we can achieve extraordinary things.

Remember, your self-belief is the key that unlocks the door to personal growth and fulfillment. Nurture it, cherish it, and let it guide you on your path to success. With a strong sense of self-belief as your compass, there are no limits to what you can accomplish. So, step forward with confidence, embrace your unique potential, and start a journey of self-discovery and transformation. The world is waiting for you to make your mark, and with self-belief as your ally, you have the power to create a life that exceeds your wildest dreams.

~

CULTIVATING A GROWTH MINDSET: UNLOCKING THE DOORS TO PERSONAL TRANSFORMATION

The Seed of Potential: Embracing the Power of a Growth Mindset

Deep within each of us lies a seed of infinite potential, a wellspring of possibility waiting to be tapped. Yet, for many, this seed remains dormant, obscured by the shadows of self-doubt, fear, and limiting beliefs. The key to unlocking the doors to personal transformation and cultivating a life of boundless growth lies in the adoption of a growth mindset – a perspective that sees challenges as opportunities, failures as steppingstones, and the self as a canvas of endless possibility.

At its core, a growth mindset is a fundamental belief in the malleability of human qualities and abilities. It rejects the notion that intelligence, talent, and character are fixed, immutable traits, and an embrace of the idea that with dedication, effort, and a willingness to learn, we can continually expand the horizons of our potential. By fostering a growth mindset, we open ourselves to a world of continuous learning, adaptation, and self-discovery, where the only limits are those we impose on ourselves.

The Alchemy of Challenge: Transmuting Obstacles into Opportunities

One of the hallmarks of a growth mindset is the willingness to embrace challenges as catalysts for personal evolution. Where a fixed mindset sees obstacles as threats to self-image and evidence of inadequacy, a growth mindset recognizes them as invaluable opportunities to stretch beyond comfort zones, acquire new skills, and test the boundaries of what is possible.

In the crucible of challenge, we have the chance to forge a stronger, more resilient sense of self. Each obstacle overcome becomes a testament to our capacity for growth and adaptation, a reminder that we are capable of far more than we often believe. By approaching challenges with a spirit of curiosity, determination, and a focus on the lessons they hold, we transmute the lead of adversity into the gold of personal transformation.

The Wisdom of Failure: Mining the Depths of Setbacks

In growth, failure is not a dead end but a rich vein of wisdom waiting to be mined. For those with a fixed mindset, failure is a judgment, a confirmation of inadequacy and a reason to retreat into the safety of the known. But for those who have cultivated a growth mindset, failure is a master teacher, offering profound lessons and insights that light the path to future success.

Every setback, every stumble, every misstep holds within it the seeds of growth and self-discovery. By approaching failure with a posture of humility, openness, and a determination to extract the lessons it holds, we transform it from a source of shame to a springboard for personal evolution. In the words of Thomas Edison, "I have not failed. I've just found 10,000 ways that won't work." With a growth mindset, we come to see failure not as a verdict but as a necessary and valuable part of the journey toward mastery.

The alchemy of a growth mindset lies in its power to transmute the base metals of challenge and failure into the gold of wisdom, resilience, and self-realization. By embracing obstacles as opportunities and setbacks as lessons, we open ourselves to a life of continuous learning, adaptation, and growth, where every experience becomes a chance to expand the boundaries of what we thought possible.

The Nourishment of Positivity: Cultivating an Empowering Inner Dialogue

At the heart of a growth mindset is the recognition that our thoughts and beliefs have a profound impact on our experience of reality. The stories we tell ourselves about who we are, what we're capable of, and what the future holds shape the lens through which we perceive and interact with the world.

To cultivate a growth mindset, we must become conscious gardeners of our inner dialogue, tending to the seeds of positivity and uprooting the weeds of self-doubt and limitation. This involves developing an awareness of our self-talk, noticing the patterns of thought that either empower or constrain us, and choosing to nurture a narrative that supports our growth and evolution.

By replacing the language of limitation ("I can't," "I'm not good enough," "I'll never be able to") with the language of possibility ("I can learn," "I'm capable of growth," "I'm willing to try"), we begin to shift the foundation of our mindset. We create space for curiosity, experimentation, and the belief that with effort and dedication, we can expand the boundaries of our potential.

The Power of Effort and Perseverance: The Engines of Growth

A growth mindset is rooted in the understanding that effort and perseverance are the keys to unlocking our full potential. Where a fixed mindset sees talent and intelligence as the primary determinants of success, a growth mindset recognizes that it is through sustained effort and a willingness to push through challenges that we grow and thrive.

This perspective shifts the focus from outcomes to learning and development. It celebrates the courage to show up, the determination to keep going in the face of setbacks, and the resilience to pick oneself up after a fall. By embracing effort as the path to mastery and perseverance as the foundation of achievement, we cultivate a sense of agency and empowerment, recognizing that our future is not determined by our current abilities but by our willingness to grow.

In the words of Carol Dweck, the pioneering researcher of mindset psychology, "The passion for stretching yourself and sticking to it, even (or especially) when it's not going well, is the hallmark of the growth mindset. This is the mindset that allows people to thrive during some of the most challenging times in their lives."

The Feedback Loop: Embracing Guidance and Reflection

A growth mindset thrives on feedback, recognizing it as an essential nutrient for personal evolution. Where a fixed mindset may view feedback as a threat to self-image or a judgment of worth, a growth mindset sees it as a gift – an opportunity to gain valuable insights, refine skills, and chart a course for continuous improvement.

Embracing feedback requires a posture of humility, curiosity, and a genuine desire to learn and grow. It means setting aside the ego's need for validation and focusing instead on the lessons and insights that feedback holds. By seeking out feedback from trusted sources, be they mentors, colleagues, or even constructive critics, we open ourselves to a wealth of knowledge and perspective that can catalyze our growth and development.

Equally important is the practice of self-reflection – the willingness to turn the lens of honest appraisal inward and examine our own thoughts, beliefs, and behaviors. By cultivating a habit of regular introspection, we become more attuned to our strengths and areas for growth, more aware of the patterns and habits that shape our lives, and more empowered to make the choices and changes that align with our highest aspirations.

The Community of Growth: Surrounding Yourself with Inspiration

The journey of cultivating a growth mindset is not one we undertake alone. The people we surround ourselves with, the conversations we engage in, and the environments we immerse ourselves in all play an important role in shaping our attitudes, beliefs, and behaviors.

To foster a growth mindset, it is essential to seek and surround ourselves with individuals who embody the qualities and perspectives we wish to cultivate. These inspire us with their resilience in the face of challenges, their enthusiasm for learning and growth, and their unwavering belief in the power of effort and perseverance. They are the mentors, the role models, and the collaborators who challenge us to stretch beyond our perceived limitations and explore the outer reaches of our potential.

By immersing ourselves in a community of growth, we create an ecosystem of support, encouragement, and accountability. We expose ourselves to new ideas, perspectives, and possibilities, and we find the courage and inspiration to step outside of our comfort zones and embrace the challenges that lead to personal transformation.

The Lighthouse of Purpose: Setting Goals and Celebrating Progress

A growth mindset is fueled by a sense of purpose – a clear and compelling vision of the person we wish to become and the impact we wish to make in the world. This sense of purpose serves as a lighthouse, guiding us through the choppy waters of challenges and setbacks, and illuminating the path toward our highest aspirations.

To harness the power of purpose, it is essential to set clear, meaningful goals that align with our values and stretch us toward growth. These goals become the milestones on our journey of personal evolution, the markers by which we measure our progress and celebrate our achievements.

Yet, in the pursuit of these goals, success is not a destination but a journey of continuous learning and self-discovery. A growth mindset celebrates progress, not just outcomes. It finds joy in the effort, the learning, and the growth that occurs along the way, recognizing that each step taken, each challenge overcome, and each lesson learned is a victory.

By focusing on progress over perfection, we cultivate a sense of momentum and motivation that propels us forward, even in the face of setbacks and adversity. We learn to embrace the journey as much as the destination, finding fulfillment.

~

NURTURING POSITIVITY: A GARDEN OF GROWTH AND RESILIENCE

The Sunlight of the Soul: Cultivating a Positive Mindset

Our attitudes and perspectives shape the colors and textures of our reality, like threads in a tapestry. Just as a garden thrives under the nurturing rays of the sun, our minds and hearts flourish when bathed in the warm light of positivity. This chapter serves as a guide to cultivating a garden of positivity within, offering practical strategies and insights to help you sow the seeds of optimism, resilience, and joy in every part of your life.

At its core, a positive mindset is a choice – a conscious decision to focus on the good, to find opportunity in challenge, and to believe in the power of possibility. It is a way of being that recognizes the inherent potential for growth and transformation in every moment, and that seeks to harness that potential through the alchemy of thought, emotion, and action.

Cultivating a positive mindset is not about denying the existence of difficulties or challenges, but about developing the inner resources and perspectives necessary to navigate them with grace, resilience, and a steadfast commitment to growth. It is about learning to see the world through the lens of possibility, to find the hidden gifts in adversity, and to nurture a deep trust in one's own capacity to learn, adapt, and thrive.

The Ecosystem of Work: Fostering Positivity in the Professional Realm

One of the key arenas in which the cultivation of positivity can have a profound impact is the workplace. Our professional lives are often characterized by a complex interplay of challenges, opportunities, and relationships, each of which can either fuel or deplete our sense of well-being and engagement.

To nurture a positive mindset in the workplace, it is essential to develop practices that help us stay grounded, focused, and inspired in the face of daily pressures and demands. One such practice is the use of morning mantras or affirmations – simple, powerful statements that anchor us in our strengths, values, and intentions. By beginning each workday with a moment of reflection and self-affirmation, we set a tone of positivity and purpose that can infuse our actions and interactions throughout the day.

Another key practice is the cultivation of gratitude, the intentional recognition and appreciation of the good in our professional lives. This can take the form of a gratitude journal, in which we regularly note down the parts of our work that we are thankful for – from supportive colleagues and meaningful projects to opportunities for growth and development. By consciously focusing on the positive elements of our work experience, we train our minds to see the abundance and possibility that surrounds us, even in challenges.

Equally important is the practice of celebrating milestones and achievements, no matter how small. In work, it is all too easy to move from one task to the next without acknowledging the progress and successes along the way. By taking the time to recognize and celebrate our accomplishments, we reinforce a sense of competence, value, and forward momentum, fueling our motivation and engagement.

The Garden of Connection: Nurturing Positive Relationships

Just as a garden thrives on the interconnectedness of its various elements – the soil, the water, the sun, and the living creatures that inhabit it – our lives are enriched by the web of relationships that surround and support us. From family and friends to colleagues and community members, the people in our lives have a profound impact on our sense of well-being, belonging, and purpose.

To cultivate positivity in our relationships, it is essential to develop habits of presence, empathy, and active engagement. One such habit is the practice of active listening – the art of giving our full, undivided attention to the person we are communicating with, without judgment, interruption, or distraction. By creating a space of deep, authentic connection in our interactions, we foster a sense of mutual understanding, respect, and trust that can transform even the most challenging relationships.

Another powerful practice is the cultivation of kindness – the intentional choice to extend compassion, generosity, and care to those around us. Whether through small acts of thoughtfulness or larger gestures of support, the practice of kindness has a ripple effect, spreading positivity and goodwill far beyond the initial interaction. By making kindness a daily habit, we create a culture of warmth, empathy, and mutual support that can transform our relationships and communities.

Equally important is the practice of mindfully choosing the company we keep – surrounding ourselves with individuals who embody the qualities and perspectives we wish to cultivate in ourselves. By seeking and nurturing relationships with people who inspire, challenge, and uplift us, we create an ecosystem of positivity that supports our own growth and development.

The Inner Landscape: Cultivating Positivity in Personal Development

Ultimately, the cultivation of a positive mindset is an inside job – a process of inner transformation that unfolds through the daily choices we make in our thoughts, beliefs, and actions. It is a journey of self-discovery and self-mastery, in which we learn to harness the power of our minds and hearts to create a life of meaning, purpose, and fulfillment.

One of the key practices in this journey is the art of setting goals with intention and grace. By defining clear, compelling visions of the person we wish to become and the life we wish to create, we give ourselves a sense of direction and purpose that can guide and motivate us through even the most challenging times. At the same time, it is essential to approach goal setting with a spirit of flexibility, self-compassion, and a focus on progress over perfection. By celebrating the small victories along the way and maintaining a growth mindset in the face of setbacks, we cultivate the resilience and adaptability necessary to thrive in an ever-changing world.

Another important practice is the art of learning from letdowns – the ability to find the hidden gifts and lessons in moments of disappointment, failure, or adversity. By approaching challenges with a spirit of curiosity and a commitment to growth, we transform them from obstacles to opportunities, from stumbling blocks to steppingstones on the path of personal evolution.

Perhaps most important, the cultivation of positivity in personal development requires a deep commitment to self-care – the ongoing practice of nurturing our physical, emotional, mental, and spiritual well-being. Whether through exercise, meditation, creative pursuits, or simply taking time to rest and recharge, the act of focusing on self-care is a powerful affirmation of our own worth and value. It is a recognition that we cannot pour from an empty cup, and that by tending to our own needs and desires, we create a foundation of vitality and resilience that lets us show up more fully in every part of our lives.

The Harvest of Joy: A Journey of Lifelong Growth

Cultivating a positive mindset is a lifelong journey – a daily practice of planting seeds of hope, nurturing them with intention, and harvesting the fruits of joy, resilience, and fulfillment. This journey requires patience, perseverance, and a deep trust in growth, even when the path ahead may seem uncertain or challenging.

By integrating the strategies and practices outlined in this chapter into the fabric of your daily life, you open yourself to a world of possibility and potential. You become the master gardener of your own mindset, tending to the soil of your thoughts, beliefs, and emotions with loving care and attention.

As you walk this path of personal transformation, remember that the cultivation of positivity is not about denying the reality of life's challenges, but about developing the inner resources and perspectives necessary to meet them with grace, resilience, and an unwavering commitment to growth. It is about learning to find the beauty and opportunity in every moment, to trust in the inherent goodness of life, and to nurture a deep sense of connection and purpose that sustains you through every season of change.

The journey of cultivating a positive mindset is a journey of coming home to yourself – of discovering the radiant essence of joy, love, and potential that has always lived within you. It is a journey of learning to see the world through the eyes of wonder, gratitude, and possibility, and of embracing the fullness of your own humanity with compassion, courage, and an open heart.

As you tend to the garden of your mind and heart, may you blossom in ways you never dreamed possible. May you discover the power of your own positivity to transform not only your own life, but the lives of all those you touch. And may you walk this path with a sense of lightness, curiosity, and a deep trust in the unfolding of your own unique journey.

For the cultivation of positivity is not a destination, but a way of being – a daily choice to embrace the beauty, wonder, and infinite potential of this precious life. It is a commitment to the lifelong journey of growth, self-discovery, and the revelation of your own radiant spirit. So, plant the seeds, tend the soil, and watch in awe as the garden of your life bursts forth in a glorious expression of color, fragrance, and unending possibility.

Case Study:

Meet Sarah, a young woman who found herself at a crossroads in her personal and professional life. Despite her intelligence and potential, Sarah struggled with self-doubt and a persistent negative outlook that colored her experiences and held her back from pursuing her dreams.

One day, a friend recommended a book on the transformative power of attitude. Intrigued, Sarah began to dig into the pages, and what she discovered resonated deeply with her. The book explored the profound influence that attitude has on every part of life, from relationships and personal growth to professional success and overall well-being.

As Sarah continued to read, she began to recognize how her own negative attitudes had been shaping her reality. She realized that her pessimistic outlook and self-limiting beliefs were not only holding her back but also affecting the quality of her relationships and her ability to find fulfillment in her work.

Determined to make a change, Sarah started to put the strategies into practice and practices outlined in the book. She began by cultivating a greater awareness of her thoughts and emotions, noticing when negative self-talk or limiting beliefs would arise. Rather than getting caught up in these patterns, she learned to challenge and reframe them, replacing negative thoughts with more empowering and optimistic ones.

Sarah also made a conscious effort to focus on gratitude and appreciation, taking time each day to reflect on the positive aspects of her life and the people and experiences that brought her joy. She started a gratitude journal, where she would write down three things she was thankful for each evening before bed. Over time, this practice helped to shift her overall mindset and perspective, letting her see the abundance and possibility that surrounded her.

In her professional life, Sarah began to approach challenges and setbacks with a newfound sense of resilience and determination. Instead of getting discouraged by obstacles, she started to view them as opportunities for growth and learning. She sought feedback and mentorship from colleagues and supervisors, using their insights to continually refine her skills and approach.

As Sarah continued to cultivate a more positive and growth-oriented attitude, she noticed a profound shift in her relationships as well. By bringing a more optimistic and compassionate presence to her interactions, she found that her connections with others deepened and flourished. She became known as someone who could be counted on for support, encouragement, and a refreshing perspective, even in challenging times.

Over time, Sarah's commitment to nurturing a positive attitude began to yield remarkable results. She took on new challenges and opportunities at work, and her contributions were recognized and celebrated by her team. In her personal life, she developed a greater sense of self-acceptance and self-love, which attracted healthier, more fulfilling relationships.

Looking back on her journey, Sarah realized that the transformation she had undergone was not just about adopting a more positive outlook – it was about shifting her relationship with herself and the world around her. By recognizing the power of her own attitudes and beliefs, and by making a conscious choice to cultivate a mindset of growth, resilience, and possibility, she had unlocked a wellspring of potential within herself.

Sarah's story serves as a powerful reminder of the transformative influence that our attitudes can have on every part of our lives. By embracing the practices and principles of positive thinking, and by committing to the lifelong journey of personal growth and self-discovery, we all have the power to shape our realities and create lives of purpose, fulfillment, and boundless possibility. The key lies in recognizing that our attitudes are not fixed or predetermined, but a reflection of the choices we make in each moment – choices with the power to transform not only our own lives but the lives of all those we touch.

∾

PART TWO WRAP-UP:

KEY POINTS:

• Attitude is the lens through which we perceive and navigate life, shaping our thoughts, emotions, and actions.

• Self-belief, or self-efficacy, is the confidence in one's ability to succeed and overcome challenges, and it greatly influences motivation, resilience, and performance.

• Attitude and self-belief are closely intertwined; our attitudes shape our self-belief, and our self-belief influences our attitudes and behaviors.

• Developing a growth mindset, which views abilities and intelligence as malleable and capable of improvement through effort and learning, is important for personal growth and success.

• Cultivating resilience and perseverance is essential for maintaining a positive attitude and strong self-belief in the face of setbacks and challenges.

• Surrounding oneself with positive influences, such as supportive people and uplifting environments, can significantly affect one's attitude, self-belief, and personal growth.

• Setting realistic goals and consistently working toward them, while celebrating progress along the way, is key to building and maintaining self-belief.

• Embracing the power of positive thinking and self-belief can lead to profound personal transformation, unlocking one's full potential and fostering a more fulfilling life.

Action Items:

• Practice self-awareness and identify negative thought patterns and limiting beliefs that may be hindering your self-belief and growth.

• Challenge negative self-talk and reframe it with positive affirmations and empowering thoughts.

• Cultivate a growth mindset by embracing challenges as opportunities for learning and development, and by viewing setbacks as temporary and valuable lessons.

• Set realistic and achievable goals that align with your values and aspirations, and break them down into manageable steps to maintain motivation and build self-belief.

• Practice gratitude by regularly acknowledging the positive aspects of your life and expressing appreciation for the people and experiences that bring you joy.

• Surround yourself with supportive and uplifting individuals who encourage your growth and believe in your potential.

• Develop resilience by focusing on your strengths, learning from failures, and maintaining a positive outlook in the face of adversity.

• Celebrate your progress and accomplishments, no matter how small, to reinforce your self-belief and maintain motivation.

• Continuously seek opportunities for personal and professional development, and approach new experiences with a curious and open mindset.

• Share your journey and insights with others, inspiring them to cultivate a positive attitude and harness their own self-belief for personal growth and success.

In our next part...

... we'll start a fascinating exploration of the mind's incredible ability to shape our reality and unlock our fullest potential. We'll dive into the groundbreaking concept of neuroplasticity, which reveals that our brains are not fixed and immutable, but rather highly adaptable and capable of profound transformation throughout our entire lives. Prepare to be amazed as we uncover the power of our thoughts and beliefs to literally rewire our neural pathways, letting us break free from limiting patterns and cultivate a mindset of growth, resilience, and boundless possibility.

But the journey doesn't stop there. We'll also explore the life-changing effects of gratitude and appreciation, and how these simple yet powerful practices can transform our mental, emotional, and even physical well-being. Through cutting-edge research and real-life examples, you'll discover how cultivating a grateful heart can help you tap into a deep well of inner peace, joy, and abundance, even in the face of life's greatest challenges. So get ready to experience the incredible alchemy of your own mind, as you learn to harness the power of your thoughts and emotions to create a life of purpose, passion, and unparalleled fulfillment.

∼

PART THREE
THE QUANTUM LEAP:

HARNESSING THE
TRANSFORMATIVE POWER
OF YOUR MIND

THE MALLEABLE MIND: **A Paradigm Shift in Neuroscience**

In the realm of personal transformation, maybe no discovery has been more profound or revolutionary than that of neuroplasticity – the brain's remarkable capacity to rewire itself in response to experience, learning, and even thought. This paradigm-shifting insight has forever changed our understanding of the relationship between mind and reality, unveiling the tremendous power we have to shape our own cognitive and emotional landscapes.

For centuries, the prevailing view of the brain was that of a static, unchangeable entity – a complex machine whose structure and function were largely fixed by the time we reached adulthood. But as the field of neuroscience has evolved, so has our perception of the brain's potential for change and adaptation. The discovery of neuroplasticity has shattered the myth of the immutable mind, revealing instead a dynamic, malleable organ constantly reshaping itself in response to the stimuli it encounters.

At its core, neuroplasticity refers to the brain's ability to reorganize its neural networks – the intricate web of connections between neurons that underlies all of our thoughts, feelings, and behaviors. Through a process known as synaptic plasticity, the brain can strengthen or weaken these connections based on the frequency and intensity of their use. The more we engage in a particular thought pattern, emotional response, or behavior, the stronger and more efficient the corresponding neural pathways become.

This insight has profound implications for our understanding of attitude and its role in shaping our lived experience. If the brain is a malleable entity, constantly adapting to the input it receives, then our attitudes – the lenses through which we perceive and interpret reality – have the power to literally rewire our neural circuitry, creating a feedback loop that reinforces and perpetuates our chosen mindset.

The Alchemy of Positive Thought: Sculpting Neural Pathways of Resilience

One of the most exciting applications of neuroplasticity is in the realm of positive thinking and its impact on mental and emotional well-being. By intentionally cultivating attitudes of optimism, gratitude, and resilience, we engage in a form of mental alchemy, transmuting the raw material of experience into gold.

Research has shown that individuals who consistently engage in positive thought patterns show increased activity in areas of the brain associated with emotional regulation, problem-solving, and resilience. Over time, these patterns of activation strengthen the corresponding neural networks, making it easier and more automatic to access these states of mind in the face of stress or adversity.

By choosing to focus on the positive aspects of our experience – the blessings, the opportunities for growth, the inherent goodness in ourselves and others – we are literally sculpting our brains to be more receptive to and reflective of these qualities. We are creating a mental and emotional ecosystem primed for resilience, adaptability, and thriving.

This is not to suggest that positive thinking is a panacea for all of life's challenges, or that we should ignore or deny the real difficulties and injustices that exist in the world. Rather, it is a recognition that our attitudes and perspectives have a profound impact on how we navigate and respond to these challenges, and that by consciously choosing to cultivate a mindset of possibility and potential, we empower ourselves to meet adversity with grace, courage, and creativity.

The Influence of Environment: Nurturing a Neuroplastic Ecosystem

While the power of thought in shaping our neural landscape cannot be overstated, it is equally important to recognize the role that our external environment plays in the process of neuroplastic change. Just as the brain is constantly adapting to the stimuli it receives from within, it is also highly responsive to the input it receives from the world.

The environments we inhabit – physical, social, and cultural – have a profound impact on the development and maintenance of our neural networks. Exposure to enriching, supportive, and stimulating environments has been shown to promote neuroplasticity, helping with the growth of new neural connections and the strengthening of existing ones. But environments that are impoverished, stressful, or toxic can have the opposite effect, inhibiting neuroplastic processes and reinforcing maladaptive patterns of thought and behavior.

This insight highlights the importance of intentionally cultivating environments that support and reinforce the attitudes and mindsets we wish to embody. By surrounding ourselves with people, places, and experiences that reflect our values and aspirations, we create a neuroplastic ecosystem that nurtures our growth and development. We immerse ourselves in a feedback loop of positivity and potential, in which our external reality begins to mirror and magnify the best within us.

This cultivation of a supportive environment extends beyond our immediate physical and social surroundings to encompass the mental and emotional spaces we inhabit as well. By engaging in practices such as mindfulness, meditation, and self-reflection, we create an internal environment conducive to neuroplastic change. We develop the capacity to observe our thoughts and emotions with curiosity and compassion, to challenge limiting beliefs and assumptions, and to consciously choose the attitudes and perspectives that align with our highest purpose.

The Journey of Self-Directed Neuroplasticity: Embracing the Transformative Power of Attitude

Ultimately, the journey of harnessing the power of neuroplasticity is one of self-empowerment and self-directed transformation. It is a recognition that we are not passive recipients of our mental and emotional states, but active participants in creating our own reality.

By embracing the principles of neuroplasticity, we open ourselves to the possibility of profound personal growth and transformation. We become the architects of our own minds, consciously sculpting the neural pathways that shape our perceptions, responses, and experiences. We develop the capacity to meet life's challenges with resilience, adaptability, and grace, secure knowing that we have the power to choose our attitudes and to shape our destiny.

This journey is not always easy, and it requires a deep commitment to self-awareness, self-reflection, and self-mastery. It demands that we confront our own limiting beliefs, fears, and patterns of thought, and that we cultivate the courage to step outside of our comfort zones in pursuit of growth and transformation.

But the rewards of this journey are immeasurable. As we begin to harness the power of neuroplasticity, we tap into a wellspring of inner strength, creativity, and resilience we may never have known we had. We develop a greater sense of agency and autonomy in our lives, recognizing that we have the power to shape our own reality through the attitudes and perspectives we choose to cultivate.

The revelation of neuroplasticity is not just a scientific discovery, but a call to action – an invitation to take responsibility for the quality of our own minds and to become active participants in the unfolding of our own lives. It is a reminder that we are not merely products of our circumstances, but co-creators of our own experience, with the power to transform ourselves and our world through the alchemy of attitude.

As we start this journey of self-directed neuroplasticity, let us do so with a sense of curiosity, compassion, and courage. Let us embrace the challenges and opportunities that arise as invitations to grow, to learn, and to expand the boundaries of what we believe to be possible. And let us remember that, in every moment, we have the power to choose the attitudes and perspectives that will shape our reality, sculpting a life of meaning, purpose, and boundless potential.

THE RADIANCE OF RESILIENCE: ILLUMINATING THE SCIENCE OF POSITIVE THINKING

The Power of Perspective: A Beacon in the Darkness

Our true character is often shaped by the difficult moments we face in life. Yet even in adversity, a power can illuminate the path forward, a beacon that can guide us toward hope, healing, and growth. That power is the radiance of positive thinking – the unwavering belief in the possibility of a brighter future, even in the face of overwhelming odds.

At its core, positive thinking is a perspective – a way of interpreting and responding to the world grounded in optimism, gratitude, and a deep faith in the human capacity for resilience and transformation. It is a conscious choice to focus on the good, even in the bad; to find the lesson and the opportunity in every challenge; and to maintain a steadfast commitment to growth and learning, no matter what life may bring.

But positive thinking is more than just a feel-good philosophy or a naive denial of reality. It is a scientifically confirmed approach to mental and physical well-being that has been shown to have profound effects on every part of our lives. From the strength of our immune systems to the resilience of our minds, the power of positive thinking is a force that can literally transform our biology, our psychology, and our experience of the world.

The Physiology of Positivity: How Thoughts Shape Our Health

One of the most remarkable discoveries in mind-body medicine is the extent to which our thoughts and emotions can influence our physical health. Through a complex network of neural and hormonal pathways, the brain constantly communicates with the rest of the body, sending signals that can either promote or undermine our well-being.

When we engage in positive thinking, we activate a cascade of physiological responses that have been shown to boost immune function, reduce inflammation, and promote healing. By reducing the production of stress hormones like cortisol and adrenaline and increasing the release of feel-good neurotransmitters like serotonin and dopamine, positive thinking creates a biological environment conducive to health and resilience.

This is not just a matter of subjective experience – the evidence for the health benefits of positive thinking is strong and compelling. In one landmark study, researchers at the University of California, Berkeley found that individuals who engaged in regular practices of loving-kindness meditation – a form of positive thinking that involves cultivating feelings of compassion and goodwill toward oneself and others – showed significant increases in the activity of genes associated with immune function and a decrease in the activity of genes associated with inflammation.

Other studies have found similar results, linking positive thinking to a wide range of health benefits, from improved cardiovascular function and lower blood pressure to reduced risk of chronic diseases like diabetes and cancer. The message is clear: by cultivating a positive outlook, we are not only improving our mental and emotional well-being, but we are also taking a proactive step toward safeguarding our physical health.

The Psychology of Resilience: Navigating Life's Challenges with Grace

The benefits of positive thinking extend far beyond the realm of physical health. Maybe even more profound is the impact that a positive outlook can have on our mental and emotional well-being, particularly in the face of life's inevitable challenges and setbacks.

Research has consistently shown that individuals who engage in positive thinking are better equipped to cope with stress, adversity, and trauma. By maintaining a hopeful and optimistic perspective, even in the darkest of times, these individuals can find meaning and purpose in their struggles, and use their challenges as opportunities for growth and transformation.

This is not to say that positive thinking is a magic bullet that can eliminate all of life's difficulties. Pain, loss, and suffering are an inevitable part of the human experience, and no amount of positive thinking can change that fact. But what positive thinking can do is to change our relationship to these experiences – to help us find the strength, courage, and resilience to meet them with grace and to emerge from them with a greater sense of purpose and clarity.

One of the key mechanisms through which positive thinking promotes mental and emotional resilience is through the cultivation of a growth mindset. Individuals with a growth mindset view challenges and setbacks not as failures or indictments of their worth, but as opportunities for learning and development. They approach life with a sense of curiosity and openness and will take risks and embrace discomfort in the pursuit of their goals and dreams.

This mindset starkly contrasts with the fixed mindset, which views talents and abilities as static and unchangeable. Individuals with a fixed mindset often feel helpless in the face of adversity, believing they are powerless to change their circumstances or improve their lot in life. They may become mired in negative thinking patterns, such as self-doubt, self-criticism, and pessimism, which can further undermine their resilience and well-being.

By cultivating a growth mindset through the practice of positive thinking, we open ourselves up to a world of possibility and potential. We see challenges not as threats, but as opportunities; not as limitations, but as invitations to grow and evolve. And we develop a deep sense of self-efficacy and self-worth, knowing we have the power to shape our own reality and to create a life of meaning, purpose, and fulfillment.

The Practice of Positivity: Cultivating a Radiant Mind

Cultivating a positive outlook is not always easy, particularly in a world that often seems filled with negativity, uncertainty, and fear. It requires a deep commitment to self-awareness, self-reflection, and self-mastery, and a willingness to challenge our own limiting beliefs and assumptions about ourselves and the world.

But fortunately, positive thinking is a skill that can be learned and cultivated, like any other. By engaging in practices that promote positivity, gratitude, and resilience, we can literally rewire our brains to default to a more optimistic and hopeful perspective, even in the face of life's greatest challenges.

Some of the most powerful practices for cultivating positive thinking include:

• **Gratitude Journaling:** Taking time each day to reflect on the things we are grateful for, no matter how small or seemingly insignificant, can help to shift our focus away from negativity and toward the abundance and blessings in our lives.

• **Mindfulness Meditation:** By learning to observe our thoughts and emotions with curiosity and compassion, we can begin to detach from negative thinking patterns and cultivate a greater sense of peace and equanimity.

• **Positive Affirmations:** Repeating positive statements about ourselves and our lives, such as "I am worthy of love and respect" or "I have the strength to overcome any challenge," can help to reprogram our subconscious minds and promote a more positive self-image.

• **Acts of Kindness:** Engaging in acts of kindness and generosity toward others has been shown to promote feelings of happiness, connection, and purpose, and to enhance our overall sense of well-being.

• **Seeking Positive Influences:** Surrounding ourselves with people, experiences, and environments that reflect our values and aspirations can help to reinforce our commitment to positive thinking and give us the support and encouragement we need to stay the course.

By incorporating these practices into our daily lives, we begin to cultivate a radiant mind – a mind filled with light, hope, and possibility, even in the darkest of times. We develop the resilience and adaptability to weather life's storms with grace and courage, and to emerge from them stronger, wiser, and more compassionate than before.

The Promise of Positivity: A Call to Radiance

Ultimately, the power of positive thinking lies not just in its ability to transform our own lives, but in its potential to create a ripple effect of positivity and resilience that extends far beyond ourselves. When we cultivate a radiant mind and a hopeful heart, we become a beacon of light for others – a source of inspiration, compassion, and strength that can help to illuminate even the darkest corners of the world.

In a world that often seems filled with darkness and despair, the practice of positive thinking is more than just a personal journey – it is a call to action, a summons to bring more light and love into the world. By embodying the principles of positivity, gratitude, and resilience, we become agents of change and transformation, helping to create a world that is more just, more compassionate, and more radiant than ever before.

So let us embrace the power of positive thinking, not as a naive denial of life's challenges, but as a courageous affirmation of our own strength and potential. Let us cultivate a radiant mind and a hopeful heart and let us use our light to illuminate the path forward for ourselves and for all those whose lives we touch.

For the promise of positive thinking is not just a promise of personal well-being and fulfillment, but a promise of a world transformed by the radiance of resilience, the luminescence of love, and the eternal light of the human spirit. May we all have the courage and the conviction to embrace the transformative power of positive thinking, to radiate resilience in the face of adversity, and to illuminate the world with the boundless light of our shared humanity.

Let us walk this path together, supporting and uplifting one another, as we work to create a future that is more compassionate, more connected, and more radiant than we ever dreamed possible. For the true measure of our lives is not in the challenges we face, but in the grace, the wisdom, and the love with which we meet them. So let us go forth with open hearts and hopeful minds, knowing that every thought, every word, and every action has the power to shape our reality and to transform the world. May we all have the courage and the commitment to be the change we wish to see, to light the way for others, and to leave this world a little brighter than we found it.

THE ALCHEMY OF EXPECTATION: HARNESSING THE TRANSFORMATIVE POWER OF SELF-FULFILLING PROPHECIES

The Mirror of the Mind: Reflecting Our Beliefs into Reality

Our beliefs about ourselves and the world hold immense power to shape our human experience. These beliefs are the lenses through which we perceive reality, the filters that shape our thoughts, emotions, and actions, and the blueprints that guide us toward our destinies. And yet, for all their power, these beliefs are not static or immutable – they are dynamic, malleable, and constantly evolving in response to the feedback loop of our own expectations and experiences.

At the heart of this dynamic lies a phenomenon that has fascinated psychologists, philosophers, and spiritual teachers for centuries – the concept of the self-fulfilling prophecy. A self-fulfilling prophecy is a belief or expectation that, because of being held, actually brings about the outcome it predicts. It is a stunning illustration of the mind's ability to shape reality, to manifest its deepest convictions and desires, and to alchemize thought into tangible form.

The implications of this phenomenon are profound and far-reaching. If our beliefs have the power to shape our reality, then we are not merely passive observers of our lives, but active co-creators of our own destinies. We are the authors of our own stories, the architects of our own futures, and the alchemists of our own transformation.

The Science of Self-Fulfillment: Excavating the Roots of Expectation

The concept of the self-fulfilling prophecy is not merely a philosophical or spiritual abstraction – it is a scientific reality that has been extensively studied and documented in fields ranging from psychology and sociology to medicine and beyond. Some of the most compelling evidence for the power of expectation comes from the groundbreaking work of researchers Robert Rosenthal and Lenore Jacobson, who conducted experiments in the 1960s that would forever change our understanding of the relationship between belief and reality.

In their most famous study, known as the "Pygmalion Effect," Rosenthal and Jacobson administered a standard IQ test to a group of elementary school students, and then randomly selected a subset of those students and told their teachers that they had been identified as "academic spurters" – students poised for rapid intellectual growth and academic success in the coming year. In reality, these students did not differ from their peers in terms of their actual intellectual abilities or potential.

What happened next was nothing short of astonishing. During the school year, the students who had been labeled as "academic spurters" actually began to outperform their peers in virtually every academic domain. They scored higher on standardized tests, received better grades, and were even described by their teachers as being more curious, engaged, and enthusiastic about learning.

The implications of this study were profound. It suggested that the expectations and beliefs we hold about others – and that others hold about us – can actually shape our behavior and performance in ways that make those expectations come true. The mere act of believing in someone's potential can actually help to unlock that potential and bring it to fruition.

But the power of expectation does not end there. Subsequent research has shown that our beliefs and expectations can shape our reality in a wide range of domains, from physical health and well-being to inter-personal relationships and professional success. For example, studies have shown that patients who are given a placebo – a "fake" treatment they believe to be real – can actually experience significant improve-ments in their symptoms and overall health, simply because of their belief in the treatment's efficacy.

Similarly, research has shown that our beliefs and expectations about our own abilities and potential can have a profound impact on our performance and success in various domains. Individuals who believe that intelligence and talent are fixed traits that cannot be developed usually shy away from challenges and give up easily in the face of fail-ure, while those who believe that abilities can be cultivated through hard work and dedication are more likely to persevere and ultimately meet their goals.

The Alchemy of Attitude: Transmuting Belief into Reality

So, what is the mechanism behind this remarkable phenomenon? How do our beliefs and expectations actually translate into real outcomes and experiences? The answer lies in the complex interplay between our thoughts, emotions, and actions – the alchemy of attitude that trans-mutes the ethereal into the concrete.

At the most basic level, our beliefs and expectations shape our percep-tions and interpretations of the world. When we believe that we are capable, worthy, and destined for success, we are more likely to notice and capitalize on opportunities that align with those beliefs. We are more likely to take risks, to persevere in the face of setbacks, and to maintain a positive and optimistic outlook even in the face of adversity.

But our beliefs and expectations also shape our actions and behaviors in more direct and tangible ways. When we believe that we can achieve a particular goal or outcome, we are more likely to take the steps to make that belief a reality. We are more likely to invest time and energy into developing the skills and knowledge we need, to seek mentors and allies who can support and guide us, and to take consis-tent and purposeful action toward our goals.

Our beliefs and expectations can actually change our physiology and neurochemistry in ways that support and reinforce our desired outcomes. When we hold positive beliefs and expectations, our brains release neurotransmitters and hormones that promote feelings of happiness, motivation, and resilience. We are more likely to experience a sense of flow and engagement in our activities, to feel a greater sense of connection and purpose, and to bounce back more quickly from setbacks and challenges.

Our beliefs and expectations create a self-reinforcing feedback loop that shapes our reality in profound and lasting ways. The more we believe in our own potential and the possibility of positive outcomes, the more likely we are to take actions and cultivate mindsets that support those beliefs – and the more evidence we generate to reinforce and strengthen those beliefs.

The Power of Prophecy: Crafting the Future with Intention

Harnessing the power of self-fulfilling prophecies is not always easy or straightforward. Our beliefs and expectations are often shaped by a complex web of factors, including our experiences, our social and cultural conditioning, and the messages and feedback we receive from others. Breaking free from limiting beliefs and cultivating a mindset of possibility and potential requires a deep commitment to self-aware-ness, self-reflection, and self-mastery.

But the rewards of this work are immeasurable. By learning to consciously craft our beliefs and expectations, we open ourselves up to a world of limitless possibility and potential. We become the prophets of our own futures, the creators of our own realities, and the alchemists of our own transformation.

Some of the key practices for harnessing the power of self-fulfilling prophecies include:

• **Cultivating Self-Awareness:** Taking time to reflect on our beliefs, assumptions, and expectations, and to challenge those that may be limiting or self-defeating.

• **Setting Clear Intentions:** Defining specific, measurable, and meaningful goals and outcomes that align with our deepest values and aspirations.

• **Visualizing Success:** Using the power of imagination to vividly and consistently envision ourselves achieving our desired outcomes, and to generate the emotional states and physiological responses that support those outcomes.

• **Affirming Possibility: Repeating positive affirmations and mantras that reinforce our beliefs in our own potential and the possibility of positive outcomes.**

• **Taking Inspired Action:** Consistently taking purposeful and strategic actions that align with our beliefs and expectations, and that generate momentum and progress toward our goals.

By incorporating these practices into our daily lives, we begin to harness the transformative power of self-fulfilling prophecies. We become the architects of our own realities, the authors of our own stories, and the alchemists of our own futures.

The Call to Greatness: Embracing the Responsibility of Co-Creation

Ultimately, the understanding of self-fulfilling prophecies is not just a tool for personal transformation, but a call to greatness – a summons to embrace our role as co-creators of our lives, relationships, and destinies. By recognizing the tremendous power and responsibility that our beliefs and expectations hold, we open ourselves up to a worldview that is grounded in possibility, suffused with hope, and infused knowing that we can make a profound and lasting difference in our own lives and in the lives of those around us.

But this worldview is not a solipsistic or self-absorbed one. Rather, it is a deeply interconnected and interdependent one, a recognition that our individual beliefs and expectations are inextricably intertwined with those of the people and communities around us. When we believe in the potential of others, we help to unlock that potential and catalyze their growth and transformation. And when we align our beliefs and expectations with the greater good, we become agents of positive change and possibility in the world.

So let us embrace the call to greatness that lies at the heart of the self-fulfilling prophecy. Let us recognize the incredible power and responsibility we hold as co-creators of our own lives and futures. And let us use that power wisely, compassionately, and purposefully, ever striving to align our beliefs and expectations with the highest good for ourselves, for others, and for the world. May we become the prophets of possibility, the weavers of new realities, and the alchemists of a future that is more just, more beautiful, and more radiant than we have ever dared to imagine.

For the true measure of our lives is not in the beliefs we hold, but in the realities, we create through the force of those beliefs. It is in the lives we touch, the love we share, and the light we bring into the world. And it is in the legacy we leave behind – a legacy of hope, of possibility, and of the enduring power of the human spirit to shape its own destiny.

So let us go forth with courage, with conviction, and with the unwavering belief that our expectations can and will become our realities. Let us dare to dream boldly, to believe fiercely, and to act with the full force of our being. And let us trust that in doing so, we are not only shaping our own lives, but contributing to the grand tapestry of human experience, weaving threads of possibility and potential that will ripple out across space and time, inspiring and uplifting all those who come after us.

This is the true power and promise of the self-fulfilling prophecy – not just to change our own lives, but to change the world. May we wield that power with wisdom, with love, and with the unshakable conviction that a brighter future is always within our reach, if only we have the courage to believe in it and the determination to make it so.

～

THE METAMORPHOSIS OF MIND: EMBRACING THE TRANSFORMATIVE POWER OF GROWTH MINDSET

The Alchemy of Belief: Transmuting Limitations into Possibilities

In the grand tapestry of human potential, there is perhaps no force more powerful or transformative than the beliefs we hold about ourselves and our capacities for growth and change. These beliefs are the invisible architects of our lives, shaping our thoughts, emotions, and actions in profound and often unconscious ways. They are the lenses through which we perceive the world, the filters that determine what we see as possible or impossible, and the hidden scripts that guide our choices and behaviors.

At the heart of this inner landscape lies a fundamental distinction with the power to either limit or liberate us – the difference between a fixed mindset and a growth mindset. A fixed mindset sees abilities, intelligence, and talents as static and immutable traits, carved in stone and impervious to change. A growth mindset, on the other hand, is one that embraces our capacities' being malleable and expandable, that we can develop and improve through effort, learning, and perseverance.

The implications of this distinction are nothing short of revolutionary. When we adopt a growth mindset, we open ourselves up to a world of boundless possibility and potential. We see challenges not as threats to our self-image, but as opportunities for learning and growth. We become more resilient in the face of setbacks and failures, viewing them not as indictments of our worth, but as valuable feedback and chances to improve. We cultivate a love of learning and a willingness to stretch beyond our comfort zones, knowing that this is where true growth and transformation happen.

A growth mindset is a catalyst for personal alchemy – a way of transmuting the lead of our perceived limitations into the gold of our highest potential. This mindset says "I can" instead of "I can't," that embraces effort and struggle as the keys to mastery, and that sees the journey of growth and self-discovery as the ultimate reward.

The Science of Self-Expansion: Cultivating a Mindset of Growth

The idea of growth mindset is not merely a motivational platitude or self-help cliché – it is a scientific reality that has been extensively studied and confirmed by researchers in the fields of psychology, education, and neuroscience. At the forefront of this research is the pioneering work of Stanford psychologist Carol Dweck, whose decades of studies have illuminated the transformative power of mindset in shaping our abilities, achievements, and overall well-being.

In one of her most famous experiments, Dweck and her colleagues gave a group of fifth graders a series of increasingly difficult puzzles to solve. Some children were praised for their intelligence ("You must be smart at this"), while others were praised for their effort ("You must have worked really hard"). The results were striking – the children who were praised for their effort were far more likely to embrace challenges, persist in the face of setbacks, and ultimately perform better on later tests of their abilities.

This simple yet profound finding cuts to the heart of the growth mindset philosophy – the belief that our abilities are not fixed but can be developed through dedication and hard work. When we embrace this belief, we change our relationship to challenge and failure. Instead of seeing them as threats to our self-image or indictments of our worth, we see them as opportunities for growth and learning.

But the power of growth mindset extends far beyond the realm of academic achievement. Studies have shown that cultivating a growth mindset can have a profound impact on our physical health, our emotional resilience, our relationships, and our overall success and fulfillment in life. For example, research has found that individuals with a growth mindset are more likely to:

• Persevere in the face of setbacks and failures, seeing them as opportunities for learning and improvement rather than signs of inadequacy.

• Embrace challenges and take on difficult tasks, knowing that this is where true growth and development happen.

• Seek feedback and criticism, using it as a valuable tool for self-improvement rather than a threat to their ego.

• Cultivate a love of learning and a willingness to step outside their comfort zones, knowing that this is where the greatest opportunities for growth and transformation lie.

• Develop stronger, more supportive relationships with others, based on a shared commitment to growth, learning, and mutual encouragement.

A growth mindset is not just a feel-good philosophy – it is a scientifically confirmed approach to unlocking our full potential and creating a life of purpose, passion, and possibility.

The Alchemy of Effort: Transmuting Struggle into Strength

Cultivating a growth mindset is not always easy or comfortable. It requires us to confront our deepest fears and insecurities, to push beyond our perceived limitations, and to embrace the discomfort and struggle that comes with true growth and change. It demands that we reframe our relationship to effort and hard work, seeing them not as signs of weakness or inadequacy, but as the keys to our success and fulfillment.

This is where the true alchemy of growth mindset lies – in the willingness to transmute the lead of our struggles and setbacks into the gold of our strengths and triumphs. In the recognition, every challenge we face, every obstacle we overcome, and every failure we learn from is an opportunity to develop new skills, cultivate new insights, and expand our sense of what is possible.

Some of the key practices for cultivating an alchemical mindset of growth and transformation include:

• **Embracing Challenges as Opportunities for Growth:** Instead of shying away from difficult tasks or situations, actively seek them out as chances to stretch beyond your comfort zone and develop new capacities.

• **Reframing Failure as Feedback:** When you encounter setbacks or failures, resist the temptation to see them as reflections of your worth or abilities. Instead, view them as valuable feedback and opportunities for learning and improvement.

• **Cultivating A Love of Learning:** Approach every experience and interaction as a chance to learn and grow, whether it's mastering a new skill, gaining a fresh perspective, or deepening your understanding of yourself and others.

• **Seeking Out Feedback and Criticism:** Actively solicit feedback from others and use it as a tool for self-reflection and improvement. Embrace criticism as a gift, knowing it can help you identify blind spots and areas for growth.

• **Celebrating Effort and Progress:** Focus on acknowledging and celebrating your efforts and progress, rather than fixating on outcomes or results. Recognize that every step forward, no matter how small, is a triumph and a testament to your commitment to growth.

By incorporating these practices into our lives, we begin to cultivate a mindset of growth and possibility that can transform every part of our experience. We become the alchemists of our own transformation, transmuting the raw materials of our struggles and setbacks into the gold of our highest potential.

The Call to Growth: Embracing the Journey of Self-Expansion

Ultimately, the cultivation of a growth mindset is not a destination, but a lifelong journey of self-discovery and self-expansion. It is a call to continually push beyond our perceived limitations, to embrace the discomfort and uncertainty that comes with true growth, and to recognize that our potential is always greater than we can imagine.

But this journey is not a solitary one. By embracing a growth mindset, we open ourselves up to a world of connection, collaboration, and mutual support. We see others not as competitors or threats, but as fellow travelers on the path of self-discovery, each with their own unique gifts and challenges to share.

And as we deepen our commitment to growth and self-expansion, we also begin to recognize the profound impact that our mindset has on the world. When we approach life with a spirit of curiosity, openness, and possibility, we become agents of positive change and transformation, inspiring others to embrace their own potential and join us on the journey of growth.

So let us embrace the call to growth that lies at the heart of the growth mindset philosophy. Let us recognize that our potential is always greater than we can imagine, and that every challenge and setback is an invitation to expand our capacities and deepen our understanding of ourselves and the world.

Let us cultivate a love of learning and a willingness to step outside our comfort zones, knowing that this is where the greatest opportunities for growth and transformation lie. And let us support and celebrate each other on this journey, recognizing that we are all in this together, each with our own unique gifts and challenges to share.

As we do so, we open ourselves up to a life of boundless possibility and potential, a life in which every struggle is an opportunity for growth, every failure is a chance for learning, and every triumph is a testament to the transformative power of the human spirit. We see that our true potential lies not in our innate abilities or talents, but in our willingness to embrace the journey of growth and self-discovery, to push beyond our perceived limitations, and to cultivate a mindset of curiosity, resilience, and possibility.

In this way, the cultivation of a growth mindset becomes not just a personal quest, but a collective calling – a shared commitment to unlocking the full potential of ourselves and others, and to creating a world in which every individual has the opportunity to thrive and flourish. It is a vision of a society that values growth, learning, and compassion above all else, and that recognizes the profound interconnectedness of our individual and collective journeys.

So let us embrace this calling with open hearts and minds, knowing that the path of growth is not always easy, but that it is always worth it. Let us support and inspire each other on this journey, celebrating our successes and learning from our failures, and never losing sight of the infinite potential that lies within each of us.

And let us remember that the true measure of our lives is not in the destinations we reach, but in the growth, we experience along the way. It is in the challenges we overcome, the lessons we learn, and the person we become. It is in the impact we have on the lives of others, and the legacy we leave behind.

This is the transformative power of the growth mindset – the power to change not just ourselves, but the world. May we all have the courage and the wisdom to embrace it, and to step boldly into the boundless possibilities of a life lived in the spirit of growth, compassion, and love.

∼

THE ALCHEMY OF ATTITUDE: TRANSFORMING NEGATIVITY INTO VITALITY AND WELL-BEING

THE SHADOW OF THE MIND: Unveiling the Toll of Toxic Thoughts

In the intricate dance of life, there is perhaps no partner more influential or omnipresent than the thoughts that inhabit our minds. These invisible companions are the silent choreographers of our emotions, behaviors, and ultimately, our health and well-being. And while we may often think of our physical and mental health as separate domains, the truth is that they are inextricably intertwined, each influencing and shaping the other in profound and often unconscious ways.

At the heart of this mind-body connection lies the power of our thoughts – the internal narratives and mental patterns that color our perceptions, guide our actions, and shape our physiological responses. And while we may like to believe that our thoughts are purely private and inconsequential, the reality is that they have a tangible and often dramatic impact on every aspect of our lives, from our relationships and careers to our physical health and longevity.

Nowhere is this impact clearer or more harmful than in the realm of negative thinking – the persistent patterns of pessimism, self-doubt, and defeatism that can take root in our minds and cast a shadow over every part of our lives. These toxic thoughts are the silent saboteurs of our well-being, eroding our resilience, dampening our vitality, and setting the stage for a host of physical and mental health problems.

The Physiology of Pessimism: How Negative Thoughts Hijack Our Health

At the biological level, negative thoughts are powerful triggers for the stress response – the complex cascade of hormonal and physiological changes that prepare our bodies to face perceived threats and challenges. When we engage in persistent negative thinking, we essentially trick our bodies into believing we are under constant threat, chronically activating the stress response that can have devastating consequences for our health.

One of the key players in this process is cortisol – the primary stress hormone released in response to perceived threats and challenges. In small doses, cortisol is essential for our survival, helping to regulate our metabolism, immune function, and cognitive performance. But when cortisol levels remain elevated for prolonged periods – as they do in individuals who engage in chronic negative thinking – the effects can be nothing short of catastrophic.

Research has consistently shown that chronic exposure to high levels of cortisol can lead to a wide range of health problems, including:

• **Cardiovascular Disease:** Negative thoughts and chronic stress have been linked to an increased risk of hypertension, heart attack, and stroke, likely due to the damaging effects of cortisol on the cardiovascular system.

• **Immune Dysfunction:** Cortisol suppresses the immune system, leaving individuals who engage in chronic negative thinking more vulnerable to infections, autoimmune disorders, and even certain types of cancer.

• **Cognitive Decline:** High levels of cortisol have been shown to damage the hippocampus – the brain region responsible for memory and learning – leading to an increased risk of cognitive decline and dementia.

• **Metabolic Disorders:** Chronic stress and negative thinking have been linked to an increased risk of obesity, insulin resistance, and type 2 diabetes, likely due to the effects of cortisol on appetite and glucose metabolism.

• **Mental Health Problems:** Negative thoughts are a hallmark of many mental health disorders, including depression, anxiety, and post-traumatic stress disorder (PTSD), and can both contribute to and exacerbate these conditions.

Chronic negative thinking sets in motion a vicious cycle of stress, inflammation, and disease that can rob us of our vitality, resilience, and overall well-being. It is a silent killer that operates beneath the surface of our awareness, slowly eroding our health and happiness from the inside out.

The Behavioral Toll: How Negativity Breeds Unhealthy Habits

But the impact of negative thoughts extends far beyond the realm of physiology. Our thoughts and beliefs also shape our behaviors and lifestyle choices, often in ways that compound the harmful effects of chronic stress and inflammation.

When caught in the grip of negative thinking, we are more likely to engage in unhealthy coping mechanisms and self-destructive behaviors, such as:

• **Overeating And Poor Nutrition:** Negative thoughts and chronic stress have been linked to an increased appetite for high-fat, high-sugar foods and a lower motivation to prepare healthy meals and engage in mindful eating practices.

• **Substance Abuse:** Individuals who struggle with negative thinking are more likely to turn to alcohol, drugs, or other substances as a way of numbing their emotions and escaping their mental distress.

• **Sedentary Behavior:** Negative thoughts can sap our energy and motivation, making it more difficult to engage in regular physical activity and exercise – behaviors essential for maintaining physical and mental health.

• **Social Isolation:** When trapped in negative thought patterns, we may withdraw from social interactions and relationships, depriving ourselves of the support, connection, and sense of belonging critical for our well-being.

These unhealthy behaviors and lifestyle choices create a self-perpetuating cycle of negativity and ill health, further reinforcing the destructive thought patterns and emotional states that drive them. Negative thinking not only directly affects our physiology, but also indirectly shapes our behaviors in ways that amplify and exacerbate its harmful effects.

The Call to Transformation: Cultivating a Mindset of Positivity and Resilience

Given the pervasive and destructive impact of negative thinking on our health and well-being, cultivating a more positive and resilient mindset is not merely a matter of personal growth or self-improvement – it is an important necessity for our physical, mental, and emotional vitality.

But how do we begin to shift our thoughts and beliefs in a more positive direction, especially when we may have spent years or even decades trapped in patterns of negativity and self-defeat? The journey of transformation is not always easy or straightforward, but it is eminently possible with the right tools, strategies, and support.

Some of the key practices for cultivating a mindset of positivity and resilience include:

• **Mindfulness And Meditation:** By developing a regular practice of mindfulness and meditation, we can learn to observe our thoughts and emotions with greater clarity and detachment, rather than getting caught up in their destructive patterns. This lets us cultivate a greater sense of inner peace, perspective, and emotional resilience.

• **Cognitive Restructuring:** Through techniques such as cognitive-behavioral therapy (CBT), we can learn to identify and challenge the negative thoughts and beliefs that underlie our mental and emotional distress. By replacing these thoughts with more balanced and realistic perspectives, we can begin to break free from the cycle of negativity and cultivate a more positive and empowering mindset.

• **Gratitude and Appreciation:** By cultivating a sense of gratitude and appreciation for the good things in our lives – no matter how small or seemingly insignificant – we can begin to shift our focus away from negativity and toward the abundance and beauty that surrounds us. This practice has been shown to have powerful benefits for our mental and physical health, including reduced stress, improved immune function, and greater overall well-being.

• **Social Connection and Support:** By building strong, supportive relationships with others and seeking out opportunities for social connection and engagement, we can tap into the powerful healing and resilience-building effects of human connection. This can involve joining a support group, contacting friends and loved ones, or simply trying to connect with others in our daily lives.

• **Physical Activity and Self-Care:** By engaging in regular physical activity and focusing on self-care practices such as healthy eating, enough sleep, and stress management, we can help to counteract the physiological effects of negative thinking and build greater resilience and vitality from the inside out.

Ultimately, the journey of transforming negativity into positivity and resilience requires patience, persistence, and a willingness to confront our own mental and emotional patterns with honesty and compassion. This journey may involve setbacks, challenges, and moments of doubt – but it is ultimately worth every step.

For when we begin to shift our thoughts and beliefs in a more positive direction, we open ourselves up to a world of greater possibility, vitality, and well-being. We see challenges as opportunities for growth and learning, rather than as threats or obstacles. We begin to approach life with a sense of curiosity, openness, and adventure, rather than with fear, anxiety, or despair.

And perhaps most importantly, we begin to recognize that our thoughts and beliefs are not fixed or immutable – they are fluid and changeable, shaped by our own choices and actions in each moment. This recognition is the key to unlocking our own transformative potential – the power to alchemize negativity into positivity, suffering into resilience, and limitation into boundless possibility.

So let us embrace the call to transformation that lies at the heart of this chapter – the invitation to reshape our thoughts, beliefs, and behaviors in service of our highest well-being and most vibrant potential. Let us recognize that, no matter how deeply entrenched our patterns of negativity may seem, we always have the power to choose a different path – a path of positivity, resilience, and boundless growth.

This path may not always be easy, and it may require us to confront uncomfortable truths and challenge long-held beliefs about ourselves and the world. But this path is eminently worth taking – for when we begin to align our thoughts and actions with our deepest values and aspirations, we tap into a wellspring of vitality, creativity, and purpose that can transform every part of our lives.

We see that our struggles and challenges are not obstacles to be feared or avoided, but opportunities for growth and self-discovery. We begin to approach life with a sense of curiosity, openness, and wonder, rather than with cynicism, judgment, or despair. And we begin to recognize that our true power lies not in our ability to control or manipulate the world, but in our capacity to choose our own thoughts, beliefs, and responses in each moment.

This is the essence of the alchemy of attitude – the understanding that, by consciously shifting our mental and emotional patterns, we can transform the lead of negativity and limitation into the gold of positivity, resilience, and boundless potential. This practice requires patience, persistence, and a willingness to step outside our comfort zones – but it can ultimately lead us to a life of greater joy, fulfillment, and meaning.

So let us embrace this practice with open hearts and minds, knowing that every thought we think and every action we take has the power to shape our reality and influence the world. Let us support and inspire one another on this journey of transformation, celebrating our successes and learning from our challenges along the way.

And let us never forget that no matter how dark or difficult our circumstances may seem, we always have the power to choose the thoughts and beliefs that will guide us forward – toward a brighter, more beautiful, and more abundant future. May we all find the courage and wisdom to embrace this power, and to use it in service of our own highest good.

THE ALCHEMY OF APPRECIATION: TRANSFORMING LIFE THROUGH THE POWER OF GRATITUDE

The Grateful Heart: Unlocking the Treasures Within

Among the many emotions humans experience, gratitude stands out as one of the most powerful and transformative. This simple yet profound sentiment can shift our perspective, heal our wounds, and illuminate the beauty and abundance that surround us in every moment. This key unlocks the treasures of the heart, revealing the hidden blessings and opportunities we so often overlook in the busyness and distractions of daily life.

At its core, gratitude is a practice of presence – a willingness to inhabit and appreciate the here and now, rather than dwelling on the past or worrying about the future. This recognition, even in life's challenges and difficulties, there is always something to be thankful for – whether it be the warmth of the sun on our skin, the love of a friend or family member, or the simple gift of another day to live and breathe and experience the wonders of the world.

But gratitude is more than just a fleeting feeling or a pleasant sentiment – it is a powerful tool for personal and collective transformation, with deep roots in both ancient wisdom traditions and modern scientific research. As we will explore in this chapter, the practice of gratitude has been shown to have profound effects on our mental, emotional, and even physical well-being, from reducing stress and anxiety to boosting our immune system and enhancing our relationships with others.

The Science of Appreciation: How Gratitude Rewires the Brain

In recent years, the study of gratitude has become a burgeoning field of scientific inquiry, with researchers from a wide range of disciplines exploring the complex ways this emotion shapes our thoughts, feelings, and behaviors. What they have found is nothing short of remarkable – a growing body of evidence that suggests that gratitude is not just a nice feeling, but a fundamental driver of human flourishing and well-being.

At the neurological level, studies have shown that the practice of gratitude can actually rewire our brains, activating regions associated with positive emotions, social bonding, and reward processing. For example, a study conducted by researchers at the University of California, Los Angeles, found that participants who kept a daily gratitude journal for just three weeks showed significant increases in activity in the medial prefrontal cortex – a brain region associated with positive valuation and decision making.

Other studies have found that gratitude practices can lead to increased levels of neurotransmitters such as dopamine and serotonin, which are associated with feelings of pleasure, happiness, and well-being. By focusing our attention on the things we are grateful for, we are training our brains to seek and savor the positive aspects of our lives, rather than dwelling on the negative or stressful.

But the benefits of gratitude extend far beyond the realm of neuroscience. Many studies have found that individuals who regularly practice gratitude report higher levels of positive emotions, life satisfaction, and overall well-being, as well as lower levels of depression, anxiety, and stress. They also usually have stronger social connections and more supportive relationships, as well as greater resilience in the face of life's challenges and setbacks.

One particularly powerful study, conducted by researchers at the University of Pennsylvania, found that participants who wrote and delivered a heartfelt letter of gratitude to someone who had made a difference in their lives experienced significant increases in happiness and decreases in depressive symptoms, with the effects lasting for up to a month after the intervention. This suggests that the benefits of gratitude are not just momentary or fleeting but can have a lasting impact on our overall mental and emotional well-being.

The Alchemy of Appreciation: Transforming Our Lives and Our World

But the transformative power of gratitude extends far beyond the individual level. As we cultivate a deeper sense of appreciation and thankfulness in our own lives, we begin to radiate that energy outward, influencing the people and the world in profound and often unexpected ways.

When we approach life with a grateful heart, we naturally become more compassionate, empathetic, and generous toward others. We are more likely to notice and appreciate the small acts of kindness and beauty that occur around us every day, and to respond in kind with our own gestures of love and support. In this way, gratitude becomes a self-reinforcing cycle of positivity and connection, drawing us closer to others and inspiring them to pay it forward in their own lives.

At the same time, the practice of gratitude can help us to cultivate a greater sense of perspective and resilience in the face of life's challenges and difficulties. When we focus on the things we are thankful for, rather than dwelling on our problems or complaints, we see our lives in a new light – as a tapestry of blessings and opportunities, rather than obstacles and setbacks.

This shift in perspective can be empowering, giving us the strength and courage to face our fears, overcome our limitations, and pursue our deepest dreams and aspirations. It can also help us to find meaning and purpose in even the darkest of times, knowing that every experience – no matter how painful or difficult – holds within it the seeds of growth, learning, and transformation.

Ultimately, the alchemy of appreciation is about more than just feeling good or having a positive attitude – it is about shifting our relationship to ourselves, to others, and to the world. It is about recognizing the inherent beauty, value, and interconnectedness of all things, and living our lives in alignment with that understanding.

Cultivating a Practice of Gratitude: Simple Strategies for Profound Transformation

So how can we begin to cultivate a deeper sense of gratitude in our own lives, and tap into the transformative power of appreciation? While there is no one-size-fits-all approach, there are several simple yet powerful practices that can help us to develop a more grateful and appreciative mindset:

Keep A Gratitude Journal: One of the most effective ways to cultivate gratitude is to make it a daily practice. Set aside a few minutes each day to write down three to five things you are grateful for – no matter how small or seemingly insignificant. Over time, this practice can help to rewire your brain to focus on the positive aspects of your life, and to develop a deeper sense of appreciation and contentment.

Express Your Appreciation to Others: Another powerful way to cultivate gratitude is to express it to the people in your life. Make a habit of regularly thanking others for their kindness, support, and contributions – whether it be a heartfelt letter, a simple "thank you," or a small gesture of appreciation. Not only will this strengthen your relationships and spread positivity to others, but it will also deepen your own sense of gratitude and connection.

Practice Mindfulness and Presence: Gratitude is ultimately about being present and engaged with the world. By practicing mindfulness and presence – whether through meditation, deep breathing, or simply paying attention to the sensations and experiences of the present moment – we can begin to cultivate a deeper sense of appreciation and wonder for the beauty and richness of life.

Reframe Challenges as Opportunities: When faced with difficulties or setbacks, it is easy to fall into patterns of negativity and complaint.

However, by consciously reframing these challenges as opportunities for growth, learning, and transformation, we can begin to cultivate a more resilient and appreciative mindset. Ask yourself: "What can I learn from this experience? How can I use it to become a stronger, wiser, and more compassionate version of myself?"

Cultivate A Sense of Awe and Wonder: Finally, one of the most powerful ways to tap into the alchemy of appreciation is to cultivate a sense of awe and wonder for the world. Whether it be through spending time in nature, engaging in creative pursuits, or simply marveling at the everyday miracles of life, allowing ourselves to be filled with a sense of wonder and reverence can help to shift our perspective and deepen our appreciation for the incredible gift of existence.

The Ripple Effect of Gratitude: Transforming the World One Heart at a Time

As we begin to integrate these practices into our daily lives, we may start to notice a profound shift not only in our own well-being and outlook, but also in the world. As more people tap into the transformative power of gratitude and appreciation, we begin to create a ripple effect of positivity and connection that extends far beyond our individual selves.

We see the world not as a place of scarcity and competition, but as a place of abundance and collaboration. We start to approach our relationships not with judgment and criticism, but with empathy and understanding. And we see our own lives not as problems to be solved, but as a grand adventure to be lived with curiosity, passion, and purpose.

In this way, the alchemy of appreciation becomes not just a personal practice, but a collective movement toward a more grateful, compassionate, and interconnected world. It becomes a way of life that recognizes the inherent worth and dignity of all beings, and that seeks to create a future in which every person has the opportunity to thrive and reach their full potential.

Case Study:

Meet John, a highly successful entrepreneur who, despite his outward achievements, struggled with a deep sense of unfulfillment and inner turmoil. For years, John had been driven by a relentless pursuit of success, pouring all of his energy into building his business and accumulating wealth and status. Yet, as he reached the pinnacle of his professional life, he couldn't shake the nagging feeling that something was missing.

One day, a friend recommended a book on the concept of neuroplasticity and the transformative power of a growth mindset. Intrigued, John began to dig into the material, and what he discovered resonated deeply with him. The book explored the idea that our brains are not fixed and immutable, but rather highly adaptable and capable of change throughout our entire lives.

As John continued to explore this idea, he began to reflect on his own mindset and beliefs. He realized that, for much of his life, he had been operating from a fixed mindset – believing that his talents, abilities, and even his own sense of worth were static and unchangeable. This belief had driven him to constantly seek external validation and to view challenges and setbacks as threats to his identity and self-image.

Armed with this new understanding, John made a conscious decision to begin cultivating a growth mindset. He started to approach challenges and obstacles as opportunities for learning and development, rather than as indictments of his own worth or abilities. He embraced the idea that he could continue to grow, evolve, and expand his own potential, no matter his age or background.

As John began to apply these principles to his life and work, he noticed a profound shift in his own sense of fulfillment and well-being. He became more resilient in the face of setbacks, more open to feedback and criticism, and more willing to take risks and step outside his comfort zone. He also became more empathetic and compassionate toward others, recognizing that everyone is on their own unique journey of growth and development.

Inspired by his own transformation, John began to integrate the principles of neuroplasticity and growth mindset into his company culture. He encouraged his team members to embrace challenges, to view failure as a necessary part of the learning process, and to continually seek opportunities for growth and development. He also became more intentional about fostering a culture of psychological safety and open communication, recognizing these were essential ingredients for innovation and success.

Because of these efforts, John's company began to thrive in ways he had never imagined possible. Not only did they achieve new levels of financial success and market share, but they also became known as a place where people could come to learn, grow, and reach their full potential. John himself became a sought-after speaker and thought leader, sharing his own journey of transformation and inspiring others to embrace the power of a growth mindset.

Looking back on his journey, John realized that the true gift of neuroplasticity and the growth mindset was not just the external success and achievement it had brought him, but the profound inner transformation it had sparked. He had discovered a new sense of purpose and meaning in his life, one grounded in the idea that we are all works in progress, with the infinite potential to learn, grow, and evolve.

John's story is a powerful reminder of the transformative power of our beliefs and mindsets. By embracing our being all capable of change and growth, and by cultivating a mindset of curiosity, resilience, and continuous learning, we open ourselves up to a world of limitless possibility and potential. We become the architects of our own lives, the authors of our own stories, and the creators of our own destinies.

PART THREE WRAP-UP:

Key Points:

• Neuroplasticity is the brain's ability to rewire itself in response to experiences, learning, and thoughts, challenging the notion that the brain is static and unchangeable.

• Our attitudes and beliefs have the power to shape our reality through the concept of self-fulfilling prophecies, where our expectations influence our outcomes.

• A growth mindset, which views abilities and intelligence as malleable, is important for personal development and success, as opposed to a fixed mindset, which sees them as static traits.

• Negative thoughts and chronic stress can harm physical and mental health, leading to various health problems and unhealthy coping mechanisms.

• Cultivating a practice of gratitude has been scientifically proven to have profound effects on mental, emotional, and physical well-being, rewiring the brain for positivity and resilience.

Action Items:

• Embrace the idea of neuroplasticity by engaging in activities that promote learning, growth, and self-discovery, recognizing that your brain can change and adapt throughout your life.

• Identify and challenge your limiting beliefs and self-fulfilling prophecies, replacing them with empowering expectations and positive affirmations that align with your goals and values.

• Cultivate a growth mindset by embracing challenges as opportunities for learning, viewing setbacks as valuable feedback, and focusing on the process of continuous improvement rather than fixating on innate abilities or outcomes.

• Practice mindfulness and self-awareness to identify negative thought patterns and their impact on your well-being, and actively work to replace them with more positive, realistic, and compassionate perspectives.

• Incorporate gratitude into your daily life by keeping a gratitude journal, expressing appreciation to others, reframing challenges as opportunities for growth, and cultivating a sense of awe and wonder for the world around you.

• Surround yourself with positive influences, seek mentors and role models who embody a growth mindset, and engage in activities and environments that support your personal and professional development.

• Encourage others to embrace the transformative power of neuroplasticity, self-fulfilling prophecies, and a growth mindset, creating a ripple effect of positivity and empowerment in your personal and professional life.

In our next part...

... we'll start a transformative journey of self-discovery and personal growth as we explore the realm of negative attitudes and limiting beliefs. These invisible barriers can hold us back from reaching our full potential, but with the right tools and mindset, we have the power to break free from their grip. Get ready to dig into identifying and challenging these self-imposed limitations, and discover how cultivating self-awareness, self-compassion, and a growth mindset can revolutionize your life.

As we navigate this path together, you'll learn practical strategies for reframing negative thoughts, setting empowering goals, and harnessing the power of visualization. We'll also explore the importance of creating a personalized action plan and establishing a strong support system to keep you motivated and accountable on your journey. By embracing these techniques and committing to your personal growth, you'll unlock a world of boundless potential and create a life that aligns with your values and aspirations. So, let's dive in and discover how transforming your mindset can lead to extraordinary results in every part of your life.

PART FOUR
UNLEASHING YOUR POTENTIAL: CONQUERING LIMITING BELIEFS AND EMBRACING PERSONAL GROWTH

THE INSIDIOUS NATURE OF NEGATIVE ATTITUDES: HOW THEY HOLD US BACK

IN THE DEPTHS of the human psyche, there lurk forces that can either propel us toward our highest potential or keep us forever bound in the chains of limitation. These forces are our attitudes – the deeply ingrained beliefs, assumptions, and mental habits that shape our perceptions, our emotions, and our actions in the world.

While some attitudes are empowering and expansive, lifting us up on the wings of possibility, others are negative – weighing us down with doubt, fear, and pessimism, and holding us back from the life we desire. These negative attitudes are like dark clouds that obscure the radiant sun of our true nature, casting shadows of insecurity, apathy, and despair across the landscape of our lives.

At their core, negative attitudes are born from a fundamental misunderstanding of who we are and what we are capable of. They are the product of past wounds, societal conditioning, and the limiting stories we tell ourselves about our own worth and potential. They whisper to us in the voice of the inner critic, telling us we are not good enough, that we will never succeed, that we will fail or be rejected.

The result is a profound disconnection from our own innate wisdom, creativity, and resilience. When we are in the grip of negative attitudes, we become small and contracted, unable to see the vast possibilities that life is offering us in every moment. We become reactive rather than proactive, letting our fears and doubts dictate our choices and shape our reality.

The Cost of Negativity: How Self-Limiting Beliefs Sabotage Our Success

The impact of negative attitudes on our lives cannot be overstated. In every arena of human endeavor – from relationships to careers to personal growth – these self-limiting beliefs act as invisible barriers, holding us back from the success, fulfillment, and joy that are our birthright.

In our relationships, negative attitudes can lead us to assume the worst about others, to project our own insecurities and fears onto our partners and friends, and to sabotage the connections that give life meaning and purpose. We may find ourselves caught in cycles of conflict and misunderstanding, unable to give or receive love because of the walls we have built around our hearts.

In our careers, negative attitudes can prevent us from taking risks, pursuing our passions, and claiming our true value. We may settle for less than we deserve, doubt our own competence and knowledge, or avoid opportunities for growth and advancement because of the fear of failure or rejection. We may find ourselves stuck in unfulfilling jobs or stagnant careers, never reaching the levels of success and impact we know we are capable of.

And in our personal growth and evolution, negative attitudes can keep us forever trapped in old patterns and limiting beliefs, unable to break free from the conditioned responses and habitual thoughts that keep us small and stuck. We may resist change, avoid discomfort, or numb ourselves with distractions and addictions, all the while knowing deep down we are meant for something more.

The Alchemy of Awareness: How Mindfulness Can Transform Negative Attitudes

But fortunately, negative attitudes are not fixed or permanent. They are simply habits of mind that can be transformed through the power of awareness, intention, and practice. By bringing mindfulness and compassion to our inner landscape, we can begin to alchemize the lead of our limiting beliefs into the gold of self-empowerment and positive change.

The first step in this process is simply to learn of the negative attitudes operating within us. This can be challenging, as these beliefs are often so deeply ingrained that we may not even realize they are shaping our perceptions and behaviors. But by cultivating a practice of mindfulness and self-reflection, we can begin to shine a light on the shadowy corners of our psyche and see the thoughts and feelings holding us back.

One powerful tool for this process is meditation – the simple act of sitting in stillness and observing the mind without judgment or resistance. As we meditate, we may begin to notice the patterns of negative self-talk, the habitual fears and doubts, the stories we tell ourselves about who we are and what we are capable of. By simply seeing these thoughts and feelings with curiosity and compassion, we begin to create a space of awareness around them – a space in which transformation becomes possible.

Another key practice is self-inquiry – the willingness to question our own assumptions and beliefs, and to explore the deeper truths that lie beneath the surface of our conditioned minds. We may ask ourselves: "Is this belief really true? What evidence do I have to support it? What would my life look like if I let go of this limiting story and embraced a more empowering perspective?"

Through this process of mindful awareness and self-inquiry, we begin to loosen the grip of negative attitudes on our lives. We see that these beliefs are not fixed or absolute, but mental constructs that can be challenged, reframed, and ultimately released. We begin to tap into the innate resilience and creativity of our true nature, and to realize that we have the power to shape our own reality through the choices we make and the attitudes we embrace.

Strategies for Overcoming Negative Attitudes: A Toolkit for Transformation

Transforming negative attitudes is not always easy. These beliefs can be deeply entrenched and may require consistent effort and practice to uproot and replace them with more empowering perspectives. But there are many tools and strategies that can support us in this process and help us to cultivate a more positive and expansive mindset.

One powerful approach is cognitive reframing – the practice of consciously shifting our interpretations and perceptions of events and experiences. When we find ourselves stuck in a negative attitude or limiting belief, we can ask ourselves: "How else could I view this situation? What is the opportunity or lesson hidden within this challenge? What would be a more empowering and constructive way to respond?"

By intentionally reframing our experiences in a more positive light, we begin to train our minds to look for the good, the hopeful, and the possible in every situation. We see obstacles as opportunities for growth, failures as feedback for learning, and challenges as invitations to rise to our highest potential.

Another key strategy is to cultivate a support system of positive influences and relationships. When we surround ourselves with people who believe in us, encourage us, and model the attitudes and behaviors we aspire to, we are more likely to stay motivated, inspired, and on track with our goals. We can seek mentors, coaches, or therapy professionals who can offer guidance and perspective, and join communities or groups that share our values and aspirations.

At the same time, it is important to set healthy boundaries with people or situations that reinforce negative attitudes or drain our energy and enthusiasm. This may mean learning to say no to commitments or relationships that no longer serve us, or creating space and time for self-care and renewal when we feel overwhelmed or depleted.

Perhaps most important, overcoming negative attitudes requires a deep commitment to self-compassion and self-acceptance. When we can learn to treat ourselves with kindness, understanding, and forgiveness – even in the face of setbacks or failures – we create a foundation of inner strength and resilience that can weather any storm. We see ourselves not as flawed or broken, but as imperfect beings who are always learning, growing, and evolving.

The Doorway to Freedom: Embracing the Journey of Personal Transformation

Ultimately, the journey of transforming negative attitudes is a journey of personal liberation. It is a path of letting go of the false beliefs and limiting stories that have held us back and stepping into the fullness of our authentic power and potential. It is a journey of reclaiming our birthright as creative, compassionate, and infinitely capable beings, and learning to live from a place of inner freedom and joy.

This journey is not always easy, and it requires courage, commitment, and a willingness to face our own shadows and fears. But the rewards are immeasurable – a life of greater purpose, passion, and possibility, and a deep sense of connection to ourselves, others, and the world.

As we start this path of transformation, we may encounter obstacles and challenges along the way. We may slip back into old patterns and negative attitudes or facing resistance from others threatened by our growth and change. But with each step forward, we are building the muscles of resilience, self-awareness, and self-mastery that will serve us for a lifetime.

And as we begin to shed the layers of negativity and limitation that have obscured our true nature, we may start to catch glimpses of the radiant being that we are – a being of infinite creativity, compassion, and potential, here to shine our unique light in the world.

So let us embrace the journey of transforming negative attitudes with openness, curiosity, and a sense of adventure. Let us be willing to face our fears, question our assumptions, and step into the unknown with courage and trust. And let us remember that every moment is an opportunity to choose a new perspective, a new attitude, and a new way of being in the world.

This journey of personal transformation is not always easy, but it is infinitely rewarding. It requires us to be honest with ourselves, to acknowledge our limiting beliefs and negative patterns, and to make a conscious choice to release them. It invites us to explore new ways of thinking, feeling, and responding to life's challenges, and to cultivate a mindset of growth, resilience, and adaptability.

As we start this path of self-discovery and personal evolution, we may encounter obstacles and setbacks along the way. But let us remember these challenges are not roadblocks, but opportunities for learning, growth, and transformation. Each time we face a difficult situation with a positive attitude and a willingness to learn, we strengthen our ability to navigate life's ups and downs with grace and wisdom.

As we transform our own attitudes and perspectives, we become a positive force in the world. Our inner light radiates outward, touching the lives of others and inspiring them to embrace their own journey of personal growth and transformation. By being an example of positivity, resilience, and compassion, we contribute to the healing and upliftment of our communities and the world.

So let us approach this journey with a spirit of enthusiasm, creativity, and joy. Let us be open to new experiences, new ideas, and new ways of being. Let us celebrate our progress, no matter how small, and be gentle with ourselves when we stumble or fall. And let us trust that as we continue to grow and evolve, we are not only creating a better life for ourselves but also contributing to the betterment of the world.

The journey of transforming negative attitudes is a journey of self-love, self-discovery, and self-realization. It is a journey that leads us to the heart of who we are, to the essence of our being, and to the limitless potential that lies within us. And as we embrace this journey with open hearts and minds, we open ourselves up to a world of infinite possibilities, where joy, love, and abundance are our constant companions, and where we can shine as the radiant, magnificent beings we were born to be.

BREAKING FREE FROM THE SHACKLES OF LIMITING BELIEFS

LIMITING beliefs are like invisible chains that hold us back from reaching our true potential. These deeply ingrained thoughts and beliefs can permeate various parts of our lives, from our careers and relationships to our personal growth and development. But where do these limiting beliefs come from, and how can we break free from their grasp?

Let's start by examining the roots of limiting beliefs. Often, they can be traced back to our childhood experiences and upbringing. Imagine a young child constantly bombarded with negative messages about their abilities or self-worth. Over time, these messages can become internalized, forming the foundation of limiting beliefs that follow them into adulthood. These beliefs manifest as feelings of inadequacy, fear of failure, or a lack of self-confidence, holding the individual back from pursuing their dreams and reaching their full potential.

But childhood experiences aren't the only culprits. Societal norms and expectations also play a significant role in shaping our limiting beliefs. The messages we absorb from media, peers, or authority figures can subtly influence our perception of what we can or cannot achieve. For example, someone may believe that certain careers are off-limits to them because of their gender, race, or socioeconomic background. These societal constraints can create invisible barriers, preventing individuals from exploring their true passions and talents.

Personal experiences and past failures can further reinforce limiting beliefs. When we face rejection or setbacks, it's easy to fall into the trap of believing that success is unattainable. We may start to doubt our abilities and avoid taking risks or pursuing our goals altogether. This fear of failure can create a self-fulfilling prophecy, where we limit our own potential and opportunities for growth.

But here's the good news: limiting beliefs are not set in stone. We have the power to challenge and overcome them. The first step is to learn of these beliefs and acknowledge their presence in our lives. Reflect on the thoughts and beliefs that hold you back. What are the stories you tell yourself about your abilities, worth, or potential?

Once you've identified your limiting beliefs, it's time to explore their origins. Ask yourself, "Where did this belief come from? Is it based on facts or merely assumptions?" By understanding the root cause of these beliefs, you can begin to reframe them and replace negative thoughts with positive affirmations.

Remember, challenging limiting beliefs requires patience and self-compassion. It's not about perfection; it's about progress. Seek support from a therapist, coach, or trusted friend who can provide guidance and encouragement along the way. Surround yourself with individuals who believe in your potential and inspire you to reach for the stars.

As you break free from the shackles of limiting beliefs, you'll discover a newfound sense of liberation and possibility. You'll see opportunities where there were once obstacles, and you'll find the courage to pursue your dreams with confidence and determination.

So, take a deep breath, and start this transformative journey of self-discovery. Challenge those limiting beliefs that have held you back for far too long. Embrace your unique strengths, talents, and potential. And most important, believe in yourself and your ability to create the life you desire.

Remember, you are the architect of your own destiny. With each limiting belief you overcome, you pave the way for personal growth, success, and fulfillment. The world is waiting for you to step into your greatness, unencumbered by the weight of self-doubt and fear. So, break free from those invisible chains, and embrace the incredible possibilities that await you. Your journey to unlocking your full potential starts now.

~

OVERCOMING LIMITING BELIEFS: EMPOWERING YOURSELF IN EVERY ASPECT OF LIFE

Limiting beliefs are like invisible barriers that hold us back from reaching our true potential. These negative and often irrational thoughts can seep into various parts of our lives, from our relationships and careers to our self-worth and personal growth. Let's explore common examples of limiting beliefs and discover how we can challenge and overcome them.

When it comes to relationships, limiting beliefs can be insidious. Thoughts like "I am not lovable or worthy of love" or "I will never find someone who truly cares about me" can create a self-fulfilling prophecy, causing us to sabotage potential connections or settle for less than we deserve. These beliefs are not based on truth but rather on experiences or negative self-talk. By cultivating self-love and embracing our inherent worthiness, we open ourselves up to the possibility of healthy and fulfilling relationships.

In the realm of career, limiting beliefs can hold us back from pursuing our dreams and reaching our full potential. Thoughts like "I am not smart enough to succeed in my desired career" or "I am too old to make a career change" can create self-doubt and hinder our progress. However, remember that intelligence and capability are not fixed traits. With dedication, learning, and perseverance, we can acquire the skills and knowledge necessary to excel in any field. Age is a number, and it's never too late to start a new career path or pursue our passions.

Self-worth is another area where limiting beliefs can have a profound impact. Thoughts like "I am not good enough as I am" or "I do not deserve happiness or success" can erode our confidence and prevent us from embracing our unique qualities and strengths. Our worth is not determined by external factors or comparisons to others. We are inherently valuable and deserving of love, happiness, and success. By practicing self-compassion and celebrating our achievements, we can cultivate a strong sense of self-worth and resilience.

Regarding health and fitness, limiting beliefs can sabotage our efforts to focus on our well-being. Thoughts like "I will never be able to lose weight and be healthy" or "I don't have enough time to prioritize my health and fitness" can create a defeatist mindset and discourage us from acting. However, recognize that small, consistent steps can lead to significant improvements in our health. By establishing attainable objectives, discovering activities that bring us joy, and prioritizing self-care, we can conquer these constraining thoughts and welcome a healthier way of life.

Creativity is another area where limiting beliefs can stifle our potential. Thoughts like "I lack the necessary creativity or talent to pursue my passion" or "My ideas are not sufficiently appreciated by others" can prevent us from exploring our artistic or entrepreneurial endeavors. However, creativity is not a fixed trait, and talent can be developed through practice and dedication. By embracing our unique perspectives and taking risks, we can overcome these limiting beliefs and unleash our creative potential.

Identifying and challenging limiting beliefs is an important step in personal growth and development. It requires self-awareness, introspection, and a willingness to question the thoughts that hold us back. By replacing negative beliefs with empowering ones, we can break free from the invisible barriers that limit our potential.

Remember, your beliefs shape your reality. By consciously choosing to embrace positive and empowering beliefs, you unlock the door to a life filled with possibilities and growth. Surround yourself with supportive individuals who believe in your potential, seek resources and mentors to guide you, and most important, believe in yourself.

You have the power to overcome any limiting belief that stands in your way. Embrace your inherent worth, pursue your passions with confidence, and know that you can achieve greatness in every part of your life. The journey of personal growth is ongoing, but with each limiting belief you overcome, you step closer to unlocking your full potential and creating the life you desire.

~

BREAKING FREE FROM LIMITING BELIEFS: A JOURNEY OF SELF-DISCOVERY AND EMPOWERMENT

LIMITING beliefs are the invisible chains that hold us back from reaching our true potential. They are the negative and often irrational thoughts that infiltrate various parts of our lives, from our relationships and careers to our self-worth and personal growth. But fortunately, we have the power to break free from these chains and start a transformative journey of self-discovery and empowerment.

Let's start by examining the impact of limiting beliefs in different areas of our lives. In relationships, thoughts like "I am not lovable or worthy of love" or "I will never find someone who truly cares about me" can create a self-fulfilling prophecy. These beliefs can cause us to sabotage potential connections or settle for less than we deserve. However, by recognizing these beliefs are rooted in experiences or negative self-talk rather than truth, we can begin to cultivate self-love and embrace our inherent worthiness. By doing so, we open ourselves up to the possibility of healthy and fulfilling relationships.

Regarding our careers, limiting beliefs can be equally harmful. Thoughts like "I am not smart enough to succeed in my desired career" or "I am too old to make a career change" can create self-doubt and hinder our progress. But intelligence and capability are not fixed traits.

With dedication, learning, and perseverance, we can acquire the skills and knowledge necessary to excel in any field. Age is a number, and it's never too late to pursue our passions and start a new career path.

Self-worth is another area where limiting beliefs can have a profound impact. Thoughts like "I am not good enough as I am" or "I do not deserve happiness or success" can erode our confidence and prevent us from embracing our unique qualities and strengths. However, our worth is not determined by external factors or comparisons to others. We are inherently valuable and deserving of love, happiness, and success. By practicing self-compassion and celebrating our achievements, we can cultivate a strong sense of self-worth and resilience.

In health and fitness, limiting beliefs can sabotage our efforts to focus on our well-being. Thoughts like "I will never be able to lose weight and be healthy" or "I don't have enough time to prioritize my health and fitness" can create a defeatist mindset and discourage us from acting. However, recognize that small, consistent steps can lead to significant improvements in our health. By setting realistic goals, finding activities we enjoy, and making time for self-care, we can overcome these limiting beliefs and embrace a healthier lifestyle.

Creativity is yet another area where limiting beliefs can stifle our potential. Thoughts like "I am not creative or talented enough to pursue my passion" or "My ideas are not good enough for others to appreciate" can prevent us from exploring our artistic or entrepreneurial endeavors. But creativity is not a fixed trait, and talent can be developed through practice and dedication. By embracing our unique perspectives and taking risks, we can overcome these limiting beliefs and unleash our creative potential.

So, how do we break free from the shackles of limiting beliefs? The first step is awareness. Reflect on the thoughts and beliefs that hold you back. Write them down and examine them objectively. Ask yourself, "Is this belief serving me or hindering my growth?" Once you've identified your limiting beliefs, it's time to challenge them. Look for evidence that contradicts these beliefs. Seek examples of individuals who have succeeded despite facing similar challenges.

Next, reframe your limiting beliefs into empowering ones. Instead of thinking, "I am not lovable," affirm, "I am worthy of love and deserve healthy relationships." Replace "I am too old to make a career change" with "I have a wealth of experience and knowledge that I can bring to a new career path." By consciously reshaping your thoughts, you create a new narrative that supports your growth and potential.

Surrounding yourself with positivity and support is important in overcoming limiting beliefs. Seek individuals who uplift and encourage you, whether it's friends, family, or mentors. Engage in activities and hobbies that bring you joy and boost your confidence. Cultivate a mindset of gratitude, focusing on the blessings and opportunities in your life.

Remember, overcoming limiting beliefs requires patience and self-compassion. There may be setbacks and moments of self-doubt along the way, but it's important to be kind to yourself and celebrate your progress. Each step you take toward challenging and overcoming your limiting beliefs is a victory.

As you continue on this journey of personal growth, remember that your beliefs are not set in stone. They are malleable and can be reshaped with conscious effort and practice. Embrace the power of neuroplasticity, knowing that your brain can form new neural pathways and adopt new beliefs.

In addition to challenging your own limiting beliefs, consider the impact you can have on others. By sharing your journey and experiences, you can inspire and empower those around you to overcome their own limiting beliefs. Together, we can create a ripple effect of positive change and growth.

So, take a deep breath, and start this transformative journey of breaking free from limiting beliefs. Embrace the discomfort that comes with challenging your thoughts and stepping outside your comfort zone. Trust in your resilience and ability to adapt and grow.

As you shed the chains of limiting beliefs, you'll discover a newfound sense of freedom and possibility. You'll approach challenges with confidence, knowing you have the strength and capability to overcome them. You'll pursue your dreams with passion and determination, unhindered by self-doubt or fear.

Remember, your beliefs are the lens through which you see the world. By consciously choosing to adopt empowering beliefs, you shape your reality and unlock your full potential. Embrace the incredible journey of self-discovery and transformation that awaits you.

The world needs your unique talents, perspectives, and contributions. Don't let limiting beliefs hold you back any longer. Step into your power, believe in yourself, and watch as you create a life beyond your wildest dreams. Your journey to greatness starts now, one empowering belief at a time.

~

TRANSFORMING LIMITING BELIEFS INTO EMPOWERING BELIEFS: A STEP-BY-STEP GUIDE

LIMITING beliefs can be the invisible barriers that hold us back from reaching our full potential. They are the negative and often irrational thoughts that can seep into various parts of our lives, hindering our progress and reducing our self-confidence. However, by putting effective strategies into practice, we can overcome these limiting beliefs and reframe them into empowering ones that propel us toward success and personal growth.

The first important step in overcoming limiting beliefs is to identify them. Reflect on your thoughts and attitudes and pinpoint any negative beliefs that may be affecting your life. These beliefs could be related to your abilities, worthiness, or potential for success. Once you have identified a limiting belief, it's time to challenge it.

Ask yourself, "Is this belief based on facts or assumptions?" and "What evidence do I have to support or refute this belief?" By questioning the validity of the belief, you begin to weaken its hold on your mind. Often, you may find that the limiting belief is rooted in experiences or negative self-talk rather than reality.

The next step is to reframe the limiting belief into a more empowering and positive one. For example, instead of telling yourself, "I'm not good enough," reframe it to "I am capable and deserving of success." By consciously replacing the negative belief with a positive one, you start to reprogram your subconscious mind and create a new narrative that supports your growth and potential.

To reinforce this new empowering belief, practice affirmations regularly. Affirmations are positive statements you repeat to yourself, such as "I am confident and capable" or "I believe in myself." By consistently repeating these affirmations, you gradually rewire your brain to embrace the positive belief and override the limiting one.

Visualization is another powerful tool in overcoming limiting beliefs. Create a mental image of yourself succeeding and feeling confident. Visualize yourself overcoming obstacles and meeting your goals. By engaging in this mental rehearsal, you train your mind to believe in your abilities and support your new empowering beliefs.

Surrounding yourself with supportive and positive people is important in this journey. Seek individuals who believe in you and challenge your limiting beliefs. Share your goals and aspirations with them and let their encouragement and motivation fuel your progress. A strong support system can make a significant difference in your ability to overcome limiting beliefs.

Acting is key to solidifying your new empowering beliefs. Break down your goals into manageable steps and consistently take action toward achieving them. Each small step you take builds confidence and proves to yourself that you can overcome challenges. Celebrate your progress along the way, no matter how small, and use it as evidence to reinforce your new beliefs.

Self-care is an essential part of overcoming limiting beliefs. Focus on activities that nourish your mind, body, and soul. Engage in practices that boost your self-esteem and confidence, such as exercise, meditation, journaling, or spending time in nature. When you take care of yourself holistically, you create a strong foundation for personal growth and belief transformation.

Finally, make it a habit to reflect on your progress and celebrate your achievements. Acknowledge the positive changes you have made in your beliefs and mindset. Recognize the growth you have experienced and the obstacles you have overcome. By regularly reflecting on your journey, you reinforce empowering beliefs and maintain momentum toward your goals.

Remember, transforming limiting beliefs into empowering ones requires patience, self-compassion, and consistent effort. There may be setbacks and moments of self-doubt along the way, but it's important to be kind to yourself and stay committed to your personal growth. Each step you take toward reframing your beliefs is a victory.

As you continue on this path of belief transformation, you'll discover a newfound sense of confidence and resilience. You'll approach challenges with a growth mindset, knowing you can overcome them. You'll pursue your dreams with passion and determination, fueled by the empowering beliefs that now guide your actions.

Your journey of transforming limiting beliefs into empowering ones has the power to create a ripple effect in your life. As you embrace a more positive and confident mindset, you inspire others to do the same. Your success and growth become a testament to the incredible potential that lies within each of us when we break free from the shackles of limiting beliefs.

So, take a deep breath, and start this transformative journey of belief reframing. Embrace the discomfort that comes with challenging your thoughts and adopting new perspectives. Trust in your ability to adapt, grow, and thrive.

The world is waiting for you to unleash your full potential. Don't let limiting beliefs hold you back any longer. Step into your power, believe in yourself, and watch as you create a life filled with endless possibilities. Your journey to greatness starts now, one empowering belief at a time.

∾

THE POWER OF SELF-AWARENESS AND SELF-COMPASSION IN OVERCOMING LIMITING BELIEFS

IN THE JOURNEY of personal growth and transformation, self-awareness and self-compassion are two essential tools that can help us break free from the shackles of limiting beliefs. These beliefs, often rooted in negative self-talk and experiences, can hold us back from reaching our full potential and living the life we desire. By cultivating self-awareness and practicing self-compassion, we create a powerful internal environment that supports the challenging and reframing of these limiting beliefs.

Self-awareness is the foundation on which personal growth is built. It involves being mindful of our thoughts, feelings, and behaviors, and understanding how they shape our experiences and perceptions of the world. When we develop self-awareness, we gain the ability to identify the limiting beliefs holding us back. We become attuned to the negative self-talk and self-criticism that often go along with these beliefs, and we can recognize when falling into patterns of thought that do not serve our highest good.

This awareness is an important first step in challenging limiting beliefs. By bringing these beliefs into conscious awareness, we can begin to question their validity and explore alternative perspectives. We can ask ourselves, "Is this belief based on facts or assumptions?" and "What evidence do I have to support or refute this belief?" By engaging in this process of self-inquiry, we start to weaken the grip of limiting beliefs on our minds and open ourselves up to the possibility of change.

However, self-awareness alone is not enough to overcome limiting beliefs. This is where self-compassion comes into play. Self-compassion involves treating ourselves with kindness, understanding, and empathy, especially in the face of challenges or failures. It is the act of extending the same compassion and care to ourselves that we would offer to a good friend or loved one.

When we encounter limiting beliefs or negative thoughts, self-compassion lets us respond to ourselves with gentleness and understanding, rather than harsh self-judgment. Instead of berating ourselves for having these beliefs or feeling stuck, we can approach ourselves with curiosity and compassion. We can acknowledge the pain or discomfort that these beliefs may cause and offer ourselves the emotional support and encouragement needed to face them head-on.

Self-compassion creates a safe and nurturing internal space for personal growth and transformation. It helps us to reframe limiting beliefs in a more constructive and empowering way. Instead of telling ourselves, "I'm not good enough," we can practice self-compassion by saying, "I am learning and growing, and I am worthy of love and success." By treating ourselves with kindness and understanding, we gradually replace negative self-talk with more positive and supportive inner dialogue.

The combination of self-awareness and self-compassion is a powerful force in overcoming limiting beliefs. When we are self-aware, we can catch ourselves believing in these limitations and actively choose to challenge them. Self-compassion then provides the emotional resilience and inner strength needed to face these beliefs without succumbing to self-criticism and self-doubt.

Developing self-awareness and self-compassion requires patience and persistence. It involves becoming more mindful of our thoughts and feelings, and consciously choosing to respond to ourselves with kindness and understanding. This may feel uncomfortable or unfamiliar at first, especially if we are accustomed to self-criticism and negative self-talk. However, with consistent practice, self-awareness and self-compassion can become habitual ways of relating to ourselves.

As we cultivate these qualities, we begin to notice a shift in our relationship with limiting beliefs. We become more adept at identifying these beliefs when they arise, and we have the tools to challenge and reframe them in a more empowering way. We see ourselves through a lens of compassion and understanding, rather than judgment and self-doubt.

The journey of overcoming limiting beliefs is a process of self-discovery and personal growth. It requires courage, vulnerability, and a willingness to confront the parts of ourselves that we may have been avoiding or suppressing. However, with self-awareness and self-compassion as our guides, we can navigate this journey with greater ease and resilience.

As we break free from the constraints of limiting beliefs, we open ourselves up to a world of possibilities. We begin to live more authentically, pursuing our dreams and goals with confidence and self-assurance. We develop a deeper sense of self-worth and self-acceptance, knowing we are inherently valuable and deserving of love and success.

The power of self-awareness and self-compassion extends far beyond the realm of personal growth. As we learn to treat ourselves with kindness and understanding, we naturally extend that same compassion to others. We become more empathetic, understanding, and supportive in our relationships, creating a ripple effect of positivity and growth in the world.

So, let us embrace the transformative power of self-awareness and self-compassion. Let us approach our limiting beliefs with curiosity and compassion, knowing we have the inner resources to challenge and overcome them. Let us be patient and persistent, trusting that each moment of self-awareness and self-compassion is a step toward greater freedom and fulfillment.

As we cultivate these qualities within ourselves, we become a beacon of hope and inspiration for others who may be struggling with their own limiting beliefs. We show change is possible, and that with self-awareness and self-compassion, we can break free from the chains of self-doubt and live the life we desire.

The journey of overcoming limiting beliefs is a lifelong process, but it is deeply rewarding and transformative. With self-awareness and self-compassion as our steadfast companions, we can face any challenge, overcome any obstacle, and create a life rich in meaning, purpose, and authentic self-expression.

So, let us embrace this journey with open hearts and minds, knowing we have the power within us to transform our lives and the world. Let us be self-aware, self-compassionate, and ever-growing, as we break free from limiting beliefs and step into the fullness of our potential.

$\sim$

BREAKING FREE FROM SOCIETAL AND CULTURAL CONSTRAINTS: EXAMINING THE INFLUENCE ON LIMITING BELIEFS

LIMITING beliefs are the invisible barriers that hold individuals back from reaching their full potential. These beliefs, often deeply ingrained in our minds, can stem from various sources, including personal experiences, past traumas, and negative self-talk. However, one of the most significant contributors to the development and perpetuation of limiting beliefs is the influence of societal and cultural factors.

From the moment we are born, we are immersed in a complex web of societal and cultural norms, values, and expectations. These external influences shape our perceptions of ourselves, others, and the world. They mold our beliefs about what is possible, acceptable, and desirable, and they can have a profound impact on our sense of self-worth, confidence, and motivation.

One of the most pervasive ways societal and cultural factors contribute to the formation of limiting beliefs is through the messages we receive from media, family, peers, and institutions. These messages, whether explicit or implicit, can reinforce stereotypes, biases, and expectations that limit our potential and self-perception.

For example, media representations of success, beauty, and happiness can create unrealistic standards that lead individuals to believe they are not good enough, smart enough, or attractive enough to meet their goals. Family dynamics and parental expectations can also play a significant role in shaping limiting beliefs, as children may internalize messages about their abilities, worth, and potential based on the feedback and attitudes they receive from their caregivers.

Cultural norms and values can also contribute to the development of limiting beliefs. In some cultures, there may be specific expectations or standards for success that can lead individuals to adopt beliefs that are self-defeating or hinder their growth. For example, in societies that place a high value on academic achievement, individuals who struggle in school may develop limiting beliefs about their intelligence or potential for success.

Similarly, cultural attitudes toward gender, race, or social class can influence the formation of limiting beliefs related to identity and achievement. Stereotypes and prejudices can lead individuals to internalize negative beliefs about their abilities or worth based on their membership in certain groups. These beliefs can limit their aspirations, self-confidence, and willingness to pursue their goals.

To break free from the constraints of limiting beliefs shaped by societal and cultural factors, it is essential to engage in a process of critical self-reflection and analysis. This involves examining the messages and narratives that have influenced our beliefs and questioning their validity and relevance to our lives.

One powerful tool for challenging limiting beliefs is to seek diverse perspectives and role models that defy stereotypes and expectations. By exposing ourselves to individuals who have overcome societal and cultural barriers to meet their goals, we can begin to expand our own beliefs about what is possible and develop a more empowering and inclusive worldview.

Another key strategy is to cultivate a strong sense of self-awareness and self-compassion. By learning to recognize and acknowledge our own limiting beliefs, we can begin to reframe them in a more positive and empowering way. This involves treating ourselves with kindness and understanding, rather than judgment and self-criticism, and recognizing that our worth and potential are not defined by external standards or expectations.

Supportive and inclusive communities can also be a powerful tool for overcoming limiting beliefs shaped by societal and cultural factors. By surrounding ourselves with individuals who affirm our worth, celebrate our uniqueness, and encourage our growth, we can begin to develop a more positive and resilient sense of self.

Ultimately, breaking free from the influence of societal and cultural factors on limiting beliefs requires a commitment to ongoing personal growth and self-discovery. It involves questioning the status quo, challenging assumptions, and embracing a more expansive and empowering vision of ourselves and the world.

By examining how societal and cultural factors shape our beliefs, we can take steps toward liberation and empowerment. We can learn to recognize and resist the messages and narratives that limit our potential, and instead embrace a more authentic and fulfilling path.

Breaking free from limiting beliefs is not always easy, and it may involve facing discomfort, uncertainty, and resistance from others. However, the rewards of living a life guided by our own values, passions, and aspirations are immeasurable.

As we work to overcome the influence of societal and cultural factors on our limiting beliefs, we not only empower ourselves but also contribute to the creation of a more just, compassionate, and equitable world. By challenging the status quo and embracing diversity and inclusion, we can help to create a society that values and nurtures the unique potential of every individual.

Examining the influence of societal and cultural factors on the development of limiting beliefs is an important step in the journey toward personal and collective liberation.

By engaging in critical self-reflection, seeking diverse perspectives, cultivating self-awareness and self-compassion, and building supportive communities, we can begin to break free from the constraints of limiting beliefs and embrace a more empowered and authentic way of being in the world.

∾

OVERCOMING LIMITING BELIEFS: INSPIRING CASE STUDIES OF PERSONAL TRANSFORMATION

LIMITING beliefs can hold individuals back from reaching their full potential and pursuing their dreams. These self-imposed barriers can manifest in various forms, such as impostor syndrome, fear of failure, or self-doubt. However, by confronting and overcoming these limiting beliefs, individuals can unlock their true potential and achieve personal and professional growth. The following case studies illuminate the transformative power of challenging limiting beliefs and the inspiring journeys of individuals who have triumphed over their inner obstacles.

Case Study 1: Jane - Overcoming Impostor Syndrome

Jane's story is a powerful example of the impact of impostor syndrome on personal and professional growth. Despite her impressive accomplishments and recognition in her competitive industry, Jane constantly battled feelings of inadequacy and self-doubt. These limiting beliefs held her back from seizing opportunities for advancement and taking on new challenges, hindering her potential for growth and success.

Recognizing the need for change, Jane took a proactive step by seeking the guidance of a therapist. Through this therapeutic process, she dug into the underlying causes of her impostor syndrome and acquired effective coping strategies to challenge her negative self-talk. A key aspect of Jane's journey was learning to practice self-compassion and celebrate her achievements, despite their magnitude. By nurturing a kinder and more supportive inner dialogue, Jane began to chip away at the foundation of her limiting beliefs.

Equipped with a renewed sense of self-belief and the unwavering support of her therapist, Jane mustered the courage to pursue leadership roles within her company. To her astonishment, her efforts were rewarded with a promotion to a managerial position. As Jane continued to excel in her new role, leading teams and projects with skill and confidence, her self-assurance blossomed. She discovered that her impostor syndrome had been a mere illusion, obscuring her true capabilities and potential.

Jane's triumph over her limiting belief not only catalyzed her own personal and professional growth but also positioned her as a beacon of inspiration for others. She now dedicates herself to mentoring colleagues who grapple with similar feelings of self-doubt, sharing her insights and strategies for overcoming impostor syndrome. Through her example, Jane shows by confronting and vanquishing limiting beliefs, individuals can unlock their full potential and make a profound impact on their own lives and the lives of others.

Case Study 2: Mark - Conquering Fear of Failure

Mark's journey illustrates the paralyzing effect of fear of failure on pursuing one's passions and dreams. Despite possessing a wealth of innovative ideas and a strong work ethic, Mark found himself shackled by the dread of not succeeding in his entrepreneurial endeavors. This limiting belief kept him limited to the sidelines, watching as others took risks and chased their ambitions.

However, Mark eventually reached a pivotal moment where he recognized that his fear of failure was holding him back from living a fulfilling life. With a resolute determination to confront his limiting belief head-on, Mark started a path of self-discovery and growth. He immersed himself in online courses on entrepreneurship and sought the wisdom of successful business owners who had navigated the challenges he feared.

Through these transformative experiences, Mark underwent a profound shift in perspective. He learned to reframe failure not as a personal shortcoming but as an invaluable opportunity for learning and growth. By embracing the idea that setbacks and obstacles were integral parts of the entrepreneurial journey, Mark gradually chipped away at the wall of fear that had held him back for so long.

Armed with newfound confidence and a growth mindset, Mark took the courageous leap into entrepreneurship. He launched his own startup, aware that challenges and setbacks would be inevitable. However, instead of being deterred by these obstacles, Mark faced them with resilience and determination. He persevered through the ups and downs, learning from each experience and adapting his approach as needed.

As Mark's business gained traction and attracted investors and customers who believed in his vision, he realized that his fear of failure had been a self-imposed limitation. By conquering this limiting belief, he had unlocked his true potential and succeeded where he had once thought was out of reach.

Mark's journey serves as a powerful testament to the transformative power of overcoming limiting beliefs. He now uses his experience to inspire and guide aspiring entrepreneurs, helping them navigate the challenges of starting a business with a growth mindset. Through his mentorship, Mark empowers others to conquer their own fears and pursue their dreams with confidence and resilience.

Chapter Summary:

The case studies of Jane and Mark showcase the profound impact of overcoming limiting beliefs on personal and professional growth. By confronting their impostor syndrome and fear of failure, respectively, these individuals broke free from the self-imposed barriers that had held them back and unlocked their true potential.

Their journeys emphasize the importance of self-awareness, seeking support, and embracing a growth mindset in the face of challenges. Through therapy, mentorship, and personal reflection, Jane and Mark gained the tools and insights necessary to reframe their limiting beliefs and cultivate a more empowering mindset.

Their stories highlight the ripple effect of personal transformation. By overcoming their own limiting beliefs, Jane and Mark not only achieved personal and professional success but also became sources of inspiration and guidance for others facing similar struggles. Their examples show that by confronting and conquering our inner obstacles, we can not only transform our own lives but also make a positive impact on the lives of those around us.

The case studies of Jane and Mark serve as powerful reminders that limiting beliefs need not define or constrain us. By taking proactive steps to challenge and overcome these self-imposed barriers, we can unlock our full potential, pursue our dreams with confidence, and inspire others to do the same.

Through self-reflection, support, and a commitment to personal growth, we all have the power to break free from the limitations of our beliefs and create the lives we desire.

BREAKING FREE FROM NEGATIVE ATTITUDES AND LIMITING BELIEFS: A TRANSFORMATIVE GUIDE TO PERSONAL GROWTH AND SUCCESS

THE INVISIBLE BARRIERS of Negative Attitudes and Limiting Beliefs

Negative attitudes and limiting beliefs are the unseen forces that can hold us back from reaching our full potential and living the life we desire. These destructive patterns, often deeply ingrained within us, have the power to shape our thoughts, emotions, and behaviors, creating invisible barriers that hinder our personal growth and limit our success.

At their core, negative attitudes are habitual ways of thinking that focus on the worst-case scenarios, magnify problems, and reduce possibilities. They can manifest as pessimism, cynicism, or a general sense of negativity that colors our perception of the world. When we constantly dwell on negative thoughts and expect the worst, we create a self-fulfilling prophecy, attracting more negativity into our lives.

Limiting beliefs are the self-imposed restrictions we place on ourselves based on our experiences, societal conditioning, or the opinions of others. These beliefs can revolve around our abilities, worthiness, or potential, convincing us we are not capable, deserving, or meant for success. They create a false sense of limitations, causing us to doubt ourselves and hold back from pursuing our dreams.

The impact of negative attitudes and limiting beliefs on our lives cannot be overstated. They can lead to a lack of confidence, low self-esteem, and a fear of failure. They can cause us to procrastinate, avoid taking risks, and miss out on valuable opportunities for growth and success. These destructive patterns can also strain our relationships, as our negativity and self-doubt can push others away and create a cycle of unfulfilling interactions.

The insidious nature of negative attitudes and limiting beliefs lies in their ability to operate beneath the surface of our conscious awareness. We may not even realize these patterns are influencing our thoughts and actions, as they have become so deeply ingrained in our psyche. This lack of awareness makes it challenging to break free from their grip and create lasting change in our lives.

However, fortunately, negative attitudes and limiting beliefs are not permanent fixtures in our lives. With self-awareness, introspection, and a willingness to change, we can begin to identify and challenge these destructive patterns. By bringing them into the light of our conscious awareness, we can start to question their validity and replace them with more empowering and positive beliefs.

The journey of overcoming negative attitudes and limiting beliefs is not always easy, as it requires us to confront the deep-seated fears and insecurities that have shaped our thinking. It involves stepping out of our comfort zones, embracing vulnerability, and being willing to see ourselves and the world in a new light. But the rewards of this trans-formative process are immeasurable.

As we begin to break free from the chains of negativity and self-doubt, we open ourselves up to a world of possibilities and growth. We start to recognize our true potential and develop the courage to pursue our dreams with confidence and resilience. We attract more positive experiences and people into our lives, as our energy shifts from one of scarcity to one of abundance.

Throughout this guide, we will explore practical techniques and exercises that will help you identify your negative attitudes and limiting beliefs, challenge their validity, and replace them with more empowering and positive patterns of thinking. We will dig into the power of self-reflection, affirmations, visualization, and other tools that can support you on your journey of personal growth and success.

As you start this transformative journey, remember that change is a process, and progress is more important than perfection. Be patient with yourself, celebrate your small victories, and trust in your ability to create lasting change in your life. With dedication, perseverance, and a commitment to your personal growth, you can break free from the invisible barriers of negative attitudes and limiting beliefs and unleash your true potential.

So, let us begin this enlightening exploration together, and empower ourselves to create a brighter future filled with endless possibilities and success. It's time to break free from the chains of negativity and soar toward a more fulfilling and purposeful life. The journey of personal transformation awaits you.

Identifying Negative Attitudes and Limiting Beliefs

The first step in overcoming negative attitudes and limiting beliefs is to learn of their presence in your life. These destructive patterns often operate beneath the surface of our conscious awareness, influencing our thoughts, emotions, and behaviors without us even realizing it. By bringing them into the light of our awareness, we can begin to challenge their validity and replace them with more empowering and positive beliefs.

Self-Reflection and Introspection:

One of the most powerful tools for identifying negative attitudes and limiting beliefs is self-reflection and introspection. This involves taking the time to pause and examine your thoughts, feelings, and behaviors objectively. Ask yourself questions such as:

- What recurring negative thoughts do I have about myself, others, or the world around me?
- In what situations do I feel most limited or held back?

- What beliefs do I have about my abilities, worthiness, or potential?
- How do these negative attitudes and limiting beliefs impact my life and relationships?

By engaging in honest self-reflection, you can start to uncover the patterns of negativity and self-doubt that may be holding you back. Keep a journal or record your observations, as this will help you gain clarity and track your progress.

Mindfulness and Observation:

Another effective way to identify negative attitudes and limiting beliefs is through mindfulness and observation. This involves paying attention to your thoughts and emotions as they arise, without judgment or attachment. When you notice a negative thought or belief surfacing, simply observe it with curiosity and detachment, as if you were an outside observer.

Ask yourself questions such as:

- What triggered this negative thought or belief?
- Is this belief based on facts or assumptions?
- How does holding onto this belief serve me?
- What would happen if I let go of this belief?

By practicing mindfulness and observation, you can develop a greater awareness of your inner landscape and start to recognize the patterns of negativity and self-doubt that may be operating within you.

Feedback from Others:

Sometimes, our negative attitudes and limiting beliefs can be so deeply ingrained that we may not recognize them on our own. In these cases, seeking feedback from trusted friends, family members, or a therapist can be valuable. Ask them if they have noticed any patterns of negativity or self-doubt in your behavior or communication.

Be open to their feedback and try not to become defensive or dismissive. Remember that their observations are coming from a place of care and concern for your well-being. Use their feedback as an opportunity for self-reflection and growth.

Examining Your Self-Talk:

The way we talk to ourselves can be a powerful indicator of our negative attitudes and limiting beliefs. Pay attention to your inner dialogue and the words you use to describe yourself and your experiences. Do you often engage in negative self-talk, such as:

- "I'm not good enough."
- "I'll never be successful."
- "I'm not worthy of love and happiness."
- "I'm a failure."

These negative self-statements reflect the limiting beliefs that may be operating within you. By learning of your self-talk, you can start to challenge and reframe these negative statements into more positive and empowering ones.

Identifying Patterns and Triggers:

As you learn of your negative attitudes and limiting beliefs, look for patterns and triggers in your life. Notice the situations, people, or experiences that usually activate these destructive patterns within you.

For example, you may notice you usually feel most limited or doubtful when faced with a new challenge or when you are in the presence of someone you perceive as more successful than you. By identifying these triggers, you can start to develop strategies for managing them and breaking free from their influence.

Remember, identifying negative attitudes and limiting beliefs is an ongoing journey of self-discovery and growth. Be patient with yourself and celebrate your progress, no matter how small. Each moment of awareness is a step toward breaking free from the chains of negativity and self-doubt and embracing a more positive and empowered way of being.

In the next chapter, we will explore practical techniques and exercises for challenging and overcoming negative attitudes and limiting beliefs. With dedication and perseverance, you can start to replace these destructive patterns with more empowering and positive beliefs, paving the way for greater personal growth and success.

CHALLENGING AND OVERCOMING NEGATIVE ATTITUDES AND LIMITING BELIEFS

Now that you have identified your negative attitudes and limiting beliefs, it's time to act and start challenging them. This process involves questioning the validity of these destructive patterns and replacing them with more empowering and positive beliefs. By consistently practicing these techniques and exercises, you can gradually shift your mindset and break free from the chains of negativity and self-doubt.

Cognitive Reframing:

Cognitive reframing is a powerful technique that involves changing the way you perceive and interpret situations. When you catch yourself engaging in negative self-talk or holding onto a limiting belief, step back and ask yourself:

- Is there another way to look at this situation?
- What are the facts, and what are my assumptions?
- How can I reframe this thought in a more positive and empowering way?

For example, instead of thinking, "I'm a failure," you can reframe it as, "I'm learning and growing from my experiences." By consciously shifting your perspective, you can start to challenge the validity of your negative attitudes and beliefs.

Evidence-Based Analysis:

Another effective way to challenge your limiting beliefs is through evidence-based analysis. This involves examining the facts and evidence that support or refute your beliefs. Ask yourself:

- What evidence do I have to support this belief?
- Is this belief based on facts or assumptions?
- Have I ever experienced a situation that contradicts this belief?

By objectively analyzing the evidence, you can see the holes in your limiting beliefs and recognize that they may not be as true as you once thought.

Positive Affirmations:

Positive affirmations are powerful statements that can help you reprogram your mind with more empowering and positive beliefs. List affirmations that challenge your negative attitudes and limiting beliefs, such as:

- "I am capable and worthy of success."
- "I trust in my abilities and embrace challenges as opportunities for growth."
- "I am deserving of love, happiness, and abundance."

Repeat these affirmations to yourself daily, either out loud or silently in your mind. The more you reinforce these positive statements, the more they will start to replace your negative beliefs.

Visualization and Mental Rehearsal:

Visualization and mental rehearsal are powerful tools for overcoming negative attitudes and limiting beliefs. Take a few minutes each day to close your eyes and visualize yourself succeeding, thriving, and living the life you desire. Imagine yourself confidently facing challenges, embracing opportunities, and meeting your goals.

As you engage in this mental rehearsal, pay attention to the positive emotions and sensations that arise. Allow yourself to experience the joy, pride, and fulfillment of your success. By consistently practicing visualization, you can start to rewire your brain and create a more positive and empowering inner world.

Surround Yourself with Positivity:

The people we surround ourselves with and the environments we inhabit can have a significant impact on our attitudes and beliefs. Make a conscious effort to surround yourself with positive, supportive, and uplifting individuals who believe in your potential and encourage your growth.

Seek mentors, role models, and communities that align with your values and aspirations. Engage in activities and hobbies that bring you joy and fulfillment. By immersing yourself in a positive and nurturing environment, you can start to absorb and embody more empowering attitudes and beliefs.

Take Action and Embrace Challenges:

One of the most effective ways to overcome negative attitudes and limiting beliefs is to act and prove them wrong. When you doubt your abilities or fear failure, challenge yourself to take a small step forward anyway. Embrace challenges as opportunities for growth and learning and celebrate your progress along the way.

As you start to collect small successes and victories, your confidence will grow, and your limiting beliefs will begin to lose their grip. Remember, action is the antidote to fear and self-doubt.

Practice Self-Compassion:

Overcoming negative attitudes and limiting beliefs is a process, and sometimes, you stumble or fall back into old patterns. In these moments, it's important to practice self-compassion and treat yourself with kindness and understanding.

Recognize that change is a journey, and setbacks are a natural part of the process. Instead of berating yourself for your mistakes, offer yourself the same compassion and support you would extend to a dear friend. Speak to yourself with patience, encouragement, and love, and remind yourself that you are doing the best you can.

Celebrate Your Progress:

As you work on challenging and overcoming your negative attitudes and limiting beliefs, take the time to celebrate your progress and successes, no matter how small they may seem. Acknowledge the efforts you are making and the positive changes you are experiencing.

Keep a journal or a "success log" where you record your achievements, breakthroughs, and moments of pride. Regularly review these entries to remind yourself of how far you have come and the incredible growth you are capable of.

Remember, overcoming negative attitudes and limiting beliefs is a life-long journey of self-discovery and personal growth. Be patient with yourself, stay committed to the process, and trust in your ability to create lasting change. With each step you take, you are breaking free from the chains of negativity and self-doubt and embracing a more positive, empowered, and fulfilling life.

In the next chapter, we will explore how to maintain and sustain your positive mindset, even in the face of challenges and setbacks. By developing a toolkit of resilience and self-care practices, you can make sure your newfound attitudes and beliefs remain strong and unwavering, guiding you toward a life of boundless possibilities and success.

MAINTAINING AND SUSTAINING A POSITIVE MINDSET

Congratulations on your journey so far! You have taken significant steps toward identifying and challenging your negative attitudes and limiting beliefs, paving the way for a more positive and empowered mindset. However, the work doesn't stop here. Maintaining and sustaining your newfound positive mindset requires ongoing effort, especially in the face of life's inevitable challenges and setbacks.

In this chapter, we will explore practical strategies and techniques for cultivating resilience, practicing self-care, and making sure your positive attitudes and beliefs remain strong and unwavering. By developing a toolkit of supportive practices, you can navigate the ups and downs of life with grace, confidence, and a steadfast commitment to your personal growth and well-being.

Cultivate a Gratitude Practice:

One of the most powerful ways to maintain a positive mindset is to cultivate a daily practice of gratitude. Take a few moments each day to reflect on the things you are thankful for, no matter how small they may seem. Write them down in a gratitude journal, share them with a loved one, or simply take a mental note.

By consistently focusing on the good in your life, you train your brain to seek and appreciate the positive, even in challenging circumstances. Gratitude helps shift your perspective from one of lack and limitation to one of abundance and possibility.

Engage in Regular Self-Care:

Self-care is essential for maintaining a positive mindset and preventing burnout. Commit to focusing on your physical, emotional, and mental well-being daily. This can include activities such as:

- Exercise and physical movement
- Healthy eating and hydration
- Adequate sleep and rest
- Mindfulness and meditation practices
- Engaging in hobbies and activities that bring you joy
- Connecting with loved ones and building supportive relationships

By consistently nurturing yourself and attending to your needs, you create a strong foundation of resilience and inner strength that can weather any storm.

Surround Yourself with Positivity:

The people we surround ourselves with and the environments we inhabit have a profound impact on our mindset and well-being. Make a conscious effort to surround yourself with positive, uplifting, and supportive individuals who believe in your potential and encourage your growth.

Seek communities and spaces that align with your values and aspirations, whether online or in-person. Engage in activities and conversations that inspire and motivate you and limit your exposure to negative influences and toxic relationships.

Practice Reframing and Positive Self-Talk:

When faced with challenges or setbacks, it's easy to fall back into patterns of negative self-talk and limiting beliefs. However, by practicing reframing and positive self-talk, you can maintain a resilient and optimistic mindset, even in difficult times.

When you catch yourself engaging in negative self-talk, take a moment to pause and reframe your thoughts in a more positive and empowering way. For example, instead of thinking, "I can't handle this," try reframing it as, "This is a challenge, but I have the strength and resources to overcome it."

Consistently practice positive self-talk and affirmations, reminding yourself of your inherent worth, capabilities, and potential. Speak to yourself with kindness, compassion, and encouragement, as you would a beloved friend.

Embrace Lifelong Learning and Growth:

A positive mindset requires a commitment to lifelong learning and personal growth. Embrace opportunities to expand your knowledge, skills, and perspectives, whether through formal education, workshops, or self-directed learning.

Engage in activities that challenge you and push you outside of your comfort zone, as this is where true growth and transformation occur. Celebrate your progress and successes along the way, and view setbacks as valuable lessons and opportunities for learning.

Develop a Support System:

Building a strong support system is important for maintaining a positive mindset and navigating life's challenges. Surround yourself with trusted friends, family members, mentors, or professionals who can offer guidance, encouragement, and a listening ear when needed.

Don't be afraid to reach out for help and support when struggling. Remember that asking for help is a sign of strength, not weakness, and that we all need the support and love of others to thrive.

Practice Mindfulness and Present-Moment Awareness:

Mindfulness and present-moment awareness are powerful tools for maintaining a positive mindset and reducing stress and anxiety. By focusing your attention on the present moment, you can let go of worries about the future or regrets about the past and find peace and contentment in the here and now.

Incorporate mindfulness practices into your daily routine, such as meditation, deep breathing, or mindful movement. Take moments throughout the day to pause, connect with your senses, and engage with the present moment.

Cultivate Resilience and Adaptability:

Life is full of unexpected twists and turns, and maintaining a positive mindset requires the ability to adapt and bounce back from adversity. Cultivate resilience by embracing challenges as opportunities for growth and learning, and by developing a "growth mindset" that views setbacks as temporary and surmountable.

Practice self-compassion and self-forgiveness when you stumble or make mistakes and remind yourself that every challenge is an opportunity to build strength, wisdom, and character.

Remember, maintaining a positive mindset is an ongoing journey, not a destination. There will be days when you feel unstoppable and full of positivity, and others when you may struggle and fall back into old patterns. Be patient and compassionate with yourself, and trust in growth and transformation.

By consistently practicing the strategies and techniques outlined in this chapter, you can develop a resilient and unwavering positive mindset that will guide you through life's ups and downs. Embrace the journey of personal growth and self-discovery, and know that with each step, you are becoming the best version of yourself, capable of creating a life of boundless joy, fulfillment, and success.

EMBRACING A LIFE OF POSITIVE TRANSFORMATION

Congratulations on your journey of self-discovery and personal growth! By identifying and challenging your negative attitudes and limiting beliefs, and cultivating a toolkit of positive mindset practices, you have laid the foundation for a life of boundless possibilities and success. In these final chapters of Part Four, we will explore how to integrate your newfound positive mindset into all areas of your life, creating a ripple effect of transformation and empowerment.

Align Your Actions with Your Positive Beliefs:

Your thoughts and beliefs are powerful, but true transformation occurs when you align your actions with your positive mindset. Make a conscious effort to live in integrity with your empowering beliefs, acting steps that reflect your newfound confidence, resilience, and self-worth.

Set goals and intentions that align with your values and aspirations and take consistent action toward their realization. Embrace challenges as opportunities for growth, and trust in your ability to overcome obstacles and achieve your dreams.

Cultivate Positive Relationships:

The relationships we have with others play a significant role in shaping our mindset and well-being. Surround yourself with positive, supportive, and uplifting individuals who believe in your potential and encourage your growth. Seek mentors, collaborators, and friends who inspire you to be your best self.

At the same time, be willing to let go of toxic or draining relationships that no longer serve your highest good. Set healthy boundaries and communicate your needs and expectations with compassion and clarity.

Embrace a Life of Purpose and Meaning:

A life of positive transformation is guided by a sense of purpose and meaning. Take the time to reflect on your values, passions, and the unique gifts you have to offer the world. Seek opportunities to contribute to something greater than yourself, whether through your work, volunteering, or creative pursuits.

When you align your actions with your purpose and values, you tap into a deep well of motivation, fulfillment, and joy. Embrace a life of service and contribution, knowing that your positive impact ripples out into the world, creating a legacy of love and light.

Practice Forgiveness and Letting Go:

Holding onto grudges, resentments, and past hurts can weigh heavily on our hearts and minds, preventing us from embracing a life of positive transformation. Practice forgiveness and letting go, both for others and for yourself.

Recognize that forgiveness does not mean condoning hurtful behavior, but releasing the negative emotions that keep you trapped in the past. By letting go of the weight of resentment and anger, you create space for healing, peace, and new possibilities to enter your life.

Embrace Lifelong Learning and Growth:

A life of positive transformation embraces lifelong learning and growth. Cultivate a curiosity and openness to new ideas, experiences, and perspectives. Seek opportunities to expand your knowledge, skills, and self-awareness, whether through formal education, workshops, or self-directed learning.

Embrace the idea that growth and change are a natural part of the human experience, and that each challenge and setback is an opportunity for learning and evolution. By consistently investing in your personal and professional development, you make sure your positive mindset remains strong and adaptive, guiding you toward a life of ever-expanding possibilities.

Celebrate Your Journey and Inspire Others:

As you embrace a life of positive transformation, take the time to celebrate your journey and the incredible growth you have experienced. Acknowledge your progress, successes, and the courage it has taken to break free from negative attitudes and limiting beliefs.

Share your story and insights with others, inspiring them to start their own journey of self-discovery and empowerment. Be a beacon of hope and positivity in your community, showing others that transformation is possible, and that a life of joy, fulfillment, and success is within reach for all of us.

Remember, embracing a life of positive transformation is an ongoing journey, not a destination. There will be ups and downs, challenges and triumphs, but with a strong foundation of positive attitudes and empowering beliefs, you have the resilience and adaptability to navigate whatever life brings your way.

Trust in the journey, trust in yourself, and know that with each step, you are creating a life of boundless love, light, and possibility. Embrace the adventure of positive transformation and watch as your world expands in ways you never thought possible.

Congratulations on your commitment to personal growth and self-discovery. May your journey be filled with joy, wonder, and endless opportunities for positive transformation. Remember, you are the author of your own story, and with a positive mindset and empowering beliefs, you have the power to create a life of extraordinary beauty and purpose. Embrace the journey and know that the best is yet to come.

~

TRANSFORMING YOUR MINDSET THROUGH GOAL SETTING AND VISUALIZATION

HAVE you ever felt held back by negative attitudes or limiting beliefs? If so, you're not alone. Many of us struggle with these challenges, but fortunately, there are powerful tools available to help us overcome them and take control of our lives. Two of the most effective strategies are goal setting and visualization.

When you set clear, specific goals for yourself, you give your mind a roadmap to follow. Start by asking yourself what you want to achieve, whether it's personal growth, career advancement, or overcoming a specific obstacle. Make sure your goals are SMART: Specific, Measurable, Achievable, Relevant, and Time-bound. This will help you stay focused and motivated as you work toward them.

Once you have your goals in mind, break them down into smaller, manageable steps. This can make them feel less daunting and increase your chances of success. Create a plan with clear action steps, and prioritize them based on their importance and urgency.

Visualization is another powerful tool for transforming your mindset. Take a few minutes each day to close your eyes and imagine yourself meeting your goals. Picture yourself succeeding and focus on the positive emotions that come with that success, such as pride, joy, and fulfillment. This practice can help rewire your brain and build your confidence in your ability to achieve your dreams.

Negative thoughts and limiting beliefs can still arise occasionally. When they do, it's important to challenge them head-on. Replace them with positive affirmations and self-talk that reinforces your belief in yourself and your ability to overcome obstacles. Surround yourself with positive influences, whether it's supportive friends, inspiring books, or uplifting podcasts. Create an environment that fosters a growth mindset and encourages you to keep pushing forward.

As you work toward your goals, don't forget to celebrate your progress along the way. Acknowledge your achievements, no matter how small they may seem, and use them as motivation to keep going. Remember that setbacks and challenges are a natural part of the journey, and they offer valuable opportunities for growth and learning.

By incorporating goal setting and visualization into your daily routine, you can transform your mindset and break free from negative attitudes and limiting beliefs. With clarity, focus, and a positive outlook, you can unlock your full potential and create the life you desire. Stay committed to your goals, stay resilient in the face of obstacles, and keep believing in yourself. You have the power to shape your own reality, and with the right tools and mindset, there's no limit to what you can achieve.

EMPOWERING YOURSELF THROUGH PERSONALIZED ACTION PLANS AND ACCOUNTABILITY

BREAKING free from negative attitudes and limiting beliefs is a journey that requires dedication, self-awareness, and a strategic approach. One of the most effective ways to support yourself in this process is by creating a personalized action plan and establishing a strong accountability system.

To begin, it's essential to conduct a thorough self-assessment of your current beliefs and attitudes. This introspective process may involve engaging in self-reflection exercises, keeping a journal, or seeking guidance from a trusted therapist or coach. By gaining a clear understanding of the negative thought patterns and self-imposed limitations holding you back, you can start to identify areas for growth and transformation.

With this newfound self-awareness, you can then set specific, achievable goals for challenging and changing these negative beliefs. Ensure that your goals are realistic, measurable, and bound by a specific timeframe. This will help you stay focused and motivated as you work toward your goals.

To make your goals more manageable, break them down into smaller, actionable steps that align with your strengths and resources. These incremental steps will serve as a roadmap, guiding you toward your desired outcomes. Remember to be patient with yourself and celebrate each milestone along the way, no matter how small it may seem.

Accountability is a key part of any successful action plan. Establish a system that works best for you, whether it involves regular check-ins with a therapist, coach, or support group, or tracking your progress through a journal or digital app. An external source of accountability can provide the motivation and support you need to stay committed to your goals, even when faced with challenges or setbacks.

In addition to professional support, don't underestimate the power of a strong personal support system. Surround yourself with friends, family members, or peers who believe in your potential and can offer encouragement and constructive feedback throughout your journey. These positive influences can help you maintain a growth mindset and provide a safe space to share your experiences and celebrate your successes.

As you navigate this path of personal transformation, carve out time for regular self-reflection. Assess your progress, acknowledge your achievements, and identify areas where you may need to adjust your action plan. Remember that setbacks and challenges are a natural part of the growth process, and each obstacle you face presents an opportunity for learning and self-discovery.

By creating a personalized action plan and cultivating a robust accountability system, you can empower yourself to break free from the negative attitudes and limiting beliefs holding you back. With commitment, self-compassion, and a strategic approach, you can transform your mindset and unlock your true potential, paving the way for a more positive, fulfilling, and purposeful life.

Case Study:

Meet Emily, a talented young professional who, despite her impressive skills and qualifications, found herself stuck in a cycle of self-doubt and unfulfilling jobs. For years, Emily had harbored a deep-seated belief she was not good enough to pursue her true passions or achieve the level of success she desired. This limiting belief, rooted in experiences of criticism and rejection, had become a self-fulfilling prophecy, holding Emily back from reaching her full potential.

One day, a close friend recommended a personal development workshop focused on identifying and overcoming negative attitudes and limiting beliefs. Intrigued by the possibility of breaking free from her self-imposed limitations, Emily decided to attend.

During the workshop, Emily engaged in a profound process of self-reflection and introspection. Through guided exercises and group discussions, she began to recognize the pervasive nature of her negative self-talk and how her limiting beliefs were shaping her reality. She realized that her fear of failure and belief she was not good enough had been preventing her from taking risks, speaking up for herself, and pursuing her true passions.

Armed with this newfound awareness, Emily committed to challenging and reframing her negative attitudes and beliefs. She started by practicing cognitive reframing, consciously shifting her perspective on experiences and current challenges. Instead of viewing setbacks as proof of her inadequacy, she saw them as opportunities for growth and learning.

Emily also incorporated positive affirmations into her daily routine, repeating empowering statements such as "I am capable and deserving of success" and "I trust in my abilities and embrace challenges as opportunities for growth." By consistently reinforcing these positive beliefs, she gradually began to replace her self-limiting thoughts with a more empowered and resilient mindset.

To support her journey of transformation, Emily sought a network of positive influences, including a mentor in her desired field and a supportive group of friends who encouraged her personal and professional growth. She also committed to focusing on self-care, engaging in regular exercise, mindfulness practices, and activities that brought her joy and fulfillment.

As Emily continued to challenge her limiting beliefs and cultivate a more positive mindset, she began to notice significant shifts in her life. She started to approach challenges with greater confidence and resilience, speaking up for herself in meetings and advocating for her ideas. She also found the courage to pursue a long-held dream of starting her own business, a venture that had always seemed out of reach due to her self-doubt.

While the journey of overcoming her negative attitudes and limiting beliefs was not always easy, Emily remained committed to her personal growth and development. She celebrated her progress and accomplishments along the way, recognizing that each step forward was a testament to her strength and resilience.

As Emily's business began to thrive and she found herself living a life more aligned with her values and passions, she realized that her transformation had not only affected her own life but also inspired others around her. She became a mentor and role model for others struggling with self-doubt and limiting beliefs, sharing her story and strategies for cultivating a more empowered and positive mindset.

Looking back on her journey, Emily recognized that breaking free from negative attitudes and limiting beliefs had been a process of self-discovery and liberation. By acknowledging and challenging her self-imposed limitations, she had unlocked a potential and sense of purpose she never knew existed. She had learned to embrace challenges as opportunities for growth and to trust in her own abilities, resilience, and worth.

Emily's story serves as a powerful reminder of the transformative impact of overcoming negative attitudes and limiting beliefs. By engaging in self-reflection, challenging limiting thoughts, cultivating a positive support system, and committing to personal growth and self-care, we all have the power to break free from the chains of self-doubt and embrace a life of greater meaning, fulfillment, and potential. This journey requires courage, vulnerability, and a willingness to confront the deepest parts of ourselves – but it is ultimately filled with endless possibility and self-discovery.

PART FOUR WRAP-UP:

KEY POINTS:

• Negative attitudes and limiting beliefs are invisible barriers that hinder personal growth and success, often operating beneath the surface of conscious awareness.

• Identifying negative attitudes and limiting beliefs involves self-reflection, introspection, mindfulness, seeking feedback from others, examining self-talk, and recognizing patterns and triggers.

• Challenging and overcoming negative attitudes and limiting beliefs requires techniques such as cognitive reframing, evidence-based analysis, positive affirmations, visualization, and disproving limiting beliefs.

• Societal and cultural factors, including media, family, peers, and institutions, can significantly influence the development and perpetuation of limiting beliefs.

• Cultivating self-awareness and self-compassion is important in the journey of overcoming limiting beliefs, as it allows for a more understanding and supportive inner dialogue.

• Maintaining a positive mindset involves practices such as gratitude, self-care, surrounding oneself with positivity, reframing, embracing lifelong learning, and developing a support system.

• Goal setting and visualization are powerful tools for transforming mindset and overcoming negative attitudes and limiting beliefs.

• Creating a personalized action plan and establishing accountability are key parts when breaking free from negative attitudes and limiting beliefs.

Action Items:

• Engage in regular self-reflection and introspection to identify negative attitudes and limiting beliefs that may be holding you back.

• Practice mindfulness and observe your thoughts and emotions without judgment to gain greater self-awareness.

• Seek feedback from trusted friends, family members, or a therapist to gain insight into patterns of negativity or self-doubt.

• Challenge negative attitudes and limiting beliefs using techniques such as cognitive reframing, evidence-based analysis, and positive affirmations.

• Cultivate a growth mindset by embracing challenges as opportunities for learning and development.

• Practice self-compassion and treat yourself with kindness and understanding, acknowledging that personal growth is a journey.

• Create a support system of positive influences, including mentors, friends, and communities that align with your values and aspirations.

• Set realistic and achievable goals that align with your values and aspirations, and break them down into manageable action steps.

• Incorporate visualization techniques into your daily routine, imagining yourself meeting your goals and experiencing the positive emotions associated with success.

• Develop a personalized action plan to address specific limiting beliefs and negative attitudes, and establish a system of accountability to stay motivated and committed to your growth.

• Engage in regular self-care practices, such as exercise, mindfulness, and pursuing hobbies that bring you joy and fulfillment.

• Continuously learn and expand your knowledge and skills, seeking opportunities for personal and professional development.

• Celebrate your progress and accomplishments along the way, acknowledging the effort and courage it takes to challenge limiting beliefs and cultivate a more positive mindset.

In our next part …

… we'll start a captivating exploration of the transformative power of positive thinking and its profound impact on our inner world. We'll dig into the fascinating link between our thoughts and emotions, uncovering how our mental patterns shape our experiences and overall well-being. Prepare to discover practical strategies for cultivating a positive mindset, such as cognitive restructuring, mindfulness practices, and surrounding yourself with uplifting influences. Together, we'll learn how to harness the power of our minds to overcome challenges, build resilience, and create a life of purpose and fulfillment.

As we navigate this journey of personal growth, we'll also explore the importance of self-care and its important role in supporting our emotional well-being. From nourishing our bodies with healthy habits to setting boundaries and prioritizing rest, we'll uncover the key ingredients for creating a balanced and thriving life. So, get ready to start a transformative adventure as we unlock the secrets to embracing the power of positive thinking and discover how small shifts in our mindset can lead to monumental changes in our lives.

◠

PART FIVE
THE ALCHEMY OF THE MIND: HARNESSING THE TRANSFORMATIVE POWER OF POSITIVE THINKING

THE FASCINATING LINK BETWEEN THOUGHTS AND EMOTIONS

Have you ever stopped to consider the incredible power your thoughts hold over your emotions and overall well-being? This concept has captivated the minds of philosophers and psychologists for centuries. The idea is simple yet profound: the way we think directly affects how we feel and the quality of our lives.

When you think about it, it's remarkable. Our thoughts are like the invisible architects of our emotional experiences. They can lift us up, filling us with joy and motivation, or drag us down into the depths of despair and anxiety. It's a phenomenon that modern psychological research has delved into extensively, confirming what ancient wisdom has long suggested – our mental state is an important determinant of our happiness and success.

The Far-Reaching Consequences of Our Thought Patterns

Let's explore this further. Imagine two individuals: one who consistently engages in negative self-talk, constantly criticizing themselves and expecting the worst, and another who makes a conscious effort to maintain a positive outlook, focusing on their strengths and opportunities for growth. Who do you think is more likely to experience feelings of contentment, resilience, and overall life satisfaction?

The answer is clear. Many studies have shown that individuals who habitually engage in negative thinking are more prone to experiencing distress, anxiety, and even depression. But those who cultivate a more positive thought pattern are usually more emotionally resilient, report higher levels of happiness, and generally feel more fulfilled in their lives.

Practical Strategies for Nurturing a Positive Mindset

So, how can we harness the power of our thoughts to enhance our emotional well-being? Fortunately, cultivating a positive mindset is a skill that can be learned and strengthened with practice. It involves more than just dismissing negative thoughts; it requires reshaping our mental landscape.

One highly effective tool is the practice of mindfulness and meditation. By regularly taking time to observe our thoughts without judgment, we can learn of our mental patterns and gently guide them in a more positive direction. It's like training our minds to focus on the good, rather than getting stuck in a cycle of negativity.

Another powerful strategy is the use of affirmations. By regularly repeating positive statements about ourselves and our abilities, we can start to internalize these beliefs and counteract the effects of negative self-talk. It's about learning to be our own cheerleader, reminding ourselves of our strengths and potential even in the face of challenges.

Visualization is another technique that can work wonders. By vividly imagining ourselves succeeding in various parts of life, we can boost our confidence and reinforce our belief in our ability to meet our goals. It's like giving our minds a blueprint for success and watching as our actions start to align with this positive vision.

Lastly, the practice of gratitude is a game-changer. When we make a habit of acknowledging the things we are thankful for, we shift our focus from what we lack to the abundance we already have. This simple shift in perspective can have a profound impact on our overall sense of contentment and appreciation for life.

Embracing Challenges as Opportunities for Growth

A key hallmark of a positive mindset is the ability to view challenges not as roadblocks, but as opportunities for personal development. When we approach difficulties with this growth-oriented perspective, we become more resilient and adaptable. We see that every struggle we face is a chance to learn, grow, and become a better version of ourselves.

This isn't to say that maintaining a positive outlook makes life's challenges disappear. Rather, it equips us with the mental and emotional tools to navigate these challenges more effectively. We become less likely to get overwhelmed or discouraged, and more likely to persevere and find creative solutions.

The Profound Impact of Positivity on Those Around Us

The benefits of a positive mindset extend far beyond our own personal growth and happiness. Our attitudes and behaviors have a ripple effect on those around us, influencing our relationships, work environments, and family dynamics.

When we radiate positivity, we become a source of inspiration and encouragement for others. Our optimism and resilience can be contagious, uplifting those in our sphere of influence and contributing to a more positive and supportive collective atmosphere.

In this way, cultivating a positive mindset is not just a gift we give ourselves, but also a way of positively affecting our communities and the world. By focusing on the good and believing in the potential for positive change, we become active participants in creating a more hopeful and uplifting reality for all.

Embracing the Journey Toward a More Fulfilling Life

Ultimately, pursuing a positive mindset is about so much more than just feeling happy. It's about equipping ourselves with the mental and emotional resources to live our best lives – to face challenges with courage, to build meaningful connections with others, and to actualize our fullest potential.

It's a continuous journey of growth and self-discovery, one that requires consistent effort and commitment. There will undoubtedly be times when maintaining a positive outlook feels challenging, when life's obstacles threaten to throw us off course. But with practice and perseverance, we can learn to redirect our thoughts, to find the lesson and the opportunity in every situation.

As we strengthen our ability to cultivate a positive mindset, we'll start to notice profound shifts in our inner world. We'll feel more grounded, more resilient, and more in control of our emotional experiences. We'll start to approach life with a greater sense of enthusiasm and possibility, knowing that our thoughts have the power to shape our reality.

So, let's make the conscious choice to harness the power of positive thinking. Let's commit to nourishing our minds with thoughts that uplift, empower, and inspire us to be our best selves. In doing so, we open ourselves up to a world of limitless potential, where every challenge is an opportunity for growth, and every day is a chance to create a life of profound meaning and fulfillment.

∾

NAVIGATING THE LABYRINTH OF NEGATIVE THOUGHTS: YOUR GUIDE TO A MORE POSITIVE MINDSET

The Subtle Traps of Negative Thinking

Imagine your mind as a garden. Just as a garden can be overrun by weeds if left unattended, our minds can become entangled in negative thought patterns that slowly strangle our joy and vitality. These patterns are often so deeply ingrained that we may not even realize their influence on our emotions and behaviors.

Let's look closely at some of these mental weeds. Self-doubt, for example, is a common culprit. Nagging voice in your head that questions your every move, undermining your confidence and making you second-guess your abilities. Then there's pessimism, the tendency to always expect the worst. Like a pair of dark-tinted glasses, pessimism colors your world in shades of negativity, making it difficult to spot the silver linings.

And let's not forget self-criticism, the relentless inner critic that magnifies your every flaw and mistake. This pattern can be especially damaging, eroding your self-esteem and making it hard to recognize and celebrate your successes.

Shining a Light on Your Thought Patterns

So, how can we begin to untangle ourselves from these negative thought patterns? The first step is awareness. Just as you can't pull out a weed if you don't know it's there, you can't change a thought pattern if you're not aware of it.

This is where the practice of mindfulness comes in. By regularly tuning into your thoughts and observing them without judgment, you can start to recognize when you're slipping into negative thinking. It's like shining a light into the corners of your mind, exposing the hidden patterns shaping your experiences.

Once you've spotted a negative thought, the next step is to challenge it. Ask yourself, "Is this thought really true? What proof do I have to back it up?" Often, you'll find that your negative thoughts are founded more on habit than on reality. For example, when you catch yourself doubting your abilities, actively look for examples that contradict this belief. Remind yourself of times when you've overcome challenges and met your goals.

Another powerful tool is reframing. This involves consciously shifting your perspective on a situation. So, instead of thinking, "I'll never get this right," you might reframe it as, "I'm learning and growing with each attempt." This simple shift can make a world of difference in how you approach challenges and setbacks.

Lastly, don't forget the importance of self-compassion. We're often so much harder on ourselves than we would ever be on a friend. Learning to treat yourself with kindness and understanding, especially in the face of mistakes or failures, can go a long way in counteracting negative self-talk.

Nurturing the Seeds of Positivity

But uprooting negative thought patterns is only half the battle. To cultivate a positive mindset, you need to actively plant and nurture positive thoughts.

One powerful way to do this is through gratitude practice. By regularly taking time to reflect on the things you're thankful for, you train your mind to focus on the good in your life. It's like watering the seeds of positivity, helping them to grow and flourish.

Affirmations are another effective tool. These are positive statements you repeat to yourself, such as "I am capable and worthy of success." By consistently reinforcing these positive beliefs, you gradually replace the negative narratives in your mind.

Finally, don't underestimate the power of your social environment. Surrounding yourself with people who uplift and inspire you can have a profound impact on your own thought patterns. Seek individuals who embody the positive thinking you want to cultivate in yourself.

The Journey to a Brighter Mindset

Transforming your mindset is a journey, not a destination. It requires consistent effort and practice. There will be days when negative thoughts seem to dominate, when it feels like you're taking one step forward and two steps back. But remember, each time you choose to challenge a negative thought or focus on gratitude, you're strengthening your positive thinking muscles.

Over time, you'll find that your default thinking patterns start to shift. Positivity will come more naturally, and you'll be better equipped to navigate life's challenges with resilience and optimism.

So, be patient with yourself. Celebrate each small victory and learn from each setback. And most important, never forget the incredible power you have to shape your own mental landscape.

By tending to your mind with awareness, compassion, and a commitment to positivity, you'll cultivate a mindset that not only enhances your own well-being but also radiates outward, positively affecting those around you.

So, take a deep breath, and step bravely into the adventure of reshaping your thoughts. A brighter, more positive future awaits.

~

THE ART OF COGNITIVE RESTRUCTURING: TRANSFORMING NEGATIVE THOUGHTS INTO EMPOWERING PERSPECTIVES

THE SHADOW of Negative Thoughts

Negative thoughts can be like dark clouds obscuring the sun, casting a shadow over our mental landscape. They have a way of coloring our perceptions, making the world seem bleak and our challenges insurmountable. But just as the sun still shines above the clouds, our capacity for positivity and resilience is always present, even when negative thoughts threaten to overshadow it.

The key to breaking free from this shadow is understanding that our thoughts are not always a reflection of reality. They are often influenced by cognitive distortions—patterns of thinking that twist and distort our perceptions. For example, overgeneralization is a common distortion where we view a single negative event as a never-ending pattern of defeat. If we fail at a task once, we might think, "I always fail. I'll never be successful."

Another distortion is black-and-white thinking, where we see things in absolute categories with no middle ground. Either we're perfect, or we're a complete failure. There's no room for anything in between. And then there's catastrophizing, where we always expect the worst possible outcome, no matter how unlikely it may be.

These distorted thoughts can trap us in a cycle of negativity, reinforcing pessimistic beliefs about ourselves and our lives. But the good news is, just as we have the power to shape our thoughts, we also have the power to reshape them.

The Transformative Power of Cognitive Restructuring

This is where the art of cognitive restructuring comes in. This technique involves identifying, challenging, and replacing negative thoughts with more balanced and empowering perspectives. It's like taking off the dark glasses of negativity and seeing the world in a new, more positive light.

The first step in this process is to learn of your negative thoughts. This might sound simple, but often these thoughts are so habitual that we don't even realize we're thinking them. When you catch yourself in a negative thought pattern, take a moment to label it. Recognizing and naming these thoughts as 'unhelpful' or 'distorted' can reduce their power over you.

Next, challenge these thoughts. Ask yourself, "Is this thought really true? What evidence do I have to support it?" Often, you'll find that your negative thoughts are based more on fear or habit than on facts. Look for alternative explanations or ways of viewing the situation. Consider what you might tell a friend if they were in your situation and had the same thought.

Then, replace the negative thought with a more balanced and empowering one. This doesn't mean putting on rose-colored glasses and ignoring reality. It's about finding a perspective that is both realistic and helpful. So, instead of thinking, "I never do anything right," you might replace that with, "I sometimes make mistakes, but I also have many successes and I'm always learning and growing."

Integrating Cognitive Restructuring into Your Life

Like any skill, cognitive restructuring takes practice. One helpful tool is keeping a thought diary. Regularly jot down the negative thoughts you experience and the circumstances in which they arise. Over time, you'll start to notice patterns and triggers for these thoughts, making it easier to catch and challenge them.

Another technique is thought stopping. When you spiral into negativity, use a designated word or phrase, like "stop" or "not helpful," to interrupt the thought. This gives you a chance to step back and apply a more rational perspective.

And don't forget the power of positive affirmations. Regularly repeating phrases that promote self-confidence and counteract negative beliefs can gradually reshape your default thinking patterns. Affirmations like, "I am capable of handling whatever comes my way," can be powerful tools in your cognitive restructuring toolkit.

The Ripple Effect of Positive Thinking

As you start to master the art of cognitive restructuring, you'll notice a profound shift in your emotional landscape. Challenges that once seemed overwhelming will start to feel more manageable. You'll be better equipped to handle stress and setbacks, bouncing back more quickly and with greater resilience.

But the benefits don't stop there. Your newfound positivity will also ripple out to those around you. As you interact with the world from a place of optimism and empowerment, you'll inspire and uplift others. Your relationships will be enriched, and you'll attract more positive experiences and opportunities.

This journey of mental transformation is ongoing. There will still be days when negative thoughts try to encroach on your mental space. But with each application of cognitive restructuring, you'll strengthen your ability to redirect your thoughts toward a more positive trajectory.

So, embrace the art of cognitive restructuring. Use it as a tool to chisel away at the negativity that blocks your path, revealing the resilience, the strength, and the boundless potential that has always been within you. With each empowering thought, you'll be one step closer to crafting a life story filled with optimism, joy, and fulfillment.

The journey to a brighter mindset starts with a single thought. Make it a positive one.

∽

GRATITUDE AND AFFIRMATIONS: PAVING THE PATH TO A MORE FULFILLING LIFE

The Alchemy of Gratitude

Imagine if a magic potion could instantly boost your happiness, melt away stress, strengthen your relationships, and even improve your health. Sounds too good to be true, right? But what if I told you that this potion is real, and it's not magic at all? It's gratitude.

Gratitude is more than just a feel-good sentiment. It's a powerful alchemy that can transform your life from the inside out. When you make a habit of recognizing and appreciating the good things in your life, you're not just counting your blessings—you're actually rewiring your brain for positivity.

Think about it: when you're focused on what you're grateful for, there's less room for negative thoughts and emotions. It's like shining a spotlight on the positives, leaving the negatives to fade into the shadows. And the more you practice gratitude, the more you train your brain to look for the good in every situation.

But the benefits don't stop there. Research has shown that gratitude can significantly increase your overall life satisfaction and happiness. It's like a happiness booster shot, without the needle. Gratitude also acts as a stressbuster, helping you manage life's challenges with more ease and resilience.

And let's not forget the ripple effect of gratitude on our relationships. When we express appreciation to others, it strengthens our connections and fosters a greater sense of bonding. It's a simple but powerful way to nurture the relationships that matter most to us.

So, how can you start tapping into the power of gratitude? One of the most effective methods is keeping a gratitude journal. Every day, take a few minutes to write down the things you're thankful for. They can be big things, like a supportive family, or small joys, like a perfect cup of coffee. The key is to make it a consistent practice.

Another way to cultivate gratitude is to make it a part of your daily reflection. Take time each day to mentally review the positive experiences and people that enrich your life. This simple habit can help cement a grateful mindset.

The Magic of Affirmations

Now, let's talk about another powerful tool for personal transformation: positive affirmations. If gratitude is about appreciating what you have, affirmations are about believing in what you can become.

Affirmations are like personal pep talks. They're statements that affirm your worth, your capabilities, and your potential. By repeating these statements regularly, you're planting the seeds of positivity in your subconscious mind.

Think of your mind as a garden, and your thoughts as the seeds. If you plant seeds of self-doubt and negativity, that's what will grow. But if you plant seeds of confidence and optimism, you'll cultivate a garden of positivity that will support and sustain you.

Affirmations can be especially powerful in boosting self-esteem and self-confidence. When you affirm your worth and abilities, you're counteracting the negative self-talk that can hold you back. You're reminding yourself of your inherent value and potential.

Affirmations can also be a great motivator. By affirming your goals and aspirations, you're reinforcing your commitment to them. You're telling yourself, "I can do this. I will do this." This can give you the extra push you need to act and persevere in the face of challenges.

So, how can you start using affirmations effectively? One way is to make them part of your morning routine. Start each day by repeating affirmations that resonate with your goals and values. This sets a positive tone for the day ahead.

You can also place visual reminders of your affirmations around your space. Stick post-it notes with your affirmations on your mirror, your computer, or anywhere you'll see them regularly. These constant reminders can help ingrain the positive messages into your subconscious.

For an even deeper effect, try combining affirmations with meditation. Take a few minutes each day to sit quietly, repeat your affirmations, and visualize yourself embodying them. This practice can help you integrate the affirmations more fully into your being.

The Journey to a Positive Life

Gratitude and affirmations are not one-time fixes. They're practices that, when cultivated over time, can profoundly shift your perspective and enhance your life experience. They're about choosing to focus on the good, believing in your potential, and shaping your mindset.

By making these practices a regular part of your life, you're not just improving your own well-being. You're also contributing to a more positive world. Your gratitude and positivity will radiate outwards, touching and inspiring those around you.

This journey to a more positive life is not always easy. There will be days when gratitude feels hard to muster, when doubts creep in despite your affirmations. But that's okay. The path to personal growth is rarely linear.

What matters is that you keep coming back to these practices, day after day. With each expression of gratitude, with each affirmation, you're strengthening your positivity muscles. You're training yourself to look for the light, even in the darkest of times.

So, embrace the power of gratitude and affirmations. Let them be your compass, guiding you toward a life of greater joy, fulfillment, and personal growth. Because when you change your mindset, you change your life. And that, my friend, is the most powerful magic.

~

CRAFTING A LIFE OF POSITIVITY: THE POWER OF YOUR SURROUNDINGS

The Invisible Sculptors of Our Lives

Imagine your life as a grand sculpture, shaped and molded by the forces around you. Every interaction, every environment, every experience leaves its mark, chiseling away at your perspective, your habits, and your overall well-being.

But what if you could take control of these invisible sculptors? What if you could deliberately choose the influences that shape your life, crafting a masterpiece of positivity and personal growth?

This is the power of surrounding yourself with positivity. It's about recognizing that your environment and social connections are not just background noise; they are active participants in your life story. And by consciously curating these elements, you can create a life rich in joy, inspiration, and fulfillment.

The Ripple Effect of Relationships

Let's start with the people in your life. The relationships you cultivate have a profound impact on your emotional and mental landscape. Surround yourself with people who uplift and inspire you, those who radiate positivity and encourage your growth.

These are the people who celebrate your successes, who lift you up when you stumble, and who challenge you to be your best self. In their presence, you feel energized, supported, and motivated to reach for your dreams.

On the flip side, it's equally important to set boundaries with those who drain your energy or pull you into negative thought patterns. This doesn't mean cutting these people out of your life, but it does mean being mindful of how much time and emotional space you give them.

Remember, your well-being should always be a top priority. It's not selfish to protect your positive space; it's a necessary act of self-care.

The Joy of Purposeful Pursuits

Another key aspect of surrounding yourself with positivity is engaging in activities that bring you joy and fulfillment. When you do things you love, you're not just having fun—you're also nurturing your soul and reinforcing a positive mindset.

So, dive into that hobby you've always wanted to try. Take that dance class, start that garden, or learn that new language. Pursuing your passions is a powerful way to infuse your life with positivity.

And don't forget the joy of giving back. Volunteering or helping others can provide a deep sense of purpose and satisfaction. It shifts your focus from your own worries to the difference you can make in the world, fostering a more positive and grateful perspective.

The Media Diet

Today, the media we consume is a significant part of our environment. And like junk food can sabotage a healthy diet, a steady stream of negative media can undermine a positive mindset.

Be mindful of the news, social media, and entertainment you consume. While it's important to stay informed, it's equally important to limit your exposure to content that consistently stresses or disturbs you.

Instead, seek media that inspires, educates, and aligns with your personal growth. Fill your feed with accounts that share uplifting stories, motivational quotes, and helpful resources. Curate a media diet that nourishes your mind and soul.

The Space You Inhabit

Your physical environment also plays a role in your mental well-being. Create a living space that is not just functional, but also uplifting. Surround yourself with colors, decorations, and personal mementos that spark joy and positive memories.

Keep your space tidy and organized. A cluttered environment can lead to a cluttered mind, while a clean and orderly space can promote mental clarity and reduce stress.

And don't underestimate the power of nature. Incorporate plants into your space, and make time to step outside and soak in the natural world. Studies have consistently shown that nature has a profound positive impact on our mental health.

The Attitude of Gratitude

One of the most powerful ways to surround yourself with positivity is to cultivate an attitude of gratitude. When you make a habit of acknowledging and appreciating the good in your life, you're training your mind to focus on the positive.

Start a gratitude journal and make it a daily practice to write down the things you're thankful for. They can be big things, like a loving family or a fulfilling career, or small joys, like a beautiful sunset or a great cup of coffee.

The more you practice gratitude, the more you'll start to notice the large amount of good that surrounds you. It's like putting on a pair of positivity glasses—suddenly, the world looks a little brighter, a little more wonderful.

Chapter Summary: The Architect of Your Positive Life

Surrounding yourself with positivity is not about creating a perfect life. It's about intentionally choosing the influences that shape your perspective and your experience of the world.

It's about surrounding yourself with people who lift you up, activities that bring you joy, and environments that inspire and energize you.

It's about nourishing your mind with positive media, cultivating a grateful heart, and creating a physical space that reflects your best self.

When you make these elements a priority, you become the architect of your own positive life. You create a foundation of joy, resilience, and personal growth that can weather any storm and celebrate any triumph.

So, start today. Look around at the invisible sculptors that shape your world, and ask yourself: are they crafting the life you want to live? If not, it's time to pick up your own chisel and start sculpting.

Surround yourself with positivity and watch as your life becomes a masterpiece of your own making.

~

RESILIENCE: YOUR INNER FORTRESS IN THE FACE OF ADVERSITY

Life's Inevitable Storms

Imagine life as a voyage across a vast ocean. The journey is filled with breathtaking vistas, serene waters, and the promise of new horizons. But as any seasoned sailor knows, no voyage is without its storms.

These storms come in many forms: setbacks, failures, losses, and challenges that threaten to push us off course or even capsize our boat. In these moments, we realize it's not just about the destination, but about how we navigate the journey.

This is where resilience comes in. Resilience is the inner fortitude that lets us weather life's storms, to not just survive them, but to emerge stronger, wiser, and more capable of handling future challenges.

The Power of Perspective

At the heart of resilience is perspective. When faced with a challenge, a resilient mindset sees not just the immediate obstacle, but the opportunity for growth and learning.

It's the difference between seeing a setback as a permanent failure and seeing it as a temporary detour. It's the ability to reframe a crisis as a chance to develop new skills, to test our mettle, and to prove to ourselves that we can overcome adversity.

This perspective is not about denying the reality of the challenge or the pain it may cause. Rather, it's about choosing to focus on what we can control, on the steps we can take to move forward, no matter how small they may seem.

The Toolkit of Resilience

So, how do we build this resilient perspective? Like any skill, resilience can be developed and strengthened. It's about equipping ourselves with a toolkit of strategies we can draw on when the storms hit.

One of the most powerful tools in this kit is problem-solving. When faced with a challenge, a resilient mindset doesn't get overwhelmed by the entire problem. Instead, it breaks it down into manageable parts, and methodically works through each one.

This approach not only makes the problem seem less daunting, but it also builds confidence as we see ourselves making progress, one step at a time.

Another important tool is the ability to seek and offer support. No one navigates life's storms alone. Resilience is not about being a solitary hero, but about knowing when and how to reach out for help.

This could mean turning to a trusted friend or family member for emotional support, seeking advice from a mentor or coach, or joining a community of others facing similar challenges.

At the same time, offering support to others can be just as empowering. When we help someone else weather their storm, we not only make a positive impact on their life, but we also remind ourselves of our own strength and capability.

Personal Growth and Self-Care

Building resilience is not just about how we handle the external storms, but also about how we nurture our internal landscape.

This means committing to continuous personal growth. It's about setting goals that align with our values and provide a sense of purpose, and then pursuing them with determination and flexibility.

It's about seeing each challenge as an opportunity to learn something new, to develop a skill, or to gain a fresh perspective. With this mindset, setbacks become steppingstones, and failures become valuable lessons.

Equally important is the commitment to self-care. Just as a sailor must maintain their vessel, we must take care of our physical and emotional well-being.

This means making time for regular exercise, healthy eating, and adequate rest. It means practicing mindfulness or meditation to calm the mind and gain clarity in the storm.

It also means being gentle with ourselves. Resilience is not about being perfect or never feeling knocked down. It's about getting back up, dusting ourselves off, and continuing the voyage.

Embracing Change

Perhaps the most challenging part of resilience is the ability to adapt to change. Life's storms have a way of changing our course, sometimes in ways we never expected or wanted.

But a resilient mindset recognizes that change is a constant part of the journey. It's not about resisting the wind, but about adjusting the sails.

This means being open to new directions, even if they differ from our original plan. It means being willing to let go of what no longer serves us, and to embrace the unknown with curiosity and courage.

The Horizon of Resilience

Building resilience is not a one-time event, but a lifelong journey. It's a voyage of self-discovery, of learning to navigate the outer world by mastering our inner world.

With each storm we weather, we add to our toolkit of resilience. We become more adept at problem-solving, more connected in our support systems, more committed to our personal growth, and more adaptable to change.

And as we continue this voyage, we see the storms not as threats, but as opportunities. We develop a deep trust in our ability to handle whatever comes our way, and a profound appreciation for the journey itself.

So as you set sail on your own life's voyage, remember that resilience is your inner fortress. This strength will carry you through the storms, the beacon that will guide you to new horizons, and the compass that will always lead you back to your true north.

Embrace the journey, trust in your resilience, and know that no matter how fierce the storm, you have the power to not just weather it, but to emerge stronger, wiser, and more alive than ever before.

MINDFULNESS AND SELF-CARE: NURTURING YOUR INNER OASIS

In the whirlwind of modern life, it's easy to get caught up in the constant rush, the endless to-do lists, and the overwhelming pressures. We often run on autopilot, disconnected from our own thoughts and emotions, and neglecting our most basic needs.

But amidst this chaos, there is a path to stillness, to self-discovery, and to inner peace. This path is paved with the practices of mindfulness and self-care.

Mindfulness: The Art of Being Present

Mindfulness is more than just a buzzword; it's a transformative practice that can reshape our relationship with ourselves and the world.

At its core, mindfulness is about being present in the moment. It's about observing our thoughts and feelings without judgment and experiencing our surroundings with a sense of openness and curiosity.

When we practice mindfulness, we step out of the endless cycle of worrying about the future or dwelling on the past. We ground ourselves in the here and now, and this present moment is the only one we have.

This simple shift in perspective can have profound effects on our mental well-being. By reducing stress, enhancing emotional resilience, and improving focus, mindfulness becomes a powerful tool in our quest for a more positive mindset.

Mindfulness in Practice

So, how do we cultivate mindfulness in our daily lives? The beauty of this practice is that it can be integrated into even the most routine activities.

One of the most accessible techniques is mindful breathing. By focusing on the sensation of the breath moving in and out of our body, we anchor ourselves in the present moment. This simple act can be a refuge during times of stress or anxiety.

Another powerful technique is the body scan meditation. By systematically relaxing each part of our body, we release physical tension and quiet the mind. This practice can be helpful before sleep, promoting a sense of calm and ease.

Mindfulness can also be practiced through observing our surroundings. By choosing an object and focusing on it with all our senses, we train our mind to be engaged in the present. This can be a leaf, a candle flame, or even a simple household object.

The key is to approach these practices with a sense of gentleness and patience. Mindfulness is a skill that develops over time, and each moment of presence is a success.

Self-Care: Honoring Your Needs

While mindfulness helps us to be present, self-care makes sure we are nurturing ourselves in that present moment. Self-care is about recognizing and meeting our own needs, whether they are physical, emotional, or spiritual.

In a world that often demands we put others first, self-care can feel indulgent or selfish. But we cannot pour from an empty cup. When we take care of ourselves, we are better equipped to handle life's challenges and to be present for the people we love.

Self-care can take many forms, and what nourishes one person may differ from another. For some, it's engaging in regular physical activity, which boosts mood and reduces stress. For others, it's nourishing the body with healthy, wholesome foods.

Getting adequate rest is a fundamental part of self-care that is often overlooked. Our bodies and minds need sleep to recover and rejuvenate, and prioritizing rest can have a profound impact on our overall well-being.

Self-care can also be found in our connection with nature. Spending time outdoors, whether it's a walk in the park or a hike in the woods, can reduce stress, improve mood, and provide a sense of perspective.

Finally, self-care involves setting healthy boundaries. This means learning to say no to commitments that deplete us, and yes to activities that replenish us. It means protecting our time and energy and focusing on our own well-being.

Your Inner Oasis

Mindfulness and self-care are not just practices; they are a way of being. They invite us to slow down, to tune into ourselves, and to treat ourselves with kindness and compassion.

When we make these practices a regular part of our lives, we create an inner oasis—a place of calm, clarity, and rejuvenation we can access no matter what storms may rage outside.

In this oasis, we find the strength to face life's challenges with resilience. We discover a deep well of inner peace that sustains us through difficult times. And we connect with a sense of joy and vitality that makes the good times even sweeter.

So, in the daily grind, remember to pause. Breathe. Check in with yourself. Ask what you need in this moment, and honor that need.

These small acts of mindfulness and self-care are not selfish; they are a necessary part of living a balanced, fulfilling life. They are the keys to unlocking your inner oasis, and to cultivating a positive, resilient mindset.

In a world always rushing, always demanding, always changing, mindfulness and self-care are the steadfast companions that will help you navigate the journey with grace, wisdom, and a deep sense of inner peace.

Embrace them and watch as your life blossoms in ways you never imagined possible.

Case Study:

Meet David, a high-achieving executive who, despite his outward success, grappled with a persistent sense of negativity and dissatisfaction. For years, David had been driven by a relentless inner critic, constantly pushing himself to work harder, achieve more, and prove his worth. Yet no matter how much he accomplished; he couldn't shake the feeling that it was never enough.

One day, a colleague recommended a workshop on the power of positive thinking and mindset transformation. Intrigued by the possibility of finding a new perspective, David decided to attend.

During the workshop, David was introduced to the concept of the thought-emotion link – the idea that our thoughts directly affect our emotional states and overall well-being. As he listened to the facilitator explain how negative thought patterns can create a self-perpetuating cycle of stress, anxiety, and dissatisfaction, David began to recognize these patterns in his own life.

Determined to break free from this cycle, David committed to practicing the strategies he learned in the workshop. He started by learning of his negative self-talk, noticing when he was engaging in self-criticism or catastrophic thinking. When he caught himself in these thought patterns, he practiced reframing them in a more balanced and compassionate way.

David also began to incorporate regular mindfulness and gratitude practices into his daily routine. He set aside time each morning for quiet reflection, focusing on his breath and centering himself in the present moment. Throughout the day, he made a point of acknowledging the small joys and successes, shifting his focus from what was lacking to what was abundant.

As David continued to practice these strategies, he noticed a gradual but profound shift in his mindset and emotional landscape. He approached challenges with a greater sense of resilience and adaptability, seeing setbacks as opportunities for growth rather than personal failures. His relationships with colleagues and loved ones also began to improve, as his newfound positivity and emotional balance allowed for more meaningful connections and interactions.

Inspired by his own transformation, David began to integrate the principles of positive thinking and mindset work into his leadership style. He made a point of recognizing and celebrating the successes of his team members, fostering a culture of appreciation and support. He also became more open about his own journey, sharing his experiences and encouraging others to focus on their mental and emotional well-being.

As David's team began to thrive under this new approach, his company took notice. He was asked to lead workshops and mentor other executives in the principles of positive leadership and mindset transformation. Through this work, David discovered a deep sense of purpose and fulfillment, knowing he was not only transforming his own life but also making a positive impact on others.

Looking back on his journey, David realized that the power of positive thinking was not about denying the challenges and complexities of life, but about choosing to meet them with a mindset of resilience, compassion, and growth. By learning to harness the power of his thoughts and cultivate a more positive emotional landscape, he had not only transformed his own experience but also become a catalyst for change in his organization and beyond.

David's story serves as a powerful reminder of the transformative potential of our own minds. By learning of our thought patterns, practicing strategies for cultivating positivity and resilience, and integrating these principles into our personal and professional lives, we all have the power to shape our experiences and create a more fulfilling, purpose-driven reality. The journey of mindset transformation is life-long, but with each step, we open ourselves to new possibilities for growth, connection, and positive impact.

~

PART FIVE WRAP-UP:

KEY POINTS:

• Our thoughts directly affect our emotions and overall well-being, creating a powerful link between our mental and emotional states.

• Negative thought patterns can lead to a self-perpetuating cycle of stress, anxiety, and dissatisfaction, hindering personal growth and fulfillment.

• Cultivating self-awareness is important in recognizing and challenging negative thought patterns, allowing for the development of a more positive mindset.

• Cognitive restructuring techniques, such as reframing negative thoughts and practicing self-compassion, can help transform limiting beliefs and promote emotional resilience.

• Regular mindfulness practices, such as meditation and gratitude, can help ground individuals in the present moment and foster a more balanced and positive outlook.

• Surrounding oneself with positive influences, engaging in purposeful activities, and creating an uplifting environment can significantly contribute to the cultivation of a positive mindset.

• Resilience is a key part of personal growth, enabling individuals to navigate life's challenges with adaptability, strength, and a focus on opportunities for learning and development.

• Self-care practices, including physical exercise, healthy eating, adequate rest, and setting boundaries, are essential for maintaining emotional well-being and supporting personal growth.

Action Items:

• Develop a daily practice of self-reflection and mindfulness to increase awareness of your thoughts and emotions, noticing patterns of negativity or self-criticism.

• Challenge negative self-talk by practicing cognitive restructuring techniques, such as reframing thoughts in a more balanced and compassionate manner.

• Incorporate regular mindfulness practices into your daily routine, such as meditation, deep breathing exercises, or body scans, to cultivate present-moment awareness and emotional balance.

• Keep a gratitude journal, regularly acknowledging the positive aspects of your life and celebrating small successes and joys.

• Surround yourself with positive influences, seeking relationships, activities, and environments that uplift and inspire you.

• Engage in purposeful pursuits and hobbies that bring you a sense of joy, fulfillment, and personal growth.

• Cultivate a growth mindset by embracing challenges as opportunities for learning and development, and reframing setbacks as temporary obstacles to overcome.

• Prioritize self-care by maintaining a balanced lifestyle that includes regular physical activity, nourishing meals, enough rest, and clear boundaries to protect your emotional well-being.

• Share your experiences and insights with others, serving as a positive influence and inspiring them to embrace the power of positive thinking and personal growth.

• Continuously seek opportunities for learning and self-discovery, remaining open to new perspectives and approaches that can support your ongoing personal and professional development.

In our next part...

... we'll start a transformative journey into the heart of gratitude and its profound impact on our lives. We'll explore how cultivating a grateful mindset can shift our perspective, letting us find joy, meaning, and abundance even in the face of life's challenges. Get ready to discover practical tools and strategies for incorporating gratitude into your daily life, from starting a gratitude journal to expressing heartfelt appreciation to others. Together, we'll learn how consistently focusing on the good can enhance our resilience, deepen our connections, and create a positive ripple effect in the world.

As we navigate this path of gratitude, we'll also explore the common obstacles that can arise, such as comparison, negativity, busyness, and personal setbacks. But fear not – we'll arm you with powerful techniques for overcoming these challenges with self-compassion, intention, and grace. By the end of our journey, you'll have a strong toolkit for cultivating gratitude as a daily practice and a way of being. So join us as we unlock the transformative power of appreciation and discover how it can reshape our lives and our world for the better.

PART SIX
THE GRATEFUL HEART: UNLOCKING THE TRANSFORMATIVE POWER OF APPRECIATION

GRATITUDE: THE KEY TO UNLOCKING LIFE'S TREASURES

It's simple to get caught up in negativity, stress, and discontent in the tapestry of life. We often focus on what's missing, what's gone wrong, or what we wish we had. But what if the key to a more joyful, fulfilling life was right in front of us all along?

Enter gratitude. More than just a passing sentiment, gratitude is a powerful tool that can transform our perception of the world and our place in it. It's the lens that allows us to see the abundance in our lives, even in the face of adversity.

The Essence of Gratitude

At its core, gratitude is about recognizing and appreciating the good in our lives. It's about taking a moment to acknowledge the gifts we've been given, whether they're as simple as a warm meal or as profound as a loving relationship.

When we practice gratitude, we shift our focus from what we lack to what we have. We see that even in the darkest of times, there are always glimmers of light. And as we train our minds to seek these positive aspects, they start to multiply.

The Ripple Effect of Gratitude

The benefits of gratitude are far-reaching, affecting not just our mental state but our physical health and social connections as well.

Studies have shown that people who regularly practice gratitude experience lower levels of stress and depression, and higher levels of happiness and life satisfaction. They are usually more resilient in the face of challenges, able to bounce back from setbacks with greater ease.

Gratitude also has a profound effect on our relationships. When we express appreciation for the people in our lives, we strengthen our bonds and create a positive feedback loop of kindness and support. We become more attuned to the needs of others and more likely to offer help and compassion.

Even our physical health can benefit from a grateful outlook. Research suggests that grateful people usually take better care of themselves, engaging in healthier behaviors like exercising regularly and attending check-ups. They also usually sleep better and have stronger immune systems.

Cultivating a Grateful Heart

So how can we make gratitude a regular part of our lives? Fortunately, it doesn't require a major life overhaul. Small, consistent practices can yield significant results.

One of the most effective methods is to keep a gratitude journal. By taking a few minutes each day to write down the things we're thankful for, we train our brains to look for the positive. Over time, this can become a natural habit, a default setting for how we view the world.

Another powerful practice is to express our gratitude directly to others. Whether it's a heartfelt thank-you, a complimentary note, or a surprise act of kindness, expressing appreciation can deepen our relationships and spread joy to those around us.

We can also cultivate gratitude through mindful attention to the present moment. By engaging our senses and noting the small pleasures in life—the warmth of the sun, the smell of fresh bread, the laughter of a child—we develop a greater appreciation for the richness of our everyday experiences.

For times when gratitude feels challenging, prompts can be a useful tool. Asking ourselves questions like "What made me smile today?" or "What am I looking forward to?" can help shift our perspective and find the silver linings in difficult situations.

The Journey of Gratitude

Ultimately, gratitude is a choice. It's a decision to focus on the good, even when the bad seems overwhelming. It's a commitment to appreciating what we have, while still striving for growth and improvement.

Like any skill, gratitude takes practice. There will be days when it comes easily, and others when it feels like a struggle. But with each small act of appreciation, we strengthen our gratitude muscle and deepen our capacity for joy.

As we start this journey of gratitude, we may find it changes more than just our own lives. Gratitude has a ripple effect, spreading positivity and kindness to those around us. By modeling appreciation and generosity, we inspire others to do the same.

In a world that often feels divided and contentious, gratitude is a unifying force. It reminds us of our common humanity, of the gifts we share and the challenges we face together. It opens our hearts to compassion, empathy, and understanding.

So let us embrace gratitude, not just as a fleeting emotion, but as a way of life. Let us wake each day with a grateful heart and go to sleep each night counting our blessings. Let us find joy in the moments and appreciate the people who make our lives richer.

In doing so, we unlock the treasures that have been within us all along. We discover that happiness is not a destination, but a choice we make in each moment. And we realize that even in a world of uncertainty, there is always, always something to be grateful for.

～

GRATITUDE: THE LUMINOUS PATH TO JOY

IN THE INTRICATE tapestry of life, it's easy to become entangled in the threads of adversity, stress, and discontent. We often dwell on what's missing, what's gone wrong, or what we yearn for. But what if the key to illuminating joy in our lives was within our reach all along?

Enter gratitude. More than a fleeting emotion, gratitude is a transformative force that can shift our perspective and cast a radiant light on the joy that permeates our lives, even in the face of life's most formidable challenges.

The Alchemy of Gratitude

At its essence, gratitude is the art of recognizing and deeply appreciating the good that surrounds us. It's about acknowledging the gifts we've been bestowed, whether they're as simple as a warm embrace or as profound as a life-changing opportunity.

When we cultivate a grateful heart, we start an alchemical process that transmutes our perception of the world. We see that even in the darkest of nights, there are always stars that shine. And as we attune our minds to seek these luminous points, they start to multiply, illuminating our path with ever-increasing radiance.

The Ripples of Gratitude

The transformative effects of gratitude extend far beyond our internal landscape, casting a warm glow on every part of our lives.

Research has consistently shown those who engage in the regular practice of gratitude experience heightened levels of happiness, contentment, and overall life satisfaction. They are usually more resilient in the face of adversity, able to navigate the storms of life with greater grace and fortitude.

Gratitude also has a profound impact on our relationships. When we express heartfelt appreciation for the people in our lives, we forge bonds strengthened by the golden threads of kindness and support. We become more attuned to the needs and contributions of others, fostering a climate of compassion and understanding.

Even our physical well-being is touched by the healing light of gratitude. Studies suggest that grateful individuals usually nurture themselves with greater care, engaging in health-promoting behaviors like regular exercise and preventive check-ups. They also usually enjoy more restful sleep and boast more robust immune systems.

Igniting the Spark of Gratitude

So how can we kindle the flame of gratitude in our daily lives? The beauty of this practice is that it doesn't require a drastic life overhaul. Small, consistent actions can yield profound results.

One of the most potent methods is the keeping of a gratitude journal. By dedicating a few moments each day to record the things we're thankful for, we train our minds to seek the positive. Over time, this becomes a natural reflex, a default lens through which we view the world.

Another transformative practice is the direct expression of our gratitude to others. Whether it's a heartfelt thank-you, a note of appreciation, or an unexpected act of generosity, voicing our gratitude can deepen our connections and ignite joy in the hearts of those around us.

We can also cultivate gratitude through the practice of mindful presence. By engaging our senses and attuning to the subtle joys of the moment—the caress of a gentle breeze, the rich aroma of a home-cooked meal, the infectious giggle of a passing child—we develop a profound appreciation for the richness that infuses our everyday experiences.

In moments when gratitude feels elusive, prompts can serve as a guiding light. Asking ourselves questions like "What unexpected blessing did I encounter today?" or "What small thing am I grateful for right now?" can help shift our focus and illuminate the silver linings that line even the darkest of clouds.

The Radiant Path Forward

Ultimately, gratitude is a choice. It's a conscious decision to focus on the light, even when shadows loom large. It's a commitment to honoring what we have, while still embracing growth and change.

Like any skill, gratitude requires practice. There will be days when it flows freely, and others when it feels like an uphill climb. But with each small act of appreciation, we strengthen our capacity for joy and expand our ability to find light in even the dimmest of circumstances.

As we step forward on this radiant path of gratitude, we may find it illuminates more than just our own lives. Gratitude has a ripple effect, radiating positivity and kindness to all who cross our path. By embodying appreciation and generosity, we become beacons of light, inspiring others to join us on this journey.

In a world that often feels shrouded in darkness, gratitude is a powerful force for illumination. It reminds us of our shared humanity, of the gifts we hold in common and the challenges we face as one. It opens our hearts to compassion, understanding, and the recognition of the profound beauty that surrounds us.

So let us embrace gratitude, not just as a passing sentiment, but as a guiding light. Let us greet each day with a heart full of appreciation and close each night with a reflection on the blessings we've encountered. Let us find joy in ordinary moments and express deep thanks for the extraordinary people who enrich our lives.

In doing so, we ignite an inner radiance that can never be extinguished. We discover that joy is not a destination, but a state of being that we can access in any moment. And we come to understand that even in a world of shadow, there is always, always a path of light waiting to be discovered.

～

GRATITUDE: THE RADIANT PATH TO JOY

In the hustle and bustle of modern life, it's all too easy to get caught up in the whirlwind of past regrets and future anxieties. We often find ourselves mentally time-traveling, dwelling on what was or fretting about. But amidst this maelstrom of thoughts, a powerful force can anchor us firmly in the present moment: gratitude.

Gratitude is more than just a fleeting acknowledgment of life's blessings; it's a proactive engagement with the present that deeply enriches our daily experiences. It's a conscious choice to shift our focus from what's lacking to what's abundant, from what we've lost to what we've gained. And in doing so, it opens the door to a profound sense of joy and contentment that can be found only in the here and now.

The Alchemy of Gratitude and Presence

When we cultivate a grateful heart, we start a transformative journey that changes our relationship with the present moment. Gratitude acts as a powerful catalyst, transmuting our ordinary experiences into moments of profound appreciation and wonder.

By seeking out things to be thankful for, we train our minds to be more attuned to the good that surrounds us. We begin to notice the small miracles that punctuate our days—the warm smile of a stranger, the comforting aroma of our morning coffee, the gentle rustling of leaves in the breeze. These moments, which might have slipped by unnoticed, become infused with a new sense of meaning and significance.

Gratitude also serves as a potent antidote to the mind's natural tendency to gravitate toward the negative. It's all too easy to get caught up in thoughts of what's missing, what's gone wrong, or what we wish were different. But when we consciously choose to focus on what we're grateful for, we create a counterbalance to these negative thought patterns. We see that even in life's challenges, there are always glimmers of goodness to be found.

Perhaps most important, gratitude cultivates a deep sense of contentment with the present moment. When we're grateful for what we have, we find that the incessant yearning for more begins to quiet. We discover that joy isn't something to be chased or reached in the future, but something that can be accessed right here, through the simple act of appreciation.

Igniting the Spark of Present Gratitude

So how can we kindle the flame of gratitude and let it illuminate our present experiences? The beauty of this practice is that it doesn't require a drastic life overhaul. Small, consistent actions can yield profound results.

One powerful method is to engage in mindful gratitude exercises. This could involve taking a few minutes each day to sit in quiet contemplation, focusing on the breath and silently acknowledging the things we're thankful for. It could also involve incorporating moments of gratitude into our existing mindfulness practices, such as focusing on feelings of thankfulness during meditation or yoga.

Another transformative practice is the use of gratitude prompts. By regularly asking ourselves questions like "What in this moment am I grateful for?" or "How is this situation benefiting me?" we train our minds to actively seek the positive in our present circumstances. Over time, this becomes a natural reflex, a default lens through which we view the world.

We can also cultivate gratitude through the practice of mindful engagement with our environment. This could involve taking regular gratitude walks, where we consciously look for things to appreciate in our surroundings. It could mean savoring our meals with a deep sense of thankfulness for the nourishment they provide. Or it could simply mean pausing throughout the day to engage our senses and marvel at the richness of the present moment.

Journaling is another powerful tool for igniting present gratitude. By setting aside time each day to document the things we're grateful for, we not only strengthen the practice of focusing on the positive, but we also establish a concrete record of the blessings in our lives. On days when gratitude feels elusive, revisiting these entries can serve as a powerful reminder of the good that surrounds us.

The Radiant Path Forward

As we step forward on this path of present gratitude, we may find it illuminates our lives in ways we never could have imagined. We may discover a new sense of joy and wonder in the ordinary moments of our days. We may find ourselves more resilient in the face of life's challenges, able to find the silver linings even in the darkest of clouds. And we may begin to radiate this spirit of appreciation to those around us, creating a ripple effect of positivity and contentment.

Ultimately, gratitude is a choice—a conscious decision to focus on the blessings of the present, even amidst the uncertainties of life. It's a commitment to finding the extraordinary in the ordinary, the sacred in the mundane. And it's a recognition that true joy isn't something to be postponed for a future date, but something that can be embraced in this very moment.

So let us resolve to make gratitude our constant companion on this journey of life. Let us greet each moment with a heart full of appreciation and let us let this spirit of thankfulness guide our steps. In doing so, we open ourselves up to the boundless joy and wonder that the present moment offers.

For it is here, in the eternal now, that we find the greatest gifts. And through the eyes of gratitude, these gifts are illuminated, casting a radiant glow on all that we experience. May we have the wisdom and the courage to embrace this light, and to let it guide us ever forward on the path of present joy. Gratitude is more than just an occasional acknowledgment of life's good fortunes; it's a proactive engagement with the present that enriches our daily experiences. This part explores how gratitude can deeply enhance our ability to immerse ourselves in the present, cultivating a life filled with joy and contentment.

GRATITUDE: THE KEY TO UNLOCKING THE TREASURES OF THE PRESENT

In the fast-paced world we inhabit, it's all too easy to get caught up in the relentless pursuit of the future or the lingering echoes of the past. We often find ourselves mentally time-traveling, our thoughts drifting to what could have been or what might be. But amidst this constant flux, a powerful practice can root us firmly in the richness of the present moment: gratitude.

Gratitude, when practiced deeply and consistently, becomes more than just a fleeting sentiment. It transforms into a potent tool for enhancing our awareness of and engagement with the present. By seeking out and appreciating the good that surrounds us, we train our minds to inhabit the here and now, unlocking a treasure trove of joy and contentment.

The Alchemy of Gratitude and Presence

When we cultivate a grateful heart, we shift our relationship with the present moment. Instead of letting our experiences pass by unnoticed or unappreciated, we begin to approach life with a heightened sense of awareness and wonder.

One of the most profound ways gratitude enhances our present awareness is through the amplification of our sensory appreciation. When we're in a state of thankfulness, we become more attuned to the subtle beauty that permeates our environment. We start to notice the way the sunlight dances through the leaves, the melodic chirping of birds, or the comforting warmth of a loved one's hand. These small moments, which might have blended into the background of our lives, suddenly take on a new brilliance and significance.

Gratitude also serves as a powerful counterbalance to our mind's inherent negativity bias. It's natural for our thoughts to gravitate toward what's lacking, what's not going according to plan, or what we wish were different. But when we consciously choose to focus on what we're grateful for, we create a shift in our mental landscape. We see that even amidst life's challenges and imperfections, there are always glimmers of goodness and grace to be found.

Perhaps most significantly, gratitude cultivates a deep sense of contentment with the present moment. When we're thankful for what we have, the incessant yearning for more begins to quiet. We realize that joy and fulfillment aren't destinations to be reached in some distant future, but experiences that can be accessed right here, through the simple act of appreciation. Gratitude teaches us to find sufficiency and even abundance in what's already present in our lives.

Practical Pathways to Present Gratitude

While the transformative power of gratitude is undeniable, it's not always easy to access in life's daily demands and distractions. That's why it's important to have practical tools and techniques that can help us cultivate a consistent practice of present-focused thankfulness.

One powerful method is to engage in mindful gratitude exercises. This could involve taking a few moments each day to sit in quiet contemplation, focusing on the breath and silently acknowledging the things we're grateful for. It could also mean incorporating gratitude into our existing mindfulness practices, such as focusing on feelings of thankfulness during yoga or while savoring a meal.

Another effective technique is the use of gratitude prompts. By regularly asking ourselves questions like "What in this moment am I thankful for?" or "How is this situation benefiting me?" we train our minds to actively seek the positive in our present circumstances. Over time, this becomes a natural reflex, a default lens through which we view the world.

We can also cultivate gratitude through the practice of mindful engagement with our environment. This might involve taking regular gratitude walks, where we intentionally look for things to appreciate in our surroundings—the beauty of a flower, the kindness of a stranger, or the simple joy of movement. By consciously attuning to the blessings that surround us, we deepen our connection to the present moment.

Journaling is another powerful tool for cultivating present gratitude. By dedicating time each day to record the things we're thankful for, we not only reinforce the habit of seeking the positive, but we also create a real record of the good in our lives. In moments when gratitude feels elusive, revisiting these entries can serve as a potent reminder of the blessings that are always present, even when they're not immediately apparent.

The Radiance of Present Gratitude

As we deepen our practice of present gratitude, we may find it illuminates our lives in profound and unexpected ways. We may discover a new sense of richness and texture in the ordinary moments of our days. We may find ourselves more resilient in the face of life's inevitable ups and downs, able to find the silver linings even in the darkest of times. And we may begin to radiate this spirit of appreciation to those around us, creating a ripple effect of positivity and joy.

Ultimately, cultivating present gratitude is a choice—a conscious decision to focus on the blessings that exist in this very moment, despite our external circumstances. It's a commitment to finding the extraordinary in the ordinary, the sacred in the seemingly mundane. And it's a recognition that true happiness isn't something to be postponed for some distant future, but something that can be experienced, right here and now.

So let us embrace the practice of present gratitude, letting it become our constant companion on this journey of life. Let us greet each moment with a heart full of appreciation and wonder and let us let this thankfulness guide our steps. In doing so, we open ourselves up to the incredible richness and beauty that the present moment offers.

For it is here, in the eternal now, that we find the greatest treasures. And through the lens of gratitude, these treasures are revealed, casting a radiant glow on all that we experience. May we have the courage and the wisdom to embrace this light, and to let it lead us ever deeper into the joyous abundance of the present.

~

GRATITUDE: THE UNSUNG HERO OF RESILIENCE

FACED with life's inevitable challenges and setbacks, it's easy to feel overwhelmed, discouraged, or even hopeless. But what if there was a simple yet powerful practice that could help us weather these storms with greater ease and grace? Enter gratitude—the often overlooked but tremendously potent tool for cultivating resilience.

Resilience, at its core, is our ability to bounce back from adversity, to adapt and thrive in the face of difficult circumstances. This quality lets us bend without breaking, to find strength and hope even in our darkest hours. And while there are many factors that contribute to resilience, one of the most transformative is the practice of gratitude.

The Alchemy of Gratitude and Resilience

When we cultivate a grateful heart, we shift our relationship with life's challenges. Instead of getting mired in what's going wrong, we train our minds to seek and appreciate what's going right. This simple shift in perspective can have a profound impact on our ability to cope with and recover from adversity.

One way gratitude enhances resilience is by helping us reframe our perceptions of difficult situations. When we're in a crisis, it's natural for our focus to narrow in on the problem at hand. We can become consumed by worry, fear, or despair, seeing only the obstacles and limitations before us. But when we consciously choose to look for things to be grateful for, even in the darkest of times, we open ourselves up to a more expansive perspective.

We see that even amidst the chaos and pain, there are still glimmers of goodness and grace. Maybe it's the support of a loved one, the resilience of our own spirit, or the small moments of beauty that continue to emerge in the world. By attuning to these blessings, we remind ourselves that our current difficulties, while real and significant, are not the whole story. We see that we have the strength and resources to persevere, to find our way through to the other side.

Gratitude also serves as a powerful emotional stabilizer, helping us maintain a sense of equilibrium even in turbulent times. When we're facing a crisis, it's easy to get swept up in a maelstrom of negative emotions—anxiety, anger, grief, despair. These feelings are natural and important to acknowledge, but when we let them consume us, they can erode our resilience and make it harder to cope with challenges.

Gratitude helps counterbalance these negative emotions by invoking feelings of appreciation, contentment, and even joy. It's not about denying or suppressing our pain, but about creating space for a wider range of emotional experiences. By regularly attuning to the good in our lives, we build up a reservoir of positive emotions we can draw on when times get tough. This emotional resilience is important for maintaining our mental health and well-being in the face of adversity.

Perhaps most important, gratitude strengthens our relationships and social support networks, which are essential parts of resilience. When we express appreciation for the people in our lives, we deepen our connections and foster a sense of intimacy and trust. We let others know that they matter to us, that their presence and support make a difference.

These strong, supportive relationships become an important lifeline during difficult times. They give us emotional comfort, practical assistance, and a sense of belonging and purpose. Knowing we have people who care about us and will stand by us through thick and thin can give us the courage and strength to face even the most daunting challenges.

Cultivating Gratitude, Nurturing Resilience

While the benefits of gratitude for resilience are clear, it's not always easy to access this practice when we're in the thick of a crisis. That's why it's so important to cultivate gratitude as a regular habit, to make it a part of our daily lives even when things are going well. By consistently attuning to the good in our lives, we build up our resilience muscles, preparing ourselves to face future challenges with greater strength and grace.

One simple but powerful way to cultivate gratitude is through daily gratitude practice. This might involve taking a few moments each day to reflect on three things you're grateful for, big or small. It could be a warm cup of coffee, a kind word from a friend, or a moment of beauty in nature. The key is to savor these blessings, to let yourself feel the emotions of appreciation and thankfulness.

Another effective method is to keep a gratitude journal, where you write down your reflections regularly. The act of putting pen to paper can help solidify these positive experiences in your mind and heart, making them more tangible and real. Over time, as you flip back through the pages of your journal, you'll have a powerful reminder of all the good in your life, even in difficult times.

You might also consider writing gratitude letters to people who have made a difference in your life. Expressing your appreciation not only strengthens your relationship with that person but also helps shift your own mindset toward one of positivity and abundance. And when you're facing a challenge, you'll know that you have a network of supportive people who believe in you and are rooting for your success.

Finally, try to bring a spirit of mindful appreciation to your daily experiences. As you move through your day, make a conscious effort to look for things to be grateful for in each moment. It might be the warmth of the sun on your skin, the laughter of a child, or the simple pleasure of a nourishing meal. By cultivating this habit of gratitude, you train your mind to see the good in every situation, even the difficult ones.

Finding Joy in the Midst of Struggle

One of the most remarkable things about gratitude is its ability to help us find joy and meaning even in great hardship. When we're facing a crisis, it is hard to imagine ever feeling happiness or contentment again. But by seeking out things to be grateful for, we open ourselves up to moments of grace and beauty that can sustain us through even the darkest of times.

This doesn't mean denying or reducing our pain but holding space for the full spectrum of human experience. We can feel grief and gratitude, sorrow and joy, fear and appreciation all at once. By embracing this complexity, we build a more nuanced and resilient relationship with life's ups and downs.

And as we move through difficult experiences with a grateful heart, we may find we emerge on the other side with a deeper sense of meaning and purpose. We may discover strengths and capacities we never knew we had, or forge connections with others that will last a lifetime. We may even find that our struggles have given us a greater appreciation for the preciousness of life, a heightened ability to savor the good moments as they arise.

The Ripple Effect of Gratitude

As we cultivate gratitude and resilience in our own lives, we may find we have a positive impact on those around us as well. When we approach challenges with a spirit of appreciation and hope, we become a beacon of light for others who may be struggling. We remind them that even in the darkest of times, there is still goodness to be found, still reasons to keep going.

And as we express our gratitude to others, we create a ripple effect of positivity and connection. We inspire them to look for the good in their own lives, to support others. In this way, our personal practice of gratitude becomes a catalyst for resilience and well-being on a larger scale.

Chapter Summary: Gratitude as a Way of Life

Ultimately, cultivating gratitude and resilience is not just a set of techniques or exercises, but a way of being in the world. It's a choice to meet life's challenges with an open and appreciative heart, to look for the good even when it's hard to find. And it's a recognition that even in our darkest moments, we are never truly alone—that there is always something to be grateful for, always a reason to keep going.

So let us embrace gratitude as a powerful ally on the path of resilience. Let us make it a daily practice, a constant companion in good times and bad. And let us trust that as we do so, we will find the strength and courage to face whatever life brings our way, and to emerge on the other side with deeper wisdom, compassion, and joy.

For the absence of struggle does not define a life well-lived, but the grace and gratitude with which we meet those struggles. May we all find that grace within ourselves, and may it light the way forward, one brave and thankful step at a time.

GRATITUDE: THE TIE THAT BINDS

In the tapestry of our lives, relationships form the vibrant threads that weave together our experiences, our joys, and our growth. These connections—whether with family, friends, colleagues, or partners—have the power to uplift us, to support us, and to bring meaning and richness to our journey. And at the heart of these life-giving bonds lies a simple yet transformative practice: gratitude.

Gratitude, when expressed with sincerity and consistency, becomes more than just a polite gesture or a social nicety. It becomes a potent force for strengthening our relationships, deepening our connections, and cultivating an atmosphere of positivity, trust, and mutual appreciation. When we take the time to acknowledge and appreciate the goodness that others bring into our lives, we create a ripple effect of kindness and joy that can transform even the most challenging relationships.

The Power of Appreciation

One of the most profound ways that gratitude enhances our relationships is by making others feel seen and valued. In the busyness of daily life, it's all too easy to take the people around us for granted, to overlook the countless small ways they contribute to our well-being and happiness. But when we make a conscious effort to express our appreciation, we send a powerful message: "You matter to me. Your presence and your actions make a difference in my life."

This message of appreciation can be validating and affirming for others. It lets them know that their efforts are noticed and cherished, that they are an integral part of our lives. And when people feel appreciated, they are more likely to invest themselves in the relationship, to go the extra mile in supporting and caring for us.

Expressing gratitude can help shift the overall tone of our relationships toward positivity and connection. When we focus on the good in others, on the things we appreciate and admire about them, we naturally create a more uplifting and supportive atmosphere. This positive focus can help counterbalance any negative interactions or misunderstandings, fostering a sense of goodwill and resilience in the face of challenges.

The Gratitude Cycle

Another beautiful part of gratitude is its ability to create a self-reinforcing cycle of kindness and generosity in relationships. When we express appreciation to others, it often inspires them to reciprocate, to look for ways to show their own gratitude and support. This can lead to a wonderful feedback loop, where each person's expressions of appreciation encourage more acts of kindness and consideration from the other.

Over time, this cycle of gratitude can transform the nature of our relationships. It can take connections that were once marked by tension, misunderstanding, or indifference and infuse them with a new sense of warmth, respect, and mutual care. It can take relationships that were already strong and make them even more intimate, trusting, and joyful.

This is because gratitude helps create a safe and supportive emotional space in our relationships. When we feel consistently appreciated and valued, we are more likely to open up, to share our thoughts and feelings honestly and vulnerably. We are more likely to trust that the other person has our best interests at heart, that they will support and confirm us even in difficult moments.

Cultivating a Grateful Heart

While the benefits of gratitude in relationships are clear, it's not always easy to make this practice a consistent part of our interactions. In the heat of conflict or the rush of daily life, we can easily forget to pause and appreciate the good in others. That's why it's so important to cultivate gratitude as an intentional habit, to weave it into the fabric of our relationships in both big and small ways.

One simple but powerful way to do this is through daily acknowledgments. This means making a conscious effort to notice and appreciate the small acts of kindness and support that others show us throughout the day. It could be thanking a colleague for their help on a project, expressing appreciation to a partner for making dinner, or acknowledging a friend's thoughtfulness in checking in on us. By making gratitude a regular part of our interactions, we train ourselves to be more attuned to the good in others and more proactive in expressing our appreciation.

Another effective method is to keep a gratitude journal specifically focused on our relationships. Taking time each day to reflect on and write about the things we appreciate about the people in our lives can help us cultivate a more consistently grateful mindset. It can also serve as a wonderful record of the many ways others have blessed and enriched our journey, a reminder to cherish and nurture these connections.

For particularly significant relationships or occasions, writing a heartfelt letter of gratitude can be a deeply moving and transformative experience, both for the writer and the recipient. Taking the time to articulate in detail what someone means to us, how they have affected our lives, can create a profound sense of connection and appreciation. And for the person receiving this letter, it can be a cherished reminder of their worth and importance, a gift they will treasure for years to come.

Gratitude doesn't always have to be expressed in grand or elaborate ways to be effective. Sometimes, the most powerful expressions of appreciation are the simplest and most heartfelt. Telling someone "thank you" and meaning it, taking a moment to acknowledge their efforts or their impact on your life, can communicate volumes. The key is to be specific, sincere, and consistent in our expressions of gratitude, to let others know that we see and value them.

The Ripple Effect of Gratitude

As we cultivate a practice of gratitude in our relationships, we may find that the benefits extend far beyond the immediate connections we are nurturing. Gratitude has a way of creating a ripple effect of positivity and kindness that touches everyone around us.

When we consistently show appreciation to others, we model a way of being that inspires them to do the same. Our gratitude can encourage them to be more appreciative in their own relationships, to pay forward the kindness and support they have received. In this way, our individual practice of gratitude becomes a catalyst for a wider culture of appreciation and connection, one that uplifts and enriches entire communities.

As we deepen our relationships through gratitude, we create a powerful support system that can sustain us through life's inevitable challenges. We build a network of people who are invested in our well-being, who will be there to lift us up and remind us of our own strength and resilience when we need it most. And in turn, we have the privilege of being that source of support and encouragement for others, of helping them weather their own storms with grace and gratitude.

Chapter Summary: The Grateful Journey

Cultivating gratitude in our relationships is not just about enhancing individual connections, but about creating a richer, more meaningful life journey. It's about choosing to focus on the beauty and blessings that surround us, even in difficulty. It's about recognizing that we are all interconnected, that our joy and fulfillment are inextricably linked to the joy and fulfillment of those around us.

By making gratitude a daily practice, a consistent way of relating to others, we open ourselves up to a world of deeper love, connection, and abundance. We create relationships that are resilient, supportive, and infused with positive appreciation. And we discover that even the smallest expressions of gratitude can have a profound impact, not just on our own lives, but on the lives of everyone we touch.

So let us start this grateful journey together, step by step and heart to heart. Let us make a commitment to appreciate the good in others, to express our gratitude with sincerity and consistency. And let us trust that as we do so, we will create a tapestry of relationships that is richer, more vibrant, and more beautiful than we ever could have imagined. For in the end, it is not the destination that matters most, but the love and appreciation we cultivate along the way.

GRATITUDE: THE ART OF LIVING APPRECIATIVELY

IN THE RUSH and tumble of daily life, it's all too easy to get caught up in what's going wrong, in what we lack, or in what we long for. We can find ourselves constantly chasing after the next goal, the next achievement, the next source of satisfaction, without ever truly appreciating the good that's already present in our lives. But what if there was a way to shift this mindset, to cultivate a deeper sense of contentment and joy in the here and now? Enter the transformative practice of gratitude.

Gratitude, at its core, is about focusing our attention on the blessings and gifts that surround us, both big and small. It's about developing a habit of appreciative living, of consciously acknowledging and savoring the good in our lives. And while this may sound simple, even obvious, the impact of this practice can be profound. By consistently orienting ourselves toward gratitude, we can change the way we experience and interact with the world.

The Alchemy of Appreciation

One of the most powerful effects of gratitude is its ability to reshape our perceptions and emotional experiences. When we make a deliberate effort to notice and appreciate the positive aspects of our lives, we see the world through a different lens. Rather than dwelling on what's lacking or frustrating, we train our minds to seek and focus on what's good, beautiful, and nourishing.

This shift in perspective can be transformative. It can help us find joy and contentment in life's challenges, to maintain a sense of hopefulness and resilience even in the face of adversity. By regularly attuning to the blessings in our lives, we build up a reservoir of positive emotions and experiences we can draw on when times get tough. We develop a greater capacity for happiness, for savoring life's simple pleasures, and for finding meaning and purpose in our daily experiences.

The practice of gratitude can have a profound impact on our relationships and interactions with others. When we approach people with a grateful heart, we're more likely to treat them with kindness, respect, and appreciation. We're more attuned to their efforts and contributions, more likely to express our thanks and admiration. This can foster a sense of warmth, connection, and mutual support in our relationships, enhancing both our own well-being and that of those around us.

Cultivating the Gratitude Habit

The benefits of gratitude are clear, but how do we actually cultivate this practice in our daily lives? Fortunately, there are countless ways to weave gratitude into our routines and interactions, from simple daily habits to more structured exercises and reflections.

One of the most effective methods is gratitude journaling. This involves taking time each day to write down a few things we're grateful for, whether they're big life events or small everyday pleasures. The act of putting pen to paper and articulating our appreciation can be powerful, helping to cement these positive experiences in our minds and hearts. Over time, as we flip back through the pages of our journal, we create a real record of the many blessings in our lives, a reminder of all the good that surrounds us.

Another powerful way to cultivate gratitude is through mindfulness and present-moment awareness. So often, we move through life on autopilot, barely noticing the beauty and richness of the world. But by making a conscious effort to pause and savor the present moment, we can tap into a deep well of appreciation and awe. This might involve taking a few minutes each morning to notice and give thanks for the simple pleasures of our daily routine—the warmth of a cup of coffee, the soft light filtering through the window, the comfort of our favorite chair. Or it might mean pausing throughout the day to notice and appreciate the people and experiences we encounter, from a kind word from a colleague to a beautiful sunset on the way home from work.

Acts of kindness and generosity can also be a wonderful way to cultivate gratitude. When we take the time to do something nice for others, whether it's writing a heartfelt thank-you note or performing a random act of kindness, we tap into a sense of appreciation and interconnection. We recognize the impact we can have on others' lives, and we feel grateful for the opportunity to make a positive difference. These acts of kindness also usually inspire reciprocal gratitude and generosity, creating a beautiful cycle of appreciation and mutual care.

For those who enjoy meditation or contemplative practices, incorporating gratitude into these routines can be especially enriching. Taking a few minutes each day to sit quietly and focus our thoughts on the people, experiences, and blessings we're grateful for can help us cultivate a deep sense of appreciation and contentment. We might focus on a particular person who has made a difference in our lives, savoring the qualities we admire in them and the ways they've supported and cared for us. Or we might reflect more broadly on the many gifts and opportunities we've been given, from our basic needs being met to the chance to pursue our passions and dreams.

The Physical Reminders of Gratitude

In addition to these daily practices and reflections, creating physical reminders of our gratitude can be a powerful way to keep appreciation at the forefront of our minds. One simple method is to start a gratitude jar, where we write down things we're grateful for on small slips of paper and add them to the jar each day. Over time, the jar becomes a visual representation of the many blessings in our lives, a tangible reminder to keep noticing and appreciating the good.

Similarly, we might display photos, mementos, or quotes that inspire feelings of gratitude and appreciation. Surrounding ourselves with these positive reminders can help keep our minds oriented toward the blessings in our lives, even in challenges or stresses.

Even our daily surroundings can become opportunities for gratitude with intentional awareness. Taking a "gratitude walk," where we make a conscious effort to notice and appreciate the beauty and wonder of the world, can be a lovely way to infuse our days with a sense of awe and thankfulness. Whether we're marveling at the intricate petals of a flower, savoring the feeling of the sun on our skin, or exchanging smiles with a passing stranger, these moments of appreciation can add up to a profound shift in our overall experience of life.

The Ripple Effect of Gratitude

As we cultivate a consistent practice of gratitude, we may start to notice a ripple effect that extends beyond our own individual experience. When we live with an attitude of appreciation and thankfulness, we naturally inspire and uplift those around us. Our gratitude becomes contagious, spreading to our families, friends, colleagues, and communities.

This ripple effect can be especially powerful when we express our gratitude directly to others. Telling someone how much we appreciate them, how much their presence and actions mean to us, can be a affirming and heartwarming experience for both parties. It deepens our connections, builds trust and mutual care, and encourages others to pay that gratitude forward in their own interactions.

In this way, our personal practice of gratitude becomes a catalyst for a wider culture of appreciation and generosity. As we each commit to living more appreciatively, to consistently seeking and savoring the good in our lives and in others, we contribute to a world that is kinder, more interconnected, and more filled with wonder and joy.

Chapter Summary: Gratitude as a Way of Being

Ultimately, cultivating gratitude is about so much more than a set of exercises or practices. It's about shifting the way we relate to ourselves, others, and the world. It's about choosing to live with an open and appreciative heart, to be present to the beauty and blessings that surround us in each moment.

This isn't always easy. Faced with life's challenges and uncertainties, it is tempting to focus on what's going wrong, to get caught up in worry, frustration, or despair. But this is where the power of gratitude shines. By consciously redirecting our attention to what we're thankful for, we remind ourselves of our own resilience, of the love and support that surrounds us, of the many opportunities we have to learn, grow, and find meaning.

So let us each commit to making gratitude a daily practice, a constant companion on our journey through life. Let us fill our journals with appreciative reflections, our relationships with heartfelt expressions of thanks, and our moments with mindful savoring. And let us trust that as we do so, we will not only enhance our own well-being and joy, but also contribute to a world that is more appreciative, more interconnected, and more alive with possibility.

For in the end, the art of living appreciatively is about recognizing the profound gift that is this life, in all its beauty and complexity. It's about meeting each moment with an open and grateful heart, and letting that gratitude guide us toward ever greater connection, purpose, and joy. May we each find our own path to this way of being, and may we walk it with grace, with wonder, and with abiding thankfulness.

~

THE GRATITUDE JOURNEY:
OVERCOMING OBSTACLES
AND CULTIVATING JOY

THE PATH to a life of gratitude is a beautiful and transformative one, but it is not always easy. Along the way, we may encounter various obstacles and challenges that can make it difficult to maintain a consistent practice of appreciation and thankfulness. These obstacles can range from internal struggles like negative self-talk and comparison to external pressures like overwhelming busyness and personal setbacks. But with awareness, intention, and the right strategies, we can learn to navigate these challenges and continue to cultivate a deep and abiding sense of gratitude.

The Comparison Trap

One of the most common obstacles to gratitude is the tendency to compare ourselves to others. In our social media-saturated world, it's all too easy to get caught up in measuring our own lives against the curated highlight reels of those around us. We see the successes, the joys, the seeming perfection of others, and we can begin to feel like our own lives lack comparison. This mindset of scarcity and inadequacy can quickly erode our ability to appreciate and give thanks for the blessings we have.

To overcome this obstacle, it's important to intentionally shift our focus inward, to our own unique journey and achievements. Rather than measuring ourselves against external benchmarks, we can practice celebrating our own milestones, acknowledging our personal growth and progress. This might involve taking time each day to reflect on what we're proud of, what we've learned, or what we've overcome. It might mean keeping a journal of our accomplishments and successes, no matter how small, to remind ourselves of our own worth and capability.

It can also be helpful to actively reframe comparisons as opportunities for inspiration and connection, rather than self-judgment. When we see others thriving, we can choose to feel motivated and uplifted by their example, to see their success as a reminder of what's possible for all of us. We can congratulate and support them, fostering a sense of community and shared celebration. By shifting our perspective in this way, we loosen the grip of comparison and make more space for authentic gratitude and joy.

The Shadow of Negativity

Another common obstacle on the gratitude journey is a pervasive sense of negativity or pessimism. When we're in the habit of focusing on what's going wrong, on what's lacking or frustrating in our lives, it is incredibly difficult to tap into authentic appreciation and thankfulness. This negative mindset can color our perceptions, making it hard to notice and savor the good that surrounds us.

To begin shifting this pattern, we can start by practicing mindful awareness of our thoughts and self-talk. Simply noticing when we're sliding into negative rumination can be a powerful first step. We can then gently redirect our attention to something positive, no matter how small. This might be the warmth of the sun on our face, the kind smile of a passerby, or the comforting smell of our favorite tea. By consistently training our minds to seek and focus on these moments of goodness, we gradually build a more appreciative and resilient outlook.

Keeping a gratitude journal can be an especially effective tool for this process. By taking time each day to write down a few things we're grateful for, we create a real record of the blessings in our lives. Over time, as we flip back through the pages, we have a powerful reminder of all the good that surrounds us, even in challenging times. This practice of intentional appreciation can help to counterbalance negative thought patterns and cultivate a more consistently positive mindset.

The Pressure of Busyness

In our fast-paced, productivity-driven world, it can often feel like there's no time for gratitude. We're so caught up in our to-do lists, our responsibilities and obligations, that we barely have a moment to pause and appreciate the present. This constant sense of overwhelm and busyness can be a major obstacle to maintaining a consistent gratitude practice.

To navigate this challenge, it's important to intentionally carve out space for appreciation, even in a hectic schedule. This might mean starting each day with a few minutes of gratitude-focused meditation or journaling, setting the tone for a more appreciative outlook. It might involve taking brief "gratitude breaks" throughout the day, pausing for a moment to notice and savor something beautiful or meaningful.

It can also be helpful to weave gratitude into our existing routines and interactions. We might make a habit of expressing our appreciation to a colleague or loved one each day, or mentally listing things we're grateful for during our commute or daily walk. By integrating these small moments of appreciation into our regular rhythms, we make gratitude a more seamless and sustainable part of our lives, even in the busiest of times.

The Weight of Setbacks

Maybe one of the most challenging obstacles to gratitude is the experience of personal setbacks and losses. When we're in the midst of grief, disappointment, or hardship, it can feel impossible to connect with a sense of appreciation or thankfulness. The weight of our pain and struggle can overshadow everything else, making gratitude feel out of reach.

In these moments, it's important to be gentle and compassionate with ourselves. It's okay to not feel grateful when we're hurting. It's okay to focus on taking care of ourselves and getting through each day. But even in the darkest of times, small glimmers of gratitude can provide a lifeline of hope and resilience.

This might mean clinging to the small comforts and supports that sustain us—a hot meal, a kind word, a moment of peace. It might mean acknowledging the growth and strength we're building as we navigate adversity, even if we wish we didn't have to. It might mean reaching out for help and connection, allowing ourselves to be held and supported by others.

As we begin to heal and recover, we can intentionally look for opportunities to appreciate the lessons and insights we've gained through our challenges. We can practice gratitude for our own resilience, for the love and support of those around us, for the gradual return of hope and possibility. By gently nurturing these seeds of appreciation, even in difficulty, we build a foundation of gratitude that can carry us through any storm.

Chapter Summary: A Journey of Intention and Grace

Cultivating a life of authentic gratitude is an ongoing journey, one that requires intention, commitment, and a willingness to navigate obstacles with grace. Sometimes, comparison, negativity, busyness, and setbacks threaten to pull us off course, to disconnect us from our sense of appreciation and joy. But by staying mindful of these challenges, and proactively using strategies to overcome them, we can continue to deepen and sustain our gratitude practice.

This journey is not about perfection, but about consistent effort and self-compassion. It's about choosing, again and again, to orient ourselves toward the good, to savor life's blessings even in its challenges. It's about recognizing that gratitude is not a destination to be reached, but a way of being cultivated and nourished each day.

As we walk this path, we may find that the obstacles themselves become opportunities for growth and deepening. We may discover reserves of resilience and appreciation we never knew we had. We may find that our capacity for joy and connection expands in ways we never imagined.

So let us approach this gratitude journey with open hearts and curious minds. Let us be gentle with ourselves when we stumble, and celebratory of ourselves when we make progress. Let us support and inspire one another along the way, sharing our struggles and our triumphs. And let us trust that with each step, each intentional act of appreciation, we are cultivating a life of profound beauty, meaning, and joy.

For in the end, the obstacles we face on the path to gratitude are not barriers to be overcome, but teachers to be learned from. They remind us of our shared humanity, of the universal challenges and opportunities we all face in seeking a life well-lived. And they invite us, again and again, to choose thankfulness, to choose appreciation, to choose joy—no matter what life brings.

May we each find the courage and commitment to walk this path, to navigate the obstacles with grace, and to cultivate a life of ever-deepening gratitude. For in doing so, we not only transform our own lives, but contribute to a world that is more appreciative, more connected, and more alive with possibility. And that is something to be grateful for.

Case Study:

Meet Laura, a successful entrepreneur who, despite her outward achievements, felt increasingly disconnected and unfulfilled. For years, Laura had been caught up in the relentless pursuit of success, always striving for the next goal, the next milestone, the next accomplishment. While this drive had propelled her to great heights in her career, it had also left her feeling chronically stressed, anxious, and dissatisfied with her life.

One day, a friend recommended a workshop on the power of gratitude and mindfulness. Intrigued by the possibility of finding a new perspective, Laura decided to attend.

During the workshop, Laura was introduced to the idea of gratitude as a daily practice, a way of intentionally focusing on and appreciating the good in one's life. As she listened to the facilitator share stories and research on the transformative effects of gratitude, Laura began to realize how much of her own life she had been taking for granted.

Inspired by what she had learned, Laura committed to incorporating gratitude into her daily routine. She started by keeping a gratitude journal, taking a few minutes each morning to write down three things she was thankful for. At first, it felt awkward and forced, but as she continued the practice, Laura noticed more things to appreciate in her life.

She began to pay attention to the small joys and comforts that had gone unnoticed – the warmth of her morning coffee, the friendly smile of her local barista, the quiet beauty of a sunset over the city skyline. She also expressed her gratitude more often to the people in her life, from her team at work to her friends and family.

As Laura continued to cultivate this practice of appreciation, she noticed a profound shift in her overall well-being. She felt less stressed and anxious, more resilient in the face of challenges and setbacks. Her relationships began to deepen and flourish as she expressed her gratitude more openly and consistently. And maybe most significantly, Laura began to feel a greater sense of contentment and fulfillment in her life, a feeling that had seemed so elusive.

Inspired by her own transformation, Laura began to share her experience with others in her community. She started a gratitude circle at her company, encouraging her team to take a few minutes each day to share what they were thankful for. She also began volunteering with a local youth organization, teaching mindfulness and gratitude practices to young people facing adversity.

As Laura's gratitude practice grew and evolved, so too did her understanding of its profound impact. She came to see that gratitude was not just a feel-good exercise, but a radical act of reframing one's experience of life. By consistently choosing to focus on and appreciate the good, she found joy and meaning even in life's inevitable challenges and uncertainties.

Looking back on her journey, Laura realized that gratitude had been the key to unlocking a deeper sense of purpose, connection, and fulfillment in her life. It had transformed her relationship with herself, others, and the world around her, opening her up to a richer and more meaningful experience of being alive.

Laura's story serves as a powerful reminder of the transformative potential of gratitude. By intentionally cultivating appreciation and thankfulness, we have the power to shift our perceptions, enhance our resilience, deepen our connections, and find greater joy and meaning in each moment. Gratitude is not a panacea for life's challenges, but it is a profound tool for navigating those challenges with grace, perspective, and an open heart.

As we each walk our own path of growth and discovery, may we remember the power of gratitude to light the way. May we approach each day with intentional appreciation, seeking and savoring the good in ourselves, others, and the world. And may we trust that in doing so, we are not only enhancing our own well-being, but contributing to a more positive, connected, and compassionate world for all.

∾

PART SIX WRAP-UP:

KEY POINTS:

• Gratitude is a powerful tool that can transform our perception of the world and our place in it, letting us find joy and meaning even in challenging circumstances.

• Consistently focusing on and appreciating the good in our lives can lead to increased happiness, resilience, and overall well-being.

• Expressing gratitude to others strengthens relationships, fosters a sense of connection and mutual support, and creates a positive ripple effect in our communities.

• Cultivating a grateful mindset involves shifting our focus from what's lacking to what's present and abundant in our lives.

• Obstacles to gratitude, such as comparison, negativity, busyness, and personal setbacks, can be navigated with intention, self-compassion, and specific strategies.

• The journey of gratitude is an ongoing practice that requires commitment, patience, and a willingness to learn from challenges.

• • •

Action Items:

• Start a daily gratitude practice, such as keeping a gratitude journal or sharing appreciations with others.

• Incorporate mindfulness and present-moment awareness into your daily routine to savor life's simple joys and cultivate a sense of wonder.

• Express gratitude directly to the people in your life through heartfelt thank-yous, kind gestures, and quality time together.

• Create visual reminders of gratitude, such as a gratitude jar or wall of photos and mementos, to keep appreciation at the forefront of your mind.

• Practice reframing challenges and setbacks as opportunities for growth, learning, and deepening your capacity for resilience and appreciation.

• Cultivate a supportive community of people who value and practice gratitude, and inspire and uplift one another on the journey.

• Engage in regular acts of kindness and generosity to spread appreciation and positivity to others.

• Be patient and compassionate with yourself as you navigate the obstacles to gratitude, remembering that growth is a process, not a destination.

• Seek resources, such as books, workshops, or mentors, to deepen your understanding and practice of gratitude.

• Regularly reflect on your gratitude journey, celebrating your progress and recommitting to your practice, even in challenging times.

In our next part...

... we'll start a transformative journey of removing toxic influences from our lives and cultivating a mindset of positivity and resilience.

We'll explore the insidious nature of toxicity, how it can seep into our relationships, environments, and even our own thought patterns, slowly eroding our sense of self-worth and limiting our potential for growth and happiness. But fear not – we'll also arm you with powerful strategies for recognizing and releasing these negative forces, from setting healthy boundaries to reframing limiting beliefs.

As we navigate this path of self-discovery and empowerment, we'll also dig into the art of rebuilding a life aligned with your deepest values and aspirations. You'll learn how to heal from the wounds of toxic experiences, to cultivate a support system that uplifts and inspires you, and to develop daily practices that nourish your mind, body, and soul. Along the way, we'll explore the transformative power of gratitude, self-compassion, and purposeful living, and how these practices can help you weather life's inevitable challenges with grace and resilience. So join us on this journey of letting go and embracing your most authentic, joyful self – it's time to reclaim your power and create the life you deserve.

∼

PART SEVEN

THRIVING AFTER TOXICITY: RELEASING NEGATIVE INFLUENCES AND EMBRACING YOUR BEST SELF

CULTIVATING A LIFE OF POSITIVITY: NAVIGATING AND RELEASING TOXIC INFLUENCES

In the journey toward a life of joy, fulfillment, and personal growth, one of the most significant challenges we face is toxic influences. These negative forces can take many forms—relationships that drain us, environments that stifle us, habits that undermine our well-being. They can seep into our lives gradually, often unnoticed, until we find ourselves weighed down by their cumulative impact. But just as a garden must be tended and weeded to flourish, so too must we learn to identify and release these toxic elements if we are to cultivate a life of authentic positivity and thriving.

The Subtle Toll of Toxicity

The effects of toxic influences can be insidious, eroding our well-being and potential in ways that are not always immediately apparent. Over time, constant exposure to negativity, criticism, or undermining can take a profound toll on our mental and emotional health. We may wrestle with increased anxiety, self-doubt, and even depression, our inner reserves of resilience and joy gradually depleted.

These impacts can ripple out into every area of our lives. In our relationships, toxicity breeds tension, conflict, and disconnection. We may find ourselves constantly on edge, bracing for the next wave of negativity or criticism. This chronic stress can make it difficult to show up as our best selves, to be present and engaged with those we care about.

In our personal growth and development, toxic influences can be stifling. When we're surrounded by people who constantly tear us down, who dismiss our dreams and ambitions, it is incredibly challenging to maintain the motivation and self-belief necessary to pursue our goals. We may start to internalize these negative messages, doubting our own capabilities and worth.

Recognizing the Red Flags

The first step in releasing toxic influences is learning to recognize them. This can be trickier than it sounds, as we often become so accustomed to these negative patterns they start to feel normal, even inevitable. But by cultivating a heightened awareness of our own emotional responses and interactions, we can start to identify the red flags that signal toxicity.

An important indicator is the way certain people or environments consistently make us feel. If we frequently leave interactions feeling drained, anxious, or upset, that's a strong sign that something is off. Healthy relationships and environments should leave us feeling uplifted, supported, and energized, not depleted and discouraged.

It can also be revealing to step back and objectively analyze the dynamics of our interactions. Are there people in our lives who consistently belittle us, dismiss our feelings, or undermine our efforts? Do we constantly walk on eggshells, afraid of triggering a negative reaction? These patterns of disrespect and emotional volatility are hallmarks of toxic relationships.

Sometimes, the toxicity in our lives comes not from a specific person, but from our overall lifestyle and environment. If our daily routines and habits are leaving us feeling stressed, unfulfilled, and out of alignment with our values and goals, that's a red flag that something needs to change. Our external circumstances can have a profound impact on our inner well-being, and cultivating a positive life requires being intentional about the spaces and activities we engage with.

Strategies for Releasing and Realigning

Once we've identified the toxic influences in our lives, the next step is taking proactive measures to manage and release them. This process will look different for everyone, depending on the specific situation and dynamics at play, but some general strategies can be helpful.

One of the most important is setting clear, firm boundaries. This means getting crystal clear on what behaviors and interactions we will and will not tolerate and communicating these boundaries assertively. If someone in our life is consistently crossing lines or disregarding our needs, we have every right to put our foot down and insist on being treated with respect. This isn't always easy, especially if we're not used to standing up for ourselves, but it's a critical skill for maintaining healthy, positive relationships.

Sometimes, the healthiest option may be to reduce or eliminate contact with toxic individuals altogether. This can be challenging, especially if the person is a family member, long-term friend, or colleague. But ultimately, we have to focus on our own well-being. If someone is consistently causing us harm and showing no willingness to change, it may be necessary to create distance, even if that means making difficult choices.

As we work to release toxic influences, it's just as important to proactively cultivate positivity in our lives. This means investing time and energy into relationships that uplift and support us, surrounding ourselves with people who bring out the best in us. It means being intentional about our environment, crafting spaces and routines that nourish our well-being and align with our values. The more we fill our lives with genuine positivity, the less room there is for toxicity to take hold.

Navigating the Journey with Compassion

Approach releasing toxic influences with a great deal of self-compassion. Recognizing and extricating ourselves from negative patterns is hard work, and this journey often involves complex emotions, difficult realizations, and challenging choices. We may feel guilty for setting boundaries, sad about letting go of certain relationships, afraid of the unknown that comes with change.

These feelings are all valid and understandable. Releasing toxicity from our lives isn't a clean, linear process—it's messy, iterative, and deeply personal. There will be steps forward and steps back, moments of clarity and moments of doubt. What matters is that we keep coming back to our commitment to cultivating a life of authentic health and happiness, that we keep choosing positivity and alignment even when it's hard.

It is helpful to remember that releasing toxic influences isn't just about us. When we do the work to create healthier patterns and dynamics, it ripples out to everyone around us. We model for others what it looks like to set boundaries, to focus on well-being, to choose environments and relationships that bring out the best in us. In this way, our personal journey toward positivity becomes a contribution to a larger cultural shift.

Chapter Summary: Tending the Garden of Our Lives

Cultivating a life of authentic positivity is an ongoing practice, a daily choice to tend to the garden of our well-being with care and intention. Just as a garden requires regular weeding and nurturing to thrive, our lives require a consistent commitment to identifying and releasing what doesn't serve us, and cultivating what does.

This isn't a one-time event, but a lifelong journey of growth and alignment. There will always be new challenges, new influences to navigate, new opportunities to choose the higher path. But the more we build the muscle of discernment, the more we get clear on our values and boundaries, the easier it becomes to recognize and release toxicity when it arises.

As we do this work, we create space for immense beauty and potential to blossom in our lives. We free up energy once consumed by negativity, making room for joy, connection, and purpose to take root and flourish. We begin to show up more fully as our authentic selves, radiating the positivity that inspires and uplifts others.

So let us approach this journey with courage and compassion, trusting in our innate wisdom to guide us toward what is healthy and true. Let us be patient with ourselves as we learn and grow, celebrating each step toward greater alignment and vitality. And let us remember that in tending to the garden of our own lives with love and care, we contribute to the collective flourishing of all.

For cultivating a life of positivity is not just a personal pursuit, but a radical act of hope and healing in a world that sorely needs more light. By doing our part to weed out toxicity and nurture joy, we become agents of change, contributing to a future that is brighter, kinder, and more beautiful for all.

So let us begin, right here and now, to release what doesn't serve and embrace what does. Let us trust in the transformative power of our own choices, and in the resilience of the human spirit to grow toward the light. And let us move forward with the conviction that a life of authentic positivity is not only possible, but our birthright—a sacred invitation to bring more goodness, more healing, more radiant possibility into the world, one courageous choice at a time.

~

THE SILENT STRUGGLE: HOW TOXIC INFLUENCES ERODE OUR WELL-BEING

IN THE PURSUIT of a fulfilling and joyful life, we often focus on cultivating positive habits, mindsets, and relationships. We seek experiences and connections that uplift us, that bring out the best in who we are and who we aspire to be. But equally important in this journey is learning to recognize and address the toxic influences that can quietly erode our well-being, often without us even realizing it.

These toxic influences can take many forms—a critical family member, a cutthroat work environment, a pattern of negative self-talk. What they all have in common is their insidious ability to undermine our mental and emotional health, to chip away at our sense of self-worth and potential. If left unchecked, these influences can create significant barriers to our personal growth and happiness, trapping us in cycles of stress, self-doubt, and stagnation.

The Corrosive Power of Toxic Relationships

One of the most potent sources of toxicity in our lives can be the relationships we hold dear. Family dynamics, romantic partnerships, close friendships—these intimate bonds have immense power to shape our well-being. When these relationships are healthy and supportive, they can be an incredible source of strength, resilience, and joy. But when they turn toxic, the effects can be devastating.

Toxic relationships often involve patterns of manipulation, criticism, neglect, or even emotional abuse. Over time, being on the receiving end of this treatment can deeply erode our sense of self-worth. We may start to internalize the negative messages, believing we are flawed, unlovable, or incapable. This can lead to heightened anxiety, depression, and a pervasive feeling of being trapped or powerless.

Toxic relationships can be draining, consuming the emotional energy we need for self-care and personal growth. When we're constantly managing another person's moods, walking on eggshells to avoid conflict, or recovering from hurtful interactions, we have little reserves left for pursuing our own goals and nurturing our well-being. We may find ourselves isolated from other supportive connections, our entire lives orbiting around the toxic dynamic.

The Stifling Impact of Negative Environments

Just as toxic relationships can undermine our well-being, so too can toxic environments. Whether it's a workplace rife with cutthroat competition, a community that thrives on gossip and judgment, or a home life filled with tension and discord, negative environments can take a profound toll on our mental health.

Constantly navigating a toxic environment can put us in a state of chronic stress. Our fight-or-flight response is triggered daily, flooding our bodies with cortisol and adrenaline. Over time, this can lead to a host of physical and mental health issues, from anxiety disorders to cardiovascular problems. We may dread each day, our joy and creativity sapped by the negative atmosphere.

Toxic environments can also stifle our personal and professional growth. When we're surrounded by criticism, pessimism, and a lack of support, it is incredibly challenging to take risks, think big, or advocate for ourselves. We may start to doubt our own abilities and ideas, shying away from opportunities fearing failure or judgment. In this way, toxic environments can become a self-fulfilling prophecy, limiting our potential and keeping us stuck in unfulfilling patterns.

Even if we're not directly targeted by the negativity in a toxic environment, simply being immersed in it can start to color our own outlook. Constant exposure to cynicism, complaining, or fear-based thinking can make it harder to maintain a positive, growth-oriented mindset. We may slip into pessimism, expecting the worst from people and situations. This negativity bias can then spill over into other areas of our lives, tainting even the good experiences with a sense of doubt or dread.

The Prison of Pessimistic Thinking

Sometimes, the most persistent toxic influence in our lives is our own mind. Patterns of pessimistic, self-critical thinking can be deeply ingrained, often stemming from early experiences or traumas. When left unchallenged, these negative thought patterns can become a mental prison, limiting our ability to see possibilities, take healthy risks, or practice self-compassion.

Pessimistic thinking often involves a lot of catastrophizing—assuming the worst-case scenario in any situation. We may find ourselves consumed with "what if" worries, fixating on all the ways things could go wrong. This anxiety can be paralyzing, leading us to avoid opportunities or experiences that could enrich our lives. We may tell ourselves we're being "realistic," but in reality, we're foreclosing on joy and growth.

Constant negative self-talk is another way pessimistic thinking can erode our well-being. When we're regularly berating ourselves, telling ourselves we're not good enough, smart enough, or worthy enough, it becomes very difficult to maintain a sense of self-esteem and agency. We may shy away from challenges, convinced of our own inadequacy. This self-criticism can also make it harder to receive compliments or support from others, as we're quick to dismiss or downplay anything that contradicts our negative self-image.

Over time, pessimistic thinking can lead to a pervasive sense of hope-lessness or helplessness. If negative outcomes are inevitable, that we're powerless to change our circumstances, we lose motivation to take positive action. This learned helplessness can keep us stuck in unful-filling or even toxic situations, as we don't believe we have the capacity to create change. It can also lead to a joyless existence, as we're unable to savor or trust the good moments when they come.

Strategies for Releasing Toxicity

Recognizing the harmful effects of toxic influences is a critical first step, but it's not enough on its own. We also need proactive strategies for releasing these influences and reclaiming our well-being. This process will look different for everyone, depending on the specific dynamics and challenges at play, but there are some general principles that can guide us.

One of the most important is learning to set and enforce healthy boundaries. This means getting clear on what we will tolerate in our relationships and environments and communicating these limits assertively. If a family member continuously puts us down, for exam-ple, we might set a boundary that we will end the conversation if the criticism continues. If a work environment is consistently toxic, we might set a boundary around how much overtime we're willing to do or look for a new job.

Building a strong support system is another key strategy. When we're facing toxic influences, it's important to have people in our corner who can offer perspective, encouragement, and a safe haven. This might mean investing more time in positive friendships, seeking mentors, or joining a support group. The more we surround ourselves with uplifting influences, the easier it becomes to recognize and resist toxicity.

Sometimes, the best way to deal with a toxic situation may be to walk away altogether. This is never an easy decision, especially when it involves close relationships or major life circumstances. But some-times, removing ourselves is the only way to protect our well-being and create space for healing. This might mean ending a relationship, quitting a job, or moving to a new community. It's a courageous act of self-care and self-respect.

Regarding pessimistic thinking, the work is largely internal. We need to learn to catch negative thought patterns as they arise and consciously replace them with more balanced, compassionate perspectives. This is where practices like cognitive reframing and mindfulness can be helpful. By learning to observe our thoughts without getting swept away by them, we can start to loosen their grip and create space for new possibilities.

It's also important to proactively fill our minds with positive inputs. This might mean seeking inspiring books, podcasts, or people who model resilience and growth. It might mean practicing gratitude, regularly reflecting on what's going right in our lives. The more we can tip the balance toward positive, uplifting influences, the easier it becomes to ward off pessimism and maintain a healthy outlook.

Ultimately, releasing toxic influences is a process of empowerment. It's about reclaiming our agency and our right to thrive, even in the face of difficult circumstances. It's about recognizing that while we may not control every situation, we always have a choice in how we respond—a choice to set boundaries, seek support, change our environment, or shift our mindset. Each time we choose to focus on our well-being, we strengthen our capacity to create a life aligned with our deepest values and aspirations.

The Journey to Joyful Living

Learning to recognize and release toxic influences is an important part of the journey to joyful, fulfilling living. It's not always a comfortable process—it often involves facing difficult truths, making tough decisions, and navigating complex emotions. But as we develop the self-awareness and courage to address toxicity in our lives, we open up immense space for healing, growth, and positive transformation.

This journey is not about achieving a perfect, problem-free life. Challenges and stressors are inevitable.

THE POWER OF BOUNDARIES: SAFEGUARDING YOUR WELL-BEING IN A TOXIC WORLD

FACED WITH TOXIC INFLUENCES, one of the most potent tools we have at our disposal is the ability to set and maintain healthy boundaries. Boundaries are the invisible lines we draw around our physical, emotional, and mental space—lines that define what we are and are not willing to accept in our interactions with others. When we have clear, consistent boundaries, we create a protective buffer between ourselves and the negativity that might otherwise seep into our lives.

The Importance of Knowing Your Limits

At the core of effective boundary setting is a deep understanding of our own limits—what we can and cannot tolerate in our relationships and environments. This is a highly individual process, as what feels toxic to one person might be tolerable to another. Some of us may have low tolerance for criticism or conflict, while others may be more sensitive to feeling controlled or smothered.

Taking the time to reflect on our own needs, values, and triggers is an essential first step. We might ask ourselves questions like: What behaviors or interactions consistently leave me feeling drained or upset? What do I need to feel safe, respected, and valued in my relationships?

What are my non-negotiables—the things I simply cannot compromise on for the sake of others?

Answering these questions honestly, without judgment, can help us gain clarity on where our boundaries need to be. This self-awareness is the foundation on which we can start to communicate and enforce our limits with others.

The Art of Assertive Communication

Once we know our boundaries, the next step is expressing them clearly and directly to others. This is where many of us can struggle, especially if we've experienced boundary violations in the past or have been conditioned to focus on others' needs over our own. We may fear being seen as selfish, difficult, or ungrateful if we speak up for ourselves.

But assertive communication is not about being aggressive or unkind. Rather, it's a way of interacting that is both honest and respectful—to ourselves and to others. When we communicate assertively, we take responsibility for our own feelings and needs, without blaming or attacking. We use "I" statements to express ourselves, focusing on the impact certain behaviors have on us rather than labeling the other person as "wrong" or "bad."

For example, instead of saying "You're always so critical!" (which puts the other person on the defensive), we might say, "I feel really discouraged when I hear negative comments about my work. I would appreciate it if we could discuss any issues constructively." This approach opens the door for dialogue and problem-solving, rather than shutdown and resentment.

The Power of Consistency

Communicating our boundaries is important, but it's only half the battle. To protect our well-being, we need to be consistent in upholding our limits, even (and especially) when it's difficult. This means being willing to follow through with consequences when our boundaries are crossed, whether that's ending a conversation, leaving a situation, or even walking away from a relationship altogether.

Consistency is key because it sends a clear message, both to others and to ourselves, that our boundaries are non-negotiable. If we only enforce our limits sometimes, or make exceptions for certain people, we teach others that our boundaries are flexible—that with enough pressure or manipulation, they can get us to bend. We also internalize the message that our needs are not truly important, that we don't deserve to have our limits respected.

Consistency can be challenging, especially in the face of resistance or backlash. Others may not always respond well to our boundaries, particularly if they're used to us being more accommodating. They may try to argue, guilt-trip, or even lash out in anger. In these moments, their reaction is not a reflection on the validity of our boundaries. We are not responsible for managing other people's emotions or expectations.

Strategies for Staying Firm

When faced with boundary pushback, a few strategies can help us stay grounded and resolved to remain calm. When we get reactive or defensive, we risk escalating the situation and losing sight of our own needs. Taking a few deep breaths, or even stepping away from the conversation temporarily, can help us maintain our composure.

It can also be helpful to clarify and repeat our boundaries, especially if there seems to be a misunderstanding. Something like, "I understand you're upset, but as I mentioned, I'm not available to talk after 9pm except for emergencies. Let's find a time tomorrow when we can discuss this further." By staying firm but respectful, we model the communication we want to see.

Sometimes, it may be appropriate to offer alternative solutions that still honor our boundaries. For example, if a friend is pushing for a last-minute get-together when we've already expressed a need for alone time, we might suggest a different day or activity that works better for us. This shows we value the relationship, even as we focus on our own needs.

However, if someone consistently ignores or tramples our boundaries, even after we've communicated clearly, it may be necessary to enforce more serious consequences. This could mean limiting our time with that person, setting stricter parameters around our interactions, or even ending the relationship if the violation is severe enough. While this can be painful, especially with people we care about, it's ultimately an act of self-respect. We teach people how to treat us by what we tolerate.

Throughout this process, it's important to remember that we need not navigate boundary challenges alone. Seeking support from trusted friends, family members, or professionals can be invaluable. They can offer an outside perspective, confirm our experiences, and remind us of our inherent worth. Surrounding ourselves with people who respect and uplift us is a powerful boundary—one that protects us from absorbing too much toxicity.

Boundaries as an Act of Self-Love

Ultimately, setting and maintaining boundaries is a profound act of self-care and self-love. It's a way of honoring our own needs, even in the face of external pressure or expectation. It's saying "my well-being matters" in a world that often encourages self-sacrifice and people-pleasing.

When we have healthy boundaries, we create space for more authentic, fulfilling relationships—with others and with ourselves. We learn to trust our own instincts, to stand up for what we believe in, to choose environments and interactions that align with our values. We free up energy that was drained by toxic dynamics, energy we can now devote to our own growth, healing, and joy.

Cultivating this emotional sovereignty is a lifelong journey, one that requires ongoing reflection, communication, and courage. Sometimes, we falter, when we give too much or tolerate what we shouldn't. But with each boundary we set and uphold, we strengthen our capacity to protect and focus on our well-being. We reinforce the truth that we are worthy of respect, care, and consideration, both from others and from ourselves.

In a world filled with toxic influences, this is a radical stance. It's a declaration of our inherent value, our right to thrive and flourish on our own terms. By learning to draw clear, consistent lines around what we will accept, we reclaim our power from those who would seek to reduce or control us. We create a sacred space within which we can heal, grow, and blossom into our fullest selves.

So let us approach boundary setting not as a punitive or isolating act, but as a profound form of self-advocacy. Let us treat our limits not as walls to keep others out, but as loving containers within which we can more fully own and express who we are. And let us remember that each time we defend our boundaries, we not only protect our own well-being, but we contribute to a world where all people feel empowered to do the same.

For the ability to set healthy boundaries is not just a personal skill, but a collective one. The more we model this self-respect and emotional responsibility, the more we give others permission to do the same. We start to create a culture where honoring each other's needs and autonomy is the norm, rather than the exception—a world where toxicity is not tolerated, because love and respect are the default.

This is the power of boundaries: not just to safeguard our individual well-being, but to reshape the fabric of our relationships and communities. By learning to hold our limits with compassion and conviction, we plant the seeds for a future where all people can thrive—not at the expense of each other, but in deep, authentic connection with one another.

So let us begin, today and every day, to cultivate the courage and clarity to know our worth, to stand in our truth, and to protect the sacred space of our hearts and minds. Let us trust that as we honor our own boundaries, we create ripples of positive change that touch all those around us. And let us move forward with the unshakable conviction we are, each and every one of us, deserving of love, respect, and space to grow into our most radiant selves.

∼

THE TRANSFORMATIVE POWER OF POSITIVE CONNECTIONS

THE CONNECTIONS we make with others are the threads that hold our lives together and give our story depth and strength. These connections, when positive and nurturing, have a profound impact on our mental, emotional, and even physical well-being. They are the invisible safety net that catches us when we stumble, the guiding light that illuminates our path in times of darkness, and the amplifier that magnifies our joy in moments of triumph.

The Benefits of a Supportive Network

Having a strong, positive support system is not a luxury, but a necessity for thriving in the face of life's challenges. When surrounded by people who genuinely care for us, who believe in our potential and want to see us succeed, we are better equipped to weather any storm.

One of the most immediate benefits of a supportive network is the emotional stability it provides. Knowing we have people to turn to, people who will listen without judgment and offer comfort and encouragement, can be grounding. It reminds us we are not alone, that our struggles and feelings are valid, and that there is hope even in the darkest of times.

This emotional support is vital when going through difficult life transitions, such as a job loss, a health crisis, or the end of a relationship. In these moments, having someone to lean on, to help us process our emotions and remind us of our strengths, can make all the difference. It can prevent us from spiraling into despair or isolation and give us the courage to keep moving forward.

Beyond providing solace in times of distress, a positive support system also plays an important role in our personal growth and development. When surrounded by people who inspire and motivate us, who challenge us to step outside our comfort zones and pursue our dreams, we are more likely to do so. We see ourselves through their eyes—as capable, talented, and worthy of success.

This external validation can be especially important when embarking on a new venture or taking a risk. Having cheerleaders in our corner, people who genuinely believe in us and our goals, can give us the extra boost of confidence we need to take that leap. And when we inevitably face setbacks or doubts along the way, their encouragement can help us stay the course.

Over time, these positive relationships can significantly enhance our resilience—our ability to bounce back from adversity and adapt to change. When we have a history of being supported and encouraged, when we've seen ourselves overcome challenges with the help of our loved ones, we start to internalize that narrative. We begin to trust in our own capacity to handle whatever life throws our way, because we know we have a team behind us.

Cultivating Positive Connections

Given the immense benefits of a strong support system, it's clear that cultivating these positive connections should be a top priority in our lives. But how do we build and maintaining these relationships, especially in a world that can often feel isolating or superficial?

The first step is to get clear on the people we want to attract into our lives. While it's wonderful to have a diverse network of friends and acquaintances, our closest support system should consist of individuals who share our values, who uplift and inspire us, and who are committed to mutual growth and respect.

This doesn't mean we should only seek people exactly like us, but those who are aligned with our core principles and life goals. We might ask ourselves: Who are the people I admire for their kindness, their integrity, their passion? What communities or activities usually attract individuals with these qualities?

By being intentional about the environments, we place ourselves in and the people we choose to engage with, we increase our chances of forming meaningful, positive connections. This could mean joining a volunteer organization, taking a class that aligns with our interests, or attending events focused on personal development or social impact.

As we begin to meet people who resonate with us, it's important to approach these interactions with authenticity and vulnerability. While it is tempting to present a curated version of ourselves, especially when we're eager to make a good impression, true connection happens when we will show up as we are—flaws, fears, and all.

This doesn't mean we need to bare our deepest secrets to every new acquaintance, but that we are open and honest about our thoughts, feelings, and experiences. When we share our stories, our struggles, and our aspirations, we invite others to see us and to share in kind. We create space for genuine understanding and empathy to blossom.

Another key aspect of building positive relationships is reciprocity. While we all need support at times, healthy connections are a two-way street. Being a good friend or ally means not only being willing to receive help, but also offering it.

This can take many forms—lending a listening ear, offering practical assistance, or simply being a consistent source of encouragement and positivity. By showing up for others in the same way we'd like them to show up for us, we show our investment in the relationship and help ensure a balanced, mutually nourishing dynamic.

As our supportive relationships deepen, it's also important to establish and maintain healthy boundaries. Even the most positive connections can become strained or toxic if there isn't a clear understanding of each person's needs, expectations, and limits.

This requires open, honest communication. We need to be willing to express what we need to feel respected and supported, as well as what we are and are not comfortable with in terms of time, energy, or emotional investment. At the same time, we need to be receptive to and respectful of the boundaries of others.

By having these candid conversations and being consistent in our actions, we create a foundation of trust and mutual understanding. We show we value the relationship enough to protect it from resentment or burnout, and that we trust each other to honor the parameters we've set.

The Ripple Effect of Positivity

As we nurture these positive, supportive connections in our lives, a beautiful thing starts to happen—we begin to radiate that same positivity outward. When we feel seen, heard, and uplifted by our loved ones, we naturally want to pay that forward. We become more attuned to the needs of others, more generous with our time and energy, and more committed to being a force for good in the world.

This ripple effect can be incredibly powerful. As we support and encourage those around us, they are better equipped to do the same for others. We start to create a culture of compassion, a network of individuals who are invested in each other's well-being and success.

This is potent when we celebrate and share our successes with our support system. When we invite others to revel in our joys and triumphs, we not only deepen our bond with them, but we also create an atmosphere of abundance and possibility. We remind each other that good things are happening all the time, and that we each have the capacity to create positive change in our own lives and in the world.

Over time, these ripples of positivity can extend far beyond our immediate circle. As we go out into the world feeling supported, empowered, and enlivened by our connections, we bring that energy to all our interactions. We become leaders in our communities, catalysts for positive change, and beacons of hope for those who may be struggling.

In this way, investing in our support system is not just a personal pursuit, but a collective one. By cultivating relationships rooted in love, respect, and mutual growth, we contribute to a world where all people feel seen, valued, and supported in reaching their highest potential.

Building these positive connections take time, effort, and ongoing nurturing. It requires us to reach out, to be consistent in our communication and care, and to be willing to work through any challenges or conflicts that arise.

But when we consider the immense benefits—the emotional resilience, the personal growth, the amplified joy and impact—this is one of the most worthwhile investments we can make. Our supportive relationships are the foundation on which we build a life of meaning, purpose, and authentic happiness.

So let us make the cultivation of positive connections a daily practice and a lifelong commitment. Let us seek those who inspire us to be our best selves and be that inspiration for others in return. Let us approach our relationships with open hearts, ready to give and receive the incredible gifts of support, encouragement, and unconditional love.

For it is the quality of our connections that determines the quality of our lives. When woven into a web of positivity, when held and uplifted by those who see the best in us, we find the courage to face any challenge, the resilience to overcome any setback, and the joy to celebrate every victory along the way.

In the embrace of our positive support system, we find not just solace and strength, but a reflection of our own boundless potential. We see that we are capable of extraordinary things, not despite our struggles and imperfections, but because of the love and belief that surrounds us.

So, let us cherish these connections, these beautiful threads that hold us together and make our lives a masterpiece woven with the colors of compassion, understanding, and unwavering support. Let us nurture these relationships with gratitude, knowing they are the foundation on which we can build our dreams and aspirations.

In times of doubt or uncertainty, may we turn to our support system, knowing that their belief in us will reignite the flame of our own self-belief. May we draw strength from their encouragement, finding the courage to face our fears and take bold steps toward our goals. And may we, in turn, be a source of light and inspiration for others, offering our own love and support to those who need it most.

For when surrounded by a network of positive influences, we are reminded that we are never truly alone on this journey of life. We have the power to lift each other up, to celebrate each other's successes, and to provide a soft place to land when the road gets tough. Together, we can create a tapestry of resilience, hope, and shared purpose, knowing that our combined strength is greater than any obstacle we may face.

So let us embrace our positive support system as a precious gift, a reminder of the love and goodness that exists. Let us cultivate these relationships with care and attention, investing our time and energy into the people who bring out the best in us. And let us never underestimate the transformative power of a kind word, a listening ear, or a heartfelt gesture of support.

It is the quality of our connections that determines the quality of our lives. When we surround ourselves with people who believe in us, who inspire us to be our best selves, and who walk beside us through the ups and downs of life, we create a masterpiece of love, resilience, and shared purpose. And in that masterpiece, we find the strength to overcome any challenge, the courage to pursue our wildest dreams, and the joy of knowing we are loved and supported, now and always.

~

CRAFTING YOUR HAVEN: THE ART OF DESIGNING A LIFE-ENHANCING ENVIRONMENT

THE SPACES we inhabit are not merely physical structures—they are extensions of our very selves. They are the stages on which the dramas of our lives unfold, the canvases on which we paint our hopes, dreams, and aspirations. When we take the time to mindfully curate these environments, to infuse them with elements that uplift and inspire us, we create not just a place to live or work, but a sanctuary for our souls.

The Power of Positive Surroundings

The impact of our surroundings on our well-being cannot be overstated. Studies have consistently shown that the environments we inhabit can significantly influence our mood, productivity, and overall quality of life. A space that feels cluttered, chaotic, or uninspiring can leave us feeling drained, anxious, and disconnected from our sense of purpose.

On the flip side, an environment designed with intention, that reflects our values and supports our goals, can be empowering. It can serve as a constant reminder of who we are and who we aspire to be. It can energize and motivate us, sparking our creativity and fostering a deep sense of contentment and belonging.

So how do we craft these life-enhancing spaces? The process starts with a willingness to let go of what no longer serves us, and to make room for what does.

The Art of Decluttering

One of the most transformative steps we can take in creating a positive environment is to simplify our space. This means letting go of items that no longer hold meaning or purpose, that weigh us down more than they lift us up.

The act of decluttering can be challenging, especially if we have emotional attachments to certain possessions. But as we learn to release what is no longer aligned with our current selves, we create space—both physically and energetically—for new growth and possibilities to emerge.

Once we've pared down to the essentials, the next step is to organize what remains in a way that feels intuitive and supportive. This could mean grouping items by function, color, or frequency of use. The key is to design a system that works for our unique needs and lifestyle, one that reduces friction and makes it easy to maintain a sense of order and clarity.

Bringing the Outside In

As we continue to shape our environment, we can draw inspiration from the natural world. Incorporating elements of nature into our space—whether through plants, natural light, or organic materials—can have a profoundly calming and restorative effect.

Indoor plants are powerful allies in crafting a positive atmosphere. Not only do they add visual beauty and vibrancy, but they also purify the air and have been shown to reduce stress, improve concentration, and enhance overall well-being.

Similarly, maximizing our exposure to natural light can be beneficial. Sunlight helps regulate our circadian rhythms, boosts our mood, and can even improve our sleep quality. We should aim to let in as much natural light as our space allows, maybe even reorienting our furniture to make the most of bright, sunny spots.

The Psychology of Color

Another key consideration in designing our environment is color. The hues we surround ourselves with can have a subtle but significant impact on our emotional state and energy levels.

Softer, muted tones like pale blues, greens, and earth colors are often associated with feelings of tranquility and relaxation. These colors can be particularly well-suited for spaces where we want to unwind and de-stress, like bedrooms or bathrooms.

In areas where we want to feel energized and focused, like home offices or creative studios, we might choose brighter, more stimulating colors. Shades like yellow, orange, and red can promote feelings of vitality and enthusiasm.

Ultimately, the goal is to choose a color palette that resonates with us on a personal level, that makes us feel good in our space. We can draw inspiration from the colors found in nature, from our favorite art pieces, or from the places where we feel most at peace.

Designing for Comfort and Joy

As we thoughtfully select colors and natural elements to incorporate into our environment, we can also look for ways to create dedicated spaces for relaxation, rejuvenation, and the pursuits that bring us joy.

This might mean carving out a cozy reading nook, complete with plush cushions and a soft throw blanket. Or maybe it's designating an area for meditation or yoga practice, with candles, incense, and inspiring imagery.

If we have hobbies or creative passions, we can design a space that supports and encourages these endeavors. A well-organized crafting table, a music corner with our favorite instruments, or a writing desk stocked with beautiful journals and pens—these are all ways to honor what lights us up and to make space for more of it in our daily lives.

The key is to be intentional about creating areas that feel inviting and nurturing, spaces that we can't wait to spend time in. When we have environments that actively support our self-care and personal growth, we're far more likely to focus on these essential parts of a happy, fulfilling life.

Cultivating Mindful Spaces

Crafting a positive environment isn't just about our physical surroundings—it's also about the mental and emotional atmosphere we cultivate. Even the most beautifully designed space can feel heavy if our minds are cluttered with negative thoughts or stress.

This is where the practice of mindfulness becomes invaluable. By learning to be present and attentive to our inner state, we can start to notice and gently redirect patterns of thinking that don't serve us. We can create mental space for gratitude, compassion, and joy to flourish.

One powerful way to reinforce this internal shift is through mindful decor. We can select items for our space that serve as reminders to stay grounded and connected to what matters most. This could be an inspiring quote framed on the wall, a cherished photograph, or a small altar with objects that hold deep personal significance.

We can also make a practice of visually highlighting the things we're grateful for. A gratitude wall or journal prominently displayed in our space can prompt us to regularly reflect on and appreciate the good in our lives, even amidst challenges.

Protecting Our Peace

As important as what we choose to include in our environment is what we choose to reduce or eliminate. In today's hyperconnected world, one of the biggest threats to our mental wellbeing is the constant barrage of media and digital noise.

Making a conscious effort to set boundaries around our media consumption—limiting exposure to negative news, curating our social media feeds to be uplifting, and designating device-free zones in our homes—can go a long way in protecting our peace and cultivating a positive mindset.

We might also consider implementing regular digital detoxes, carving out time to unplug completely and reconnect with the real joys of our environment. Engaging all our senses—savoring the scent of fresh flowers, relishing the feel of soft fabrics, enjoying the sound of soothing music—can be a powerful way to ground ourselves in the present and cultivate a deep appreciation for the simple pleasures that surround us.

The Ever-Evolving Sanctuary

As we start the journey of crafting our ideal environment, it's important to remember that our spaces, like ourselves, are constantly evolving. What feels nurturing and inspiring to us today may shift as we grow and change.

The key is to approach our environment with a sense of curiosity and openness, to be willing to continually reassess and refine our spaces to reflect our current needs and aspirations. This might mean sometimes decluttering, rearranging furniture to create new flow and energy, or introducing fresh elements that spark our excitement.

By viewing our environments as living, breathing extensions of ourselves, we can cultivate a deep sense of attunement and partnership with our spaces. We can learn to trust that as we change, our sanctuaries will change with us, forever supporting and reflecting our highest selves.

Ripples of Positivity

As we pour love and intention into crafting our personal environments, a beautiful ripple effect begins to occur. By creating spaces that make us feel good, that inspire and uplift us, we naturally start to radiate that positivity outward.

We become more patient, more compassionate, more energized to make a difference in the world. We see possibilities where before we saw only obstacles. We become a force for good, not just in our own lives, but in the lives of all those we touch.

In this way, the act of designing our environment is not a self-indulgent luxury, but a profound form of service. By caring for ourselves and our spaces, we become better equipped to care for others and the planet we share.

So as we thoughtfully select each element of our surroundings, let us remember the far-reaching impact of our choices. Let us infuse our spaces with reminders of our values, our hopes, and our most cherished dreams. Let us craft environments that don't just reflect who we are, but who we aspire to be—for ourselves, for our loved ones.

THE POWER WITHIN: CULTIVATING A MINDSET FOR RESILIENCE AND JOY

OUR MINDS ARE the most powerful tools we have. They are the lenses through which we perceive and interpret the world, the narrators of our inner stories, and the architects of our emotional landscapes. When we learn to harness the power of our thoughts, to cultivate a mindset rooted in positivity and resilience, we unlock a wellspring of potential that can transform every aspect of our lives.

The Anatomy of a Positive Mindset

At its core, a positive mindset is not about denying life's challenges or putting on a facade of perpetual happiness. Rather, it's a way of relating to our experiences that lets us navigate adversity with grace, to find opportunity in obstacles, and to maintain a sense of hope and perspective even in the darkest of times.

Individuals with a positive mindset usually share certain key features. They are self-aware, able to recognize and challenge their own negative thought patterns. They are proactive, focusing their energy on what they can control rather than dwelling on what they cannot. They are resilient, viewing setbacks as temporary and as opportunities for growth. And they are deeply grateful, consistently orienting their attention toward the good in their lives.

While some people may naturally lean toward this outlook, the truth is that a positive mindset is a skill that can be developed and strengthened. Like any muscle, it grows with consistent exercise and strategic training.

Spotting the Saboteurs

The first step in this training is learning to identify the negative thought patterns that can undermine our best efforts. These cognitive distortions can take many forms, but some common ones include:

• **Catastrophizing:** Imagining the worst possible outcome of a situation.

Overgeneralizing: Viewing a single negative event as a never-ending pattern of defeat.

Discounting the Positive: Insisting that your accomplishments or positive qualities "don't count."

• **Emotional Reasoning:** Assuming that your negative emotions reflect reality.

• **"Should" Statements:** Holding yourself to a strict list of what you should and shouldn't do.

• **Labeling:** Attaching a negative label to yourself based on errors or imperfections.

Learning of these thought patterns is a critical first step, because we cannot change what we do not acknowledge. One powerful way to build this awareness is through the practice of journaling. By regularly writing down our thoughts and reactions, we start to notice recurring themes and triggers. We can begin to catch ourselves in the act of negative thinking, creating a space between stimulus and response.

The Art of Reframing

Once we've identified our negative thought patterns, we can start to actively challenge and reframe them. This process, known as cognitive restructuring, involves examining the evidence for and against our thoughts, considering alternative perspectives, and ultimately developing a more balanced and realistic outlook.

For example, let's say we've made a mistake at work and our immediate thought is, "I'm a total failure." We can challenge this thought by asking ourselves:

- Is this a correct, objective description or an exaggeration?
- What evidence do I have this thought is true? What evidence do I have that it's false?
- Is there another way of looking at this situation?
- What would I say to a friend in a similar situation?

Through this questioning process, we might arrive at a reframe such as, "I made a mistake, but that doesn't define me. I can learn from this and do better next time." This new thought, while still acknowledging the reality of the situation, is more constructive and empowering.

Another powerful tool for reframing is the practice of visualization. By vividly imagining ourselves handling a challenging situation with confidence and competence, we start to internalize a new narrative. We see ourselves not as victims of circumstance, but as capable agents of change.

The Gratitude Advantage

As we work to reframe our negative thoughts, we can simultaneously cultivate a more positive overall outlook by focusing on gratitude. Many studies have shown that regularly expressing gratitude can significantly increase happiness, improve relationships, and even boost physical health.

One of the simplest and most effective ways to harness the power of gratitude is through keeping a gratitude journal. By taking time each day to write down three things we're thankful for, we train our brains to scan for the positive. We start to notice and appreciate the small joys and blessings we might otherwise overlook in the bustle of daily life.

Another strategy is to set gratitude reminders throughout our day. This could be as simple as a note on our bathroom mirror, a daily alarm on our phone, or a ritual like saying grace before meals. By consistently prompting ourselves to reflect on what we're grateful for, we make gratitude a habit and infuse our days with a regular dose of positive perspective.

Embracing Imperfection

One of the biggest barriers to a positive mindset is the trap of perfectionism. When we hold ourselves to unrealistic standards, when we must excel in every endeavor and never make a misstep, we set ourselves up for constant disappointment and self-criticism.

Learning to embrace our imperfections, to view ourselves with compassion and understanding, is a crucial part of developing a resilient and positive outlook. This doesn't mean we abandon our goals or stop striving for excellence. Rather, it means we redefine success in terms of growth, effort, and authenticity rather than flawless performance.

Practically, this can involve setting realistic, achievable goals for ourselves and celebrating our progress along the way. It can mean reframing setbacks as learning opportunities rather than failures. And it can involve practicing self-compassion, treating ourselves with the same kindness and understanding we would extend to a dear friend.

One powerful self-compassion exercise is to imagine what a loved one struggling is going through, and then direct those same words of comfort and encouragement toward ourselves. By learning to be our own ally and cheerleader, we build a foundation of self-worth that can weather any storm.

The Voice Within

As we challenge our negative thoughts, focus on gratitude, and embrace our imperfections, we can further enhance our positive mindset by engaging in positive self-talk. The inner dialogue we have with ourselves is powerful, shaping our beliefs, emotions, and actions in profound ways.

One way to harness this power is through affirmations - positive statements we repeat to ourselves to challenge negative beliefs and build self-confidence. These could be phrases like, "I am capable and strong," "I choose to focus on the good," or "I trust in my ability to handle whatever comes my way."

The key to effective affirmations is to phrase them in the present tense, as if they are already true, and to choose statements that resonate deeply with us. By consistently repeating these positive messages to ourselves, we start to internalize them, gradually shifting our overall mindset in a more optimistic and empowered direction.

In addition to affirmations, we can also practice catching and countering our negative self-talk in the moment. When we notice ourselves engaging in harsh self-criticism or pessimistic predictions, we can consciously replace those thoughts with more constructive and compassionate alternatives. Over time, this practice can help us develop a more automatically positive inner dialogue.

The Company We Keep

As much as our mindset is an inside job, it is also profoundly influenced by the people and environments we surround ourselves with. Just as negativity can be contagious, so too can positivity. When we fill our lives with individuals who uplift, inspire, and believe in us, we create a powerful support system for our own growth and well-being.

This might involve cultivating friendships with people who share our values and goals, who challenge us to be our best selves. It could mean seeking mentors or role models who embody the qualities and mindsets we aspire to. And it can involve setting loving boundaries with individuals who consistently drain our energy or pull us into patterns of negativity.

Similarly, we can actively seek environments and experiences that nourish our positive mindset. This could include attending workshops or retreats, joining a supportive community or group, or simply surrounding ourselves with art, music, and media that inspire and elevate us.

The Mindful Moment

One of the most transformative tools for cultivating a positive mindset is the practice of mindfulness and meditation. By learning to be present in the moment, to observe our thoughts and emotions with curiosity and non-judgment, we can begin to disentangle ourselves from the grip of negative patterns.

Through regular meditation, we train our minds to be more focused, more calm, and more aware. We learn to recognize thoughts as simply mental events, rather than truths that define us. We discover that we can choose which thoughts to engage with and which to let pass by like clouds in the sky.

This ability to step back and observe our inner experience is empowering. It lets us respond to life's challenges with greater clarity and resilience, rather than getting swept away by knee-jerk reactions and negative spirals.

Practically, this can involve setting aside time each day for a formal meditation practice, even if it's for a few minutes. It can also mean bringing mindful awareness into our daily activities - focusing on the task at hand, noticing the sensations in our bodies, and gently bringing our attention back to the present moment whenever we get caught up in worry or rumination.

Another powerful mindfulness tool is the practice of mindful breathing. Whenever we find ourselves in a stressful or emotionally charged situation, we can use our breath as an anchor, a way to ground ourselves in the present. By taking a few deep, conscious breaths, we activate our body's relaxation response, reducing stress and letting us approach the situation with greater calm and clarity.

The Journey Continues

Cultivating a positive mindset is a lifelong journey, a daily choice to steer our thoughts and focus in a constructive direction. It requires patience, self-compassion, and a willingness to keep showing up, even on the difficult days.

But the rewards of this practice are immeasurable. As we learn to shift our mental habits, we open ourselves up to greater joy, resilience, and fulfillment. We become better equipped to navigate life's inevitable ups and downs, to find meaning and growth in even the toughest challenges.

We begin to recognize that our thoughts and beliefs are not fixed realities, but malleable patterns we have the power to shape. We discover that we are not defined by our mistakes or limitations, but by our capacity for learning, growth, and positive change.

As we continue on this path, a positive mindset is not a destination to be reached, but a way of being cultivated, moment by moment, day by day. It's a commitment to choosing hope over fear, gratitude over complaint, and self-compassion over self-judgment.

This journey is deeply personal. What works for one person may not work for another. We each need to find the tools, practices, and perspectives that resonate most deeply with us, that support our unique needs and aspirations.

This might involve experimenting with different mindfulness techniques, exploring various styles of affirmations, or finding the self-care rituals that most nourish and recharge us. It may involve seeking the teachers, books, or communities that inspire and support us on our path.

Ultimately, the cultivation of a positive mindset is a profound act of self-love and self-empowerment. It is a declaration that we are worthy of joy, peace, and fulfillment, and that we have the inner resources to create those experiences, despite our external circumstances.

As we continue to strengthen our positive mental habits, we not only transform our own lives, but we also become a beacon of hope and inspiration for others. We start to radiate the qualities we wish to see more of in the world - compassion, resilience, joy, and love.

In this way, the cultivation of a positive mindset is not just a personal practice, but a global one. Each of us has the power to be a ripple of positive change, to contribute to a collective shift toward greater understanding, harmony, and well-being.

So let us approach this journey with open hearts and curious minds. Let us be gentle with ourselves, celebrating our progress and learning from our missteps. Let us fill our mental gardens with seeds of positivity, tending to them daily with patience and care.

And let us trust that as we do this inner work, as we learn to harness the power of our minds for good, we are not only transforming ourselves, but the world. One thought, one choice, one moment at a time, we are creating a future of greater possibility, for ourselves and for all.

❧

RISING FROM THE ASHES: REBUILDING YOUR LIFE AFTER TOXIC RELATIONSHIPS

THE DECISION TO remove toxic influences from our lives is monumental. This choice requires immense courage, self-awareness, and a deep commitment to our own well-being. Whether we're leaving an abusive relationship, setting boundaries with a manipulative family member, or walking away from a toxic work environment, the act of saying "no more" is a powerful declaration of self-love and self-respect.

But what comes next? How do we rebuild our lives after such a significant upheaval? How do we heal from the wounds of the past and create a future that is brighter, healthier, and more fulfilling?

The journey of rebuilding is not an easy one. This path is often strewn with challenges, setbacks, and moments of doubt. But it is also a journey of incredible growth, self-discovery, and transformation. It's a chance to reclaim our power, redefine our narratives, and create a life that reflects our deepest values and aspirations.

The Healing Journey

The first step on this path is healing. When we've been in a toxic situation for a long time, it's common to feel a mix of emotions - relief, grief, anger, confusion, fear. We may question our own judgment, struggle with feelings of guilt or shame, or feel overwhelmed by starting over.

These feelings are normal and valid. Healing is not a linear process, and it's okay to have good days and bad days. The key is to be patient and compassionate with ourselves, to allow ourselves the time and space to process our experiences and emotions.

One of the most powerful tools in this process is seeking support. This could involve working with a therapist or counselor who can provide a safe, non-judgmental space to explore our feelings and experiences. It could mean joining a support group where we can connect with others who have gone through similar situations. Or it could simply involve contacting trusted friends and family members who can offer a listening ear and a shoulder to lean on.

Another important part of healing is learning to practice self-care. When we've been in a toxic situation, we may have neglected our own needs and desires to cater to someone else's. Rebuilding our lives is a chance to reconnect with ourselves, to rediscover what brings us joy, peace, and fulfillment.

This could involve developing a regular exercise routine, exploring a new hobby or creative outlet, or establishing a daily meditation or journaling practice. It could mean focusing on rest and relaxation, treating ourselves to small indulgences, or learning to say "no" to requests or invitations that don't serve us.

The key is to approach self-care not as a luxury, but as a necessity - a fundamental way of honoring and nurturing ourselves as we navigate the challenges of healing and growth.

Personal Growth and Self-Discovery

As we begin to heal from the wounds of the past, we often find that the journey of rebuilding is also a profound opportunity for personal growth and self-discovery. Free from the constraints and manipulations of a toxic situation, we have the chance to reevaluate our lives, our values, and our goals.

This process of self-reflection can be both exciting and daunting. We may question long-held beliefs, confronting limiting patterns of behavior, or grappling with existential questions about our purpose and path in life.

One powerful way to navigate this process is through the practice of journaling. By regularly writing down our thoughts, feelings, and experiences, we can gain clarity and insight into our own minds and hearts. We can begin to identify recurring themes, uncover hidden desires and fears, and track our progress.

Another tool for growth is setting new goals for ourselves. When we've been in a toxic situation, our goals and dreams may have been suppressed or dismissed. Rebuilding our lives is a chance to reclaim those aspirations, to define success on our own terms.

This could involve setting professional goals, such as pursuing a new career path or starting our own business. It could mean setting personal goals, like traveling to a new country, learning a new language, or running a marathon. Or it could involve relational goals, such as building stronger friendships, reconnecting with family members, or even opening ourselves up to the possibility of a new, healthy romantic partnership.

The key is to choose goals that resonate with us, that reflect our authentic desires and values. And as we work toward these goals, it's important to celebrate our progress along the way, to acknowledge each small victory as a testament to our strength and resilience.

Cultivating a Positive Mindset

As we heal and grow, one of the most transformative shifts we can make is in our mindset. When we've been in a toxic situation, it's easy to get caught in patterns of negative thinking - to focus on our failures, limitations, and fears.

But as we rebuild our lives, we have the opportunity to consciously cultivate a more positive, empowered mindset. This doesn't mean denying the reality of our challenges or putting on a fake smile. Rather, it means choosing to focus on the good in our lives, to reframe obstacles as opportunities, and to trust in our own capacity for resilience and growth.

One powerful tool for cultivating a positive mindset is the practice of gratitude. By regularly taking time to reflect on the things we're thankful for - whether it's a supportive friend, a beautiful sunset, or a small personal victory - we train our brains to scan for the positive. We begin to notice and appreciate the blessings in our lives, even in the midst of difficulty.

Another strategy is to reframe our self-talk. When we catch ourselves engaging in negative inner dialogue - criticizing ourselves, predicting failure, or rehashing past hurts - we can consciously choose to replace those thoughts with more constructive ones. We can remind ourselves of our strengths, our progress, and our potential. We can speak to ourselves with the same kindness and encouragement we would offer to a beloved friend.

Over time, as we continue to practice these strategies, we begin to internalize a more resilient, optimistic outlook. We develop a deeper trust in ourselves and in life's unfolding. We become less reactive to external circumstances and more grounded in our own inner wisdom and strength.

Handling Setbacks and Challenges

No journey of rebuilding is without its setbacks and challenges. There will be days when we feel overwhelmed, discouraged, or tempted to slip back into old patterns. There will be moments when the task of creating a new life feels daunting, even impossible.

In these moments, it's important to have strategies in place to cope and maintain our momentum. One such strategy is developing a toolkit of healthy coping mechanisms. This could include practices like deep breathing, meditation, exercise, or spending time in nature. It could involve creative outlets like writing, painting, or playing music. Or it could mean reaching out for support from a trusted friend or professional.

The key is to have many tools that we can turn to in times of stress, so we don't resort to unhealthy coping mechanisms like substance abuse, self-isolation, or self-harm.

Another important strategy is learning to reframe setbacks as learning opportunities. When we encounter a challenge or roadblock, it's easy to get discouraged and feel like we've failed. But if we can shift our perspective and ask ourselves, "What can I learn from this? How can I grow from this experience?" we open ourselves up to new insights and possibilities.

We see that setbacks are not a reflection of our worth or capability, but simply a part of the learning and growth process. We develop a more resilient, adaptable mindset that lets us bounce back from difficulties and continue.

Seeking Inspiration and Support

As we navigate the ups and downs of rebuilding our lives, it is incredibly helpful to seek inspiration and support from others who have walked similar paths. Whether it's through reading memoirs, listening to podcasts, or connecting with mentors or role models, hearing the stories of those who have overcome adversity can provide both comfort and practical guidance.

These narratives can remind us we are not alone, that our struggles are valid and shared by many. They can offer insights into strategies and mindsets that have helped others to heal, grow, and thrive. And they can inspire us to keep going even in the darkest of times, to trust that a brighter future is possible.

In addition to seeking inspiration, it's also important to build a strong support network as we rebuild our lives. This could involve strengthening existing relationships with friends and family members who uplift and encourage us. It could mean seeking new connections through support groups, community organizations, or shared interest clubs.

The key is to surround ourselves with people who see our potential, who believe in our dreams, and who provide a safe space for us to be authentic and vulnerable. These relationships can offer not just emotional support, but also practical assistance, whether it's helping us move into a new apartment, connecting us with job opportunities, or simply showing up with a listening ear and an open heart.

Embracing the Journey

Ultimately, the journey of rebuilding our lives after removing toxic influences is a deeply personal and transformative one. This path requires courage, compassion, and a profound commitment to our own growth and well-being.

This journey will ask us to confront our deepest fears, to heal our most profound wounds, and to let go of the beliefs and patterns that no longer serve us. It will challenge us to step outside our comfort zones, to take risks and embrace uncertainty, and to trust in our own resilience and strength.

But it is also a journey of incredible possibility and potential. As we shed the weight of toxic relationships and situations, we create space for new, healthy connections to blossom. As we heal our wounds and reclaim our power, we tap into a deep well of inner wisdom and creativity. And as we clarify our values and vision for the future, we begin to craft a life that is authentic, fulfilling, and aligned with our deepest truths.

This journey is not a quick fix or a one-time event. It is a lifelong process of learning, growth, and self-discovery. There will be moments of doubt and difficulty, setbacks and challenges. But there will also be moments of profound joy, connection, and transformation.

The key is to approach this journey with patience, self-compassion, and a spirit of curiosity. To celebrate our victories, learn from our missteps, and trust in the unfolding of our unique path. To seek the support, resources, and inspiration that nourish us along the way, and to offer the same to others navigating their own journeys of healing and growth.

As we do this, we not only transform our own lives, but we also contribute to a larger shift in our communities and our world. We become a living testament to the power of resilience, the possibility of change, and the enduring human capacity for healing and hope.

So let us embrace this journey with an open heart and a courageous spirit. Let us trust in the wisdom of our own souls, the support of those who love us, and the guiding light of our highest aspirations. And let us remember that with each step we take, each choice we make, we are not only rebuilding our lives - we are creating a legacy of healing, growth, and transformation that will ripple out into the world in ways we can scarcely imagine.

The path may not be easy, but it is one of the most rewarding and meaningful journeys we can undertake. It is an invitation to reclaim our power, our purpose, and our most authentic selves. And it is a reminder that no matter where we've been or what we've endured, we always have the capacity to rise, to heal, and to create a life of profound beauty, meaning, and joy.

Case Study:

Meet Lila, a vibrant and creative woman in her mid-30s who, despite her many talents and achievements, felt stagnant and unfulfilled. For years, Lila had poured her energy into a high-stress job and toxic relationships, neglecting her own needs and desires. She had grown accustomed to putting others first, to reducing her own feelings and aspirations, and to tolerating behavior that left her feeling drained and went down.

One day, after a painful interaction with her partner, Lila had a moment of profound clarity. She realized that the life she was living was not the one she wanted, that the people and situations she was tolerating were holding her back from the growth and joy she craved. With a mixture of fear and exhilaration, Lila embarked on a journey of removing toxic influences from her life.

The first step was ending her unhealthy romantic relationship. Though the breakup was painful, and the aftermath was challenging, Lila found solace in reconnecting with friends and family members who had been pushed to the periphery during her relationship. She began to rediscover hobbies and interests that had fallen by the wayside, savoring the freedom to spend her time and energy on pursuits that nourished her.

At work, Lila started setting clearer boundaries and advocating for her needs. When her efforts were met with resistance or dismissal, she made the bold decision to leave her toxic work environment and start her own business – a dream she had long harbored but never felt empowered to pursue.

As Lila navigated these major life changes, she also began to cultivate a new mindset and environment. She decluttered her living space, creating a sanctuary that reflected her evolving tastes and supported her well-being. She started a daily gratitude practice, focusing on the abundance and opportunities in her life rather than dwelling on lack or limitations. And she surrounded herself with inspiring books, artwork, and people who uplifted and motivated her.

The journey was not without its challenges. There were moments of doubt and loneliness, setbacks and frustrations. But Lila met these challenges with a growing sense of resilience and self-trust. She sought support from a therapist and joined a women's empowerment group, finding strength in connecting with others on similar paths of growth and self-discovery.

As time passed, Lila began to notice profound shifts in her life. She felt lighter, more energized, and more at peace with herself. Her new business was thriving, and she was building a community of clients and collaborators who shared her values and vision. She was attracting healthier, more supportive relationships, and deepening her connections with the people who mattered to her.

Perhaps most significantly, Lila had a newfound sense of self-love and self-respect. She no longer tolerated mistreatment or settled for less than she deserved. She spoke her truth, even when it was difficult, and trusted her intuition to guide her toward what was right for her. She embraced her imperfections and celebrated her victories, recognizing that both were essential parts of her growth journey.

Looking back on her transformation, Lila realized that removing toxic influences from her life was not a singular event, but an ongoing process of choosing herself, again and again. It was a commitment to honoring her own needs, desires, and boundaries, even when it meant disappointing others or venturing into unknown territory. It was a daily practice of aligning her thoughts, her environment, and her relationships with her highest values and aspirations.

Lila's story is a powerful reminder we all have the capacity to change our lives by changing what we tolerate and what we focus on. By daring to remove the people and situations that drain us, we create space for new, nourishing influences to enter. By cultivating a mindset and environment that support our growth, we become a magnet for more positivity and possibility. And by honoring our own worth and potential, we give others permission to do the same.

The journey of removing toxic influences and rebuilding our lives is a courageous and transformative one. It asks us to confront our fears, to grieve our losses, and to trust in our own resilience and wisdom. It requires patience, self-compassion, and a willingness to embrace change and uncertainty. But it is also a journey of immense freedom, empowerment, and joy – a reclamation of our right to thrive and to create a life that reflects our deepest truths.

As we navigate this path, may we draw strength from the stories of those like Lila who have walked it before us. May we seek the support, resources, and inspiration that nourish us along the way. And may we always remember that no matter where we start or what we encounter, we have the power within us to rise, to heal, and to build a life of profound beauty and meaning – one choice, one step, one day at a time.

≈

PART SEVEN WRAP-UP:

KEY POINTS:

• Toxic influences, such as negative relationships, environments, and mindsets, can significantly hinder personal growth, well-being, and fulfillment.

• Recognizing and acknowledging toxicity in one's life is the first step toward making positive changes and reclaiming personal power.

• Removing toxic influences is a courageous and transformative process that requires self-awareness, boundary setting, and a commitment to personal well-being.

• Healing from the impact of toxic experiences involves seeking support, practicing self-care, and allowing oneself time and space to process emotions and experiences.

• Cultivating a positive mindset, through practices such as gratitude, reframing negative thoughts, and surrounding oneself with uplifting influences, is essential for rebuilding a life aligned with one's values and aspirations.

• Rebuilding one's life after removing toxic influences is an ongoing journey of personal growth, self-discovery, and empowerment.

• Setbacks and challenges are a normal part of the growth process and can be reframed as opportunities for learning and development.

• Seeking inspiration and support from others who have navigated similar experiences can provide guidance, encouragement, and a sense of community on the journey of personal transformation.

Action Items:

• Reflect on the presence of toxic influences in your life, and honestly assess their impact on your well-being and personal growth.

• Set clear, firm boundaries with individuals or situations that consistently drain your energy or undermine your self-worth.

• Seek support from trusted friends, family members, or professionals to help you navigate the challenges of removing toxic influences and healing from their impact.

• Develop a self-care plan that includes activities and practices that nourish your physical, emotional, and mental well-being.

• Cultivate a daily gratitude practice, focusing on the positive aspects of your life and the opportunities for growth and learning.

• Challenge negative self-talk and reframe limiting beliefs by practicing self-compassion and positive affirmations.

• Surround yourself with uplifting influences, such as inspiring books, podcasts, or people who embody the qualities and mindsets you wish to cultivate.

• Set meaningful goals for your personal growth and development, and celebrate your progress along the way.

• Embrace setbacks and challenges as opportunities for learning and growth, and develop healthy coping strategies to navigate difficult moments.

• Seek communities, resources, and mentors that can support and inspire you on your journey of personal transformation.

In our next part…

… we'll dive into the transformative power of embracing challenges and turning obstacles into opportunities for growth and self-discovery. We'll explore how adopting a resilient mindset can help you navigate life's inevitable setbacks with grace and determination, letting you emerge stronger and wiser from each experience. Get ready to learn practical strategies for cultivating perseverance, maintaining a positive outlook, and leveraging the lessons hidden within every challenge.

As we start this journey of personal development, we'll also uncover the importance of continuous learning and adaptability in the face of change. You'll discover how setting realistic goals, seeking support, and celebrating your victories, no matter how small, can keep you motivated and focused on your growth. By the end of this part, you'll have a powerful toolkit for transforming adversity into a catalyst for your success and well-being, enabling you to create a life of purpose, fulfillment, and endless possibilities.

PART EIGHT
THE ALCHEMY OF ADVERSITY: TRANSFORMING CHALLENGES INTO OPPORTUNITIES FOR GROWTH

INTRODUCTION TO OVERCOMING CHALLENGES

LIFE's inherent challenges offer profound opportunities for growth and self-discovery. Instead of perceiving obstacles as mere hindrances, viewing them as essential catalysts for personal development can significantly change our approach to life's difficulties.

In the journey of rebuilding our lives after removing toxic influences, challenges are an inevitable part of the process. We may face setbacks, doubts, and moments of uncertainty as we navigate the uncharted territory of creating a new life for ourselves. But it is in these very challenges we find the greatest opportunities for transformation and growth.

Understanding the Value of Challenges

Challenges, whether they appear in our personal lives, careers, or relationships, test our resilience and adaptability. Each obstacle presents a unique opportunity to develop critical skills and deepen our understanding of ourselves and the world.

Growth Through Adversity: Challenges push us beyond our comfort zones, forcing us to adapt and grow. This growth is often as developed resilience, new skills, or a better understanding of our capabilities.

When we face difficulties in our journey of rebuilding, we are called to tap into inner strengths we may not have known we had. We learn to problem-solve, to think creatively, and to persevere in the face of uncertainty. These are skills that will serve us not just in the immediate challenge, but in all areas of our lives going forward.

Self-Discovery: Overcoming obstacles often requires us to tap into our inner resources, revealing strengths we may not have realized we possessed. This process of self-discovery can increase our confidence and self-efficacy. As we navigate the challenges of creating a new life, we may discover passions, talents, and values that had been suppressed in our previous situations. We may find we are more capable, more creative, and more resilient than we ever believed possible. This self-discovery is a gift that can inform and enrich our lives long after the immediate challenge has passed.

Resilience Building: Each challenge we overcome builds our resilience, making us better equipped to handle future difficulties. This resilience is essential for navigating the complexities of life. In rebuilding our lives, we are likely to face many challenges - financial, emotional, relational, and practical. But with each obstacle we overcome, we develop a greater sense of our own strength and capability. We learn that we can handle difficult situations, that we can adapt and persevere. This resilience becomes a reservoir we can draw on in future times of stress or uncertainty.

Strategies for Turning Obstacles into Opportunities

Reframe Your Perspective: Shift your mindset to view challenges as opportunities. Ask yourself, "What can I learn from this situation?" or "How can this challenge make me stronger?" When we face a setback in our journey of rebuilding, it's easy to get discouraged or feel like we've failed. But if we can reframe the situation as an opportunity for learning and growth, we open ourselves up to new possibilities. Maybe a job loss is a chance to explore a new career path. Maybe a relationship ending is a chance to deepen our relationship with ourselves. By consciously shifting our perspective, we can transform obstacles into catalysts for positive change.

Set Realistic Goals: Break down the challenge into manageable parts and set achievable goals. This approach can help maintain motivation and prevent feelings of overwhelm. Rebuilding our lives can feel daunting when viewed as a whole. But if we can break it down into smaller, achievable steps, it becomes more manageable. Setting realistic goals also helps us to celebrate our progress along the way, rather than getting fixated on a distant end point. By focusing on what's right in front of us, we can maintain a sense of momentum and accomplishment.

Seek Learning Opportunities: Every obstacle offers a chance to learn something new, whether it's a skill, a life lesson, or insight into your personality. Embrace the learning part of the challenge. If we're struggling to adjust to a new living situation, maybe it's a chance to learn about home repair or interior design. If we're navigating a difficult conversation with a family member, maybe it's an opportunity to practice assertive communication or boundary setting. By approaching challenges with a learning mindset, we can gain valuable skills and insights that enrich our lives far beyond the immediate situation.

Leverage Support Networks: Don't face challenges alone. Lean on friends, family, or colleagues for support, advice, and encouragement. Sometimes, just knowing you're not alone can make a significant difference. In the journey of rebuilding, it's especially important to have a strong support system. This could include a therapist, a support group, or trusted loved ones who can offer a listening ear and practical assistance. Letting others help us not only eases the practical burden of challenges, but also reminds us we are cared for and valued.

Celebrate Small Victories: Recognize and celebrate your progress, no matter how small. This can boost your morale and motivation to continue pushing forward. In a major life overhaul, it's easy to get focused on the end goal and overlook the smaller milestones along the way. But each step forward is worthy of celebration. Maybe it's successfully navigating a difficult conversation or setting up your new living space the way you want it or sticking to a new self-care routine for a week. Acknowledging these victories helps to maintain a sense of progress and accomplishment.

Maintain a Positive Attitude: Keep a positive attitude through affirmations, gratitude, and mindfulness. A positive mindset can significantly affect your ability to tackle challenges effectively. This doesn't mean denying the difficulty of the situation, but choosing to focus on the good that can come from it. Practices like daily gratitude, positive self-talk, and mindfulness can help to keep us grounded in the present moment and open to possibilities. When we approach challenges with a sense of optimism and curiosity, we are more likely to spot opportunities for growth and transformation.

Encouragement and Motivation

Remember, everyone faces challenges, but not everyone sees them as opportunities for growth. By embracing obstacles with a proactive and positive mindset, you can not only overcome them but also emerge stronger and more capable. Keep pushing forward, stay adaptable, and use each challenge as a steppingstone toward achieving your personal and professional goals. The journey through challenges is where true growth occurs.

When rebuilding our lives, challenges are not a sign that we're doing something wrong - they are a sign that we are doing something courageous and transformative. Each obstacle we face is a testament to our strength, our resilience, and our commitment to creating a life that aligns with our deepest values and aspirations.

So, when you find yourself in the midst of a challenge, remember that you are not alone. Remember that you have within you the wisdom, the strength, and the creativity to not just survive, but to thrive. Remember that each challenge is an invitation to grow, to learn, and to become the most empowered version of yourself.

Embrace the journey, trust the process, and know that with each challenge you overcome, you are one step closer to the life you envision for yourself. You are one step closer to a life of authenticity, fulfillment, and unbounded possibility.

The path of rebuilding is not an easy one, but it is a path worth taking. It is a path of courage, of resilience, and of profound personal transformation. And with each challenge you turn into an opportunity, you are not just changing your own life - you are becoming a beacon of hope and inspiration for others navigating their own journeys of growth and healing.

So, keep going. Keep growing. Keep turning obstacles into opportunities. The life you are creating for yourself is a testament to your strength, your courage, and your boundless capacity for transformation. Embrace the challenges, for they will shape you into the person you are meant to become.

~

UNDERSTANDING THE
POWER OF MINDSET

OUR MINDSET SHAPES our perception of challenges and our capacity to overcome them. It influences our daily interactions, our approach to problem-solving, and our resilience in the face of adversity.

In the journey of rebuilding our lives after removing toxic influences, our mindset is one of the most powerful tools we have. The way we think about ourselves, our circumstances, and our ability to change can make the difference between feeling stuck and overwhelmed, or feeling empowered and motivated to create the life we want.

Fixed Mindset vs. Growth Mindset

Fixed Mindset:

• **Belief:** Abilities are static and unchangeable.

• **Impact:** Individuals with a fixed mindset may avoid challenges, fearing failure as a negative reflection on their inherent abilities.

• **Result:** This mindset can limit personal growth as it discourages stepping out of comfort zones and engaging with potentially enriching experiences.

When rebuilding our lives, a fixed mindset can be limiting. We may tell ourselves that we're not strong enough to leave a toxic situation, that we'll never find happiness or success, or that we're destined to repeat past patterns. This thinking keeps us stuck and prevents us from seeing and seizing opportunities for growth and change.

Growth Mindset:

• **Belief:** Abilities and intelligence can be developed through dedication and hard work.

• **Impact:** Embraces challenges and sees failures as valuable learning opportunities.

• **Result:** Promotes lifelong learning and resilience, enhancing personal and professional growth.

But a growth mindset is empowering when we're navigating major life transitions. With a growth mindset, we can develop new skills, build new relationships, and create new patterns of living. We see challenges as opportunities to learn and grow, and we're more resilient in the face of setbacks. This mindset lets us approach the rebuilding process with a sense of curiosity, adaptability, and hope.

Strategies to Develop a Growth Mindset

A growth mindset is a transformative process that can change how you face life's challenges:

Embrace Challenges:

• **Action:** Actively seek new challenges that push the boundaries of your comfort zone.

• **Benefit:** Each challenge is a chance to grow and refine your skills.

In rebuilding our lives, we will inevitably face many challenges - finding new housing, navigating changed relationships, establishing new routines and support systems. By embracing these challenges as opportunities for growth, rather than as threats to our wellbeing, we maintain a sense of agency and empowerment. We can actively seek challenges that help us develop new skills and strengths.

View Failures as Learning Opportunities:

• **Action:** Reflect on failures to extract lessons and insights.

• **Benefit:** Transforming setbacks into learning opportunities fosters resilience and perseverance.

There will probably be many moments in the rebuilding process where we feel like we've failed - a job interview that doesn't go well, a relapse into old patterns, a conflict with a loved one. But with a growth mindset, we can reframe these experiences as opportunities for learning and self-reflection. We can ask ourselves what we can do differently next time, what support we might need, or what the experience reveals about our values and priorities. This helps us to maintain momentum and motivation in the face of challenges.

Cultivate a Love for Learning:

• **Action:** Engage in continuous education and seek knowledge for the sake of learning.

• **Benefit:** Keeps you intellectually stimulated and prepared to adapt to change.

A love of learning is a powerful asset in the rebuilding process. It lets us approach new situations with curiosity and openness, rather than fear or resistance. We can seek information and resources that help us navigate this new chapter of life - whether that's through reading self-help books, attending workshops, or engaging with supportive communities. Continuously expanding our knowledge and skills helps us feel equipped to handle whatever challenges come our way.

Practice Self-Compassion:

• **Action:** Treat yourself with kindness and understanding during times of difficulty.

• **Benefit:** Encourages a healthy relationship with yourself and mitigates the impact of negative self-talk.

Rebuilding our lives can be an emotionally taxing process, and it's likely that we'll have moments of doubt, frustration, or self-criticism. Self-compassion is essential for maintaining a growth mindset through these difficult times. This means treating ourselves with the same kindness and understanding we would offer to a dear friend - acknowledging our pain, reminding ourselves that setbacks are part of the human experience, and affirming our inherent worth and capability. Self-compassion helps us to bounce back from challenges and to maintain a positive, growth-oriented outlook.

Surround Yourself with Positivity:

• **Action:** Build relationships with mentors and peers who encourage your growth.

• **Benefit:** A supportive environment can enhance motivation and provide guidance during challenging times.

The people we surround ourselves with have a profound impact on our mindset and our ability to grow through challenges. As we rebuild our lives, it's important to cultivate relationships with people who support our journey - whether that's a therapist, a mentor, a support group, or friends and family members who believe in our ability to change and grow. These positive relationships can provide encouragement, perspective, and practical guidance as we navigate new terrain. They remind us that we're not alone, and that growth is always possible.

Chapter Summary: Harnessing the Power of Mindset

The transition from a fixed mindset to a growth mindset doesn't happen overnight but is a rewarding investment in your personal development. By embracing the principles of a growth mindset, you open yourself up to a world of possibilities where every obstacle is an opportunity to learn, grow, and become more adept at navigating the complexities of life. Let your mindset be the catalyst for transformation as you turn life's obstacles into steppingstones for success.

In the journey of rebuilding our lives, a growth mindset is an invaluable ally. It lets us approach challenges with resilience, adaptability, and a sense of empowerment. It helps us to reframe setbacks as opportunities for learning and growth, and to maintain a sense of hope and possibility even in the face of difficulties.

Cultivating a growth mindset is a daily practice - it requires self-awareness, self-compassion, and a willingness to step outside our comfort zones. But the rewards are immeasurable. With a growth mindset, we not only navigate the challenges of rebuilding with greater ease and resilience - we also open ourselves up to a life of continuous learning, development, and fulfillment.

So as you start this brave journey of rebuilding, remember the power of your mindset. Embrace challenges, learn from failures, cultivate self-compassion, and surround yourself with positivity. Know that with every challenge you face, you are growing stronger, wiser, and more capable of creating the life you envision for yourself.

Your mindset is the lens through which you view your life, your challenges, and your potential. By choosing to adopt a growth mindset, you are choosing to see every obstacle as an opportunity, every setback as a setup for a comeback, and every challenge as a chance to become the most resilient, empowered version of yourself.

Trust in the transformative power of your mindset. Let it be your north star as you navigate the uncharted territories of your new life. And know that with a growth mindset, there is no limit to what you can learn, who you can become, and what you can achieve. Your journey of rebuilding is also a journey of becoming - and with a growth mindset, it's a journey of limitless possibility.

$\sim$

RECOGNIZING COMMON CHALLENGES AND OBSTACLES

Life is replete with challenges that can manifest in various parts of our lives, from personal and professional realms to health-related issues. Understanding these common obstacles can help us prepare and develop strategies to navigate them effectively.

When rebuilding our lives after removing toxic influences, we are likely to face a unique set of challenges. These may include the emotional aftermath of the toxic situation, the practical challenges of starting over, and the internal obstacles that can arise as we navigate this new chapter. By recognizing these common challenges, we can normalize our experiences and develop targeted strategies for overcoming them.

Personal Challenges

Self-Doubt and Low Self-Esteem:

• **Example:** Consider Jane, who has recently left an emotionally abusive relationship. Despite knowing she made the right decision; she struggles with self-doubt and feelings of worthlessness. The years of criticism and gaslighting have taken a toll on her self-esteem, making it difficult for her to trust her own judgment and believe in her ability to create a better life.

In rebuilding our lives, self-doubt and low self-esteem can be significant obstacles. We may question our ability to make good decisions, to succeed on our own, or to create healthy relationships. These doubts are often the echoes of the toxic influences we've left behind. With time, self-compassion, and supportive resources, we can rebuild our sense of self-worth and learn to trust ourselves again.

Grief and Loss:

• **Anecdote:** Mark has recently cut ties with a toxic family member. While he knows it was necessary for his well-being, he struggles with feelings of grief and loss. He misses the good times and the sense of familiarity, even as he acknowledges the harm the relationship caused. He wonders if he'll ever feel whole again without this person in his life.

Removing toxic influences, even when necessary, can involve a profound sense of loss. We may grieve the relationship we wished we had, the dreams we had for the future, or the sense of belonging we found, even in a dysfunctional situation. This grief is a natural part of the healing process. By honoring our feelings and seeking support, we can gradually transform our grief into a renewed sense of self and purpose.

Practical Challenges

Financial Instability:

• **Example:** After leaving a toxic work environment, Sarah finds herself without a stable income. She has savings, but the uncertainty of her financial future is a significant source of stress. She worries about how she'll pay her bills, whether she'll find a new job, and if she made the right decision in leaving.

Rebuilding our lives often involves practical challenges, like financial instability. We may have to leave a job, a living situation, or a relationship that provided financial security, even if it was toxic. This can be frightening and stressful, but our well-being is worth more than any material security. By reaching out for support, making a plan, and taking things one step at a time, we can navigate this uncertainty and build a more stable foundation for our new life.

Redefining Relationships:

• **Anecdote:** After distancing herself from a toxic friend group, Lisa feels lonely and unsure of how to build new connections. She knows her old friendships were unhealthy, but they were also familiar. She's uncertain how to navigate social situations without falling back into old patterns or attracting similar types of people.

As we remove toxic influences, we may need to redefine many of our relationships. This can involve setting new boundaries, learning new communication skills, and being discerning about the people we allow into our lives. It can be a challenging and sometimes lonely process, but it's also an opportunity to build healthier, more fulfilling connections. By being patient with ourselves, seeking supportive communities, and staying true to our values, we can gradually build a network of relationships that uplift and inspire us.

Health-Related Challenges

Coping with Trauma:

• **Example:** After leaving an abusive situation, Michael struggles with symptoms of trauma. He has flashbacks, nightmares, and difficulty feeling safe. He knows he needs help to process what he's been through, but he's unsure where to turn or how to begin healing.

Toxic situations, whether they involve abuse, neglect, or chronic stress, can leave us with the lingering effects of trauma. As we rebuild our lives, we may struggle with anxiety, depression, PTSD, or other mental health challenges. These are normal responses to abnormal situations, and that healing is possible. Seeking professional help, whether through therapy, support groups, or other resources, can be a brave and transformative step in our journey of rebuilding.

Self-Care and Stress Management:

• **Anecdote:** As Emily navigates the challenges of rebuilding her life, she neglects her own needs. She's so focused on practical tasks and trying to stay positive she forgets to eat regular meals, get enough sleep, or take time for activities that bring her joy. She feels exhausted, overwhelmed, and on the verge of burnout.

When rebuilding, it is easy to put our own needs last. We may feel pressure to be strong, to keep pushing forward, and to prove that we made the right decision. However, self-care and stress management are essential for our resilience and well-being. By focusing on our physical, emotional, and mental health, we give ourselves the resources we need to navigate challenges and build a life that sustains us. This can involve developing a self-care routine, learning stress management techniques, and being compassionate with ourselves when we need rest or support.

Navigating These Challenges

Recognizing these common challenges is the first step in overcoming them. Here are strategies to help navigate these obstacles:

• **Seek Support:** Whether it's professional counseling, a mentor, or a support group, external help can provide guidance and accountability. In rebuilding our lives, having a supportive network is important. This can include friends and family who understand our situation, as well as professionals who can offer objective guidance and coping strategies. Knowing that we're not alone and that help is available can make all the difference in navigating the challenges of this journey.

• **Set Realistic Goals:** Break your goals into manageable steps that can help you gradually overcome your challenges without feeling overwhelmed. In rebuilding, it's important to be patient with ourselves and to celebrate each small victory. Setting realistic, incremental goals can help us maintain a sense of progress and empowerment, even when the bigger picture feels daunting.

• **Practice Self-Compassion:** Be kind to yourself. Acknowledge that setbacks are part of the journey and do not define your worth or capabilities. Rebuilding our lives is a brave and difficult process. There will be moments of doubt, frustration, and exhaustion. By treating ourselves with the same compassion we'd offer a dear friend, we can weather these challenges with greater resilience and grace. Self-compassion lets us learn from setbacks, to forgive ourselves for mistakes, and to keep hope and determination.

• **Develop Resilience:** Learn from each experience to build your resilience. Understanding that challenges are opportunities for growth can transform your approach to facing them. Every challenge we face in rebuilding our lives has the potential to make us stronger, wiser, and more adaptable. By viewing obstacles as opportunities for growth, we can maintain a sense of purpose and empowerment even in the face of difficulty. Resilience is not about avoiding challenges, but about developing the skills and mindset to meet them with courage and flexibility.

Chapter Summary: Embracing Challenges as Opportunities

By understanding and recognizing the common challenges in various areas of our lives, we can better equip ourselves to tackle them head-on. Remember, each challenge carries a lesson and an opportunity to grow stronger and wiser. Embrace these opportunities and let them guide you to a more fulfilled and resilient life.

In the journey of rebuilding after toxic influences, challenges are inevitable. We will face internal obstacles, like self-doubt and grief, as well as external ones, like financial instability and the need to redefine relationships. We may struggle with the aftermath of trauma and the ongoing need for self-care and stress management.

But with each challenge we face, we also have an opportunity to develop new strengths, insights, and capacities. We can learn to trust ourselves, to build healthier connections, to advocate for our needs, and to cultivate deep wells of resilience. We can discover our own courage, creativity, and adaptability in the face of change and uncertainty.

As we navigate these challenges, it's essential to be patient and compassionate with ourselves. Rebuilding is not a linear process, and there will be setbacks and difficult days. But by staying connected to our support systems, setting realistic goals, practicing self-care, and maintaining a growth mindset, we can gradually transform these obstacles into opportunities for profound personal transformation.

Remember, you are not alone in this journey. Many have walked this path before you and have found their way to a life of greater joy, authenticity, and fulfillment. By embracing the challenges of rebuilding as invitations to grow, heal, and discover your own

∼

STRATEGIES FOR RESILIENCE AND PERSEVERANCE

When faced with life's inevitable challenges, building resilience and fostering perseverance are essential for overcoming them successfully. Here's how you can develop these important skills through practical strategies and techniques:

When rebuilding our lives after removing toxic influences, resilience and perseverance are more than just helpful skills - they are essential survival tools. The journey of rebuilding is often marked by setbacks, uncertainties, and emotional challenges that can test our resolve and make us question our path. By cultivating resilience and perseverance, we give ourselves the strength and adaptability to weather these storms and keep moving toward the life we envision.

Setting Realistic Goals

• **Importance:** Setting achievable goals provides a sense of direction and a measurable standard of progress, which can be motivating during tough times.

• **How to Implement:** Break your larger goals into smaller, manageable tasks that make the journey seem less daunting. Celebrate small victories along the way to maintain momentum and motivation.

When rebuilding our lives, it's important to set goals that are both meaningful and attainable. We may have grand visions of the life we want to create, but we need to break these down into concrete, manageable steps. For example, if our goal is to build a new career after leaving a toxic work environment, we might start by updating our resume, contacting professional contacts, and identifying job opportunities that align with our values and skills.

By setting realistic milestones and celebrating each achievement along the way, we maintain a sense of progress and empowerment. This is important in the rebuilding process, as it can often feel like we're starting from scratch or taking one step forward and two steps back. Recognizing and honoring our incremental victories helps us maintain perspective and motivation, even when the bigger picture feels overwhelming.

Seeking Support

• **Importance:** No one is an island, and having a support system can make a significant difference in how effectively you navigate challenges.

• **How to Implement:** Build a network of supportive friends, family, or professionals who understand and encourage your goals. Don't hesitate to reach out for help when you need it, whether it's for advice, encouragement, or simply a listening ear.

In rebuilding our lives, having a strong support system is non-negotiable. We need people who understand what we've been through, who believe in our potential, and who can offer guidance and encouragement when we're feeling lost or discouraged. This might include friends or family members who have stood by us through the toxic situation, a therapist who can help us process our experiences, or a support group of individuals who have gone through similar challenges.

Be proactive in building and maintaining these support networks. This might involve contacting old friends, joining community organizations, or seeking professional resources. It also means being open and honest about our needs and struggles and being willing to accept help when it's offered. Remembering we need not navigate this journey alone can be a profound source of strength and resilience.

Practicing Self-Care

• **Importance:** Regular self-care is important for maintaining both physical and mental health, enabling you to face challenges with greater vitality and a clearer mind.

• **How to Implement:** Integrate activities into your routine that help reduce stress and improve well-being, such as exercise, meditation, hobbies, or enough rest. Remember, self-care is not selfish—it's necessary.

Self-care is often one of the first things to fall by the wayside when we're in survival mode, but it's also one of the most important factors in our resilience and perseverance. When we're rebuilding our lives, we're often dealing with intense emotions, practical challenges, and the ongoing effects of trauma or stress. Taking care of ourselves physically, emotionally, and mentally gives us the resources we need to keep going, even when things are tough.

This can look different for everyone, but some common self-care practices include getting enough sleep, eating nourishing foods, engaging in physical activity, spending time in nature, practicing mindfulness or meditation, and making time for hobbies or activities that bring us joy. It also means setting boundaries, asking for help when we need it, and giving ourselves permission to rest and recharge.

Remember, self-care isn't a luxury or a reward for when we've "earned" it. It's a fundamental necessity for our well-being and our ability to navigate challenges with resilience and grace.

Staying Positive

• **Importance:** Maintaining a positive outlook can help you manage stress and setbacks enabling you to stay focused and motivated.

• **How to Implement:** Practice gratitude by regularly noting things you are thankful for; this can shift your perspective from what's going wrong to what's going right. Use affirmations to reinforce a positive self-image and outlook.

Staying positive in the face of adversity is easier said than done, but it's an important skill in the rebuilding process. When we've been through toxic situations, it's easy to get stuck in negative thought patterns, expecting the worst or doubting our own capabilities. But by consciously cultivating a positive outlook, we can reframe our challenges as opportunities for growth and maintain hope and motivation even in difficult times.

One powerful practice is gratitude. Even in the darkest of times, there are always things we can be thankful for - a supportive friend, a moment of beauty, a personal strength we've discovered. By regularly acknowledging these things, whether through journaling, sharing with others, or simply appreciating them, we train our brains to look for the good. This doesn't mean denying the hard things, but it helps us maintain perspective and see the possibilities and the problems.

Affirmations can also be a useful tool for staying positive. These are simple statements that affirm our worth, our capabilities, and our potential. They might be phrases like "I am resilient," "I am capable of creating the life I want," or "I trust in my journey." By repeating these affirmations, especially in moments of doubt or stress, we reinforce a positive self-image and outlook.

Remember, positivity isn't about pretending everything is perfect. It's about choosing to focus on what we can control, what we have to be grateful for, and what we're learning through our challenges. It's a practice, not a perfect state, and one that can make a profound difference in our ability to persevere.

Adapting and Being Flexible

• **Importance:** Flexibility is a key part of resilience. Being adaptable in the face of changing circumstances can help you manage stress and overcome challenges.

• **How to Implement:** Stay open to new methods, ideas, and approaches, especially when faced with setbacks. Learn to pivot and adjust your strategies as necessary, viewing each change as a learning opportunity rather than a failure.

Rebuilding our lives after toxic influences is rarely a linear or predictable process. We will face unexpected challenges, setbacks, and changes of plan. Our ability to adapt and be flexible in the face of these changes allows us to keep even when our original roadmap no longer applies.

This means being open to trying new things, even if they're outside our comfort zone. It means being willing to adjust our goals or strategies when our initial plans aren't working. It means viewing setbacks as opportunities to learn and grow, rather than as failures or dead-ends.

For example, if we're struggling to find a job in our chosen field after leaving a toxic work environment, being adaptable might mean considering a different industry, seeking additional training or education, or exploring freelance or entrepreneurial options. If a relationship isn't providing the support we need in our healing process, being flexible might mean setting new boundaries, seeking new connections, or redefining what we need from our social network.

The key is to stay focused on our overall vision and values, while being willing to adjust our path as needed. By staying open, curious, and willing to learn, we develop the flexibility and adaptability that are cornerstones of resilience.

Encouragement for the Journey

Building resilience and perseverance is not about never failing but about bouncing back after setbacks. It's about the courage to continue that counts. Remember, each challenge you overcome is a testament to your strength and a step toward greater growth.

In the journey of rebuilding, there will be moments when you feel like giving up. There will be days when the challenges seem insurmountable, and the future feels uncertain. In these moments, remember the resilience and perseverance you've already shown in getting to this point. Remember the toxic influences you've had the courage to leave behind, the new life you're working to create, and the unshakable worth and potential you carry.

Each setback you face is an opportunity to learn, to grow, and to prove to yourself just how strong and capable you are. Each goal you achieve, no matter how small, is a testament to your determination and your ability to create change. Each day you choose to keep going, to take care of yourself, to reach out for support, and to believe in your journey, you are building the resilience and perseverance that will carry you through.

This journey is not about perfection. It's about progress, growth, and the courage to keep showing up for yourself, even in the face of adversity. It's about learning to be kind to yourself, to celebrate your strengths, and to forgive your missteps. It's about surrounding yourself with people who see your worth and support your healing, and about learning to be that person for yourself, too.

There will be days when you feel like you're taking two steps forward and one step back. There will be moments of doubt, fear, and exhaustion. But there will also be moments of profound pride, joy, and self-discovery. Sometimes, you surprise yourself with your own strength, resilience, and capacity for change.

Through it all, remember that you are not alone. You are part of a community of survivors, of individuals who have faced the darkness and chosen to keep reaching for the light. Draw strength from their stories, their support, and their belief in your potential.

And most importantly, draw strength from yourself. Remember that you have survived so much, and that each day you choose to keep going is a victory. Remember that your worth is not defined by your challenges, but by the courage, compassion, and determination you bring to facing them.

This journey of rebuilding is not a sprint, but a marathon. It requires patience, persistence, and a willingness to keep putting one foot in front of the other, even when the path ahead is unclear. But with each step, you are moving closer to the life you deserve - a life of safety, healing, and joy.

So, keep going. Keep setting goals and celebrating victories. Keep reaching out for support and offering it to others. Keep practicing self-care and self-compassion. Keep believing in your own resilience and potential.

And most of all, keep showing up for yourself, even in the toughest of times. Because that is the heart of resilience - the unwavering commitment to your own healing, growth, and happiness, no matter what challenges come your way.

You've got this. And you are worth every step of this journey.

TURNING SETBACKS INTO OPPORTUNITIES

Setbacks and failures are inevitable parts of life, but they can also serve as powerful catalysts for growth and success. By reframing how we perceive these challenges, we can transform them into opportunities for personal development and achievement.

This is especially true when rebuilding our lives after toxic situations. The journey of healing and growth is rarely linear, and setbacks are a natural part of the process. But by learning to view these challenges as opportunities for learning and self-discovery, we can maintain our momentum and motivation, even in the face of adversity.

Inspirational Success Stories

J.K. Rowling:

• **Story:** Before achieving fame with the Harry Potter series, J.K. Rowling faced many rejections from publishers. She persisted despite these setbacks, driven by her passion and belief in her stories.

• **Lesson:** Rowling's experience teaches us that perseverance in the face of rejection can eventually lead to success. Use rejection as a motivator to improve and persist.

Rowling's story is a powerful reminder that success often comes after multiple failures and rejections. When rebuilding, we may face rejection or disappointment in many forms - a job application turned down, a friendship that doesn't pan out, a goal that takes longer to achieve than we hoped. But by maintaining our belief in ourselves and our vision, and by using each rejection as fuel for our determination, we can keep moving forward.

Steve Jobs:

• **Story:** Steve Jobs was famously ousted from Apple, the company he co-founded. This setback didn't deter him; instead, he founded NeXT and Pixar, leading to new successes that eventually brought him back to Apple.

• **Lesson:** Jobs' comeback story exemplifies how a setback can be a setup for a comeback. When faced with failure, look for new opportunities to innovate and grow.

Jobs' experience shows that even the most devastating professional setbacks can open up new doors and opportunities. For those rebuilding after leaving a toxic work environment, this is an important lesson. Losing a job or a career path can feel like the end of the world, but it can also be the beginning of a new chapter. By staying open to new possibilities and being willing to innovate and take risks, we can find new avenues for success and fulfillment.

Oprah Winfrey:

• **Story:** Oprah was fired from her first television job as a news anchor. Instead of letting this derail her aspirations, she pursued a career in daytime TV, eventually becoming a global media leader.

• **Lesson:** Oprah's resilience shows us that sometimes, a career setback can redirect you to opportunities that align more closely with your strengths and passions.

Oprah's story is a testament to the power of resilience and adaptability. Sometimes, a setback is actually a redirection to our true path. For those rebuilding after toxic relationships or experiences, this can be a powerful realization. The end of a relationship or a community that wasn't serving us can be painful, but it can also free us up to discover connections and experiences that are more authentic and nurturing.

Actionable Advice to Leverage Setbacks

Reflect and Learn:

• Take time to analyze what went wrong and why. This reflection can provide insights that improve your skills or strategies.

When rebuilding, reflection is an important tool. When we face a setback, it's important to step back and ask ourselves what we can learn from the experience. This might involve examining our own actions and choices, seeking feedback from others, or simply sitting with our emotions and letting insights emerge. By treating each setback as a learning opportunity, we can gain wisdom and self-awareness that will serve us well.

Stay Resilient:

• Develop a resilient mindset that sees failure as a temporary state. Focus on long-term goals rather than short-term setbacks.

Resilience is the cornerstone of successful rebuilding. It's the ability to bounce back from setbacks, to keep going even when things are tough, and to maintain hope and determination in the face of adversity. To cultivate resilience, it's important to develop a long-term perspective. Remind yourself that this setback is temporary, and that your ultimate goals and values are still within reach. Surround yourself with supportive people, engage in self-care practices, and celebrate your strengths and successes, no matter how small.

Seek Feedback:

• Constructive criticism is invaluable. Seek feedback to understand different perspectives and areas for improvement.

When rebuilding, it's easy to get stuck in our own perspective or to be overly self-critical. Seeking feedback from trusted sources can provide valuable insights and help us see our situation in a new light. This might involve asking for input from a therapist, a mentor, or a supportive friend. Be open to constructive criticism, but also remember to filter feedback through your own inner wisdom and values. Not all advice will be relevant or helpful, but by staying open to new perspectives, we can learn and grow.

Adjust Your Path:

• Be willing to change your plans based on what you learn from setbacks. Flexibility can lead to better-suited opportunities and outcomes.

Rebuilding often involves a lot of trial and error. What worked for us in the past may no longer serve us, and what we thought we wanted may be different from what we actually need. By staying flexible and open to adjusting our path, we can navigate setbacks more easily and find our way to a life that fulfills us. This might mean letting go of old dreams or expectations, trying new things, or taking a different route to our goals. The key is to stay true to our core values and vision, while being willing to adapt our strategies as needed.

Maintain a Positive Outlook:

• Stay optimistic and view challenges as growth opportunities. A positive attitude will not only keep you motivated but also attract the right resources and people to support your journey.

Finally, maintaining a positive outlook is essential for leveraging setbacks into opportunities. This doesn't mean denying or reducing the pain or difficulty of our experiences but choosing to focus on the potential for growth and learning. By reframing challenges as opportunities, we open ourselves up to new possibilities and solutions. We attract supportive people and resources, and we maintain the motivation and inspiration to keep going.

Chapter Summary: Embracing the Lessons of Failure

Embracing setbacks as natural and valuable parts of the learning process is important. By viewing each failure as a steppingstone to greater achievements, we can continue to pursue our goals with renewed vigor and insight. Remember, the most successful people are not those who never fail, but those who never give up.

This is especially true for those rebuilding after toxic influences. The journey of healing and growth is not about perfection, but about resilience, self-discovery, and the courage to keep showing up for ourselves. Each setback we face is an opportunity to deepen our self-awareness, to clarify our values and goals, and to develop the skills and strengths we need to thrive.

So, the next time you face a disappointment or a failure, remember this is not the end of your story. It is simply a plot twist, a chance to learn and grow and redirect yourself to a path that is even better suited to your unique gifts and purpose.

Embrace the lessons of failure, and trust in your own resilience and potential. With each setback you overcome, you are one step closer to the life you desire and deserve. Keep going, keep growing, and remember - your comeback story is already in the making.

NAVIGATING THROUGH ADVERSITY

When faced with major life challenges, navigating through adversity can feel overwhelming. However, with the right tools and strategies, you can effectively manage these challenges and emerge stronger. Here are practical tips for dealing with adversity:

When rebuilding after toxic influences, navigating adversity is a central part of the journey. The process of healing and creating a new life often involves facing deep-seated pain, challenging ingrained patterns, and overcoming significant obstacles. Having a toolkit of strategies for managing adversity can make all the difference in our ability to persevere and thrive.

Maintain a Positive Mindset

• **Strategy:** Focus on maintaining a hopeful outlook, even in difficult circumstances. This can help you see opportunities for growth and solutions rather than just problems.

• **Action:** Practice mindfulness or positive affirmations to reinforce a constructive mindset.

Maintaining a positive mindset in the face of adversity is not about denying the reality of our challenges, but about choosing to focus on the potential for growth and healing. When rebuilding after toxic influences, it's easy to get stuck in a negative spiral - focusing on what we've lost, the pain we've endured, or the obstacles in our path. But by consciously shifting our mindset to one of hope and possibility, we open ourselves up to new solutions and opportunities.

Mindfulness practices can be helpful. By learning to observe our thoughts and emotions without judgment, we can catch ourselves in negative patterns and gently redirect our focus. Positive affirmations can also be a powerful tool - by repeating phrases that affirm our strength, resilience, and worthiness, we gradually internalize these beliefs and shift our overall outlook.

Identify and Understand the Problem

• **Strategy:** Clearly define what the challenge or problem is. This helps in developing a targeted approach to tackle it.

• **Action:** Break down the issue into smaller, manageable parts and focus on them to address the most critical parts first.

When we're in the midst of adversity, it can feel like an overwhelming and insurmountable problem. But by taking the time to clearly identify and understand the specific challenge we're facing; we can start to develop a more manageable approach.

When rebuilding, this might involve unpacking the different layers of trauma, dysfunction, or practical challenges we're dealing with. It might mean identifying specific triggers, patterns, or obstacles holding us back. By breaking these down into smaller, more clearly defined parts, we can start to prioritize our focus and develop targeted strategies for each part of the problem.

Seek Support

• **Strategy:** Leverage your personal and professional networks for support. Sharing your challenges can provide both emotional relief and practical solutions.

• **Action:** Reach out to friends, family, mentors, or professional counselors who can offer guidance and support.

Navigating adversity is not a solo journey, especially when rebuilding after toxic influences. We need the support, guidance, and perspective of others to help us through the tough times and to remind us of our own strength and resilience.

This might involve contacting trusted friends or family members who can offer a listening ear and emotional support. It might mean seeking a therapist or counselor who can provide professional guidance and help us process our experiences. It could also involve joining a support group or connecting with others who have been through similar challenges.

The key is to remember that we need not go through this alone. Building a strong support network is an important part of navigating adversity and rebuilding our lives.

Practice Self-Care

• **Strategy:** Prioritizing your physical and mental well-being can enhance your ability to cope with stress and recover from setbacks.

• **Action:** Engage in regular physical activity, ensure adequate rest, and participate in hobbies or activities you enjoy.

Self-care is often one of the first things to fall by the wayside when we're facing adversity, but it's also one of the most important tools we have for managing stress, building resilience, and supporting our overall well-being.

When rebuilding after toxic influences, self-care is crucial. We may be dealing with the physical and emotional aftermath of trauma, the stress of practical challenges like finding new housing or employment, and the overall strain of creating a new life. Taking care of ourselves on a basic level - getting enough sleep, eating nourishing foods, moving our bodies, and engaging in activities that bring us joy - can provide a foundation of stability and strength to help us weather the storms.

Self-care also involves setting boundaries, saying no to things that drain us, and focusing on our own needs and well-being. It means giving ourselves permission to rest, to feel our emotions, and to take things one day at a time. By making self-care a non-negotiable part of our routine, we build our capacity to handle adversity and show up for ourselves in the ways that matter most.

Set Realistic Goals

• **Strategy:** Setting achievable goals gives you a sense of direction and a clear pathway to follow, which can be helpful in times of uncertainty.

• **Action:** Create short-term goals that contribute to overcoming adversity and celebrate small victories along the way.

When we're in the midst of adversity, it's easy to feel lost or overwhelmed, unsure of which way to turn or what steps to take. Setting realistic goals can provide a sense of direction and purpose, helping us to focus our energy and efforts productively.

When rebuilding, these goals might be related to our healing journey - such as committing to therapy, practicing a new self-care habit, or reaching out for support when we need it. They might be practical goals - like saving up for a deposit on a new apartment, updating our resume, or learning a new skill. Or they might be personal growth goals - like setting boundaries in relationships, expressing our needs more assertively, or cultivating a new hobby or interest.

The key is to make these goals realistic and achievable, breaking them down into smaller steps we can work toward. And just as importantly, it's about celebrating our progress along the way. Each small victory - whether it's making it through a tough day, reaching out for help, or accomplishing a task we set for ourselves - is worth acknowledging and honoring. These small wins add up over time, building our confidence, momentum, and resilience.

Stay Flexible

• **Strategy:** Being adaptable in your approach lets you navigate changing circumstances more effectively.

• **Action:** Be willing to adjust your plans as new information and resources become available.

Navigating adversity often requires flexibility and adaptability. Circumstances can change quickly, new challenges can arise, and what worked for us in the past may no longer be effective. Being willing to adjust our approach and try new strategies is key to staying resilient and finding our way forward.

When rebuilding, this might mean being open to new forms of support or healing modalities, even if they're unfamiliar or outside our comfort zone. It might involve adjusting our goals or timelines based on changing circumstances or new insights. It could mean letting go of certain expectations or attachments to make room for new possibilities.

The key is to stay focused on our overall vision and values, while being willing to adapt our path as needed. By staying open, curious, and willing to learn, we develop the flexibility and resilience to navigate whatever challenges come our way.

Develop Coping Mechanisms

• **Strategy:** Effective coping mechanisms can help you manage stress and maintain mental health during tough times.

• **Action:** Techniques such as deep breathing, journaling, or engaging in therapy can be beneficial.

Dealing with adversity is stressful, and chronic stress can take a significant toll on our physical and mental health. Effective coping mechanisms are important for managing stress and maintaining our well-being as we navigate tough times.

Different coping strategies work for different people, so find what resonates for you. Some common techniques include:

Deep breathing or other relaxation practices to calm the nervous system

Journaling to process emotions and gain clarity

Engaging in creative activities like art, music, or writing to express feelings and find new perspectives

Spending time in nature to ground and center yourself

Talking to a therapist or counselor to work through challenges and develop new coping skills

The key is to have a range of tools in your toolkit, so you can draw on different strategies depending on your needs and circumstances. And remember, coping mechanisms are not about numbing or avoiding difficult feelings, but about finding healthy ways to process and manage them.

Chapter Summary: Harnessing Resilience

Navigating through adversity is not just about surviving but also about learning and growing from the experience. By adopting these strategies, you can build resilience and develop a stronger, more adaptable approach to facing life's challenges. Remember, each obstacle you overcome is an opportunity to refine your problem-solving skills and enhance your capacity to deal with future adversities.

In the journey of rebuilding after toxic influences, harnessing resilience is perhaps the most important skill. It's what lets us keep going even when things are hard, to find hope and meaning in pain, and to trust in our own capacity for healing and growth.

Building resilience is not about becoming invulnerable or immune to stress and pain. Rather, it's about developing the skills and resources to cope effectively with adversity, to adapt to change, and to bounce back from setbacks. It's about cultivating a mindset of growth and possibility, even in the face of significant challenges.

When rebuilding after toxic influences, resilience is about more than just surviving - it's about thriving. It's about reclaiming our sense of self, our agency, and our hope for the future. It's about learning to trust ourselves again, to set healthy boundaries, and to create a life that aligns with our deepest values and aspirations.

Building resilience is a process, not a destination. It requires patience, self-compassion, and a willingness to keep showing up for ourselves, even when things are tough. It means celebrating our strengths and successes, while also embracing our vulnerabilities and areas for growth. It means surrounding ourselves with supportive people and resources, while also learning to be our own best advocate and ally.

Ultimately, resilience is about the courage to keep going, to keep growing, and to keep believing in ourselves and our potential. It's about the recognition that we are stronger than we realize, and that every challenge we face is an opportunity to deepen our self-awareness, our wisdom, and our capacity for joy and connection.

As you navigate the journey of rebuilding, remember that resilience is not something you either have or you don't - it's a muscle you can strengthen with practice and intention. Every time you face a setback and keep going, every time you reach out for help or offer compassion to yourself, every time you step toward your goals and values - you are building resilience.

Trust , and trust in yourself. You have the strength, the wisdom, and the courage to not only survive adversity, but to thrive in the face of it. Keep going, keep growing, and know that you can create a life of authentic joy, meaning, and connection - no matter what challenges lie ahead.

~

EMBRACING THE GROWTH JOURNEY

As we conclude this part, it's essential to emphasize the importance of embracing the journey of growth and viewing challenges not just as hurdles but as catalysts for personal development and transformation. Life's obstacles are important opportunities to learn, evolve, and enhance our resilience.

This is especially true when rebuilding after toxic influences. The journey of healing and reclaiming our lives is rarely a straight path - it's filled with twists, turns, and unexpected challenges. But by learning to view these challenges as opportunities for growth, we can maintain a sense of purpose and forward momentum, even in the face of adversity.

The Value of Challenges

Challenges push us beyond our comfort zones, forcing us to confront our fears and limitations. This confrontation is not a moment of defeat but an opportunity for victory through personal growth. By facing these challenges head-on, we gain invaluable insights into our capabilities and potential.

When rebuilding, we may face many challenges that feel overwhelming or impossible to overcome. We may be confronted with painful emotions, ingrained patterns of thought and behavior, or practical obstacles that seem insurmountable. But by reframing these challenges as opportunities for growth, we open ourselves up to new possibilities and solutions.

Every time we face a fear, set a boundary, or take a step toward our goals, we are building our capacity for resilience and self-trust. We are proving to ourselves that we are stronger than we realized, and that we have the power to create change in our lives. These moments of confrontation and victory, however small, are the building blocks of our transformation.

Transforming Setbacks into Success

Each obstacle we overcome teaches us a new lesson about perseverance, problem-solving, and the importance of maintaining a positive outlook. These lessons shape us into more adaptable, resourceful, and resilient individuals, better prepared for future challenges.

In the journey of rebuilding, setbacks are inevitable. We may experience relapses into old patterns, encounter resistance from others, or face unexpected roadblocks on our path. But by viewing these setbacks as learning opportunities, we can maintain our momentum and motivation.

Every setback holds a lesson - about our triggers, our coping mechanisms, our areas for growth, or the resources and support we need to succeed. By approaching these setbacks with curiosity and self-compassion, we can extract the wisdom they hold and use it to inform our path forward.

Over time, we learn to trust in our own resilience and problem-solving skills. We develop a more flexible and adaptable mindset, knowing we have the tools and the strength to overcome whatever challenges arise. We start to see setbacks not as failures, but as opportunities to refine our approach and recommit to our goals.

Encouragement for the Journey Ahead

View Challenges as Steppingstones:

• Recognize that each challenge is a steppingstone toward greater knowledge and strength. With every hurdle you cross, you build a sturdier foundation for your future.

When rebuilding, it's important to maintain a long-term perspective. The challenges we face in the moment can feel all-consuming, but they are ultimately temporary. By viewing each challenge as a stepping stone, we remind ourselves that this is just one part of a larger journey of growth and transformation.

Every challenge we overcome, no matter how small, is a victory worth celebrating. It's a testament to our strength, our resilience, and our commitment to creating a better life for ourselves. By focusing on these victories, we build momentum and motivation to keep going, even when things get tough.

Celebrate Every Victory:

• No victory is too small to celebrate. Each achievement on your journey is a testament to your perseverance and commitment to growth.

In the journey of rebuilding, it's easy to get caught up in how far we still have to go. We may compare ourselves to others or feel like our progress is too slow or insignificant. But by learning to celebrate every victory, no matter how small, we cultivate a sense of pride and accomplishment that fuels our ongoing growth.

Did you set a boundary today that was hard for you? Celebrate it! Did you reach out for support when you were struggling? Celebrate it! Did you step toward a goal, even if it was a baby step? Celebrate it!

Each victory is a testament to your courage, your resilience, and your commitment to your own healing and growth. By acknowledging and honoring them, you reinforce the belief that you can create change in your life, one small step at a time.

Remain Curious and Open-Minded:

• Approach each new challenge with curiosity rather than fear. Embracing a mindset of exploration can transform potentially daunting experiences into exciting opportunities.

Curiosity is a powerful antidote to fear and resistance. When we approach challenges with a sense of openness and exploration, we create space for new insights and solutions to emerge.

When rebuilding, this might mean being willing to try new coping strategies, even if they feel unfamiliar or uncomfortable at first. It might mean exploring new perspectives on our experiences, or seeking information and resources that challenge our assumptions. It could mean staying open to feedback from others, even when it's hard to hear.

By cultivating a curious and open-minded approach, we develop a greater sense of flexibility and adaptability in the face of challenges. We learn to see obstacles not as roadblocks, but as puzzles to be solved or opportunities for learning and growth.

Foster Continuous Learning:

• Commit to lifelong learning as a way to continuously evolve. Whether through formal education, personal reading, or hands-on experiences, every learning opportunity enriches your journey.

The journey of rebuilding is ultimately a journey of learning and self-discovery. It's about unlearning old patterns and beliefs, and replacing them with new skills, insights, and ways of being. By committing to lifelong learning, we ensure this process of growth and evolution never stops.

This might involve pursuing formal education or training in areas that support our healing and growth - such as therapy, coaching, or personal development courses. It could mean reading books or articles that expand our understanding of ourselves and the world. It might mean seeking new experiences and perspectives that challenge us to grow and evolve.

The key is to approach learning with a sense of curiosity and openness, knowing that every new insight or skill is a valuable addition to our toolkit for navigating life's challenges.

Cultivate Resilience and Flexibility:

• Develop resilience by bouncing back from setbacks with renewed vigor. Flexibility lets you navigate the unpredictable waters of change with grace and poise.

Finally, cultivating resilience and flexibility is perhaps the most important skill for embracing the growth journey. Resilience allows us to bounce back from setbacks and keep going, even when things are hard. Flexibility enables us to adapt to changing circumstances and find new paths forward when our original plans are disrupted.

When rebuilding, resilience and flexibility are essential. We may face setbacks and challenges that feel overwhelming at times, but by developing these qualities, we make sure we can weather any storm.

This might mean practicing self-compassion and forgiveness when we stumble or make mistakes. It could involve learning to reframe setbacks as opportunities for learning and growth. It might mean being willing to adjust our goals or strategies based on new information or changing circumstances.

By cultivating resilience and flexibility, we develop a greater sense of trust in ourselves and our ability to handle whatever challenges come our way. We learn to see change and uncertainty not as threats, but as opportunities for growth and transformation.

Chapter Summary: A Call to Action

Let us embrace the journey of growth with enthusiasm and optimism. Recognize that each challenge, no matter how formidable, holds the key to unlocking new doors of opportunity and insight. As you continue on your path, remember that the challenges you face are not just obstacles but invitations to rise up and become a stronger, wiser, and more resilient individual.

Embrace these challenges as your allies in the journey of life. They are the steppingstones that lead to a richer, more fulfilling experience. With each step forward, you become more equipped to handle whatever lies ahead, not just surviving but thriving in the face of adversity.

This is especially true in the journey of rebuilding after toxic influences. The path may be long and winding, filled with unexpected twists and turns. But by embracing the growth journey - by viewing challenges as opportunities, celebrating every victory, staying curious and open-minded, committing to lifelong learning, and cultivating resilience and flexibility - you make sure every step is leading you toward a life of greater authenticity, joy, and fulfillment.

So let this be your call to action: embrace the growth journey with all of its challenges and rewards. Trust in your own strength and resilience, knowing you have the power to transform even the greatest obstacles into steppingstones toward your dreams.

Keep going, keep growing, and remember - your story is still unfolding. With each new challenge you face and overcome, you are writing the next chapter of your journey. Make it one of courage, resilience, and unwavering commitment to your own healing and happiness.

You've got this. Embrace the journey, for it is yours and yours alone. Your path may be unique, with its own set of challenges and triumphs, but this path will lead you to a deeper understanding of yourself and your place in the world.

As you navigate this journey of growth and self-discovery, remember to be kind and patient with yourself. Change is rarely easy, and there will be moments when you may feel discouraged or overwhelmed. In those moments, remember that growth is not a linear process - it is a series of ups and downs, victories and setbacks, all woven together into the tapestry of your unique story.

Embrace the ups and the downs, the joys and the sorrows, knowing that each experience is a valuable part of your journey. Celebrate your victories, no matter how small, and learn from your setbacks, knowing they are opportunities for growth and reflection.

Surround yourself with people who support and encourage you on your path. Seek mentors, friends, and loved ones who believe in your potential and who inspire you to keep growing and evolving. Build a community of support and accountability, knowing you need not navigate this journey alone.

Trust in yourself and your own inner wisdom. You have within you all the strength, courage, and resilience you need to overcome any challenge and achieve any goal. Trust in your ability to heal, to grow, and to create a life that is authentic and fulfilling.

Embrace the journey, for it is a beautiful and sacred one. It is a journey of becoming, of discovering who you are and who you are meant to be. It is a journey of learning to love and accept yourself, flaws and all, and of creating a life that reflects your deepest values and aspirations.

So take a deep breath, put one foot in front of the other, and keep going. Embrace the challenges and the victories, the ups and the downs, knowing that each step is taking you closer to the person you are meant to become.

Your journey is yours, and it is beautiful. Embrace it with all your heart, and trust you have everything you need to create a life of joy, meaning, and purpose. You've got this - now go out there and make it happen!

Case Study:

Meet Jake, a hardworking entrepreneur who found himself at a crossroads after his startup company faced a series of unexpected setbacks. Despite pouring his heart and soul into the venture, external market factors and internal team challenges led to the company's eventual closure. Jake was devastated, feeling like a failure and questioning his ability to bounce back from this significant blow.

As he grappled with the aftermath of this setback, Jake realized that he had two choices: he could let this failure define him and rob him of his confidence, or he could view it as an opportunity for growth and learning. With the encouragement of a trusted mentor, Jake chose the latter path.

He began by stepping back and objectively assessing what had gone wrong. He sought feedback from his former team members, investors, and customers, listening with an open mind and a willingness to learn. Through this process, Jake identified several areas where he could have made better decisions or been more proactive in addressing challenges.

Armed with these insights, Jake set about turning his setback into a steppingstone for future success. He enrolled in a business management course to fill in gaps in his knowledge and skills. He started networking with other entrepreneurs, learning from their experiences and building valuable connections. And he began brainstorming new business ideas, applying the lessons he had learned from his previous venture.

As he navigated rebuilding, Jake faced many moments of doubt and discouragement. There were days when the challenges seemed insurmountable and the path forward unclear. But Jake had developed a toolkit of strategies for building resilience and perseverance.

He practiced reframing his negative thoughts, replacing self-criticism with self-compassion and failure-focused thinking with opportunity-focused thinking. He broke down his goals into manageable steps, celebrating each small victory along the way. And he surrounded himself with a supportive network of friends, family, and mentors who believed in him and his vision.

Slowly but surely, Jake saw the fruits of his labors. His network began to yield exciting new business opportunities. His growing knowledge and skills gave him the confidence to take on new challenges. And his resilient mindset let him approach obstacles with creativity and determination rather than fear and doubt.

One year after his startup's closure, Jake launched a new venture - one that built on the lessons he had learned and the relationships he had cultivated. This time, he was better prepared for the challenges of entrepreneurship. He had a clearer vision, a stronger skill set, and a more resilient spirit.

As his new company began to gain traction and succeed, Jake looked back on his journey with a sense of pride and gratitude. He realized that his greatest failure had actually been his greatest gift - a catalyst for profound personal and professional growth. He had emerged from the experience not just a better entrepreneur, but a better leader, learner, and human.

Jake's story is a powerful illustration of the transformative potential of viewing challenges as opportunities. By embracing a growth mindset, a willingness to learn, and a commitment to resilience, he turned his worst setback into a launchpad for his greatest success.

His journey also highlights the importance of seeking support, practicing self-care, and maintaining a long-term perspective in the face of adversity. By reaching out for help, taking care of his own needs, and keeping his eyes on the horizon, Jake weathered the storms of uncertainty and emerge stronger on the other side.

Ultimately, Jake's experience is a testament to the innate resilience and potential that lies within each of us. It is a reminder that no setback is final, and no failure is fatal. With the right mindset, strategies, and support, we all have the capacity to transform our challenges into opportunities and our obstacles into steppingstones.

As we navigate our own journeys of growth and resilience, may we draw inspiration and courage from stories like Jake's. May we face our setbacks with curiosity and compassion, extract the lessons they hold, and use them as fuel for our success. And may we always remember that within every challenge lies an invitation to learn, to grow, and to become the most empowered versions of ourselves.

For through the crucible of adversity, we forge our greatest strength, wisdom, and resilience. It is through the process of overcoming that we discover our true potential and purpose. And through the journey of continuous growth, we create lives of authentic meaning, contribution, and joy.

So let us embrace the challenges on our path, knowing they are not barriers to our success, but the very steppingstones that will lead us to it. Let us trust, in ourselves, and in the indomitable human spirit that lets us turn every setback into a setup for a comeback.

And let us move forward with the conviction that our best days, our biggest triumphs, and our most meaningful impact always lie ahead of us - as long as we have the courage to keep learning, keep growing, and keep rising to meet each new challenge as an opportunity to become our best selves.

~

PART EIGHT WRAP-UP:

KEY POINTS:

• Challenges and setbacks are inevitable in life, but they can be transformed into valuable opportunities for growth and learning.

• Adopting a growth mindset, which views challenges as opportunities for development rather than threats to success, is important for overcoming obstacles and achieving goals.

• Resilience and perseverance are essential skills for navigating adversity and can be cultivated through practices such as setting realistic goals, seeking support, and maintaining a positive outlook.

• Reflecting on and learning from setbacks, rather than being discouraged by them, lets individuals gain valuable insights and improve their problem-solving skills.

• Celebrating small victories and maintaining a long-term perspective can help individuals stay motivated and focused on their growth journey.

• Embracing continuous learning, through formal education, personal reading, or hands-on experiences, enriches personal development and equips individuals to handle future challenges more effectively.

• Cultivating flexibility and adaptability enables individuals to navigate change and uncertainty with greater ease and grace.

• Seeking support from others, practicing self-care, and maintaining a balanced lifestyle are important for managing stress and promoting overall well-being during challenging times.

Action Items:

Identify a recent challenge or setback you have faced and reflect on what you can learn from the experience.

Set realistic, achievable goals for personal or professional growth, and break them down into manageable steps.

Develop a support network of individuals who can offer encouragement, guidance, and accountability as you work toward your goals.

Practice reframing negative thoughts or self-talk into more positive, growth-oriented statements.

Celebrate your successes, no matter how small, and acknowledge the progress you have made in your growth journey.

Identify areas where you can embrace continuous learning, whether through formal education, reading, or new experiences, and commit to engaging in these activities regularly.

Practice self-care activities that promote physical, mental, and emotional well-being, such as exercise, meditation, or pursuing hobbies.

Cultivate resilience by focusing on your strengths, maintaining a long-term perspective, and bouncing back from setbacks with a determination to learn and grow.

Embrace flexibility by staying open to new ideas, approaches, and solutions, especially when faced with unexpected challenges or changes.

Regularly assess your progress and adjust your strategies as needed, while maintaining a commitment to your overall growth and development.

In our next part...

... we'll dive into the transformative power of emotional intelligence (EQ) and explore how developing this important skill set can help you navigate life's challenges with greater ease and resilience. We'll dig into the key parts of EQ, such as self-awareness, empathy, and self-regulation, and discover practical strategies for cultivating these essential skills in your daily life. Get ready to learn how to harness the power of your emotions and build stronger, more meaningful connections with others.

As we start this journey of emotional growth, we'll also uncover the importance of building emotional resilience in the face of adversity. You'll gain valuable insights into managing stress, bouncing back from setbacks, and maintaining peak performance, even in the most challenging situations. By the end of this part, you'll have a powerful toolkit for enhancing your emotional intelligence and unlocking your full potential for personal and professional success. So, let's dive in and discover how mastering your emotions can transform your life in profound and lasting ways.

~

PART NINE
MASTERING YOUR EMOTIONS: HARNESSING THE POWER OF EMOTIONAL INTELLIGENCE FOR PERSONAL AND PROFESSIONAL GROWTH

EMOTIONAL INTELLIGENCE UNVEILED

EMOTIONAL INTELLIGENCE (EQ) is a pivotal skill set that involves recognizing, understanding, and managing our own emotions, as well as discerning and influencing the emotions of others. This capability lets us navigate social complexities, build stronger relationships, and make decisions informed by more than just logic.

When rebuilding after toxic influences, developing emotional intelligence is especially important. Toxic environments often detach us from our own emotions and reactions, making it challenging to navigate the obstacles of healing and growth. By cultivating greater EQ, we can reclaim our emotional autonomy and develop healthier ways of relating to ourselves and others.

The Role of EQ in Managing Reactions

Self-awareness: This is the ability to understand your own emotions and their impact on your thoughts and behavior. Self-awareness lets you recognize triggers that might lead to impulsive reactions.

For those rebuilding after toxic influences, self-awareness is often the first step in the healing process. It involves learning to tune into our own emotions and physical sensations, and to recognize the patterns of thought and behavior that may be holding us back. By developing greater self-awareness, we can start to identify our own needs and boundaries and make choices that align with our values and goals.

Self-regulation: This involves managing your emotions in healthy ways, adapting to changing circumstances, and following through on commitments. It enables you to think before reacting, thus preventing impulsive behaviors that could lead to negative outcomes.

Self-regulation is especially important for those who have experienced toxic relationships or environments. Toxic influences often train us to react impulsively or to suppress our emotions altogether, leading to a cycle of unhealthy behavior. By developing self-regulation skills, we can learn to react to difficult circumstances with greater thoughtfulness and intention, instead of allowing our emotional impulses to guide us.

Motivation: People with high EQ are usually motivated by things beyond external rewards like fame, money, or recognition. They are resilient, optimistic, and driven by an inner ambition.

For those rebuilding after toxic influences, finding intrinsic motivation can be a challenge. Toxic environments often strip us of our sense of agency and self-worth, making it difficult to find the drive to pursue our goals and dreams. By developing a stronger sense of inner motivation, we can reclaim our sense of purpose and direction, and find the courage to keep going even in the face of setbacks and challenges.

Empathy: The capacity to understand or feel what another person is experiencing from within their frame of reference. Empathy is critical in managing reactions effectively as it allows for better handling of interpersonal relationships.

Empathy is a key skill for navigating the complexities of relationships, especially when rebuilding after toxic influences. Toxic environments often foster a sense of isolation and disconnection, making it difficult to form healthy and supportive relationships. By developing greater empathy, we can learn to connect with others more authentically and meaningfully and build the relationships that support our ongoing growth and healing.

Social skills: Being adept at managing relationships to move people in desired directions, whether in leading, negotiating, or working as part of a team.

Finally, developing strong social skills is essential for those rebuilding after toxic influences. Toxic environments often leave us feeling socially anxious or awkward, unsure of how to navigate the complexities of interpersonal relationships. By developing greater social skills, we can learn to communicate, set healthy boundaries, and build the relationships that support our personal and professional growth.

Why EQ is Essential for Effective Reaction Management

• **Better Control of Emotions:** EQ provides the tools needed to temper reactions in real-time, offering a chance to step back and choose how to act instead of being swept away by emotions.

For those rebuilding after toxic influences, learning to control our emotional reactions is a critical step in the healing process. Toxic environments often foster a sense of emotional chaos and unpredictability, making it difficult to regulate our own emotions and reactions. By developing greater EQ, we can learn to respond to challenging situations more thoughtfully and intentionally, rather than being driven by our emotional impulses.

• **Improved Decision Making:** With a better grasp of your emotional state, you can make more calculated decisions that are not just based on the heat of the moment.

When rebuilding after toxic influences, making healthy and empowered decisions is essential for creating a life that aligns with our values and goals. Toxic environments often train us to decide based on fear, obligation, or guilt, rather than our own authentic desires and needs. By developing greater EQ, we can learn to make decisions grounded in our own self-awareness and emotional wisdom, rather than being driven by external pressures or expectations.

• **Enhanced Relationships:** High EQ involves effective communication and understanding of others, which help in mitigating conflicts and enhancing interactions.

For those rebuilding after toxic influences, learning to form healthy and supportive relationships is a key part of the healing process. Toxic environments often leave us feeling isolated and disconnected, unsure of how to connect with others meaningfully. By developing greater EQ, we can learn to communicate, set healthy boundaries, and build the relationships that support our ongoing growth and healing.

• **Greater Self-Understanding:** By understanding your emotions, you can pinpoint why certain things trigger you and how to handle them, which is important in personal and professional growth.

Finally, developing greater self-understanding is perhaps the most important benefit of cultivating EQ when rebuilding after toxic influences. Toxic environments often leave us feeling disconnected from ourselves, unsure of our own thoughts, feelings, and needs. By developing greater self-awareness and emotional intelligence, we can reclaim our sense of self and develop a deeper understanding of who we are and what we want in life.

Developing Your EQ

• **Reflect on Your Emotions:** Regularly take time to reflect on your emotional responses and consider why you reacted a certain way.

For those rebuilding after toxic influences, reflecting on our emotional responses can be a powerful tool for healing and growth. By taking time to explore our emotions and reactions, we can start to identify patterns of thought and behavior that may be hindering our progress and develop new strategies for responding to challenging situations in a more healthy and empowered way.

• **Practice Mindfulness:** This can help increase your awareness of your thoughts and feelings and improve your ability to manage them.

Mindfulness is a key skill for developing greater EQ, especially when rebuilding after toxic influences. By learning to tune into our own thoughts and feelings in the present moment, we can develop greater self-awareness and emotional regulation skills. This can involve practices like meditation, deep breathing, or simply taking a few moments throughout the day to check in with ourselves and notice how we're feeling.

• **Seek Feedback:** Getting an outside perspective on your emotional responses can be enlightening and help you grow.

For those rebuilding after toxic influences, seeking feedback from trusted friends, family members, or professionals can be a valuable tool for growth and healing. By getting an outside perspective on our emotional responses and patterns of behavior, we can gain new insights and develop strategies for change. This can involve working with a therapist or coach, joining a support group, or simply having honest conversations with loved ones about our experiences and goals.

• **Work on Your Empathy:** Try to see situations from others' perspectives, which can help in understanding and managing reactions during emotional interactions.

Finally, developing greater empathy is a key skill for navigating the complexities of relationships, especially when rebuilding after toxic influences. By learning to see situations from others' perspectives, we can develop a deeper understanding of their thoughts, feelings, and needs, and respond more compassionately and effectively. This can involve practices like active listening, perspective-taking, and compassionate communication.

Chapter Summary

Developing emotional intelligence is not just beneficial but essential in managing reactions effectively. By cultivating greater EQ, you not only enhance your ability to handle your emotions and reactions in challenging situations but also improve your interactions and relationships with others. This journey of emotional growth not only fosters personal development but also enhances your overall quality of life.

When rebuilding after toxic influences, developing emotional intelligence is especially important. By cultivating greater self-awareness, self-regulation, motivation, empathy, and social skills, we can reclaim our emotional autonomy and develop healthier ways of relating to ourselves and others. This journey of emotional growth is not always easy, but it is a necessary component in the healing process and a crucial stage in creating a life of greater happiness, purpose, and contentment.

So let this be your invitation to start the journey of developing your emotional intelligence. Reflect on your emotions, practice mindfulness, seek feedback from others, and work on your empathy. Trust that every action you make is leading you towards a deeper self-awareness and a stronger ability to handle the obstacles of life with grace, resilience, and wisdom.

Remember, developing emotional intelligence is not a destination, but a lifelong journey of growth and self-discovery. By committing to this journey, you are not only investing in your own healing and happiness, but also in your ability to create positive change in the world around you.

As you continue on this path, be patient and compassionate with yourself. Emotional intelligence is a process of unlearning old patterns and habits, and replacing them with new ways of thinking, feeling, and relating. There will be moments of challenge and discomfort, but these are also opportunities for growth and transformation.

Celebrate your successes, no matter how small, and learn from your setbacks. Surround yourself with people who support and encourage you on this journey and seek resources and tools that can help you continue to grow and evolve.

Remember that every step you take toward greater emotional intelligence is a step toward a life of greater authenticity, connection, and purpose. By developing your ability to understand and manage your own emotions, and to empathize with and inspire others, you are not only transforming your own life but also contributing to a more compassionate and emotionally intelligent world.

So, embrace this journey with curiosity, courage, and commitment. Trust in your own innate wisdom and resilience and know that you have the power to create a life of profound emotional depth and richness.

As you navigate the ups and downs of this path, hold fast to the vision of the person you are becoming - someone who is emotionally aware, empowered, and deeply connected to themselves and others. Someone who can weather life's storms with grace and resilience, and who can inspire others to do the same.

This is the promise of emotional intelligence - a life of greater joy, meaning, and connection, not just for yourself but for all those whose lives you touch. So, keep going, keep growing, and trust in the journey. Your emotional intelligence is a gift to yourself and to the world, and it is a journey worth taking, one day at a time.

～

THE IMPORTANCE OF SELF-AWARENESS IN EMOTIONAL INTELLIGENCE

Self-awareness is a foundational pillar of emotional intelligence (EQ) and plays a pivotal role in how individuals understand and manage their emotions. This self-awareness is important for recognizing and processing one's emotional state and its impact on behavior and thought processes.

When rebuilding after toxic influences, self-awareness is especially important. Toxic environments often leave us disconnected from our own emotions and reactions, making it difficult to navigate the challenges of healing and growth. By cultivating greater self-awareness, we can reclaim our emotional autonomy and develop healthier ways of relating to ourselves and others.

Understanding Self-Awareness

Self-awareness involves a clear understanding of your personality, including strengths, weaknesses, thoughts, beliefs, motivation, and emotions. It enables individuals to recognize different feelings as they occur, the reasons behind these emotions, and how they affect their thoughts and actions.

For those rebuilding after toxic influences, developing self-awareness can be a challenging but essential process. It involves learning to tune into our own emotions and physical sensations, and to recognize the patterns of thought and behavior that may be holding us back. This can be uncomfortable as it requires confronting painful memories and experiences. However, by developing greater self-awareness, we can start to identify our own needs and boundaries and make choices that align with our values and goals.

Benefits of Self-Awareness in Emotional Intelligence

Improved Emotional Control:

• By recognizing your emotions, you can better manage and control them. Understanding the triggers that affect your emotional state is key to managing reactions in stressful or challenging situations.

For those rebuilding after toxic influences, learning to control our emotional reactions is a critical step in the healing process. Toxic environments often foster a sense of emotional chaos and unpredictability, making it difficult to regulate our own emotions and reactions. By developing greater self-awareness, we can learn to respond to challenging situations more thoughtfully and intentionally, rather than being driven by our emotional impulses.

Enhanced Decision Making:

• Being self-aware lets you make decisions informed by your feelings and needs rather than dictated by fleeting emotions. This leads to more calculated and thoughtful decisions.

When rebuilding after toxic influences, making healthy and empowered decisions is essential for creating a life that aligns with our values and goals. Toxic environments often train us to decide based on fear, duty, or guilt, rather than our own authentic desires and needs. By developing greater self-awareness, we can learn to make decisions grounded in our own emotional wisdom, rather than being driven by external pressures or expectations.

Increased Self-Confidence:

• Knowing your strengths and limitations helps to build confidence. When you have a better understanding of yourself, you are more likely to pursue opportunities that align with your capabilities.

For those rebuilding after toxic influences, developing self-confidence can be a challenge. Toxic environments often leave us feeling worthless or inadequate, making it difficult to trust in our own abilities and strengths. By cultivating greater self-awareness, we can start to identify our own unique talents and qualities and develop a stronger sense of self-worth and self-confidence.

Better Relationships:

• Self-awareness fosters empathy because understanding your own emotions helps you relate to others on an emotional level. This empathy can lead to stronger and more effective interpersonal relationships.

For those rebuilding after toxic influences, learning to form healthy and supportive relationships is a key part of the healing process. Toxic environments often leave us feeling isolated and disconnected, unsure of how to connect with others meaningfully. By developing greater self-awareness and empathy, we can learn to communicate set healthy boundaries, and build the relationships that support our ongoing growth and healing.

Effective Communication:

• When you understand your emotions, you can communicate more effectively. You are better equipped to express how you feel without anger or passivity, which can help in both personal and professional relationships.

When rebuilding after toxic influences, learning to communicate effectively is essential for advocating for our own needs and boundaries. Toxic environments often train us to suppress our emotions or express them in unhealthy ways, making it difficult to communicate assertively. By developing greater self-awareness, we can learn to express ourselves more authentically and effectively and build the relationships that support our ongoing growth and healing.

Developing Self-Awareness

Reflect on Your Emotions:

• Regularly take time to consider your emotional reactions to events. Journaling or meditation can help with this reflection.

For those rebuilding after toxic influences, reflecting on our emotional responses can be a powerful tool for healing and growth. By taking time to explore our emotions and reactions, we can start to identify recurring patterns of thought and behavior that may be impeding our progress and develop innovative approaches for handling difficult circumstances in a more flexible manner.

Ask for Feedback:

• Sometimes it's hard to see ourselves objectively, so feedback from trusted friends, family, or colleagues can be invaluable in understanding our emotional responses.

For those rebuilding after toxic influences, seeking feedback from trusted friends, family members, or professionals can be a valuable tool for growth and healing. By getting an outside perspective on our emotional responses and patterns of behavior, we can gain new insights and develop strategies for change. This can involve working with a therapist or coach, joining a support group, or simply having honest conversations with loved ones about our experiences and goals.

Practice Mindfulness:

• Mindfulness practices encourage you to live in the moment and learn of your thoughts and feelings. This can heighten your self-awareness.

Mindfulness is a key skill for developing greater self-awareness, especially when rebuilding after toxic influences. By learning to tune into our own thoughts and feelings in the present moment, we can develop greater emotional awareness and regulation skills. This can involve practices like meditation, deep breathing, or simply taking a few moments throughout the day to check in with ourselves and notice how we're feeling.

Set Personal Development Goals:

• Use your understanding of your emotions to set personal development goals that push you to grow beyond your current emotional responses.

Finally, setting personal development goals is a powerful way to translate our growing self-awareness into real action steps. By identifying the areas where we want to grow and develop, we can create a roadmap for our ongoing healing and transformation. This can involve setting goals around emotional regulation, communication skills, self-care, or any other area where we want to create positive change in our lives.

Chapter Summary: Embracing the Journey of Self-Discovery

Self-awareness is an ongoing journey of personal exploration and growth. By investing time and effort into understanding your emotions, you can enhance your emotional intelligence, leading to improved decision-making, stronger relationships, and a more fulfilling life. Remember, the more aware you are of your emotions, the better equipped you are to manage them effectively, turning potential obstacles into opportunities for personal and professional growth.

When rebuilding after toxic influences, developing self-awareness is especially important. By cultivating a deeper understanding of our own emotions and reactions, we can reclaim our sense of self and develop healthier ways of relating to ourselves and others. This journey of self-discovery is not without challenges, but it is an integral part of the healing process and a crucial step in creating a life of greater joy, meaning, and fulfillment.

So let this be your invitation to embrace the journey of self-discovery. Reflect on your emotions, seek feedback from others, practice mindfulness, and set personal development goals. Trust that every step you take is bringing you closer to a deeper understanding of yourself and a greater capacity for navigating the challenges of life with grace, resilience, and wisdom.

Remember, developing self-awareness is not a destination, but a life-long journey of growth and transformation. By committing to this journey, you are not only investing in your own healing and happiness, but also in your ability to create positive change in the world around you. So, keep going, keep growing, and trust in the journey. Your self-awareness is a gift to yourself and to the world, and it is a journey worth taking, one day at a time.

Strategies for Managing Reactions

Effectively managing reactions is important for maintaining emotional balance and making thoughtful decisions. This is especially important when rebuilding after toxic influences, as toxic environments often train us to react impulsively or defensively to stressful situations. By developing effective strategies for managing our reactions, we can reclaim our emotional autonomy and respond to challenges in a more grounded and empowered way.

Here are several techniques that can help you control your emotional responses and prevent knee-jerk reactions in stressful situations:

Deep Breathing Exercises

Deep breathing is a simple yet powerful tool to reduce stress and manage emotional reactions.

- **Technique:**

Diaphragmatic Breathing: Breathe deeply into your diaphragm rather than your chest to increase oxygen intake and trigger a relaxation response in the body.

Box Breathing: Inhale for a count of four, hold the breath for four, exhale for four, and hold again for four. This technique is useful in high-stress environments.

- **Benefits:** Calms the nervous system, reduces stress, and helps regain emotional control.

For those rebuilding after toxic influences, deep breathing can be a valuable tool for managing the intense emotions that often arise in the healing process. By focusing on the breath and intentionally slowing down our physiological response to stress, we can create a sense of calm and groundedness in the face of difficult emotions.

Mindfulness Practices

Mindfulness encourages you to experience the present moment, without judgment, which can significantly enhance your ability to manage reactions.

• **Techniques:**

Mindful Breathing: Focus only on your breath, the sensations of air entering and leaving your nostrils.

Body Scan: Gradually tune into each part of your body, noticing any sensations, tension, or discomfort, which can help divert your mind from distressing emotions.

• **Benefits:**

Increases awareness of emotional triggers.

Reduces overall anxiety and stress, enhancing response mechanisms to adverse situations.

For those rebuilding after toxic influences, mindfulness can be a powerful tool for developing greater self-awareness and emotional regulation skills. By learning to tune into our own thoughts and feelings in the present moment, we can start to identify the patterns of thought and behavior that may be holding us back and develop new strategies for responding to challenging situations in a more healthy and empowered way.

Journaling

Writing down your thoughts and feelings can serve as an emotional outlet and a way to dissect complex feelings.

• **Technique:** Regularly dedicate time to express your emotions through writing. Detail not just what you feel, but also why you think you feel that way.

- **Benefits:**

Helps process emotions and clarify thoughts.

Let's you track patterns in your emotional responses, potentially uncovering triggers and effective coping mechanisms.

For those rebuilding after toxic influences, journaling can be a valuable tool for processing difficult emotions and experiences. By taking time to explore our thoughts and feelings on paper, we can gain new insights into our own patterns of behavior and develop strategies for change. This can be especially helpful in the early stages of healing, when our emotions may feel overwhelming or confusing.

Progressive Muscle Relaxation

This technique involves tensing and then relaxing each muscle group in the body, promoting physical and mental relaxation.

- **Technique:**

Tense each muscle group for five to ten seconds, then relax for 30 seconds, progressively working through the whole body.

- **Benefits:**

Reduces physical tension that can go along with emotional stress.

Helps break the ongoing cycle of physical responses to stress, such as tight muscles, which can feed back into feelings of anxiety.

For those rebuilding after toxic influences, progressive muscle relaxation can be a helpful tool for managing the physical symptoms of stress and anxiety. By learning to intentionally relax our bodies, we can create a sense of calm and safety in the face of difficult emotions. This can be especially important in trauma recovery, where physical tension and hyperarousal are common symptoms.

Chapter Summary: Embracing Emotional Management

By integrating these strategies into your daily routine, you can improve your ability to manage reactions in both personal and professional contexts. Each technique offers a unique way to cope with emotional challenges, making sure you remain calm and collected, even in stressful situations. Practicing these techniques regularly not only helps in immediate situations but also contributes to long-term emotional resilience and intelligence.

When rebuilding after toxic influences, developing effective strategies for managing reactions is an essential part of the healing process. By learning to respond to stress and difficult emotions in a more grounded and intentional way, we can reclaim our sense of agency and develop healthier patterns of behavior. This can involve a combination of deep breathing, mindfulness, journaling, progressive muscle relaxation, and other techniques that resonate with our individual needs and preferences.

Remember, managing reactions is a skill that can be developed over time with practice and patience. It is not about suppressing or denying our emotions but learning to respond to them in a more healthy and empowered way. By embracing the journey of emotional management, we can cultivate greater resilience, self-awareness, and emotional intelligence, and create a foundation for ongoing growth and healing.

So let this be your invitation to explore the strategies that work best for you. Practice deep breathing, mindfulness, journaling, and progressive muscle relaxation, and notice how these techniques impact your ability to manage reactions in stressful situations. Trust that every effort you make to cultivate greater emotional awareness and regulation is a step toward a more grounded, empowered, and fulfilling life.

Remember, managing reactions is not about perfection, but about progress. Be patient and compassionate with yourself as you navigate the ups and downs of the healing journey. Celebrate your successes, learn from your challenges, and trust in your own innate resilience and wisdom. With time, practice, and self-compassion, you can develop the emotional management skills you need to thrive in the face of life's challenges and create a life of greater joy, meaning, and connection.

∿

CULTIVATING EMPATHY

EMPATHY IS a cornerstone of emotional intelligence that significantly enriches our ability to interact and connect with others. It entails understanding and sharing the feelings of another person, which not only enhances interpersonal relationships but also fosters effective communication and conflict resolution.

When rebuilding after toxic influences, cultivating empathy is especially important. Toxic environments often leave us feeling disconnected from our own emotions and the emotions of others, making it difficult to form healthy and supportive relationships. By developing greater empathy, we can start to reconnect with our own emotional wisdom and build the relationships that support our ongoing growth and healing.

The Significance of Empathy in Emotional Intelligence

Enhances Understanding of Others:

• Empathy lets us perceive and interpret the emotions of others accurately. This deep understanding aids in navigating social interactions and responding appropriately to different emotional cues.

For those rebuilding after toxic influences, developing a deeper understanding of others' emotions can be a powerful tool for healing and growth. By learning to read and respond to emotional cues, we can start to build more authentic and supportive relationships and create a sense of safety and connection in our interactions with others.

Strengthens Relationships:

• By showing empathy, we confirm others' feelings and perspectives, which can strengthen bonds and build trust. Empathetic relationships are characterized by a deeper connection and mutual respect, pivotal for both personal and professional relationships.

For those rebuilding after toxic influences, building empathetic relationships can be a critical step in the healing process. Toxic environments often leave us feeling isolated and disconnected, unsure of how to form healthy and supportive relationships. By developing greater empathy, we can start to build the connections that offer a feeling of security, affirmation, and encouragement, and that allow us to evolve and recover in significant ways.

Improves Communication:

• Empathy contributes to more effective communication. It involves active listening, where you pay attention not just to the words being spoken but also to the emotions underlying those words. This level of understanding can help in addressing others' needs more accurately and responding in ways that are supportive and constructive.

When rebuilding after toxic influences, developing empathetic communication skills can be a powerful tool for advocating for our own needs and boundaries. By learning to listen actively and respond with compassion and understanding, we can create more meaningful and effective dialogue, and build relationships based on mutual respect and trust.

Helps with Conflict Resolution:

• In conflict situations, empathy shows the other person's point of view and understand their feelings. This understanding can pave the way for finding common ground and resolving disputes amicably, without escalating tensions.

For those rebuilding after toxic influences, learning to approach conflict with empathy and understanding can be a critical step in the healing process. Toxic environments often foster a sense of defensiveness and reactivity, making it difficult to resolve conflicts healthily and productively. By developing greater empathy, we can learn to approach conflicts with curiosity and compassion and resolve disputes that honor the needs and feelings of all involved.

Promotes Compassionate Leadership:

• In leadership roles, empathy fosters a supportive work environment that can enhance team cooperation, boost morale, and lead to higher job satisfaction and productivity among employees.

For those rebuilding after toxic influences, developing empathetic leadership skills can be a powerful way to create positive change in our personal and professional lives. By modeling compassion, understanding, and respect in our interactions with others, we can create a ripple effect of healing and growth that extends far beyond ourselves.

Ways to Cultivate Empathy

Practice Active Listening:

• Focus on the speaker, acknowledge their feelings, and respond thoughtfully. Active listening involves not only hearing but also understanding and reflecting on what is being communicated.

For those rebuilding after toxic influences, practicing active listening can be a powerful tool for developing greater empathy and understanding. By learning to tune into the emotions and experiences of others, we can start to build more authentic and supportive relationships and create a sense of safety and connection in our interactions.

Put Yourself in Others' Shoes:

• Try to imagine yourself in the other person's situation, which can help in understanding their reactions and decisions.

For those rebuilding after toxic influences, learning to put ourselves in others' shoes can be a powerful way to develop greater empathy and compassion. By imagining what it might be like to walk in someone else's shoes, we can understand their experiences and perspectives in a deeper way and respond with greater sensitivity and understanding.

Ask Open-Ended Questions:

• Encourage others to express their thoughts and feelings more comprehensively by asking questions that require more than yes or no answers.

For those rebuilding after toxic influences, asking open-ended questions can be a powerful way to build deeper connections and understanding with others. By creating space for others to share their experiences and perspectives, we can start to build relationships based on mutual trust and respect, and that support our ongoing growth and healing.

Observe Non-Verbal Cues:

• Pay attention to body language, facial expressions, and tone of voice to better understand what others might be feeling.

For those rebuilding after toxic influences, learning to read non-verbal cues can be a powerful tool for developing greater empathy and understanding. By tuning into the subtleties of others' emotional expressions, we can start to build more authentic and supportive relationships and respond with greater sensitivity and compassion.

Challenge Prejudices and Discover Commonalities:

• Work on recognizing and challenging your biases and try to find common ground with others, which can foster empathy and reduce feelings of division.

For those rebuilding after toxic influences, learning to challenge our own biases and prejudices can be a powerful way to develop greater empathy and understanding. By trying to find common ground with others, even those who seem different from ourselves, we can start to build bridges of connection and understanding that support our ongoing growth and healing.

Chapter Summary

Empathy is a powerful tool in the realm of emotional intelligence. It not only enhances our understanding and relationships with others but also equips us to manage our social interactions more effectively. By cultivating empathy, we open ourselves to a deeper connection with the world, leading to a more compassionate and fulfilling life.

When rebuilding after toxic influences, developing empathy is especially important. By learning to tune into our own emotions and the emotions of others, we can start to build the relationships that provide a sense of safety, validation, and support, and that let us grow and heal in meaningful ways. This journey of empathy cultivation is not always easy, but it is an essential part of the healing process and a key step in creating a life of greater joy, meaning, and connection.

So let this be your invitation to embrace the journey of empathy cultivation. Practice active listening, put yourself in others' shoes, ask open-ended questions, observe non-verbal cues, and challenge your own prejudices and biases. Trust that every effort you make to develop greater empathy and understanding is a step toward a more compassionate and fulfilling life.

Remember, cultivating empathy is not about perfection, but about progress. Be kind and understanding towards yourself as you navigate the ups and downs of the healing journey and have faith in your own natural ability for growth and transformation. With time, practice, and self-compassion, you can develop the empathy skills you need to thrive in your relationships and create a life of greater meaning and connection.

⚬

APPLYING EMOTIONAL INTELLIGENCE IN CHALLENGING SITUATIONS

EMOTIONAL INTELLIGENCE (EQ) is an important tool for effectively navigating difficult or stressful situations. Here are practical examples of how EQ can be applied across various challenging scenarios to manage reactions constructively, especially when rebuilding after toxic influences:

Complaint from a Client

• **Situation:** A client is upset and expresses dissatisfaction with a product or service.

• **Application of EQ:**

Empathy: Understand and acknowledge the client's feelings and frustrations.

Active Listening: Give the client your full attention, clarifying and summarizing their concerns to ensure understanding.

Problem Solving: Collaboratively discuss potential solutions or alternatives, showing commitment to resolving the issue.

• **Outcome:** This approach not only de-escalates the situation but also strengthens client trust and loyalty.

For those rebuilding after toxic influences, applying EQ in this situation can be especially challenging. Toxic environments often train us to react defensively or dismissively to complaints, rather than approaching them with empathy and a genuine desire to understand and resolve the issue. By consciously applying EQ skills in this situation, we can break free from old patterns and build more positive and productive relationships with clients.

Team Conflict

• **Situation:** A disagreement or conflict arises within a team.

• **Application of EQ:**

Perspective-taking: Encourage each team member to share their viewpoints and listen to others without judgment.

Mediation: Facilitate a dialogue that allows for constructive criticism and mutual understanding, rather than blame.

Conflict Resolution: Work together to find a compromise or solution that addresses the concerns of all parties involved.

• **Outcome:** This fosters a positive work environment and enhances team cohesion.

For those rebuilding after toxic influences, applying EQ in team conflict situations can be a powerful way to create positive change in our professional lives. Toxic environments often foster a culture of blame, defensiveness, and unhealthy competition, making it difficult to resolve conflicts productively. By consciously applying EQ skills in these situations, we can start to build a more collaborative and supportive team culture and create a sense of safety and trust among team members.

Tight Deadlines

• **Situation:** The team faces high-pressure situations with tight deadlines.

• **Application of EQ:**

Self-regulation: Manage your stress through techniques such as deep breathing or short breaks.

Prioritization: Help the team focus on tasks and set realistic goals.

Communication: Maintain clear and calm communication about progress and challenges.

• **Outcome:** Reduces panic and increases productivity, preventing burnout and ensuring timely completion of tasks.

For those rebuilding after toxic influences, applying EQ in high-pressure situations can be a critical step in the healing process. Toxic environments often create a sense of constant urgency and stress, leading to burnout and a lack of work-life balance. By consciously applying EQ skills in these situations, we can start to create a more sustainable and supportive work environment and build resilience in the face of challenges.

Performance Feedback

• **Situation:** Providing critical feedback to an employee or colleague.

• **Application of EQ:**

Sensitivity: Deliver feedback in a way that is constructive rather than critical, focusing on specific behaviors instead of personal traits.

Support: Offer guidance on how to improve and encourage questions to clarify understanding.

Encouragement: Highlight strengths and potential for future contributions.

• **Outcome:** Encourages personal development and helps maintain motivation and morale.

For those rebuilding after toxic influences, applying EQ in feedback situations can be a powerful way to build more positive and supportive relationships with colleagues and employees. Toxic environments often foster a culture of criticism and blame, making it difficult to give and receive feedback constructively. By consciously applying EQ skills in these situations, we can start to create a more growth-oriented and supportive work culture, and build relationships based on mutual respect and trust.

Personal Setbacks

• Situation: Experiencing a personal setback such as a job loss or failed project.

• **Application of EQ:**

Self-awareness: Acknowledge and accept your feelings without harsh self-judgment.

Seek Support: Reach out to friends, family, or mentors for perspective and encouragement.

Resilience: Focus on lessons learned and plan steps to move forward positively.

• **Outcome:** Enables quicker recovery from setbacks and fosters a mindset oriented toward growth and opportunity.

For those rebuilding after toxic influences, applying EQ in the face of personal setbacks can be a critical step in the healing process. Toxic environments often leave us feeling ashamed, inadequate, and alone when we experience setbacks or failures. By consciously applying EQ skills in these situations, we can start to build greater resilience and self-compassion and learn to view setbacks as opportunities for growth and learning.

Chapter Summary

In every challenging situation, emotional intelligence provides the tools to manage not only one's reactions but also to positively influence the emotions of others. By practicing and applying EQ skills such as empathy, active listening, self-regulation, and effective communication, individuals can navigate the complexities of interpersonal interactions and professional challenges more successfully. These skills enable individuals to transform potential conflicts and pressures into opportunities for growth, collaboration, and improved relationships.

For those rebuilding after toxic influences, developing greater emotional intelligence is especially important. Toxic environments often leave us feeling disconnected from our own emotions and the emotions of others, making it difficult to navigate challenging situations healthily and productively. By consciously applying EQ skills in these situations, we can start to reclaim our emotional autonomy and build the relationships and environments that support our ongoing growth and healing.

So let this be your invitation to embrace the journey of emotional intelligence cultivation, especially in challenging situations. Practice empathy, active listening, self-regulation, and effective communication, and notice how these skills impact your ability to navigate difficult situations with greater ease and resilience. Trust that every effort you make to apply EQ in your personal and professional life is a step toward a more fulfilling and meaningful existence.

Remember, applying emotional intelligence is not about perfection, but about progress. Be patient and compassionate with yourself as you navigate the ups and downs of the healing journey, and trust in your own innate capacity for growth and transformation. With time, practice, and self-compassion, you can develop the EQ skills you need to thrive in the face of life's challenges and create a life of greater joy, connection, and purpose.

∽

BUILDING EMOTIONAL RESILIENCE: YOUR KEY TO THRIVING IN CHALLENGING TIMES

LIFE CAN THROW some tough curveballs our way. Whether it's a personal setback, a stressful situation at work, or a difficult emotional experience, we all encounter adversity occasionally. But here's the thing: it's not about avoiding these challenges altogether. It's about developing the emotional resilience to navigate them with grace and come out stronger on the other side.

The Importance of Emotional Resilience

So, why does emotional resilience matter so much? Well, for starters:

Stress Management: When you have emotional resilience, you're better equipped to handle stress without letting it take over your mental well-being.

Bouncing Back from Setbacks: Resilience lets you recover more quickly from personal and professional hurdles, learning valuable lessons along the way.

Consistent Performance: In the workplace, emotional resilience helps you maintain your performance, even when the pressure is on.

Personal Growth: By viewing challenges as opportunities for growth, emotional resilience encourages a mindset of continuous learning and development.

Emotional Resilience: Your Ally in Managing Reactions

One of the key benefits of emotional resilience is that it helps you respond to difficult situations thoughtfully, rather than reacting impulsively. When you have emotional resilience, you're able to:

• **Pause and Assess:** Take a moment to understand the situation and your own emotions before responding.

• **Keep the Big Picture in Mind:** Focus on long-term goals and outcomes, rather than getting caught up in temporary setbacks.

• **Choose Optimism:** Maintain a positive outlook, which can actually influence the outcome of a situation.

Your Toolkit for Building Emotional Resilience

So, how can you develop this invaluable skill? Here are strategies to add to your resilience toolkit:

Cultivate Supportive Relationships:

• Surround yourself with people who support and accept you. A strong social network can provide an important buffer against stress.

Practice Self-Awareness:

• Engage in activities that help you understand yourself better, like mindfulness or journaling. The more you understand your emotional triggers and responses, the better you can manage them.

Nurture a Positive Mindset:

• Make a habit of practicing gratitude and focusing on the good in your life. This doesn't mean ignoring problems but finding a healthy balance.

Develop Key Skills:

• Work on building skills like problem-solving and adaptability. These will serve you well when facing life's challenges.

Don't Hesitate to Seek Help:

• If you're struggling, don't be afraid to contact a therapist or counselor. They can provide valuable tools and strategies to help you build resilience.

Embrace Continuous Learning:

• View each challenge as an opportunity to learn and grow. Every difficulty carries lessons that can help you become more resilient.

The Takeaway: Embracing Emotional Resilience for a More Fulfilling Life

Emotional resilience isn't just a static trait – it's a dynamic skill that you can develop and strengthen. By incorporating these strategies into your life, you can enhance your ability to navigate challenges with greater ease and less stress. Embracing emotional resilience won't improve how you handle difficult situations – it will enrich your overall quality of life, leading to greater satisfaction and well-being. So, start building your resilience today, and watch as you begin to thrive, no matter what life throws your way.

∾

EMOTIONAL INTELLIGENCE: UNLOCKING YOUR POTENTIAL FOR PERSONAL AND PROFESSIONAL GROWTH

PICTURE THIS: you're conversing with a colleague about a challenging project. Tensions are running high, and you can sense that both of you are feeling frustrated. But instead of letting your emotions take over, you step back. You acknowledge your colleague's perspective, express your own concerns calmly, and work together to find a solution. That right there? That's emotional intelligence in action.

The Power of Emotional Intelligence

Emotional intelligence, or EQ, is a skill that can have a profound impact on virtually every part of your life. When you develop your EQ, you'll notice improvements in:

Personal Relationships

• **Understanding and Empathy:** With higher EQ, you'll be better able to recognize and understand both your own emotions and those of others. This leads to greater empathy and deeper, more meaningful relationships.

• **Communication:** Emotional intelligence enables you to express yourself more clearly and listen more attentively. The result? Stronger, more fulfilling connections with others.

Professional Success

• **Leadership:** EQ is a game-changer regarding leadership. Leaders with high EQ are better equipped to manage teams, resolve conflicts, and motivate employees – and they usually garner more respect.

• **Workplace Dynamics:** Navigating workplace challenges, fostering teamwork, and contributing to a positive work environment all become easier when you have emotional intelligence in your toolkit.

Conflict Resolution

• **Objective Problem-Solving:** When you have high EQ, you're able to approach disputes with both rationality and compassion. This leads to more constructive conflict resolution and less personal tension.

Resilience

• **Stress Management:** Understanding and managing your emotions is a powerful tool for reducing stress, anxiety, and even depression.

• **Adaptability:** In our fast-paced world, the ability to adapt to change is important. Emotional intelligence enhances this ability, letting you face new situations with greater ease.

Decision Making

• **Balanced Reasoning:** EQ helps you consider both emotional and rational perspectives when making decisions. The result is more balanced, effective outcomes.

• **Thoughtful Responses:** Instead of reacting impulsively, emotional intelligence lets you respond thoughtfully, keeping long-term consequences and your goals in mind.

Overall Well-Being

• **Self-Awareness and Self-Regulation:** These core parts of EQ contribute to a healthier lifestyle by helping you understand and manage your emotions.

• **Personal Fulfillment:** When your emotions and actions are in alignment, as they are when you have high EQ, you'll experience greater inner peace, happiness, and overall satisfaction with life.

The Bottom Line: Emotional Intelligence is a Key to a More Fulfilling Life

Developing your emotional intelligence isn't just about getting ahead at work or being a better leader – although those are certainly benefits. It's about enriching your life in profound, personal ways. When you understand and manage your emotions effectively, you're better able to build strong relationships, handle challenges, and seize opportunities for personal and professional growth. So, start honing your EQ skills today. Your future self will thank you.

Case Study:

Emma, a talented software engineer, had always been driven by logic and rational thinking. She excelled in her field, but often struggled when navigating the complex interpersonal dynamics of her workplace. Emma found herself often frustrated by what she perceived as irrational or overly emotional behavior from her colleagues, and her blunt communication style often left others feeling unheard or dismissed.

After a challenging project where tensions with her team ran high, Emma's manager suggested that she consider working on her emotional intelligence skills. At first resistant to the idea, Emma eventually agreed to go to a workshop on EQ development.

At the workshop, Emma was introduced to the concept of self-awareness as the foundation of emotional intelligence. Through various exercises and reflective activities, she began to recognize patterns in her own emotional responses and how they might be affecting her interactions with others. She realized that her tendency to dismiss emotions as irrational was preventing her from understanding and empathizing with her colleagues' perspectives.

Armed with this new insight, Emma committed to practicing greater self-awareness in her daily life. She started keeping a journal where she could process her emotional reactions to different situations, and she began to pay more attention to her body's physiological responses to stress or frustration. Through this practice, Emma developed a deeper understanding of her own emotional landscape and how it influenced her behavior.

As Emma continued to work on her self-awareness, she also began to focus on developing empathy. In team meetings, she made a conscious effort to listen to her colleagues, not just to the content of their words but to the emotions and needs underlying their communication. She started to ask more questions to clarify understanding and to show genuine interest in others' perspectives.

At first, this shift in approach felt unnatural and even uncomfortable for Emma. But as she persisted, she began to notice a change in her interactions. Her colleagues seemed more open and receptive to her ideas, and there was a greater sense of collaboration and mutual respect within the team.

Encouraged by these positive changes, Emma also started to work on her self-regulation skills. When she felt herself getting frustrated or impatient in a difficult conversation, she would take a few deep breaths and remind herself to stay focused on the outcome rather than getting swept up in the emotion of the moment. She learned to take short breaks when needed to regain her composure and to approach challenges with a more balanced, less reactive mindset.

Over time, these practices had a profound impact on Emma's work and her relationships. She found that she communicated more effectively, even in high-pressure situations. She better understood and addressed the needs and concerns of her team members, leading to smoother project execution and a more positive team dynamic.

Emma's growth in emotional intelligence also had a ripple effect beyond her immediate work team. As she interacted with clients and stakeholders with greater empathy and emotional awareness, she found that she built stronger, more trusting relationships. This not only made her work more enjoyable but also opened up new opportunities for collaboration and partnership.

One of the most transformative parts of Emma's journey was the realization that emotions weren't a weakness or an obstacle to be overcome, but a valuable source of information and insight. By learning to tune into and understand her own emotions and those of others, she gained a powerful tool for navigating complex situations and making more holistic decisions.

As Emma reflected on her experience, she realized that developing her emotional intelligence had been one of the most impactful investments she had made in her personal and professional growth. It had let her show up more fully and authentically in her work and her relationships and had given her the resilience and adaptability to thrive in the face of challenges.

Emma's story is a powerful illustration of the transformative potential of cultivating emotional intelligence. By committing to the ongoing practice of self-awareness, empathy, and self-regulation, she unlocked new levels of personal and professional effectiveness and fulfillment.

Her journey also highlights that developing EQ is not a one-time event, but an ongoing process of growth and learning. It requires a willingness to step outside of our comfort zones, to examine our own patterns and assumptions, and to approach our interactions with curiosity and openness.

But the rewards of this work are immeasurable. As we develop our capacity to understand and manage our own emotions, to empathize with and inspire others, and to navigate challenges with resilience and grace, we tap into a wellspring of potential that can transform every part of our lives.

Whether we're leading teams, building relationships, or simply striving to be our best selves, emotional intelligence is a powerful ally on the path to success and fulfillment. By embracing the ongoing journey of EQ development, we open ourselves up to richer, more meaningful experiences of work, relationship, and life itself.

So let Emma's story be an invitation to all of us – to courageously explore the landscape of our own emotions, to approach others with empathy and understanding, and to cultivate the resilience and agility to thrive in an ever-changing world. For in this work, we find not only greater effectiveness and success, but also a deeper sense of connection, purpose, and joy.

❧

PART NINE WRAP-UP:

KEY POINTS:

• Emotional intelligence (EQ) is an important skill set that involves recognizing, understanding, and managing one's own emotions, as well as discerning and influencing the emotions of others.

• Developing emotional intelligence is particularly important when rebuilding after toxic influences, as it helps individuals navigate the challenges of healing and growth.

• Self-awareness, a key part of EQ, lets individuals recognize their emotional triggers and responses, leading to better emotional control and decision making.

• Empathy, another essential part of EQ, enhances understanding of others' feelings and perspectives, leading to stronger relationships and more effective communication.

• Strategies for cultivating empathy include active listening, putting oneself in others' shoes, asking open-ended questions, observing non-verbal cues, and challenging one's own prejudices and biases.

• Applying emotional intelligence in challenging situations, such as dealing with client complaints, team conflicts, tight deadlines, performance feedback, and personal setbacks, can lead to more positive outcomes and personal growth.

• Building emotional resilience is important for managing stress, bouncing back from setbacks, maintaining consistent performance, and fostering personal growth.

• Developing EQ skills can lead to improved personal relationships, professional success, conflict resolution, resilience, decision making, and overall well-being.

Action Items:

• Practice self-reflection and mindfulness to increase self-awareness and better understand your emotional responses to various situations.

• Engage in active listening and put yourself in others' shoes to develop empathy and strengthen your relationships.

• Challenge your own prejudices and biases, and actively seek to find common ground with others to foster understanding and connection.

• Apply EQ skills in challenging situations by managing your own emotions, communicating effectively, and finding constructive solutions.

• Cultivate supportive relationships and build a strong social network to provide a buffer against stress and support your emotional resilience.

• Develop a positive mindset by practicing gratitude, focusing on the good in your life, and viewing challenges as opportunities for growth and learning.

• Enhance your problem-solving and adaptability skills to better navigate life's challenges and build emotional resilience.

• Seek help from a therapist or counselor if you are struggling, as they can provide valuable tools and strategies for building resilience and managing emotions.

• Continuously learn and grow from your experiences, using each challenge as an opportunity to strengthen your emotional intelligence and resilience.

• Incorporate EQ development into your daily life, recognizing that it is an ongoing process of growth and self-discovery that can lead to greater personal and professional fulfillment.

In our next part...

... we'll explore the transformative power of harnessing your mindset and emotional intelligence to manifest your dreams and achieve personal and professional growth. We'll dig into the fascinating world of the Law of Attraction, visualization techniques, and inspired action, and discover how these tools can help you break free from limiting beliefs and unlock your full potential. Get ready to learn practical strategies for cultivating a positive mindset, maintaining motivation, and building resilience in the face of challenges.

As we start this journey of self-discovery and personal growth, we'll also uncover the importance of developing emotional intelligence skills such as self-awareness, self-regulation, and empathy. You'll gain valuable insights into how these skills can enhance your relationships, communication, and overall success in both personal and professional settings. By the end of this part, you'll have a powerful toolkit for aligning your thoughts, emotions, and actions to create the life you desire. So, let's dive in and explore the incredible potential within you, waiting to be unleashed.

~

PART TEN
MASTERING YOUR EMOTIONS: HARNESSING THE POWER OF EMOTIONAL INTELLIGENCE FOR PERSONAL AND PROFESSIONAL GROWTH

MANIFESTING YOUR DREAMS: THE TRANSFORMATIVE POWER OF A POSITIVE MINDSET

WE ALL HAVE DREAMS – those aspirations that fill us with excitement and hope for the future. But sometimes, the path to achieving those dreams can feel daunting. That's where the power of mindset comes in. Your mindset is not just a feel-good concept; it's an important tool in transforming your visions into reality.

Mindset and Manifestation: A Powerful Connection

Attracting Positive Outcomes:

• **The Law of Attraction:** At the core of the mindset-manifestation connection is the Law of Attraction. This principle suggests that the energy you put out into the world usually attracts similar energy back to you. A positive mindset is more likely to attract positive circumstances and opportunities.

• **Seeing Opportunities Everywhere:** When you approach life with a positive outlook, you're more attuned to the opportunities that align with your goals. You not only recognize these opportunities but also actively create them.

Building Resilience in the Face of Challenges:

• **Overcoming Obstacles:** A positive mindset is your ally when dealing with setbacks. Instead of being overwhelmed by difficulties, you see them as chances to learn, grow, and become stronger.

• **Staying Committed:** Maintaining a hopeful and optimistic perspective helps you stay committed to your goals, even when progress is slow or hurdles seem insurmountable.

Enhancing Focus and Clarity:

• **Clarifying Your Goals:** A positive mindset helps you gain clarity about what you want to achieve. By focusing on the positive outcomes you want, rather than what you want to avoid, you can define your goals more precisely.

• **Channeling Your Energy:** With a clear, positive focus, you can direct your energy more effectively toward making your dreams a reality.

Embracing New Possibilities:

• **Opening Doors to Possibilities:** A positive mindset encourages you to be receptive to different paths and opportunities you may not have thought about before. It helps you think outside the box and see potential where others might see limitations.

• **Adapting to Change:** In our ever-changing world, adaptability is key. A positive mindset fosters this essential trait, letting you navigate change with greater ease and even thrive in the face of it.

Nurturing a Positive Mindset for Manifestation

• **Visualize Your Success:** Take time regularly to visualize yourself meeting your goals. This exercise helps prepare your mind to identify and take advantage of chances that can transform your aspirations into actuality.

• **Affirm Your Abilities:** Use positive affirmations to reinforce your belief in your capacity to meet your goals. Affirmations are a powerful tool for staying focused and motivated.

• **Reflect and Process:** Engage in reflective practices like journaling or meditation. These activities can help you maintain a positive mindset by providing a space to process your thoughts and emotions constructively.

• **Find Inspiration in Others:** Look to people who have achieved goals similar to yours. Learning about their journeys can provide motivation and practical strategies to guide your own path.

Your Mindset, Your Power

Your mindset is more than just a state of mind; it's a potent force in manifesting your dreams. By nurturing a positive mindset, you not only bolster your resilience in the face of challenges but also enhance your capacity to recognize and create opportunities that align with your goals. Always remember, your mindset shapes your approach to life's ups and downs – it's the bedrock on which you can construct the life of your dreams. So keep your mind focused on the positive, and watch as your dreams take shape in reality.

~

THE MIND-DREAM CONNECTION: HARNESSING THE POWER OF POSITIVE THINKING

WE ALL HAVE ASPIRATIONS – those exciting, sometimes daunting dreams we hope to one day turn into reality. But did you know that the key to achieving those dreams might be right between your ears? That's right, we're talking about the power of your mindset. Far from being a feel-good idea, your mindset is an important tool in transforming your visions into tangible results.

The Mindset-Manifestation Link

Attracting the Good Stuff:

• **Like Attracts Like:** The Law of Attraction is at the heart of the mindset-manifestation connection. It suggests that the vibes you put out into the world usually attract similar vibes back to you. So, by maintaining a positive mindset, you're more likely to draw in positive circumstances and opportunities.

• **Opportunity Radar:** When you approach life with a glass-half-full attitude, you develop a keen eye for spotting opportunities that align with your goals. Not only do you recognize these opportunities, but you also actively create them.

Bouncing Back from Setbacks:

- **Obstacle Navigation:** A positive mindset is your best friend when handling setbacks. Instead of getting bogged down by difficulties, you view them as opportunities for growth, learning, and becoming a stronger version of yourself.

- **Unwavering Commitment:** By maintaining a hopeful and optimistic outlook, you're more likely to stay dedicated to your goals, even when progress seems slow, or obstacles appear daunting.

Laser-Sharp Focus and Clarity:

- **Goal Definition:** A positive mindset helps you gain crystal-clear clarity about what you want to achieve. By focusing on the positive outcomes you want, rather than what you want to avoid, you can define your goals with greater precision.

- **Energy Direction:** With a clear, positive focus, you can channel your energy more effectively toward making your dreams a reality.

Venturing into New Territory:

- **Expanding Your Horizons:** A positive mindset encourages you to be open to new paths and possibilities you may not have considered before. It helps you think creatively and see potential where others might see roadblocks.

- **Change Navigation:** In our ever-evolving world, adaptability is essential. A positive mindset cultivates this important trait, letting you navigate change with greater ease and even thrive in it.

Cultivating a Positive Mindset for Dream Manifestation

- **Mental Rehearsal:** Regularly take time to visualize yourself meeting your goals. This mental practice helps train your brain to recognize and seize opportunities that can turn your dreams into reality.

- **Self-Affirmation:** Use positive affirmations to reinforce your belief in your ability to meet your goals. Affirmations are a powerful tool for maintaining focus and motivation.

- **Reflective Practices:** Engage in reflective practices like journaling or meditation. These activities can help you maintain a positive mindset by providing a space to process your thoughts and emotions constructively.

• **Role Model Inspiration:** Look to people who have achieved goals similar to yours. Learning about their journeys can provide motivation and practical strategies to guide your own path.

The Bottom Line: Your Mindset is Your Superpower

Your mindset is far more than just a state of mind; it's a potent force in manifesting your dreams. By nurturing a positive mindset, you not only fortify your resilience in the face of challenges but also enhance your ability to recognize and create opportunities that align with your goals. Always remember, your mindset shapes your approach to life's ups and downs – it's the foundation on which you can build the life of your dreams. So, keep your mind focused on the positive, and watch as your dreams begin to materialize in the real world.

VISUALIZING YOUR WAY TO VICTORY: THE REMARKABLE POWER OF MENTAL IMAGERY

PICTURE THIS: you're standing on a stage, accepting an award for a project you poured your heart and soul into. The audience is applauding, and you feel a sense of pride and accomplishment wash over you. Now, what if I told you you could use this very technique – picturing your success – to help make it a reality? That's the power of visualization.

Visualization is a potent mental practice that involves creating vivid mental images of your desired outcomes. By literally seeing your success in your mind's eye before it happens, you can boost your motivation, confidence, and performance.

The Benefits of Visualization

• **Motivation Boost:** By regularly visualizing your goals, you keep your eyes on the prize. This constant reminder of what you're working toward can significantly boost your motivation.

• **Confidence Surge:** Seeing yourself meet your goals, even if only in your mind, can give your confidence a major boost. It reinforces your belief in your ability to succeed.

- **Performance Enhancement**: Mental rehearsal – visualizing the steps needed to achieve your goals – can improve your real-world performance. It helps you feel more prepared and less anxious when it's time to actually take those steps.

Effective Visualization Techniques

Vision Boards:

- **The Technique:** Gather images, quotes, and symbols that represent your goals and aspirations. Arrange these on a physical board or digital platform.

- **The Benefits:** A vision board serves as a constant visual reminder of your goals, keeping them at the forefront of your mind and reinforcing your commitment to achieving them.

Mental Rehearsal:

- **The Technique:** Close your eyes and vividly imagine meeting your goals. Engage all your senses – what do you see, hear, feel, and even smell when you reach your goals?

- **The Benefits:** Mental rehearsal prepares your mind and body for action. By simulating the success scenario, it can reduce anxiety and increase preparedness.

Guided Imagery:

- **The Technique**: Use audio recordings or scripts that guide you through detailed scenarios of success and goal achievement.

- **The Benefits:** Guided imagery is helpful for individuals who find it difficult to visualize on their own. It provides a structured narrative that paints a vivid picture of success.

Daily Visualization Practice:

- **The Technique:** Dedicate a few minutes each day to visualize your goals as already achieved. Focus on the feelings and experiences associated with success.

• **The Benefits:** A daily visualization practice reinforces a positive mindset and keeps you aligned with your goals.

Amplifying the Power of Visualization

To enhance the effectiveness of your visualization practice, combine it with other positive practices like affirmations and meditation. For example, state your goals in the present tense while visualizing, or meditate on the feelings of having achieved your goals. This can deepen the emotional impact and effectiveness of your visualization practice.

Your Mind's Eye: Your Pathway to Success

Visualizing success is not mere daydreaming – it's an active practice that can profoundly influence your psychological state and behavior, propelling you toward your goals. By regularly engaging in visualization, you not only boost your motivation but also align your subconscious mind with your goals. This makes you more attuned to opportunities and more persistent in the face of obstacles. So, harness the remarkable power of visualization. Close your eyes, see your success, and then go out there and make it happen. Your mind's eye is your pathway to turning your dreams into your reality.

~

THE LAW OF ATTRACTION: HARNESSING THE POWER OF YOUR THOUGHTS

THE LAW of Attraction is a powerful universal principle that suggests we attract into our lives whatever we focus on. Whether positive or negative, the energy we emit through our thoughts, emotions, and actions has a magnetic effect, drawing similar energies back to us. By understanding and leveraging this principle, you can significantly enhance the effectiveness of your goal-setting efforts.

Like Attracts Like: The Core of the Law of Attraction

Positive Thoughts, Positive Outcomes:

• When you maintain a positive outlook and focus on successful outcomes, you're more likely to attract opportunities that align with those positive intentions.

• This principle encourages a proactive approach to life, where you actively envision and work toward what you want, rather than focusing on what you fear or wish to avoid.

Negative Thoughts, Negative Results:

• Conversely, dwelling on fears, worries, or doubts sends out negative energy, which can manifest as obstacles or setbacks in your life.

• By recognizing and shifting negative thought patterns, you can reduce their harmful impact.

Applying the Law of Attraction to Your Goals

• **Clarity is Key:** Start with a clear, specific definition of what you wish to achieve. The more precise you are about your goals, the more effectively you can direct your thoughts and energies toward achieving them.

• **Visualization:** Regularly visualize meeting your goals. Imagine the experience in vivid detail – the emotions, the environment, the people involved. This mental practice reinforces your goals and aligns your subconscious mind with your goals.

• **Affirmations:** Use affirmations to strengthen your belief in your ability to meet your goals. State your intentions in the present tense, as if they are already happening. This helps to solidify them in your mind and in your life.

• **Gratitude:** Practice gratitude daily. Appreciating what you already have creates a positive feedback loop that attracts more to be grateful for, including the successful achievement of your goals.

Letting Go of Resistance

• **Release Doubt:** Let go of any doubts or fears related to your goals. Trust that what you want is on its way and that setbacks are merely part of the journey.

• **Openness to Opportunities:** Stay open to unexpected opportunities. The Law of Attraction often works in mysterious ways, and being flexible can help you leverage opportunities you might not have expected.

Your Thoughts are Your Magnets

Embracing the Law of Attraction in goal setting is about more than just wishful thinking. It's about creating a mindset that magnetically attracts the people, resources, and opportunities needed to meet your goals. It requires focus, positivity, action, and a belief in the possibility of achieving what you desire.

Here's how you can start harnessing the Law of Attraction today:

1. Define your goals clearly and specifically.
2. Visualize yourself meeting these goals daily.
3. Use positive affirmations to reinforce your belief in your ability to succeed.
4. Practice gratitude for what you already have.
5. Let go of doubts and stay open to opportunities.

By aligning your thoughts, emotions, and actions with your goals, you set a powerful process in motion that can profoundly affect your ability to manifest your dreams. Remember, your thoughts are your magnets. What you think about, you bring about. So focus on the positive, believe in your ability to succeed, and let the Law of Attraction work its magic.

~

BREAKING FREE FROM LIMITING BELIEFS: YOUR PATH TO UNLEASHING YOUR FULL POTENTIAL

LIMITING beliefs are those subconscious thoughts that act as invisible barriers, preventing us from achieving our full potential and manifesting our dreams. These beliefs can be insidious, quietly shaping our actions and decisions without us even realizing it. But here's the good news: by recognizing and challenging these beliefs, you can break free from their hold and unlock a world of personal growth and success.

Strategies to Overcome Limiting Beliefs

Identification:

• **Self-Reflection:** Take time to reflect on your thoughts and attitudes. Identify any recurring negative patterns that might suggest limiting beliefs, such as a tendency to doubt your capabilities or to reduce your achievements.

• **Journaling:** Writing down your thoughts can help you identify and articulate limiting beliefs you may not have been consciously aware of.

Questioning:

• **Critical Examination:** For each limiting belief, ask yourself critical questions to challenge its validity. For example, if you believe "I am not skilled enough," ask yourself, "What evidence do I have to support this belief? Have there been instances where I have successfully used my skills?"

• **Seek Counterexamples:** Look for evidence that contradicts your limiting beliefs. This could include past successes or times when you overcame similar challenges.

Reframing:

• **Positive Affirmations:** Replace limiting beliefs with empowering affirmations. For example, change "I can't handle this challenge" to "I have the skills and resources to handle this challenge effectively."

• **Visualization:** Use visualization techniques to imagine yourself successfully overcoming your limiting beliefs and meeting your goals.

Building a Supportive Environment:

• **Positive Influences:** Surround yourself with positive influences and people who uplift and encourage you. Their support can help reinforce your new, positive beliefs.

• **Mentorship:** Seek mentors who embody the success you aspire to. Their journey can provide a roadmap and inspire you to transcend your limiting beliefs.

Action-Oriented Approach:

• **Small Steps:** Start taking small, manageable actions toward your goals. Each step forward will build confidence and reduce the power of limiting beliefs.

• **Celebrate Wins:** Recognize and celebrate your achievements, no matter how small. This reinforces your capability and helps dismantle any self-doubt.

The Power of Overcoming Limiting Beliefs

Overcoming your limiting beliefs can profoundly affect your life by opening doors to new opportunities and enabling you to pursue your dreams with confidence. It enhances your emotional resilience, empowers you to take on new challenges, and improves your overall quality of life. By addressing and reshaping these beliefs, you are not only changing how you view yourself but also how you interact with the world around you.

Your Journey of Self-Discovery

Overcoming limiting beliefs is not an overnight process but a journey of continuous self-discovery and improvement. It requires introspection, courage, and a commitment to personal growth. But by starting this journey, you allow yourself to live a life that is not confined by self-imposed boundaries but enriched with limitless possibilities.

Here's how you can start your journey today:

1. Identify your limiting beliefs through self-reflection and journaling.
2. Question and challenge these beliefs by seeking evidence to the contrary.
3. Reframe negative beliefs into positive, empowering affirmations.
4. Build a supportive environment with positive influences and mentors.
5. Take small, consistent actions toward your goals and celebrate your wins.

Remember, every step you take on this path, no matter how small, is a step toward a more empowered, fulfilled version of yourself. Embrace the challenge of overcoming these beliefs as a pathway to achieving your dreams and living the life you desire. Your journey of self-discovery starts now.

~

INSPIRED ACTION: THE KEY TO UNLOCKING YOUR DREAMS

TAKING inspired action is the catalyst that transforms your dreams into reality. It's not just about taking any action, but about taking purposeful steps that are directly aligned with your goals. Inspired action is fueled by a deep motivation and a clear understanding of your desired outcomes. Here's why it's so important:

Progress Over Perfection:

• **Consistent Effort:** Instead of waiting for the perfect moment or the perfect plan, taking regular, small steps can lead to significant progress.

• **Momentum Building:** Each action, no matter how small, builds momentum and keeps you engaged with your goals, making it easier to stay on track.

Overcoming Fear and Doubt:

• **Boosting Confidence:** Each step you take reinforces your capabilities and gradually reduces the fears and doubts that may hinder your progress.

- **Active Engagement:** By engaging with your goals, you're less likely to be paralyzed by fear, as you're continuously proving to yourself that you can move forward.

Learning and Growth:

- **Feedback Loop:** Every action provides feedback. Successes show what works, and setbacks teach you what doesn't, offering invaluable insights that refine your approach.

- **Adaptability:** This continuous learning makes you more adaptable and better equipped to tackle future challenges.

Manifesting Your Vision:

- **Law of Attraction:** Inspired action is a key part of the Law of Attraction. By acting, you signal to the universe your commitment to your goals, inviting opportunities that align with your aspirations.

- **Synchronicity:** Often, action leads to serendipitous events where the right people and opportunities seem to appear at the right time.

Building Resilience:

- **Facing Challenges:** Consistent action helps you develop toughness and persistence, key traits needed to overcome obstacles.

- **Emotional Strength:** Each challenge faced and overcome fortifies your emotional resilience, enabling you to handle bigger challenges.

Embracing the Power of Inspired Action

Inspired action doesn't always feel easy or comfortable. It often requires stepping out of your comfort zone and facing uncertainties. However, the rewards are large, leading not only to the achievement of your goals but also to personal growth and self-discovery.

Here's how you can take inspired action today:

Break your goals down into small, manageable steps.

Take consistent action, no matter how small, toward your goals every day.

Embrace challenges as opportunities for growth and learning.

Stay adaptable and open to feedback.

Trust in the process and keep faith in your journey.

Embrace each step of your journey with courage and optimism. Trust that each action you take is bringing you closer to your dreams, transforming them from mere visions into physical realities. Keep pushing forward, stay adaptable, and remember that every small step counts on the path to manifesting your dreams.

By consistently taking inspired action, you not only move closer to your goals but also build a life characterized by growth, resilience, and fulfillment. Let your actions be guided by your deepest wants and watch as the path to your dreams unfolds before you. Your journey starts with a single step – take that step today, and keep walking toward your greatest aspirations.

Resilience and Motivation: Your Fuel for the Journey of Success

Maintaining motivation and resilience can sometimes be more challenging than setting the goals themselves. But with the right strategies, you can stay motivated, overcome setbacks, and maintain a resilient attitude throughout your goal-setting journey. Here's how:

Set Clear and Measurable Goals:

• **Clarity and Precision:** Clear goals provide a direct path for action and help measure progress, which can greatly enhance motivation.

• **Small Milestones:** Breaking your goals into smaller, achievable milestones can provide a sense of accomplishment and keep you motivated over the long term.

Maintain a Positive Mindset:

• **Focus on the Positive:** Concentrate on what you have achieved rather than what has gone wrong. This shift in focus can reduce feelings of discouragement and renew energy.

- **Learn from Mistakes:** View every setback as a learning opportunity. Analyzing what went wrong and strategizing how to avoid similar issues can turn setbacks into valuable lessons.

Cultivate a Supportive Environment:

- **Seek Like-minded Individuals:** Surround yourself with supportive and motivating people who encourage and inspire you.

- **Join Groups:** Engage with communities that share similar goals. This can provide motivation through shared experiences and collective encouragement.

Practice Regular Self-Care:

- **Balance is Key:** Ensure you are not neglecting your physical or mental health. Regular exercise, enough sleep, and proper nutrition are important for maintaining high energy levels and motivation.

- **Mindfulness and Relaxation:** Techniques such as meditation, yoga, or even simple breathing exercises can improve mental resilience and help manage stress.

Visualize Your Success:

- **Power of Visualization:** Regularly visualize meeting your goals. Imagine how success looks and feels. This visualization can act as a powerful motivator, making your goals feel more real and achievable.

Adapt and Stay Flexible:

- **Plan for Obstacles:** Recognize that obstacles are inevitable. Planning how to handle potential challenges can prevent them from derailing your progress.

- **Be Willing to Adjust:** If certain strategies aren't working, be open to adjusting your plans or methods. Flexibility can be key to overcoming unexpected challenges.

Reward Yourself:

- **Celebrate Milestones:** Recognize and celebrate when you reach milestones. This not only boosts morale but also reinforces the habit of working toward goals.

Stay Committed:

• **Regular Review:** Regularly review your goals and progress. Remind yourself why these goals are important to you and renew your commitment to achieving them.

• **Consistency is Critical:** Even on days when motivation wanes, the discipline to keep pushing forward can carry you through. Remember, consistency often yields results.

Your Journey, Your Growth

By integrating these strategies into your life, you can enhance your motivation and resilience in the face of challenges. Remember, goal setting is not just about reaching a destination but about growing and learning throughout the journey. Embrace each step, keep pushing forward, and let your goals light the way to personal growth and achievement.

Here's how you can start building your resilience and motivation today:

- Set clear, measurable goals with smaller milestones.
- Maintain a positive mindset and learn from mistakes.
- Surround yourself with supportive people and communities.
- Focus on self-care and stress management.
- Visualize your success regularly.
- Stay flexible and adaptable in the face of challenges.
- Celebrate your achievements, no matter how small.
- Stay committed and consistent, even on tough days.

Remember, resilience and motivation are not static qualities, but muscles that can be strengthened with practice. Every step you take, every challenge you face, is an opportunity to grow these muscles. So keep pushing forward, stay committed to your journey, and know that with each step, you're becoming a stronger, more resilient version of yourself. Your journey to success starts with a single, motivated step – take that step today.

Case Study:

Meet Samantha, a talented graphic designer who had always dreamed of starting her own design agency. Despite her skills and passion, Samantha found herself stuck in a cycle of unfulfilling freelance gigs and self-doubt. She knew she had the potential to create something incredible, but fear and uncertainty held her back from taking the leap.

One day, a friend recommended a personal development workshop focused on harnessing the power of mindset and emotional intelligence. Intrigued, Samantha decided to attend, hoping to gain new perspectives on her situation.

At the workshop, Samantha was introduced to the concept of the Law of Attraction - the idea that our thoughts and emotions have a magnetic effect, attracting experiences and opportunities that align with our mental state. This idea resonated deeply with Samantha, who realized that her own negative self-talk and limiting beliefs had been holding her back from pursuing her dreams.

Armed with this new awareness, Samantha committed to a journey of personal growth and mindset transformation. She started by identifying and challenging her limiting beliefs, such as the idea that she wasn't experienced enough to run her own agency or that the market was too saturated for her to succeed. Through journaling and self-reflection, Samantha began to recognize these thoughts as false narratives rather than objective truths.

To replace these limiting beliefs, Samantha crafted empowering affirmations that aligned with her goals and values. She started each day by stating these affirmations, such as "I am a skilled and creative designer with a unique perspective to offer" and "I attract abundant opportunities and supportive clients." By consistently reinforcing these positive beliefs, Samantha began to notice a shift in her mindset and energy.

Alongside this inner work, Samantha also took inspired action toward her goals. She contacted her network, sharing her vision for her agency and asking for support and referrals. She invested in professional development courses to sharpen her business skills and sought mentorship from experienced entrepreneurs in her field.

As Samantha took these steps, she encountered moments of doubt and fear. But instead of letting these emotions derail her, she practiced reframing them as opportunities for growth and learning. She reminded herself that each challenge was bringing her closer to her dream and that her resilience was growing with each obstacle overcome.

Throughout her journey, Samantha also surrounded herself with positivity and support. She joined a community of like-minded entrepreneurs who encouraged and inspired each other. She curated her social media feeds to focus on uplifting content and unfollowed accounts that triggered comparison or self-doubt. And she made self-care a non-negotiable priority, knowing that her ability to pursue her dreams depended on her physical, mental, and emotional well-being.

Slowly but Samantha's efforts began to bear fruit. She attracted high-profile clients drawn to her unique design aesthetic and positive energy. She formed collaborative partnerships with other creatives who shared her values and vision. And she woke up each day feeling excited and energized to work on her business, rather than drained and discouraged.

A year after that fateful workshop, Samantha officially launched her design agency. As she celebrated this milestone surrounded by friends, family, and supportive colleagues, Samantha reflected on the profound transformation she had undergone. By harnessing the power of her mindset and aligning her actions with her goals, she had not only achieved her dream but become a more confident, resilient version of herself.

Samantha's story is a powerful reminder of the transformative potential of mindset and emotional intelligence. By shifting her thoughts and beliefs, taking inspired action, and cultivating resilience and motivation, Samantha broke free from the limitations that had held her back and manifest the life and business she desired.

Her journey also highlights that personal growth and dream manifestation are not a matter of magic or wishful thinking, but of consistent, intentional effort. It's about aligning our inner world of thoughts and emotions with our outer world of actions and experiences, and trusting in the process even when faced with challenges and uncertainties.

By embracing practices like affirmations, visualization, self-reflection, and inspired action, we all have the power to shape our realities and create lives fulfilling and authentic to our deepest desires. It's not always an easy path, but it is rewarding - a journey of self-discovery, resilience-building, and, ultimately, dream manifestation.

So let Samantha's story be an invitation to all of us - to courageously examine our own mindsets and beliefs, to align our actions with our aspirations, and to trust in our own power to create the lives we desire. For when we do this inner and outer work, we open ourselves up to a world of limitless potential and possibility.

The journey of manifestation is personal, unique to each individual's dreams and circumstances. But by harnessing the universal principles of mindset, emotional intelligence, and inspired action, we all have the power to transcend our limitations, overcome our obstacles, and create lives of profound meaning and fulfillment.

So let us embrace this journey with open hearts and minds, knowing that each step we take is bringing us closer to our highest potential and deepest desires. Let us trust in ourselves, and in the unwavering support of the universe. And let us remember that, no matter where we are starting from, a life of joy, abundance, and purpose is always within reach - if we do the work to manifest it.

~

PART TEN WRAP-UP:

KEY POINTS:

• A positive mindset is an important tool in transforming dreams into reality by attracting positive outcomes, building resilience, enhancing focus and clarity, and embracing new possibilities.

• The Law of Attraction suggests that the energy and focus put into the world usually attract similar energy and opportunities back.

• Visualization is a powerful mental practice that involves creating vivid mental images of desired outcomes, boosting motivation, confidence, and performance.

• Limiting beliefs are subconscious thoughts that act as invisible barriers, preventing individuals from achieving their full potential and manifesting their dreams.

• Inspired action, fueled by deep motivation and a clear understanding of desired outcomes, is the catalyst that transforms dreams into reality.

• Maintaining motivation and resilience is important for staying on track and overcoming setbacks throughout the goal-setting journey.

• Cultivating emotional intelligence, including self-awareness, self-regulation, and empathy, is essential for personal and professional growth and success.

Action Items:

• Practice visualization techniques such as creating vision boards, engaging in mental rehearsal, and using guided imagery to reinforce your goals and align your subconscious mind with your goals.

• Identify and challenge limiting beliefs through self-reflection, journaling, questioning, and reframing negative thoughts into empowering affirmations.

• Take consistent, inspired action toward your goals by breaking them down into manageable steps, celebrating small wins, and staying adaptable and open to feedback.

• Cultivate a supportive environment by surrounding yourself with positive influences, seeking mentorship, and engaging with like-minded communities.

• Maintain a positive mindset by focusing on achievements, learning from mistakes, and regularly practicing gratitude and positive affirmations.

• Prioritize self-care and stress management through exercise, proper nutrition, mindfulness, and relaxation techniques to maintain motivation and resilience.

• Set clear, measurable goals with smaller milestones and regularly review progress to stay committed and motivated.

• Develop emotional intelligence by practicing self-awareness, self-regulation, empathy, and effective communication in personal and professional settings.

• Embrace challenges as opportunities for growth and learning, staying flexible and adaptable in the face of setbacks and obstacles.

• Trust in the process and maintain faith in your journey, knowing that each step taken brings you closer to manifesting your dreams and achieving personal growth and fulfillment.

In our next part...

... we'll dive into the fascinating world of mental strength and explore how you can harness its power to overcome challenges, meet your goals, and thrive in both your personal and professional life. We'll dig into the key parts of mental strength, such as resilience, grit, and emotional intelligence, and discover practical strategies for developing these essential qualities. Get ready to learn how to cultivate a growth mindset, reframe setbacks as opportunities, and build a strong support system to help you navigate life's ups and downs with greater ease and confidence.

As we start this journey of self-discovery and personal growth, we'll also uncover the importance of self-care and positive thinking in maintaining mental strength. You'll gain valuable insights into how to manage stress, set healthy boundaries, and develop a more optimistic outlook, even in the face of adversity. By the end of this part, you'll have a powerful toolkit for building mental strength and unlocking your full potential for success and fulfillment. So, let's dive in and explore how you can become the most resilient, adaptable, and mentally strong version of yourself.

∼

PART ELEVEN
UNLEASHING YOUR INNER STRENGTH: MASTERING THE ART OF MENTAL RESILIENCE FOR PERSONAL AND PROFESSIONAL GROWTH

UNLEASHING YOUR INNER STRENGTH

MENTAL STRENGTH IS the foundation of resilience and perseverance. It's the inner fortitude that allows you to navigate life's challenges, recover from setbacks, and keep pushing toward your goals. Here's why mental strength is so crucial:

Enhances Stress Management:

• **Coping Mechanisms:** Mental strength equips you with effective coping mechanisms to manage stress. This ability is essential in maintaining your focus and productivity under pressure.

• **Emotional Regulation:** It allows for better regulation of emotions, preventing overwhelming stress or anxiety from derailing your efforts.

Facilitates Recovery from Setbacks:

• **Resilience:** Mental strength fosters resilience, enabling you to bounce back from failures and setbacks with greater ease. It instills a sense of persistence that is crucial for long-term success.

• **Learning from Mistakes:** With mental strength, setbacks become learning opportunities. It helps you analyze what went wrong and how you can improve, rather than seeing failure as a defeat.

Supports Goal Achievement:

• **Perseverance:** Mental strength is key to perseverance. It drives you to keep pushing forward, even when progress seems slow or obstacles appear insurmountable.

• **Motivation:** It sustains your motivation over the long haul, helping you stay committed to your goals despite challenges.

Enhances Decision Making:

• **Clarity and Focus:** Mental strength provides the clarity and focus needed to make informed decisions, especially in complex or high-pressure situations.

• **Risk Assessment:** It enables you to assess risks and benefits more accurately, leading to better strategic planning.

Promotes Personal Growth:

• **Self-Awareness:** Developing mental strength involves increasing self-awareness, which is essential for personal growth. Understanding your strengths and weaknesses allows for targeted development.

• **Adaptability:** It enhances your adaptability, empowering you to adjust to change and uncertainty with confidence.

Building Your Mental Strength

Building mental strength is a dynamic process that involves several practices:

• **Mindfulness and Meditation:** Regular mindfulness practices and meditation can improve emotional regulation and stress management.

• **Challenging Negative Thoughts:** Identify and challenge limiting beliefs and negative thought patterns to foster a more positive mindset.

• **Setting Realistic Goals:** Set achievable goals that motivate you and provide a sense of accomplishment as you progress.

• **Seeking Support:** Don't hesitate to seek support from mentors, peers, or professionals. A robust support system can provide guidance and encouragement.

• **Continuous Learning:** Commit to lifelong learning and self-improvement to keep your mind sharp and adaptive.

Here's how you can start building your mental strength today:

- Practice mindfulness and meditation regularly.
- Challenge your negative thoughts and replace them with positive ones.
- Set realistic, achievable goals that motivate you.
- Build a supportive network of mentors, peers, and professionals.
- Commit to continuous learning and self-improvement.

Remember, building mental strength is not about never failing or never feeling discouraged. It's about developing the resilience to recover from setbacks, the perseverance to keep going, and the adaptability to learn and grow through challenges.

By understanding the importance of mental strength and working to cultivate it, you can significantly enhance your ability to persevere through adversity, overcome challenges, and meet your goals. This journey not only leads to success but also to a richer, more resilient life. Start building your mental strength today, and watch as your resilience and perseverance grow, empowering you to tackle any challenge that comes your way.

NURTURING A GROWTH MINDSET: THE KEY TO CONTINUOUS LEARNING AND ADAPTATION

A GROWTH MINDSET is the foundation of developing mental strength. It's the belief that your abilities and intelligence can be developed through dedication and hard work. This mindset stands in contrast to a fixed mindset, which assumes that capabilities are static and unchangeable. Here's how you can foster a growth mindset and enhance your mental strength:

Embrace Challenges:

• **Opportunity for Growth:** View challenges as opportunities to expand your abilities. Each challenge is a chance to test yourself and push beyond your current boundaries.

• **Positive Reframing:** Instead of fearing challenges, approach them with curiosity and openness. This shift in perception changes challenges from threats to exciting learning opportunities.

Persist in the Face of Setbacks:

• **Resilience:** When faced with setbacks, a growth mindset encourages persistence rather than withdrawal. It helps you see failures as temporary and informative, not as a reflection of your abilities or worth.

• **Learning from Mistakes:** Analyze what went wrong and why. Use these insights to refine your approach and strategies, treating every setback as a valuable lesson.

Effort as a Pathway to Mastery:

• **Value Effort:** Recognize that effort is a necessary part of becoming skilled and achieving mastery. It's not just about working hard but also about working smart and continuously improving.

• **Consistency Over Time:** Understand that significant improvements require time and sustained effort. Celebrate small wins along the way to keep motivation high.

Learn from Criticism:

• **Constructive Feedback:** Welcome constructive criticism as a tool for learning. It provides external perspectives that could highlight blind spots and areas for improvement.

• **Detachment:** Learn to detach your self-worth from the criticism. See it as commentary on your work or behavior, not on you as a person.

Be Inspired by the Success of Others:

• **Learning Opportunities:** Instead of feeling threatened by the success of others, use it as motivation. Analyze what they did well and how you can incorporate similar strategies into your own endeavors.

• **Collaborative Mindset:** Shift from a competitive mindset to a collaborative one. Understand that success is not a zero-sum game; the achievements of others can coexist with your own.

Practical Steps to Develop a Growth Mindset

Here are practical steps you can take to develop a growth mindset:

• **Journaling:** Regularly write down your reflections on daily experiences, focusing on what you learned and how you can improve.

• **Setting Learning Goals:** Instead of just outcome-oriented goals, set goals focused on learning and development.

• **Mindfulness Practices:** Engage in mindfulness to maintain presence and awareness, which can enhance your openness to new experiences and perspectives.

• **Diverse Challenges:** Deliberately put yourself in new and challenging situations that force you out of your comfort zone and stimulate growth.

Your Journey of Continuous Growth

By adopting and nurturing a growth mindset, you build the mental strength required to navigate life's complexities with confidence and resilience. Embracing this mindset lets you continually evolve, ensuring both personal and professional growth while maintaining a vibrant, adaptive approach to life.

Remember, developing a growth mindset is a journey, not a destination. It requires consistent effort and practice. But with each challenge embraced, each setback overcome, and each lesson learned, you're not just building skills – you're building a resilient, adaptable mindset that will serve you in every area of life.

Start nurturing your growth mindset today. Embrace challenges, persist through setbacks, value effort, learn from criticism, and be inspired by others' success. With each step, you'll be unlocking your potential for continuous learning, improvement, and adaptation. Your journey of growth starts now.

∽

SEEKING SUPPORT AND PRACTICING SELF-CARE: BUILDING A STRONG FOUNDATION FOR MENTAL HEALTH

RECOGNIZING the need for support and the importance of self-care is important in building and maintaining mental strength. Here's a deeper look into how you can effectively seek support and practice self-care:

Seeking Support

• **Utilize Your Social Network:** Reach out to friends and family who make you feel safe and supported. Discussing your challenges with them can provide relief, new solutions, or simply a different perspective that might help you see things in a new light.

• **Professional Help:** Sometimes, the support we need goes beyond what friends and family can provide. Therapists, counselors, and other mental health professionals can offer expert guidance and strategies to manage stress, anxiety, and other challenges.

• **Community and Groups:** Joining support groups where members share similar experiences can be therapeutic. Whether it's a group specifically for stress management, personal development, or a particular life challenge like grief or addiction, these communities can provide comfort and practical advice.

Practicing Self-Care

• **Regular Physical Activity:** Exercise is a powerful stress reliever. It might be a daily walk, a run, yoga, or any form of exercise you enjoy. Physical activity releases endorphins, which are chemicals in the brain that act as natural painkillers and mood elevators.

• **Mindfulness and Meditation:** These practices help you stay present and grounded, reducing the impact of stress. Techniques like deep breathing, guided imagery, or body scan meditation can be effective in managing stress and enhancing overall emotional resilience.

• **Balanced Diet and Sleep:** Never underestimate the power of a balanced diet and good sleep hygiene on your mental health. Nutritious food and adequate rest can greatly improve your mood, energy levels, and cognitive function.

• **Hobbies and Interests:** Engage in activities you love and that make you lose track of time. Whether it's painting, reading, cooking, or gardening, hobbies can provide a great escape from everyday stress and enrich your life.

• **Setting Boundaries:** Learn to say no to requests or commitments that cause excessive stress or that infringe on your downtime. Setting clear boundaries with both yourself and others is important in maintaining mental health.

Integrating Support and Self-Care into Your Life

By integrating these practices into your routine, you can create a strong foundation of support and self-care that will bolster your resilience and help you manage life's challenges more effectively. Remember, building mental strength is a journey, not a destination, and it requires commitment, patience, and kindness toward yourself.

Here are practical ways to start building your support system and self-care practices:

- Identify the people in your life who provide a safe, supportive space and try to connect with them regularly.

- If you're struggling, consider contacting a mental health professional for expert guidance and support.
- Look for support groups or communities that align with your needs and interests.
- Incorporate regular physical activity into your routine, choosing forms of exercise you enjoy.
- Practice mindfulness and meditation techniques daily, even if it's for a few minutes.
- Focus on a balanced diet and good sleep hygiene.
- Make time for hobbies and interests that bring you joy and provide a break from stress.
- Set clear boundaries with yourself and others to protect your mental health and well-being.

Remember, seeking support and practicing self-care are not signs of weakness, but rather essential parts of building and maintaining mental strength. By consistently applying these strategies and making them a part of your daily life, you'll create a solid foundation for navigating life's challenges with greater resilience and overall well-being. Your journey to a stronger, healthier mind starts with these simple yet powerful practices.

Case Study:

Meet Alex, a high-achieving marketing executive who had always prided himself on his ability to handle stress and navigate challenges. However, after personal and professional setbacks, including a difficult breakup and a missed promotion, Alex struggled to maintain his usual level of performance and positivity.

Recognizing that he needed to make a change, Alex decided to focus on building his mental strength and resilience. He began by examining his mindset and identifying areas where he could shift his perspective. Through self-reflection and journaling, Alex realized that he often fell into patterns of negative self-talk and catastrophic thinking, especially when faced with obstacles or failures.

To counteract these tendencies, Alex started practicing reframing his thoughts in a more positive and constructive light. Instead of berating himself for mistakes, he began to view setbacks as opportunities for learning and growth. He challenged his negative self-talk with evidence and perspective, asking himself questions like, "Is this thought based on facts or feelings?" and "What would I say to a friend in this situation?"

Alongside this cognitive work, Alex also committed to developing a growth mindset. He started seeking out challenges and learning opportunities, both in his personal and professional life. He enrolled in a public speaking course to push himself out of his comfort zone and took on a stretch project at work that required him to learn new skills. By embracing discomfort and focusing on the process of growth rather than the outcomes, Alex began to build a greater sense of resilience and adaptability.

To support his mental strength journey, Alex also made self-care a non-negotiable priority. He started each day with a mindfulness practice, taking a few minutes to focus on his breath and set intentions for the day ahead. He focused on regular exercise, even if it was a short walk during his lunch break and tried to fuel his body with nourishing foods.

Alex also recognized the importance of emotional intelligence in navigating challenges and building strong relationships. He started paying closer attention to his own emotional responses and those of others, practicing active listening and empathy in his interactions. When faced with stress or conflict, he focused on regulating his own emotions first, using deep breathing and self-soothing techniques to stay calm and centered.

Over time, these practices had a profound impact on Alex's mental strength and overall well-being. He found that he approached challenges with greater clarity and confidence, bouncing back from setbacks more quickly and maintaining a sense of perspective even in difficult situations. His relationships also improved, as his increased emotional intelligence let him communicate more effectively and build deeper connections with colleagues and loved ones.

One of the most transformative parts of Alex's journey was his growing sense of self-awareness and self-compassion. As he continued to work on his mental strength, he developed a kinder, more understanding relationship with himself. He learned to acknowledge his own efforts and progress, celebrating small wins and treating himself with the same grace and encouragement he would offer a good friend.

This shift in self-talk and self-treatment had a ripple effect on every area of Alex's life. He found that he was more resilient in the face of stress and change, more open to feedback and growth, and more capable of setting healthy boundaries and priorities. His work performance improved, not only because of his increased skills and knowledge but also because of his enhanced ability to manage his energy, emotions, and relationships effectively.

Looking back on his journey, Alex realized that building mental strength was not about achieving a state of unshakable positivity or eliminating all stress and challenges. Rather, it was about developing the tools, mindset, and self-awareness to navigate life's ups and downs with greater resilience, adaptability, and grace. It was an ongoing process of growth and self-discovery, one that required consistent effort and commitment but that yielded profound rewards.

Alex's story is a powerful reminder that mental strength is not an innate quality, but a skill that can be cultivated and strengthened. By focusing on mindset, self-care, emotional intelligence, and growth, we all have the capacity to build the inner resources and resilience needed to thrive in the face of life's challenges.

His journey also highlights the interconnectedness of our cognitive, emotional, and physical well-being. When we work to strengthen our minds through practices like reframing thoughts, developing a growth mindset, and cultivating self-awareness, we create a positive ripple effect that touches every part of our lives.

Ultimately, the journey of building mental strength is a deeply personal and ongoing one. It requires us to confront our own patterns and beliefs, to step outside our comfort zones, and to treat ourselves with compassion and patience as we grow and evolve. But by committing to this work, as Alex did, we open ourselves up to a life of greater resilience, fulfillment, and potential.

So let Alex's story be an invitation to all of us – to courageously examine our own mental habits and beliefs, to focus on self-care and self-discovery, and to approach life with a growth-oriented and resilient mindset. For it is through this inner work we build not only mental strength, but the capacity to navigate challenges with wisdom, to connect with others deeply, and to pursue our goals and dreams with unwavering determination.

The path to mental strength is not always an easy one, but it is a journey worth taking. With each mindset shift, each moment of self-compassion, each challenge embraced, we strengthen our capacity to handle whatever life brings our way. We become more than just survivors of our circumstances; we become active creators of our own well-being and success.

So let us all take a page from Alex's book and commit to the lifelong journey of building our mental strength. Let us approach this work with curiosity, openness, and self-love, trusting that every effort we make is an investment in our ability to thrive and flourish, no matter what challenges come our way.

For mental strength is not about perfection or invulnerability. It's about cultivating the wisdom, resilience, and adaptability to meet life on its own terms – to navigate the storms and savor the joys with equal presence and grace. It's about becoming the most emotionally intelligent, growth-oriented, and self-aware versions of ourselves, and using that inner strength to create lives and relationships of profound meaning and impact.

So let us all start this journey together, supporting and inspiring each other as we grow and evolve. Let us remember that every challenge we face, every setback we encounter, is an opportunity to deepen our mental strength and resilience. And let us trust that by doing this inner work, we are not only changing ourselves, but also contributing to a world of greater compassion, connection, and thriving.

The journey to mental strength starts with a single step – a commitment to self-awareness, growth, and care. May we all have the courage to take that step, and to keep walking forward, one mindset shift at a time. For through this journey, we will unlock our full potential and create lives of authentic joy, meaning, and impact.

TURNING OBSTACLES INTO OPPORTUNITIES: STRATEGIES FOR OVERCOMING SETBACKS

Overcoming obstacles and setbacks is an integral part of the journey toward personal growth and success. Challenges, whether they are personal, professional, or related to health, can test our resilience and force us to adapt and persevere. Here's how you can effectively overcome these hurdles:

Understand the Nature of Setbacks:

• Recognize that setbacks are not permanent, nor do they define your value or capabilities. Viewing challenges as temporary obstacles that provide learning opportunities can transform your approach to overcoming them.

Develop a Resilient Mindset:

• Cultivate resilience by embracing a growth mindset. Believe in your ability to adapt and learn from every situation. Resilience isn't about avoiding difficulty but facing it head-on with courage and the willingness to persevere.

Effective Goal Setting:

• Break down larger goals into smaller, manageable tasks. This makes the process less overwhelming and provides clear direction on moving forward. Celebrate small victories along the way to maintain motivation.

Leverage Your Support Network:

• Don't underestimate the power of support from friends, family, or professional networks. Sharing your challenges with others can provide new insights, emotional support, and encouragement.

Learn from Experience:

• Each setback provides valuable insights. Analyze what went wrong, what you could do differently, and how you can improve. This reflective practice turns theoretical learning into practical improvement.

Maintain Physical and Mental Health:

• Regular physical activity, adequate rest, and proper nutrition play a critical role in building psychological resilience. Additionally, practices like mindfulness and meditation can improve your emotional response to stress.

Stay Flexible:

• Being flexible and open to change lets you adapt when unexpected challenges arise. Flexibility helps you adjust your strategies and find new pathways toward your goals.

Seek Professional Help When Needed:

• Sometimes, overcoming a setback requires skills beyond your current capabilities. Seeking help from mentors, coaches, or therapists can give you the tools and techniques to navigate complex challenges.

Keep a Long-Term Perspective:

• Focus on long-term outcomes rather than short-term setbacks. A long-term perspective helps you see beyond the immediate difficulties and understand the value of the lessons learned through these experiences.

Turning Setbacks into Steppingstones

By adopting these strategies, you can transform the way you handle setbacks, turning obstacles into steppingstones toward success. Remember, resilience and perseverance are not inherent traits but skills that can be developed with practice and determination.

Here's how you can start overcoming setbacks today:

- Recognize that setbacks are temporary and provide learning opportunities.
- Cultivate a resilient, growth-oriented mindset.
- Break down goals into manageable tasks and celebrate small victories.
- Leverage your support network for insights and encouragement.
- Learn from each setback by reflecting on what you can improve.
- Maintain physical and mental health through exercise, rest, and mindfulness.
- Stay flexible and adaptable in the face of unexpected challenges.
- Seek professional help when needed to navigate complex challenges.
- Keep a long-term perspective, focusing on the lessons learned.

Remember, every obstacle you face is an opportunity to grow, learn, and become a stronger, more resilient version of yourself. By approaching setbacks with a positive, proactive mindset and leveraging these strategies, you'll be well-equipped to overcome any challenge that comes your way. Your journey of growth and success continues, one overcome obstacle at a time.

～

EMOTIONAL INTELLIGENCE: YOUR KEY TO MENTAL STRENGTH AND EFFECTIVE RELATIONSHIPS

EMOTIONAL INTELLIGENCE (EQ) is an important part of developing mental strength and navigating life's challenges effectively. EQ involves understanding and managing your own emotions and the emotions of others. It enhances decision making, improves relationships, and increases personal resilience. Here's why it's essential and how you can develop it:

The Importance of Emotional Intelligence

Enhanced Self-Awareness: Understanding your emotions helps you recognize your strengths and areas for improvement, leading to better personal and professional choices.

Improved Relationships: By recognizing and respecting others' feelings, you can develop stronger, more empathetic relationships.

Effective Communication: High EQ enables clearer and more effective communication, reducing misunderstandings and conflicts.

Better Stress Management: Being aware of and controlling your emotional reactions helps manage stress and maintain psychological health.

Strategies to Develop Emotional Intelligence

Self-Awareness

• **Reflect Regularly:** reflect on your emotions and reactions to understand your behavior patterns and triggers.

• **Keep a Journal:** Writing about your daily experiences and emotions can provide deeper insights into your emotional processes and triggers.

• **Mindfulness Practices:** Engage in mindfulness exercises like meditation to enhance your awareness of the present moment and your emotional state.

Self-Regulation

• **Pause Before Reacting:** Take a moment to think before responding to emotional situations, which can help manage impulsive behaviors.

• **Develop Coping Strategies:** Identify and practice stress-reduction techniques such as deep breathing, progressive muscle relaxation, or engaging in hobbies that help in managing emotions effectively.

• **Set Clear Boundaries:** Knowing and setting limits on what you can tolerate can help you manage your emotions in relation to others.

Empathy

• **Active Listening:** Focus on listening to others without immediately responding or judging, which can increase understanding and empathy.

• **Perspective-Taking:** Try to see situations from others' viewpoints to better understand their emotions and reactions.

• **Respond with Compassion:** When interacting with others, especially in conflict situations, respond with empathy and consideration for their feelings.

Social Skills

• **Practice Clear Communication:** Be clear and direct in your interactions. Use assertive communication to express your needs and feelings respectfully.

• **Conflict Resolution Skills:** Learn and apply techniques for resolving disagreements calmly and constructively.

• **Build and Maintain Relationships:** Invest time in nurturing positive relationships with diverse groups of people to enhance your social skills and networks.

Applying Emotional Intelligence in Real Life

In practical terms, apply these skills regularly at work and in personal relationships. For example, if a colleague is upset about a project, use empathy to understand their concerns and self-regulation to provide calm, constructive feedback. In personal settings, use your emotional awareness to recognize when family tensions rise and apply conflict resolution skills to address issues before they escalate.

Your Journey of Emotional Growth

Emotional intelligence is a continuous journey that enhances your mental strength, resilience, and overall effectiveness in handling life's challenges. By practicing these skills, you not only improve your personal well-being but also contribute positively to the lives of those around you.

Here's how you can start building your EQ today:

- Reflect on your emotions and reactions regularly.
- Practice mindfulness to enhance your emotional awareness.
- Pause before reacting in emotional situations.
- Develop coping strategies for stress management.
- Listen actively and practice empathy in your interactions.
- Communicate clearly and assertively.
- Learn and apply conflict resolution techniques.
- Invest in building and maintaining positive relationships.

Remember, every interaction, every challenge, and every emotional experience is an opportunity to practice and strengthen your emotional intelligence. As you continue on this path of emotional growth, you'll find yourself better equipped to handle stress, build strong relationships, and navigate life's complexities with greater resilience and mental strength. Your journey of emotional mastery starts now.

CULTIVATING GRIT AND DETERMINATION: UNLOCKING YOUR POTENTIAL FOR LONG-TERM SUCCESS

CULTIVATING grit and determination is important for anyone striving to achieve long-term goals and overcome the inevitable challenges life throws their way. Here are practical strategies to help develop these powerful traits:

Set Long-term Goals

• **Clarify Your Vision:** Establish clear, well-defined goals aligned with your passions and long-term aspirations. This clarity will fuel your motivation and commitment.

• **Break It Down:** Divide larger goals into smaller, actionable steps. Meeting these smaller goals will provide frequent reinforcement and motivation, keeping you engaged and determined.

Embrace Challenges

• **Seek Out Challenges:** Regularly engage in tasks that push you out of your comfort zone. This will help you build endurance and adaptability, which are core parts of grit.

• **Persist in the Face of Setbacks:** View each setback as a stepping stone toward your goals. Persisting despite difficulties is a key feature of grit.

Develop a Growth Mindset

• **Learn from Criticism:** Use constructive criticism as a tool for self-improvement, rather than seeing it as a setback or a negative reflection on your abilities.

• **Celebrate Effort Over Success:** Focus on the effort you put into your work, rather than the outcome. This mindset encourages persistence and reduces the fear of failure.

Foster Resilience

• **Manage Stress:** Engage in activities that reduce stress, such as physical exercise, meditation, or hobbies. Lower stress levels enable better focus and persistence.

• **Emotional Regulation:** Develop techniques to manage emotions effectively. Staying calm and optimistic, even in stressful situations, strengthens your resolve to continue toward your goals.

Build Supportive Relationships

• **Seek Mentors:** Align yourself with mentors who exemplify the qualities of grit and determination. Their guidance and encouragement can be invaluable.

• **Cultivate a Supportive Community:** Surround yourself with peers who motivate and challenge you. A community that shares your values and supports your goals can enhance your perseverance.

Keep Learning and Adapting

• **Continuous Learning:** Commit to lifelong learning to continuously improve and adapt to new challenges. This approach will keep you mentally sharp and adaptable.

• **Reflect Regularly:** Take time to reflect on your experiences. What strategies worked? What can you do differently? Reflection is important for learning and growth.

Developing Grit and Determination in Daily Life

Integrating these practices into your daily routine can significantly enhance your mental strength and resilience. Grit and determination are not just innate traits but skills that can be developed through conscious effort and perseverance.

Here are practical ways to start building grit and determination today:

- Set clear, long-term goals and break them down into actionable steps.
- Regularly seek challenges that push you out of your comfort zone.
- Persist in the face of setbacks, viewing them as opportunities for growth.
- Use constructive criticism as a tool for self-improvement.
- Celebrate the effort you put into your work, not just the outcome.
- Manage stress through activities like exercise, meditation, or hobbies.
- Develop techniques to regulate your emotions effectively.
- Seek mentors and cultivate a supportive community.
- Commit to continuous learning and regular self-reflection.

Remember, building grit and determination is a journey, not a destination. Every challenge you face, every setback you overcome, and every goal you pursue is an opportunity to strengthen these powerful traits. By consistently applying these strategies and maintaining a growth mindset, you'll unlock your potential for long-term success and personal growth. Your path to greater grit and determination starts now.

～

THE POWER OF POSITIVE THINKING: BUILDING MENTAL STRENGTH AND RESILIENCE

HARNESSING the power of positive thinking is essential for building mental strength and resilience. Positive thinking doesn't mean ignoring life's less pleasant situations; it simply involves approaching unpleasantness more positively and productively. Here's how to cultivate positivity, reframe negative thoughts, and build resilience:

Cultivating Positivity

• **Surround Yourself with Positive Influences:** Spend time with people who uplift you and avoid those who sap your energy. This includes curating your media and social media consumption to reduce negativity.

• **Create Positive Habits:** Integrate activities that enhance your mood, such as exercising, reading, or engaging in hobbies you love. These habits can shift your mood and increase your overall happiness.

Reframing Negative Thoughts

• **Recognize Negative Patterns:** Learn of the instances when your thoughts turn negative. Acknowledging these patterns is the first step in changing them.

- **Challenge These Thoughts:** Question the validity of negative thoughts. For example, if you think, "I'll never be good at this," challenge that by asking, "What evidence do I have that supports this thought?"

- **Replace with Constructive Thoughts:** Instead of saying "I can't handle this," you might say, "I know this is challenging, but I'll tackle it step by step."

Building Resilience

- **Develop a Strong Sense of Purpose:** Having clear goals and a sense of direction can provide motivation and a framework for action, particularly during tough times.

- **Learn from Setbacks:** View failures as opportunities to learn and grow rather than as a negative reflection of your abilities.

- **Practice Emotional Regulation:** Techniques like deep breathing, meditation, or progressive muscle relaxation can help you manage emotions effectively, especially in stressful situations.

Staying Resilient in the Face of Adversity

- **Stay Connected:** Maintain strong, supportive relationships that provide love and acceptance. Social support is important for resilience in tough times.

- **Be Proactive:** Don't ignore problems or try to wish them away. Instead, figure out what needs to be done, make a plan, and act.

- **Maintain a Hopeful Outlook:** Optimism is a key part of resilience. Believing that good things will happen may sound simplistic, but it can help you see beyond current struggles.

Applying Positive Thinking in Daily Life

By consistently applying these strategies, you can harness the power of positive thinking to significantly enhance your mental strength. This approach not only improves your ability to cope with stress and adversity but also contributes to an overall happier and more fulfilling life.

Here are practical ways to start harnessing the power of positive thinking today:

- Surround yourself with positive people and curate your media consumption.
- Integrate mood-enhancing activities into your daily routine.
- Recognize negative thought patterns and actively challenge them.
- Replace negative thoughts with constructive, solution-focused ones.
- Develop a strong sense of purpose and clear goals.
- View setbacks as learning opportunities for growth.
- Practice emotional regulation techniques like deep breathing or meditation.
- Maintain strong, supportive relationships.
- Address problems and making plans.
- Cultivate an optimistic outlook, focusing on the possibilities.

Remember, building mental strength through positive thinking is an ongoing process. Every day presents new opportunities to reframe your thoughts, cultivate resilience, and approach life with a more optimistic mindset. By consistently applying these strategies, you'll not only enhance your ability to navigate life's challenges but also unlock a greater sense of happiness and fulfillment. Your journey to a more positive, resilient mindset starts now.

∽

PART ELEVEN WRAP-UP:

KEY POINTS:

• Mental strength is the foundation of resilience and perseverance, enhancing stress management, helping with recovery from setbacks, supporting goal achievement, enhancing decision making, and promoting personal growth.

• Building mental strength involves practices such as mindfulness and meditation, challenging negative thoughts, setting realistic goals, seeking support, and committing to continuous learning.

• A growth mindset is important for developing mental strength, as it encourages embracing challenges, persisting in the face of setbacks, valuing effort, learning from criticism, and being inspired by others' success.

• Overcoming setbacks and obstacles is an integral part of personal growth and success, requiring strategies such as understanding setbacks, developing a resilient mindset, effective goal setting, leveraging support networks, and maintaining a long-term perspective.

• Emotional intelligence (EQ) is essential for mental strength and effective relationships, enhancing self-awareness, improving relationships, enabling effective communication, and promoting better stress management.

• Cultivating grit and determination is important for achieving long-term goals and overcoming challenges, involving strategies such as setting long-term goals, embracing challenges, developing a growth mindset, fostering resilience, building supportive relationships, and continuous learning and adaptation.

• Positive thinking is powerful in building mental strength and resilience, requiring the cultivation of positivity, reframing of negative thoughts, and staying resilient in the face of adversity.

• Seeking support and practicing self-care are important for maintaining mental strength, involving using social networks, seeking professional help, joining communities and groups, engaging in physical activity, practicing mindfulness and meditation, maintaining a balanced diet and sleep, pursuing hobbies and interests, and setting boundaries.

Action Items:

• Practice mindfulness and meditation regularly to enhance emotional awareness and manage stress effectively.

• Challenge negative thoughts and replace them with constructive, solution-focused ones to foster a positive mindset.

• Set clear, long-term goals and break them down into actionable steps to maintain motivation and progress.

• Actively seek challenges that push you out of your comfort zone to build resilience and adaptability.

• Develop strategies to regulate emotions effectively, such as deep breathing, progressive muscle relaxation, or engaging in hobbies.

• Cultivate a supportive network of mentors, peers, and professionals to provide guidance, encouragement, and support.

• Commit to continuous learning and regular self-reflection to enhance personal growth and adaptability.

• Practice self-care consistently, including regular physical activity, a balanced diet, enough sleep, and engaging in hobbies and interests.

• Set clear boundaries with yourself and others to protect your mental health and well-being.

• Reframe setbacks and failures as opportunities for learning and growth, maintaining a long-term perspective on success.

• Develop emotional intelligence by practicing self-awareness, self-regulation, empathy, and effective communication in personal and professional settings.

• Cultivate grit and determination by persisting in the face of challenges, focusing on effort over success, and maintaining a growth mindset.

• Surround yourself with positive influences and actively challenge negative thought patterns to harness the power of positive thinking.

• Seek professional help when needed to navigate complex challenges and build mental strength.

• Regularly assess your progress and adjust your strategies as needed, while maintaining a commitment to your overall growth and development.

In our next part...

... we'll explore the transformative power of conquering fear and taking bold steps toward success. We'll dig into the psychological parts of fear, understanding its impact on personal and professional growth, and discover practical strategies for overcoming fear and embracing challenges as opportunities. Get ready to learn how to identify and challenge limiting beliefs, develop a growth mindset, and cultivate the resilience needed to navigate setbacks and failures on your journey to success.

. . .

As we start this exploration of fear and courage, we'll also uncover the importance of setting SMART goals and taking calculated risks. You'll gain valuable insights into assessing your risk tolerance, breaking down large goals into manageable tasks, and creating action plans that keep you motivated and accountable. By the end of this part, you'll have a powerful toolkit for conquering fear, embracing failure as a stepping stone to success, and unlocking your full potential for personal and professional achievement. So, let's dive in and discover how you can become the most courageous, resilient, and purposeful version of yourself.

~

PART TWELVE
EMBRACING COURAGE: CONQUERING FEAR AND TAKING BOLD STEPS TOWARD SUCCESS

UNDERSTANDING THE ROLE OF FEAR IN LIMITING SUCCESS:

FEAR CAN BE a formidable barrier to personal and professional growth. It often lurks behind feelings of inadequacy and hesitance to step into unknown territories, stifling potential and opportunities for success. Understanding and managing fear is important to taking bold steps toward meeting your goals. Here are strategies to help conquer fear and harness it to fuel your journey toward success:

Acknowledging and Understanding Fear

• **Identify Your Fears:** Start by identifying what scares you about the situation. Is it the fear of failure, rejection, or the unknown? Understanding the root of your fear is the first step in overcoming it.

• **Rationalize Your Fears:** Once you know what you're afraid of, question the validity of your fears. Are they based on facts, or are they hypothetical scenarios? Rationalizing your fears can reduce their power.

Strategies to Overcome Fear

• **Gradual Exposure:** Start small by taking gradual steps toward the things that scare you. This could mean taking on slightly more challenging projects at work or speaking up in meetings. Gradual exposure helps build confidence and reduce fear.

• **Visualization:** Imagine yourself successfully overcoming your fear. Visualization is a powerful tool that conditions your brain to recognize successful outcomes as possible realities.

• **Education and Preparation:** Often, fear stems from the unknown. Educating yourself about what you're facing can demystify fears and equip you with the knowledge to handle challenges better.

• **Mindfulness and Relaxation Techniques:** Practices like deep breathing, meditation, or yoga can help manage the physical and emotional symptoms of fear, helping you maintain calm and clarity in the face of challenges.

Cultivating a Positive Support Network

• **Seek Support:** Talk about your fears with trusted friends, family, or mentors. They can provide encouragement, offer new perspectives, or share their own experiences and strategies for dealing with similar fears.

• **Professional Help:** If your fear feels overwhelming, consider seeking help from a coach or therapist who can provide professional strategies to cope with and overcome deep-seated fears.

Embracing a Growth Mindset

• **Learn from Failures:** View failures as learning opportunities rather than setbacks. Analyze what went wrong, make changes, and try again with a better approach.

• **Celebrate Small Wins:** Recognizing and celebrating progress, no matter how small, can boost your confidence and motivate you to keep moving forward.

Applying Fear Conquering Strategies in Daily Life

Fear, while a natural reaction to risk and uncertainty, shouldn't be a roadblock to your success. By using these strategies, you can turn fear into a catalyst for growth and achievement. Remember, courage isn't the absence of fear but the triumph over it. Embrace your fears as part of your growth journey, letting them propel you toward your goals rather than hold you back.

Here are practical ways to start conquering fear and taking bold steps toward success:

- Identify your fears and understand the root causes behind them.
- Question the validity of your fears and rationalize them based on facts.
- Take gradual steps toward facing your fears, building confidence.
- Use visualization to imagine yourself successfully overcoming your fears.
- Educate yourself about the challenges you're facing to reduce fear of the unknown.
- Practice mindfulness and relaxation techniques to manage fear symptoms.
- Seek support from trusted friends, family, mentors, or professionals.
- View failures as learning opportunities and celebrate small wins along the way.
- Embrace a growth mindset, seeing fears as opportunities for development.

Remember that courage is not the absence of fear, but the triumph over it.

By consistently applying these strategies and maintaining a positive, growth-oriented mindset, you'll develop the mental strength and resilience to conquer your fears and take bold steps toward success. Every fear you face, every challenge you overcome, and every goal you pursue contributes to your personal and professional growth. Your path to greater courage and success starts with these simple yet powerful practices. Embrace your fears, harness their power, and let them fuel your journey to achieving your dreams.

IDENTIFYING PERSONAL FEARS: A SELF-REFLECTIVE EXERCISE

To EFFECTIVELY IDENTIFY and begin overcoming personal fears, readers can engage in the following self-reflective exercise. This process involves several steps designed to bring clarity and awareness, ultimately empowering individuals to address the fears that impede their progress.

Steps for Identifying Personal Fears:

Create a Reflective Space: Find a quiet and comfortable place where you can be undisturbed for a period. This setting should feel safe and calming, conducive to deep reflection.

Prepare to Reflect: Equip yourself with a notebook and a pen for jotting down thoughts, or prepare to use a digital device if you prefer typing. The key is to have a way to record your insights as they come.

Engage in Mindfulness or Meditation: Begin with a few minutes of mindfulness or meditation to center your thoughts and calm your mind. Focus on your breathing and allow yourself to become present in the moment.

Ask Guiding Questions: Reflect on moments where you felt held back or unusually stressed. Ask yourself questions such as:

- What situations make me feel anxious or afraid?
- When have I stopped myself from acting because I was scared?
- What is the worst that I imagine happening in these situations?
- How do these fears affect my decisions and actions?

Write Down Your Thoughts: As you ponder these questions, write down whatever thoughts, feelings, or memories come to mind. Don't censor or judge your responses; let them flow naturally.

Identify Patterns and Common Themes: Look over your notes and identify any recurring fears or themes. For example, you might notice that fear of failure often surfaces when you consider starting new projects.

Acknowledge and Accept Your Fears: Acknowledge these fears as a part of your experience. Accepting them does not mean resigning yourself to them but recognizing them as the first step toward over-coming them.

Develop an Action Plan: Consider strategies that could help you address these fears. This might include further self-reflection, seeking support from others, engaging in professional counseling, or gradually exposing yourself to the fear in manageable steps.

Moving Forward:

After identifying your fears through this exercise, the next steps involve working to mitigate their influence over your life. This might include setting small, achievable goals that challenge these fears or discussing your feelings with a trusted friend or mentor who can offer support and accountability.

Remember, the goal of this exercise isn't to eliminate fear —fear is a natural and sometimes useful part of the human experience. Instead, it aims to prevent fear from becoming a barrier to your personal and professional fulfillment. By understanding and managing your fears, you can make more empowered choices and open up new possibilities for your future.

Practical Tips for Implementing This Exercise:

Schedule a dedicated time for this self-reflection, ensuring you won't be interrupted.

Start with a short mindfulness or meditation practice to settle your mind.

Ask yourself guiding questions and write down your thoughts without judgment.

Identify common themes or recurring fears in your responses.

Accept these fears as part of your experience, but not as defining factors.

Develop a plan to address these fears through self-reflection, support, or gradual exposure.

Set small, achievable goals that challenge your fears.

Discuss your fears and plan with a trusted friend or mentor for support and accountability.

Remember that the goal is to manage fears, not eliminate them.

Celebrate your progress and continue to reflect on and manage your fears.

By engaging in this self-reflective exercise and implementing these practical steps, you can gain a clearer understanding of your personal fears and begin to develop strategies to overcome them. This process of self-discovery and proactive management can be a powerful tool in your journey toward greater personal and professional fulfillment. Remember, every small step you take in addressing your fears is a step toward a more empowered, authentic life.

CHALLENGING LIMITING BELIEFS: A PATH TO PERSONAL GROWTH AND SUCCESS

CHALLENGING LIMITING beliefs is a transformative process that can improve your approach to success and personal fulfillment. By systematically addressing and restructuring the negative beliefs that undermine your confidence and ambition, you can adopt a more empowering and proactive mindset. Here's how you can begin this important journey:

Steps to Challenge Limiting Beliefs

Identify Your Limiting Beliefs: Reflect on the thoughts that often come up when you face a challenge or setback. These might manifest as self-doubt, fear of failure, or beliefs you lack the skills or deserve success. Keep a journal to track these thoughts over a few days or weeks to recognize patterns.

Question Their Validity: Examine these beliefs critically. Ask yourself questions like:

- "What evidence do I have that supports this belief?"
- "Are there instances where this belief has not held true?"
- "What would I tell a friend who had these thoughts?"

Reframe the Beliefs: For each limiting belief, try to formulate a positive counterpart. For example, change "I always make mistakes" to "Every mistake is a learning opportunity." This reframing helps shift your focus from self-criticism to self-improvement and growth.

Seek Evidence to Support New Beliefs: Actively look for real-life examples where your new, positive beliefs are true. This might involve taking small risks to show your capability, engaging in new learning opportunities, or simply observing others who embody these positive beliefs.

Visualize Success: Incorporate visualization techniques where you see yourself as successful and confident. Regular visualization can reinforce your new beliefs and decrease the power of old, limiting thoughts.

Create Affirmations: Develop affirmations that reinforce your new beliefs. Repeat these affirmations daily or whenever you slip back into old thought patterns.

Seek Support: Talk to mentors, coaches, or peers about your goal to overcome limiting beliefs. They can offer support, accountability, and advice based on their experiences.

Practice Persistence: Changing deep-seated beliefs takes time and persistent effort. Recognize and celebrate small victories along the way to motivate yourself.

Example Scenario: Overcoming the Fear of Public Speaking

Suppose you have a deep-seated belief you are poor at public speaking and that you embarrass yourself every time you try. Here's how you could apply the steps above:

- **Identify:** Recognize and write down your belief: "I'm terrible at public speaking."
- **Question:** Reflect on experiences. Were there occasions where you received positive feedback?
- **Reframe:** Change your belief to "Every public speaking opportunity is a chance to improve and connect with my audience."

- **Seek Evidence:** Volunteer for small speaking engagements and focus on the positive feedback.
- **Visualize:** Regularly imagine giving a successful, engaging talk.
- **Affirmations:** Daily remind yourself, "I am a confident and capable speaker."
- **Support:** Join a local Toastmasters club to practice in a supportive environment.
- **Persist:** Keep seeking opportunities to speak and refine your skills, despite setbacks.

Practical Tips for Challenging Limiting Beliefs:

- Set aside dedicated time for self-reflection and belief examination.
- Write down your limiting beliefs and their positive counterparts.
- List evidence that supports your new, empowering beliefs.
- Practice visualization and affirmations daily.
- Share your journey with supportive friends, mentors, or professionals.
- Take small, consistent steps toward challenging your beliefs through action.
- Celebrate your progress and learn from setbacks.
- Be patient and persistent; changing beliefs takes time and consistent effort.
- Regularly revisit and refine your new beliefs as you grow and learn.
- Embrace the discomfort of growth and continue to push your boundaries.

By putting these strategies into practice, you can begin to dismantle the limiting beliefs that hold you back and build a more resilient, confident self-image. This proactive approach not only fosters personal growth but also equips you to handle future challenges with greater ease and assurance. Remember, every step you take toward challenging your limiting beliefs is a step toward a more empowered, fulfilling life. Embrace the journey and trust in your ability to grow and thrive.

~

DEVELOPING A FEAR CONQUERING MINDSET: STRATEGIES FOR DAILY PRACTICE

INCORPORATING strategies such as positive self-talk, visualization, mindfulness, and gradual exposure into your daily routine can significantly enhance your ability to manage and conquer fears. Each technique offers a unique approach to strengthening your mental resilience:

Positive Self-Talk:

• **Technique:** Regularly track and adjust your inner dialogue.

• **Benefits:** Shifts your focus from self-doubt to self-empowerment, enhancing your overall confidence and ability to handle stress.

Visualization:

• **Technique:** Regularly practice envisioning yourself successfully overcoming challenges.

• **Benefits:** Prepares your mind for success, reduces anxiety associated with fear, and enhances your confidence in facing real-life situations.

Mindfulness:

• **Technique:** Engage in daily practices such as meditation, mindful breathing, or sensory exercises.

• **Benefits:** Increases your awareness of present emotions and thoughts, allows for better management of stress, and promotes a calm, centered state of mind.

Gradual Exposure:

• **Technique:** Systematically expose yourself to the fear in small, manageable increments.

• **Benefits:** Helps desensitize your reaction to fear, builds tolerance, and enhances control over your emotional responses.

Practical Applications and Tips:

• **Create a Daily Routine:** Incorporate these practices into your daily life. Start with a few minutes a day, gradually increasing the time as you become more comfortable with the exercises.

• **Keep a Journal:** Document your thoughts, feelings, and progress. Note any changes in your reactions to fear-inducing situations and celebrate your victories, no matter how small.

• **Seek Professional Guidance:** If your fears feel overwhelming, consider seeking the help of a therapist who can guide you through these techniques, particularly visualization and gradual exposure.

• **Join Support Groups:** Connecting with others also working to conquer their fears can provide more support, motivation, and accountability.

Empowering Affirmations for Conquering Fear:

- "I am capable of overcoming any challenges that come my way."
- "Every step I take in facing my fears strengthens my confidence."
- "I choose to focus on positive outcomes and possibilities."
- "I am resilient, strong, and brave in the face of adversity."

Integrating Fear-Conquering Strategies into Your Life:

- Schedule dedicated time for positive self-talk, visualization, and mindfulness practices.
- Start small, with a few minutes a day, and gradually increase the duration.
- Keep a fear-conquering journal to track your progress and celebrate your successes.
- Create a plan for gradual exposure to your fears, starting with manageable steps.
- Practice your affirmations daily, especially when facing challenging situations.
- Seek support from professionals, support groups, or trusted friends and mentors.
- Be patient and persistent; developing a fear conquering mindset takes time and practice.
- Celebrate your progress and learn from any setbacks along the way.
- Continuously update and refine your strategies as you grow and face new challenges.
- Embrace the process of personal growth and let your fears fuel your determination to succeed.

By embracing these strategies, you not only enhance your ability to conquer fears but also empower yourself to take on new challenges and opportunities with a stronger, more resilient mindset. Remember, the journey to overcoming fear is progressive, and each small step forward is a victory in building a fearless approach to life. With consistent practice and dedication, you can cultivate a mind ready to face any fear and pursue your goals with unwavering confidence.

∽

TAKING CALCULATED RISKS: STRATEGIES FOR GROWTH AND SUCCESS

TAKING calculated risks is not just about seeking thrill or danger—it's about deliberately stepping out of your comfort zone to achieve growth and success. This approach requires careful consideration and strategic planning. Here are several key strategies to help you effectively embrace and manage calculated risks:

Understand Your Risk Tolerance

• **Assessment:** Determine your personal and professional tolerance for risk. Consider factors like financial stability, emotional resilience, and the potential impact on your relationships and career.

• **Action:** Align your risk-taking activities with your level of comfort and readiness to handle potential setbacks.

Educate Yourself

• **Research:** Gather information about the situation or decision at hand. Understanding the details will help you make an informed choice and reduce the unknowns that can contribute to fear.

• **Consult:** Speak with mentors, industry experts, or peers with experience in similar situations to gain insights and advice.

Evaluate Benefits and Consequences

• **Analysis:** Weigh the potential benefits against the risks. Consider the best and worst-case scenarios, and realistically assess the likelihood of each outcome.

• **Pros and Cons:** Create a list to visualize the advantages and drawbacks, helping clarify the decision-making process.

Plan Strategically

• **Preparation:** Develop clear, actionable steps to approach the risk. Planning helps mitigate potential negative consequences and outlines a path to success.

• **Contingency Plans:** Have backup plans in place. Knowing you have alternatives can reduce anxiety and boost confidence.

Start Small

• **Incremental Steps:** Begin with smaller risks to build your confidence and understanding of what it takes to manage and benefit from taking chances.

• **Reflect:** After each risk, no matter the outcome, take time to reflect on what you learned and how it can apply to future decisions.

Build a Support System

• **Network:** Surround yourself with a supportive network that encourages your growth and provides honest feedback.

• **Emotional Support:** Ensure you have people who can provide emotional support and guidance through the ups and downs of risk-taking.

Embrace Failure as a Learning Opportunity

• **Perspective:** View failures as valuable lessons rather than setbacks. Analyze what went wrong, what went right, and how you can improve.

• **Resilience:** Cultivating resilience through experiencing failure can strengthen your ability to manage future risks more effectively.

Practical Tips for Implementing Risk-Taking Strategies:

- Assess your risk tolerance and align your actions.
- Thoroughly research and consult with experts before making decisions.
- Analyze the potential benefits and consequences of each risk.
- Develop a strategic plan and have contingency plans in place.
- Start with small risks and gradually build up to bigger ones.
- Reflect on each risk-taking experience to learn and grow.
- Build a supportive network of mentors, peers, and loved ones.
- Embrace failures as opportunities for learning and growth.
- Continuously reassess and adjust your risk-taking strategies as needed.
- Celebrate your successes and learn from your setbacks along the way.

By adopting these strategies, you're not only preparing yourself to take calculated risks but also positioning yourself to grow from each experience, whether it leads to success or provides a valuable lesson. Remember, the goal of taking risks is not to eliminate fear but to understand and manage it so it doesn't prevent you from reaching your full potential. With a strategic approach and a growth mindset, you can harness the power of calculated risk-taking to unlock new opportunities, foster personal and professional development, and ultimately meet your goals with greater confidence and resilience.

$\sim$

EMBRACING FAILURE AS A STEPPINGSTONE:

REFRAMING failure as an opportunity for growth is essential for fostering resilience and perseverance. By embracing failure, we can enhance our problem-solving skills, develop emotional resilience, and learn to navigate obstacles more effectively. Here's a deeper look into how we can transform our perception of failure and setbacks into a positive force for personal development:

Understanding Failure

• **Normalizing Failure:** Recognize that failure is a common and natural part of the learning process. By normalizing it, we reduce the stigma and fear associated with making mistakes.

• **Analyzing Outcomes:** Each failure provides valuable data. Analyzing what went wrong and why can offer insights critical for future success.

Strategies for Embracing Failure

• **Growth Mindset:** Cultivate a growth mindset by viewing skills and abilities as qualities that can be developed through dedication and hard work. This perspective encourages viewing challenges as opportunities to grow.

• **Emotional Agility:** Develop emotional agility by learning to approach uncomfortable emotions with curiosity and openness. This helps in managing negative emotions related to failure and turning them into constructive feedback.

• **Resilience Building:** Strengthen resilience by setting small, incremental goals that lead to larger goals. This gradual approach helps build confidence and reduce the fear of large failures.

Practical Exercises

• **Failure Autopsy:** Regularly conduct a "failure autopsy" where you reflect on a setback and identify both the factors that led to the failure and the lessons learned. This exercise can help demystify failure and integrate useful lessons into future endeavors.

• **Visualization:** Practice visualization exercises where you imagine encountering a setback and then handling it successfully. This mental rehearsal can build psychological preparedness and confidence.

Creating a Supportive Environment

• **Seek Constructive Feedback:** Regularly seek feedback not just on successes but also on failures. Constructive criticism can be invaluable in learning and improvement.

• **Share Failure Stories:** Create a culture, whether at work or in personal circles, where sharing stories of failure is encouraged. This helps to destigmatize failure and highlight it as a part of the growth process.

Practical Tips for Embracing Failure:

- Acknowledge and accept failures as a natural part of the learning process.
- Analyze each failure to identify lessons and areas for improvement.
- Cultivate a growth mindset and view challenges as opportunities for development.

- Practice emotional agility by approaching negative emotions with curiosity and openness.
- Build resilience through setting small, incremental goals and celebrating progress.
- Conduct regular "failure autopsies" to reflect on setbacks and extract valuable lessons.
- Use visualization exercises to mentally prepare for potential failures and build confidence.
- Actively seek constructive feedback on both successes and failures.
- Create a supportive environment that encourages sharing failure stories and lessons learned.
- Maintain persistence and focus on continuous learning and improvement.

By shifting how we perceive and react to failure, we can transform it from a source of fear and embarrassment into a powerful tool for learning and innovation. The key is to maintain persistence, learn from every experience, and keep moving forward with an enriched understanding and renewed focus. Embracing failure not only builds resilience but also paves the way for a culture of continuous improvement and enduring success. By normalizing failure, analyzing outcomes, developing a growth mindset, and creating a supportive environment, we can harness the power of failure as a steppingstone to personal and professional growth, ultimately leading to greater achievements and fulfilment in all parts of life.

TAKING BOLD STEPS TOWARD SUCCESS: A ROADMAP FOR SETTING AND ACHIEVING SMART GOALS

SETTING SMART goals and taking bold actions toward them is important for success. Here's a detailed roadmap for implementing these goals effectively and overcoming fear and obstacles along the way:

Setting SMART Goals

Specific: Define your goals with precision. Clear and detailed descriptions help focus efforts and foster understanding.

Measurable: Establish concrete criteria for measuring progress. Determine how you will know when the goals are met.

Achievable: Ensure that your goals are attainable. This involves assessing your current resources and capabilities and setting realistic expectations.

Relevant: Align your goals with your values and long-term goals. This makes sure your efforts are focused on what's important to you.

Time-Bound: Set deadlines for your goals. Having a timeline increases urgency and prompts action.

Practical Steps for Implementation

Break It Down: Divide large goals into smaller, manageable tasks. This can reduce overwhelm and provide clear next steps.

Create a Timeline: Plot out deadlines for each task and milestone. This helps maintain momentum and tracks progress.

Accountability: Share your goals with a mentor, friend, or peer group. Accountability can increase your commitment and inspire action.

Overcoming Fear and Obstacles

Acknowledge Fear: Recognize and accept your fears as a natural part of the process. Understanding the sources of your fear can help you address them more effectively.

Reframe Challenges: View obstacles as opportunities to learn and grow. Each challenge is a chance to improve your skills and adapt your strategies.

Stay Flexible: Be willing to adjust your plans when faced with setbacks. Flexibility can help you navigate difficulties more effectively.

Seek Support: Don't hesitate to ask for help or guidance. Others can offer valuable insights, encouragement, and support.

Maintain Persistence: Stay committed to your goals, even when progress is slow. Persistence is key to overcoming challenges.

Encouragement and Motivation

- **Celebrate Progress:** Take time to acknowledge and celebrate your successes, no matter how small. This can boost your morale and motivation.

- **Reflect on Your Journey:** Regular reflection on what you've learned and how you've grown can reinforce your resolve and remind you of why your goals are worth pursuing.

Actionable Tips for Goal Achievement:

Write down your SMART goals and place them in a visible location for daily reminders.

Create a detailed action plan with specific tasks, deadlines, and milestones.

Schedule dedicated time for working on your goals and focus on them in your daily routine.

Find an accountability partner or join a support group to stay motivated and on track.

Regularly assess your progress and adjust your plan as needed.

Practice positive self-talk and visualization techniques to overcome fear and self-doubt.

Celebrate your successes, no matter how small, to maintain momentum and motivation.

Learn from setbacks and failures and use them as opportunities for growth and improvement.

Continuously educate yourself and seek resources and mentors to support your journey.

Maintain a growth mindset and embrace challenges as opportunities for personal development.

By following these strategies and embracing a proactive approach, you can not only set SMART goals but also effectively navigate the journey toward achieving them, turning potential setbacks into steppingstones for success. Remember, success is not just about reaching the destination but also about the personal growth and resilience you develop along the way. Stay focused, stay committed, and keep taking bold steps toward your goals, knowing that each step, no matter how small, is bringing you closer to your ultimate vision of success.

Case Study:

Stephanie had always dreamed of starting her own business, but fear held her back. She worried about the risks, the potential for failure, and whether she had what it takes to succeed. Despite her passion and innovative ideas, Stephanie found herself stuck in a comfortable but unfulfilling corporate job, watching as others pursued their entrepreneurial dreams.

One day, a friend recommended a workshop on conquering fear and taking bold steps toward success. Intrigued, Sarah decided to attend, hoping to gain new perspectives on her situation.

At the workshop, Stephanie learned about the role of fear in limiting potential and holding people back from pursuing their goals. The facilitator explained that fear is a natural human response to uncertainty and risk, but that it can be managed and even harnessed as a motivator for growth.

Through various exercises and discussions, Stephanie began to identify and understand her specific fears around starting a business. She realized that her fear of failure was rooted in a deep-seated belief she wasn't capable or deserving of success. She also recognized that her fear of the unknown was keeping her from taking even small steps toward her dream.

Armed with this new self-awareness, Stephanie began to develop strategies for overcoming her fears. She started by setting small, achievable goals for herself, such as researching potential business ideas and contacting mentors in her industry. As she took these initial steps, Stephanie practiced reframing her fears as opportunities for learning and growth.

When doubts and anxieties arose, Stephanie used techniques like positive self-talk and visualization to counter them. She began to imagine herself as a successful entrepreneur, handling challenges with confidence and resilience. She also started a daily gratitude practice, focusing on the strengths and resources she already had that could help her on her journey.

As Stephanie continued to work on her mindset and take consistent action toward her goals, she began to notice a shift in her perspective. The risks and uncertainties of starting a business began to feel less daunting, and more like exciting challenges to be navigated. She sought out opportunities to learn and grow, rather than shying away from them.

One of the most transformative parts of Stephanie's journey was learning to embrace failure as a necessary part of the growth process. Through the workshop and her own research, Stephanie came to understand that all successful entrepreneurs face setbacks and failures along the way. The key, she realized, was to view these experiences as valuable lessons and opportunities for improvement, rather than as definitive defeats.

This mindset shift let Stephanie approach her business ventures with a greater sense of resilience and adaptability. When her first product launch didn't go as planned, instead of being discouraged, Stephanie analyzed the situation, gathered feedback, and used those insights to refine her approach. She learned to celebrate her progress and efforts, rather than tying her self-worth only to outcomes.

As Stephanie continued to take bold steps toward her goals, she also recognized the importance of building a strong support system. She joined entrepreneurial networks and sought mentors who could offer guidance and encouragement. Surrounding herself with others also pursuing their dreams helped Stephanie stay motivated and accountable.

Over time, Stephanie's consistent efforts and growth-oriented mindset began to yield results. Her business gained traction, attracting clients and positive attention within her industry. While the journey was not without its challenges and setbacks, Stephanie approached each obstacle with greater confidence and determination.

Looking back on her journey, Stephanie realized that conquering her fears had been a process of self-discovery and empowerment. By learning to understand and manage her anxieties, reframe challenges as opportunities, and embrace failure as a steppingstone to success, she had not only built a thriving business but also transformed her own sense of self.

Stephanie's story is a powerful reminder that fear, while a natural part of the human experience, need not hold us back from pursuing our dreams. By developing a toolkit of strategies for understanding and managing fear, setting SMART goals, and taking consistent action, we all have the capacity to overcome our limiting beliefs and achieve extraordinary things.

Her journey also highlights the importance of cultivating a growth mindset, one that embraces challenges and failures as opportunities for learning and development. By shifting our perspective in this way, we open ourselves up to a world of possibility and resilience.

The path to conquering fear and succeeding is not always a straight line. It requires patience, persistence, and a willingness to adapt and learn from setbacks. But as Stephanie's experience shows, the rewards of this journey are immeasurable – not just in terms of external achievements, but in the profound personal growth and self-discovery that occurs along the way.

So let Stephanie's story be an invitation to all of us – to courageously examine our own fears and limiting beliefs, to set bold and meaningful goals for ourselves, and to take consistent, purposeful action toward those goals. Let us remember that every challenge we face, every obstacle we overcome, is an opportunity to develop our resilience, creativity, and strength.

By embracing the strategies and mindset shifts that Stephanie employed, we too can learn to harness the power of our fears and transform them into fuel for our growth and success. We can build lives and careers that are not only externally rewarding, but that also reflect our deepest values and aspirations.

This journey of conquering fear and pursuing our dreams is not for the faint of heart. It requires courage, introspection, and a willingness to step outside of our comfort zones. But as Stephanie's story reminds us, the rewards of this journey are boundless – a life of purpose, fulfillment, and continuous growth.

So let us each take a page from Stephanie's book and begin examining our fears, setting bold goals, and taking meaningful action. Let us support and encourage one another on this path, celebrating our victories and learning from our setbacks. And let us remember that within each of us lies the potential for extraordinary growth and achievement – if only we will embrace the journey with openness and courage.

The path to conquering fear and achieving our dreams starts with a single step – a commitment to self-discovery, growth, and bold action. May we all find the strength and determination to take that step, and to keep walking forward, one brave choice at a time. For through this journey, we not only achieve external success, but also become the most empowered, resilient, and authentic versions of ourselves.

PART TWELVE WRAP-UP:

• Fear can be a formidable barrier to personal and professional growth, stifling potential and opportunities for success.

• Acknowledging and understanding fear involves identifying its roots, rationalizing fears based on facts, and accepting them as part of the experience.

• Strategies to overcome fear include gradual exposure, visualization, education and preparation, mindfulness and relaxation techniques, seeking support, and embracing a growth mindset.

• Challenging limiting beliefs is a transformative process that involves identifying beliefs, questioning their validity, reframing them positively, seeking evidence to support new beliefs, visualizing success, creating affirmations, seeking support, and practicing persistence.

• Developing a fear conquering mindset requires daily practices such as positive self-talk, visualization, mindfulness, and gradual exposure to fears.

• Taking calculated risks involves understanding risk tolerance, educating oneself, evaluating benefits and consequences, planning strategically, starting small, building a support system, and embracing failure as a learning opportunity.

• Embracing failure as a steppingstone to success involves normalizing failure, analyzing outcomes, cultivating a growth mindset, developing emotional agility, building resilience, conducting failure autopsies, using visualization exercises, seeking constructive feedback, and creating a supportive environment.

• Setting SMART (Specific, Measurable, Achievable, Relevant, Time-Bound) goals and taking bold actions toward them is important for success, requiring breaking down goals, creating timelines, ensuring accountability, overcoming fear and obstacles, staying flexible, seeking support, maintaining persistence, celebrating progress, and reflecting on the journey.

Action Items:

• Identify your fears and understand their root causes through self-reflection and journaling.

• Gradually expose yourself to fear-inducing situations, starting with manageable steps, to build confidence and resilience.

• Practice visualization techniques, imagining yourself successfully overcoming fears and meeting your goals.

• Educate yourself about the challenges you face and prepare to reduce fear of the unknown.

• Incorporate mindfulness and relaxation techniques into your daily routine to manage fear and stress effectively.

• Seek support from trusted friends, family, mentors, or professionals to gain encouragement, guidance, and accountability.

• Challenge your limiting beliefs by questioning their validity, reframing them positively, and seeking evidence to support new, empowering beliefs.

• Develop a fear conquering mindset through daily practices such as positive self-talk, affirmations, and gradual exposure to fears.

• Assess your risk tolerance and take calculated risks by thoroughly researching, planning strategically, and starting with small steps.

• Embrace failure as a learning opportunity by analyzing outcomes, cultivating a growth mindset, developing emotional agility, and seeking constructive feedback.

• Set SMART goals and create detailed action plans with specific tasks, deadlines, and milestones.

• Break down large goals into smaller, manageable tasks and celebrate progress along the way to maintain motivation.

• Stay flexible and adaptable in the face of setbacks, viewing them as opportunities for growth and learning.

• Maintain persistence and commitment to your goals, even when progress is slow or challenges arise.

• Continuously reflect on your journey, learn from experiences, and adjust your strategies as needed to support ongoing personal and professional growth.

In our next part...

... we'll start a transformative journey toward embracing an attitude of abundance and unlocking the secrets to a prosperous, fulfilling life. We'll explore the powerful shift from a scarcity mentality to one of abundance, and discover practical strategies for cultivating gratitude, reframing limiting beliefs, and aligning your actions with your deepest intentions. Get ready to learn how to set clear, meaningful financial goals and make inspired decisions that propel you toward the wealth and success you desire.

• • •

As we dive into this exploration of abundance, we'll also uncover the essential features of a prosperous mindset, such as resilience, optimism, growth-orientation, and financial literacy. You'll gain valuable insights into how to develop these traits within yourself and harness their power to create a life of true abundance. By the end of this part, you'll have a comprehensive toolkit for overcoming scarcity thinking, embracing the flow of abundance, and manifesting your most ambitious dreams. So, let's start this exciting journey together and discover the boundless potential that awaits you on the other side of an abundant mindset.

~

PART THIRTEEN
EMBRACING ABUNDANCE: UNLOCKING THE SECRETS TO A PROSPEROUS MINDSET AND THRIVING FINANCIAL FUTURE

UNDERSTANDING THE CONCEPT OF AN ATTITUDE OF ABUNDANCE:

ADOPTING an attitude of abundance is transformative, fostering a life enriched with wealth, opportunities, and contentment. Here's a deeper exploration of how this mindset can be cultivated and its impact:

Cultivating an Attitude of Abundance

Recognize Abundance Around You:

• Start by acknowledging the abundance that already exists in your life. This could be anything from natural resources, opportunities for personal growth, or the abundance of love and support from friends and family.

• Regularly practicing gratitude by maintaining a gratitude journal or sharing what you are thankful for with others can help cement the recognition of abundance.

Shift Your Focus:

• Redirect your focus from what you lack to what you have. This shift in perspective encourages a positive emotional state and enhances your ability to attract more abundance.

• Celebrate others' successes. Viewing other people's achievements as a source of inspiration rather than competition fosters an abundant mindset.

Abandon Scarcity Thinking:

• Identify and challenge any scarcity-based beliefs. These might include thoughts like "there isn't enough for everyone" or "if someone else succeeds, I will fail."

• Replace these thoughts with affirmations that emphasize abundance, such as "There is plenty for everyone, and my success contributes to the success of others."

Be Open to Possibilities:

• Stay open to unexpected opportunities. An abundance mindset is flexible and adaptive, understanding that opportunities for wealth and growth can come from unforeseen places.

• Continuously educate and improve yourself to be ready to seize opportunities as they arise.

Impact of an Attitude of Abundance

Enhanced Creativity and Innovation:

• By believing in limitless possibilities, you're more likely to venture into new ideas and innovative solutions without the fear of scarcity.

Increased Resilience:

• Viewing challenges as opportunities rather than insurmountable obstacles can help you recover from setbacks more quickly.

Better Relationships:

• An abundance mindset encourages sharing and generosity, traits that strengthen relationships and build trust.

Greater Satisfaction and Happiness:

• Focusing on abundance can lead to higher life satisfaction, as you appreciate and maximize what you have instead of fixating on what's missing.

Practical Tips for Embracing an Abundance Mindset:

- Practice daily gratitude by keeping a journal or sharing with others.
- Reframe negative thoughts and limiting beliefs into positive affirmations.
- Celebrate the successes and achievements of others.
- Focus on what you have rather than what you lack.
- Engage in acts of generosity and kindness toward others.
- Continuously learn and develop yourself to seize new opportunities.
- Surround yourself with positive, abundant-minded individuals.
- Set ambitious goals and believe in your ability to achieve them.
- Embrace challenges as opportunities for growth and learning.
- Regularly visualize and affirm your ideal life of abundance and prosperity.

Overall, an attitude of abundance encourages a richer, more fulfilling life. It lets individuals transcend the limitations of scarcity, opening up new vistas for personal and professional growth. By embracing and practicing this mindset, you align yourself with the wealth of opportunities the world offers, leading to a more prosperous and joyful existence.

Remember, abundance is not just about financial wealth but also the richness of experiences, relationships, and personal growth. By shifting your mindset and focusing on the abundance around you, you can attract more positivity, success, and fulfillment into your life.

OVERCOMING SCARCITY MENTALITY: A STEP-BY-STEP GUIDE TO EMBRACING ABUNDANCE

OVERCOMING LIMITING beliefs rooted in scarcity thinking is important for anyone looking to fully embrace wealth and prosperity. Here's a step-by-step guide to shift your mindset toward abundance:

Identify Limiting Beliefs

• **Awareness:** Start by acknowledging the limiting beliefs that influence your perception of wealth and opportunities. These could ingrain ideas like "Money is the root of all evil," or "You have to work hard to be rich."

• **Reflection:** Reflect on how these beliefs have shaped your behavior and decision-making regarding wealth and prosperity.

Challenge Scarcity Mentality

• **Question Your Beliefs:** Ask yourself if these beliefs are your own or if they've been adopted from external influences like family or societal norms.

• **Seek Contradictory Evidence:** Look for evidence that disproves your limiting beliefs. For example, if you believe that "money corrupts," research or talk to people who have used their wealth for good.

Cultivate a Mindset of Abundance

• **Gratitude:** Practice daily gratitude to shift focus from what you lack to what you have. This can significantly change your perception of abundance.

• **Positive Affirmations:** Use affirmations that reinforce abundance, such as "There is plenty for everyone," or "I attract prosperity with ease."

Visualize Prosperity

• **Mental Imagery:** Regularly visualize yourself achieving wealth and prosperity. Imagine living your ideal life and how it feels to have met your financial goals.

• **Create a Vision Board:** Put together a vision board that represents your goals and dreams. This can serve as a constant reminder and inspiration.

Educate Yourself

• **Financial Literacy:** Invest in learning about money management, investment strategies, and wealth creation. Knowledge is a powerful tool against scarcity thinking.

• **Personal Development:** Work on personal growth to enhance your self-esteem and belief in your ability to achieve prosperity.

Surround Yourself with Positivity

• **Supportive Network:** Build a network of supportive, like-minded individuals who encourage and inspire you to reach your potential.

• **Limit Negative Influences:** Minimize contact with those who reinforce scarcity thinking or undermine your confidence.

Take Action

• **Set Concrete Goals:** Use SMART (Specific, Measurable, Achievable, Relevant, Time-bound) criteria to set goals that foster growth and prosperity.

• **Step-by-Step Approach:** Break your goals into actionable steps to avoid feeling overwhelmed and keep track of your progress.

Practical Exercises for Overcoming Scarcity Mentality:

- Write down your limiting beliefs about money and wealth, then challenge each one with contradictory evidence.
- Start a gratitude journal and write down three things you're grateful for each day.
- Create a list of abundance affirmations and repeat them daily, especially when faced with scarcity thoughts.
- Spend 10-15 minutes each day visualizing your ideal life of prosperity and abundance.
- Read books or go to seminars on financial literacy and personal development.
- Join a mastermind group or find a mentor who embodies an abundance mindset.
- Set three SMART financial goals for the next 6 months and create an action plan to achieve them.
- Practice giving and sharing your resources, whether it's time, money, or knowledge.
- Regularly review your progress and celebrate your successes, no matter how small.
- Continuously work on personal growth and self-improvement to reinforce your abundance mindset.

Adopting an attitude of abundance is not just about wishing for more but actively reshaping your mindset to open up to prosperity. By consciously working on overcoming your scarcity mentality, you empower yourself to pursue wealth and success without the mental constraints that once held you back. Remember, abundance is a state of mind, and by consistently practicing these steps and exercises, you can transform your relationship with wealth and create a life of true prosperity and fulfillment.

〜

HARNESSING THE POWER OF GRATITUDE AND APPRECIATION FOR ABUNDANCE

GRATITUDE AND APPRECIATION are powerful tools that can transform our perception and help attract wealth and prosperity into our lives. By cultivating a consistent practice of gratitude, we can create a positive ripple effect that enhances our overall well-being and opens us up to abundant possibilities. Here are effective practices and exercises to help you harness the power of gratitude:

Daily Gratitude Journaling

• **Practice:** Dedicate a few minutes each day to write down what you are thankful for. Focus on both big and small things—from a successful project at work to a beautiful sunset.

• **Benefit:** This helps shift your focus from what's missing in your life to what's present, fostering a sense of contentment and abundance.

Gratitude Affirmations

• **Practice:** Start your day with positive affirmations focused on gratitude. Examples include "I am grateful for my ability to create wealth," or "I appreciate every opportunity that comes my way."

• **Benefit:** Repeating these affirmations can rewire your brain to recognize and appreciate abundance, enhancing your openness to prosperity.

Gratitude Meditation

• **Practice:** Engage in a daily meditation session focusing on things you are grateful for. This can be as simple as breathing deeply and mentally acknowledging the gifts in your life.

• **Benefit:** Meditation not only reduces stress but also enhances your emotional connection to feelings of gratitude, which can attract more positive experiences.

Send Thank You Notes

• **Practice:** Make it a habit to send thank-you notes or messages to people who have helped or inspired you. This can be through email, text, or traditional mail.

• **Benefit:** Expressing gratitude to others increases your positive social interactions and deepens relationships, creating a supportive network that can propel you toward success.

Gratitude Visits

• **Practice:** Periodically, visit or call someone specifically to thank them for how they've positively affected your life.

• **Benefit:** This practice not only strengthens bonds but also reinforces your own feelings of gratitude, enriching your emotional well-being.

Appreciation Pause

• **Practice:** Throughout your day, take brief pauses to appreciate your immediate environment or recent interactions that were positive.

• **Benefit:** These pauses can help you maintain a constant state of gratitude, which keeps you attuned to the abundance in your life.

Gratitude Reflection

• **Practice:** At the end of each week, reflect on all the positive things that happened. You might write them down, discuss them with a friend, or simply think about them quietly.

• **Benefit:** Regular reflection reinforces your gratitude practice and helps cement the habit of recognizing and celebrating abundance.

Actionable Steps to Cultivate Gratitude:

- Set aside 5-10 minutes each morning to write in your gratitude journal.
- Choose 3-5 gratitude affirmations and repeat them daily, especially when faced with challenges.
- Incorporate a 10-minute gratitude meditation into your daily routine.
- Send at least one thank-you note or message per week to someone who has positively affected your life.
- Schedule a monthly gratitude visit or call with a friend, family member, or mentor.
- Set reminders throughout your day to take appreciation pauses and acknowledge the good around you.
- Dedicate time each Sunday to reflect on the positive experiences and accomplishments of the past week.
- Share your gratitude practices with others and encourage them to join you in cultivating appreciation.
- Create a gratitude jar or box where you can store notes of appreciation to review when you need a boost.
- Continuously seek new opportunities to express gratitude and appreciate the abundance in your life.
- Incorporating these practices into your routine can fundamentally change your approach to life, turning gratitude into a daily norm. As you become more attuned to the abundance around you, you'll likely find that opportunities for wealth and prosperity begin to flow more freely into your life.

Remember, gratitude is a powerful magnet for attracting positive experiences and abundance. By consistently practicing appreciation, you can transform your mindset, enhance your well-being, and open yourself up to a world of limitless possibilities.

~

SHIFTING FROM A MINDSET OF LACK TO ONE OF ABUNDANCE:

TRANSITIONING from a scarcity mindset to one of abundance is about changing how you perceive and interact with the world. Let's break down the common thought patterns that signify a scarcity mindset and explore effective strategies to cultivate an abundance mindset:

Common Scarcity Mindset Patterns

• **Fear of Insufficiency:** Believing that there will never be enough, leading to constant worry about running out of resources or opportunities.

• **Zero-Sum Thinking:** Viewing success and resources as limited, where if someone else wins or succeeds, you lose.

• **Overemphasis on Limitations:** Focusing more on limitations and barriers rather than possibilities and opportunities.

• **Envy and Comparison:** Habitually comparing oneself unfavorably to others, which can lead to feelings of inadequacy and resentment.

Strategies to Cultivate an Abundance Mindset

Visualization

• **Technique:** Regularly visualize meeting your goals and living in abundance. Imagine your life filled with success and happiness.

• **Impact:** Visualization promotes a positive mental outlook and primes your brain to recognize and seize opportunities.

Positive Affirmations

• **Technique:** Use daily affirmations that focus on abundance, such as "I attract success and prosperity with ease," or "There is plenty for everyone, including me."

• **Impact:** Affirmations can reshape your thought patterns, making you more receptive to abundance.

Reframing

• **Technique:** Actively reframe scarcity-driven thoughts. For example, change "I can't afford this" to "How can I afford this?"

• **Impact:** Reframing helps you to see challenges as opportunities, encouraging a more proactive and positive approach.

Gratitude Practice

• **Technique:** Maintain a gratitude journal where you list things you are thankful for each day.

• **Impact:** Gratitude shifts your focus from what you lack to what you have, enhancing feelings of contentment and abundance.

Goal Setting

• **Technique:** Set realistic and meaningful goals aligned with your values and visions of abundance.

• **Impact:** Goals give you a roadmap to follow, which can help direct your actions and thoughts toward abundance.

Limiting Exposure to Negativity

• **Technique:** Be mindful of your inputs—reduce interactions with negative influences and consume media that uplifts and inspires.

- **Impact:** Protecting your mental space from negativity helps maintain a positive and abundant mindset.

Practical Exercises for Cultivating an Abundance Mindset:

- Spend 10-15 minutes each day visualizing your ideal life of abundance and success.
- Write down 3-5 abundance affirmations and repeat them daily, especially when faced with scarcity thoughts.
- Identify three recent scarcity-driven thoughts and reframe them into abundance-oriented perspectives.
- Keep a gratitude journal and write down at least three things you're grateful for each day.
- Set three meaningful goals that align with your vision of abundance and create an action plan to achieve them.
- Audit your media consumption and social interactions and make a conscious effort to limit exposure to negativity.
- Engage in acts of kindness and generosity, as giving reinforces the belief that there is enough to share.
- Celebrate your successes and the successes of others, recognizing there is plenty of abundance to go around.
- Surround yourself with positive, abundance-minded individuals who inspire and encourage you.
- Continuously educate yourself on topics related to personal growth, success, and abundance.

By incorporating these strategies and exercises into your daily life, you can significantly shift your mindset toward one that not only recognizes abundance but also creates more of it in your life. This transformation can lead to greater happiness, satisfaction, and success. Remember, abundance is not just about material wealth but also the richness of experiences, relationships, and personal growth. By embracing an abundance mindset, you open yourself up to a world of limitless possibilities and potential.

NAVIGATING THE PATH TO FINANCIAL SUCCESS: THE POWER OF CLEAR GOALS AND INTENTIONAL ACTION

When it comes to embracing wealth and prosperity, having a well-defined roadmap is essential. Just like embarking on a journey to a new destination, your financial journey requires clear directions and a solid plan. This is where the art of setting goals and intentions comes into play.

Think of your financial goals as the checkpoints along your route. Each goal should be carefully crafted, considering your current financial situation and your long-term aspirations. When setting these goals, it's important to be specific. Instead of simply stating, "I want to be wealthy," challenge yourself to define what wealth means to you. Is it a specific savings target? Is it the ability to retire comfortably at a certain age? By adding specificity to your goals, you create a tangible target to work toward.

However, it's not enough to simply set ambitious goals. Your goals must also be grounded in reality. While it's admirable to dream big, setting unrealistic expectations can lead to frustration and disappointment. Take the time to assess your current financial situation and break down your larger goals into smaller, achievable milestones. This approach lets you celebrate your progress along the way and maintains your motivation.

Another important part of goal setting is adding a time dimension. By assigning a deadline to each goal, you create a sense of urgency and accountability. This timeline acts as a gentle reminder, keeping you focused and on track. Regularly reviewing your progress against these deadlines lets you make necessary changes and makes sure you're consistently moving toward your desired outcomes.

To further solidify your commitment to your financial goals, make a habit of writing them down. The act of putting pen to paper transforms your abstract ideas into concrete statements. This physical representation of your goals serves as a constant reminder of what you're working toward. Keep your written goals in a visible place, such as on your desk or in your wallet, to keep them at the forefront of your mind.

In addition to setting clear goals, the practice of intention setting can add a deeper layer of meaning to your financial pursuits. Intention setting involves clarifying the underlying reason behind your goals. It's about understanding the "why" that fuels your desire for wealth and prosperity. By aligning your actions with your values and visualizing the positive impact that financial success will have on your life, you infuse your journey with purpose and significance.

Embracing the power of clear goals and intentional action is a transformative step in your financial journey. By setting specific, realistic, and time-bound goals, writing them down, and aligning them with your intentions, you create a roadmap that guides you toward your desired destination. Stay committed to your plan, remain adaptable in the face of challenges, and trust in your ability to manifest the wealth and prosperity you envision. Your dedication and intentional approach will pave the way to a financially abundant future.

∾

ALIGNING ACTIONS WITH INTENTIONS: THE TRANSFORMATIVE POWER OF INSPIRED FINANCIAL DECISIONS

Clear goals and intentions are a part of the equation for financial success. The true magic lies in translating those intentions into concrete actions. This is where the idea of inspired action comes into play. Inspired action is about moving forward with purpose, enthusiasm, and alignment with your deepest financial aspirations.

To start this transformative journey, start by gaining clarity on your financial intentions. Take the time to reflect on what you desire. Is it the security of a substantial savings account? The freedom to pursue your entrepreneurial dreams? Or maybe the joy of a comfortable retirement? By clearly defining your goals, you create a solid foundation for inspired action.

Once your intentions are set, harness the power of visualization. Close your eyes and imagine yourself already living in a state of financial abundance. Engage all your senses as you picture yourself surrounded by the fruits of your labor. Allow yourself to feel the excitement, gratitude, and satisfaction that come with meeting your goals. This practice of embodying your desired outcome can ignite a powerful motivational spark within you.

With your intentions clear and your vision in mind, it's time to break down your grand aspirations into manageable steps. Create a strategic plan that outlines the specific actions you need to take to bring your financial goals to fruition. Each step should be purposeful and achievable, letting you make steady progress. Remember, even the smallest actions, when taken consistently, can lead to significant results.

As you navigate your financial journey, cultivate a mindset of positivity and gratitude. Celebrate each milestone, no matter how small, and express gratitude for the opportunities and resources that come your way. This attitude of abundance will not only keep you motivated but also attract more positive energy into your life. When challenges arise, meet them with a sense of optimism and a determination to find creative solutions.

In moments of uncertainty, trust your intuition to guide you. Your inner wisdom holds valuable insights that can steer you toward opportunities aligned with your goals and values. Pay attention to the subtle signs and synchronicities that may point you in the right direction. By developing a keen sense of intuition, you can make inspired financial decisions with greater confidence.

Taking inspired action often requires stepping outside your comfort zone. Embrace calculated risks as opportunities for growth and expansion. While it's important to approach financial decisions with careful consideration, don't let fear hold you back from exploring new avenues. By taking well-thought-out risks, you open yourself up to the possibility of unexpected successes and breakthroughs.

Remember, the path to financial prosperity is a journey of continuous growth and learning. Stay committed to your vision, even in the face of setbacks. Believe in your ability to manifest abundance and trust that your inspired actions will lead you closer to your goals with each passing day. As you align your actions with your intentions, you'll discover the transformative power of inspired financial decisions.

Embrace the journey, stay focused on your destination, and let the magic of inspired action propel you toward a life of financial abundance and fulfillment.

UNLOCKING THE SECRETS OF A PROSPEROUS MINDSET: CULTIVATING THE HABITS OF WEALTH AND ABUNDANCE

THE JOURNEY toward financial prosperity is not only dependent on external factors such as income or investments. It begins within, with the cultivation of a mindset that aligns with wealth and abundance. By examining the common features found in individuals who have embraced financial success, we can gain valuable insights into how to shape our own thoughts and beliefs.

One of the most striking qualities of those with a prosperous mindset is their unwavering resilience. They understand that the path to success is rarely smooth, and setbacks are an inevitable part of the journey. Instead of being discouraged by challenges or failures, they view them as opportunities for growth and learning. To cultivate this resilience in your own life, start by reframing your perspective on adversity. Embrace the lessons that come with each obstacle and develop a positive outlook that lets you bounce back stronger than before.

Optimism is another hallmark of a wealthy mindset. Successful individuals have an unshakable belief in their ability to create the life they desire. They approach each day with a sense of hope and possibility, knowing that their thoughts and actions have the power to shape their reality. To nurture this optimistic outlook, engage in positive self-talk and surround yourself with uplifting influences. Visualize your goals and dreams with vivid detail, allowing yourself to feel the excitement and gratitude that come with achieving them.

A growth-oriented mindset is yet another key characteristic of those who have embraced wealth. They recognize that personal and professional development is a lifelong journey, and they actively seek opportunities to expand their knowledge and skills. They view challenges as chances to stretch beyond their comfort zone and failures as valuable lessons that propel them forward. To cultivate a growth mindset, embrace a love for learning and a willingness to step outside your comfort zone. Seek new experiences, pursue feedback, and never stop striving to become the best version of yourself.

Individuals with a prosperous mindset also operate from a place of abundance rather than scarcity. They understand that the universe is vast and generous, and there is more than enough success and wealth to go around. Instead of focusing on what they lack, they express gratitude for the blessings in their lives and trust that their needs will be met. To shift your own mindset toward abundance, make a habit of acknowledging the good in your life and visualizing a future filled with prosperity and opportunities.

Finally, financial literacy is a cornerstone of a wealthy mindset. Successful individuals focus on understanding the principles of money management, investing, and wealth-building. They take proactive steps to educate themselves and seek the guidance of experts when needed. To enhance your own financial literacy, commit to learning about budgeting, saving, and creating multiple streams of income. Read books, go to workshops, and surround yourself with mentors who can guide you on your financial journey.

Cultivating a prosperous mindset is a transformative process that requires intention, effort, and consistency. By embodying the features of resilience, optimism, growth, abundance, and financial literacy, you align yourself with the energy of wealth and success. Remember, your mindset is the foundation on which your financial reality is built. Nurture it with care, feed it with positive thoughts and actions, and watch as your dreams of prosperity unfold before your eyes.

Case Study:

Meet Pete, a hardworking IT professional who had always dreamed of financial freedom and abundance. Despite his success in his career, Pete constantly worried about money and feeling like there was never enough. He knew he needed to make a change, but he wasn't sure where to start.

One day, a friend recommended a seminar on adopting an attitude of abundance. Intrigued, Pete decided to attend, hoping to gain new insights into his financial mindset.

At the seminar, Pete learned about the power of shifting from a scarcity mentality to one of abundance. The speaker explained that a scarcity mindset is rooted in the belief that there is never enough, leading to constant fear and limitation. In contrast, an abundance mindset recognizes the vast opportunities and resources available, fostering a sense of gratitude and openness to possibilities.

Pete realized that his own thinking had been deeply entrenched in scarcity. He often compared his financial situation unfavorably to others, focusing on what he lacked rather than appreciating what he had. He also usually viewed money as a finite resource, believing that if someone else succeeded financially, it meant less opportunity for him.

Determined to make a change, Pete began putting the strategies into practice he learned at the seminar. He started by practicing daily gratitude, taking time each morning to write down three things he was thankful for. This simple habit helped shift his focus from lack to appreciation, and he soon noticed abundance in areas he had previously overlooked.

Pete also began challenging his limiting beliefs around money. When thoughts like "I'll never be able to afford that" or "I'm not good with money" arose, he questioned their validity. He asked himself, "Is this belief based on facts or fear?" and "What evidence do I have to support this thought?" By consciously reframing his beliefs, Jake started to open up to new financial possibilities.

Visualization became another powerful tool in Pete's abundance tool-kit. He set aside time each day to imagine himself living the financially abundant life he desired. He pictured himself debt-free, with a thriving investment portfolio and the freedom to pursue his passions. As he engaged in this practice, Pete began to feel a sense of excitement and motivation, as if his dreams were already on their way to becoming reality.

To further solidify his commitment to abundance, Pete created a vision board filled with images and affirmations representing his financial goals. He placed this board in a prominent location, using it as a daily reminder of his intentions and desires. Each time he looked at it, he felt a renewed sense of purpose and determination.

As Pete continued to work on his mindset, he also took practical steps to enhance his financial knowledge and skills. He read books on personal finance, went to workshops on investing, and sought mentors who had achieved the level of abundance he aspired to. By educating himself and surrounding himself with positive influences, Pete began to feel more confident and empowered in his financial journey.

The path to abundance was not always smooth. There were moments of doubt and setbacks along the way. But instead of letting these challenges derail him, Pete chose to view them as opportunities for growth and learning. He reframed "failures" as feedback, using them to adjust his strategies and strengthen his resilience.

Over time, Pete's consistent efforts began to yield remarkable results. He attracted new opportunities for income and investment, as if the universe was conspiring to support his abundant mindset. His relationships also began to flourish, as his newfound positivity and gratitude made him a magnet for like-minded individuals.

Perhaps most important, Pete's internal experience of life transformed. No longer weighed down by the heaviness of scarcity and fear, he approached each day with a sense of joy, excitement, and possibility. He discovered that true abundance was not just about financial wealth, but about the richness of experiences, relationships, and personal growth.

Looking back on his journey, Pete realized that adopting an attitude of abundance had been a transformative choice. By consciously shifting his mindset and aligning his actions with his intentions, he had unlocked a world of opportunity and fulfillment he had never known before. His story serves as a powerful reminder that our thoughts and beliefs have the power to shape our reality, and that by choosing abundance, we open ourselves up to a life of limitless potential.

Pete's experience also highlights the importance of combining inner work with outer action. While cultivating an abundant mindset is important, it must come with practical steps and a commitment to continuous learning and growth. By setting clear financial goals, educating himself, and taking inspired action, Pete turned his mental shift into real results.

The journey to true abundance is an ongoing process, not a one-time event. It requires consistent effort, self-reflection, and a willingness to embrace change. But as Pete discovered, each step on this path brings greater clarity, confidence, and fulfillment.

His story invites us all to examine our own relationship with money and success. It challenges us to identify the limiting beliefs and scarcity mindsets that may be holding us back, and to consciously choose a different perspective. It reminds us that abundance is not something we chase, but something we cultivate from within.

By embracing the practices of gratitude, visualization, belief reframing, and continuous learning, we too can start a transformative journey toward a more abundant life. We can learn to recognize and appreciate the wealth that already surrounds us, while also opening ourselves up to new opportunities and possibilities.

Ultimately, adopting an attitude of abundance is about far more than just financial prosperity. It's about creating a life of purpose, joy, and fulfillment. It's about recognizing our own inherent worthiness and capacity for success. And it's about choosing to see the world through a lens of possibility and potential, rather than limitation and lack.

As we navigate our own paths to abundance, let us remember that the power to create the life we want lies within us. By aligning our thoughts, beliefs, and actions with the energy of abundance, we become magnetic to all the good that life offers. We become co-creators of our own reality, shaping our experiences with the power of our intentions and expectations.

So let us approach this journey with openness, curiosity, and a deep trust in the abundance of the universe. Let us celebrate each milestone and lesson along the way, knowing they are all part of the rich tapestry of our growth and evolution. And let us inspire others with our own stories of transformation, reminding them that an abundant life is not only possible, but truly within reach.

The path to abundance is not always easy, but it is always worth it. With each mindset shift and inspired action, we move closer to the life of our dreams. We discover that true wealth is not measured by the digits in our bank accounts, but by the depth of our gratitude, the breadth of our impact, and the richness of our experiences.

In embracing abundance, we become a force for positive change in the world. We inspire others with our optimism, generosity, and unwavering belief in the goodness of life. We become living proof that abundance is not reserved for the lucky few, but a birthright available to us all.

So let us step forward with courage and conviction, knowing that an abundant life awaits. Let us trust in the journey, embrace the lessons, and celebrate the victories. And let us remember that, with an attitude of abundance, there are no limits to the prosperity, joy, and fulfillment we can create.

The world is ready for our abundant energy. Let us rise to the occasion and shine our light, knowing that in doing so, we not only transform our own lives but inspire countless others to do the same. The journey to abundance starts within, but its impact ripples out to touch all those around us. May we approach this path with gratitude, grace, and a profound appreciation for the magic and potential that lies within us all.

∽

PART THIRTEEN WRAP-UP:

KEY POINTS:

• Adopting an attitude of abundance fosters a life enriched with wealth, opportunities, and contentment.

• Cultivating an attitude of abundance involves recognizing abundance around you, shifting your focus, abandoning scarcity thinking, and being open to possibilities.

• Overcoming scarcity mentality is important for embracing wealth and prosperity, requiring identifying limiting beliefs, challenging them, cultivating a mindset of abundance, visualizing prosperity, educating oneself, surrounding oneself with positivity, and acting.

• Gratitude and appreciation are powerful tools for attracting abundance, involving practices such as daily gratitude journaling, affirmations, meditation, sending thank-you notes, gratitude visits, appreciation pauses, and gratitude reflection.

• Shifting from a mindset of lack to one of abundance involves recognizing scarcity mindset patterns, using strategies like visualization, positive affirmations, reframing, gratitude practice, goal setting, and limiting exposure to negativity.

• Navigating the path to financial success requires setting clear, specific, realistic, and time-bound goals, writing them down, and aligning them with intentions.

• Inspired financial decisions involve gaining clarity on intentions, visualizing desired outcomes, breaking down goals into manageable steps, cultivating positivity and gratitude, trusting intuition, and embracing calculated risks.

• Cultivating a prosperous mindset involves embodying features such as resilience, optimism, growth-orientation, abundance mentality, and financial literacy.

Action Items:

• Practice daily gratitude by keeping a journal and writing down three things you're grateful for each day.

• Identify limiting beliefs about money and wealth, challenge them with contradictory evidence, and replace them with abundance affirmations.

• Visualize your ideal life of prosperity and abundance for 10-15 minutes daily.

• Set SMART (Specific, Measurable, Achievable, Relevant, Time-bound) financial goals and create an action plan to achieve them.

• Engage in acts of generosity and kindness, such as sending thank-you notes or expressing appreciation to others.

• Reframe scarcity-driven thoughts into abundance-oriented perspectives.

• Limit exposure to negative influences and surround yourself with positive, abundance-minded individuals.

• Continuously educate yourself on personal finance, wealth-building strategies, and personal development.

• Practice positive affirmations and visualization techniques to reinforce an abundant mindset.

• Cultivate resilience by viewing challenges as opportunities for growth and learning from setbacks.

• Develop a love for learning and seek opportunities for personal and professional growth.

• Trust your intuition and embrace calculated risks when making financial decisions.

• Celebrate your successes, no matter how small, and express gratitude for the blessings in your life.

• Continuously assess and refine your financial goals and strategies as you progress on your journey to abundance.

• Share your abundance mindset and practices with others, inspiring them to cultivate gratitude and prosperity in their own lives.

In our next part...

... we'll dive into the transformative power of positive connections and explore how nurturing meaningful relationships can profoundly affect our overall well-being, happiness, and sense of belonging. We'll uncover the key elements of building and maintaining strong, supportive connections, such as effective communication, emotional intelligence, and empathy. You'll learn practical strategies for cultivating a positive mindset, resolving conflicts with grace and understanding, and fostering a deep sense of connection with others.

As we start this journey of relational growth, we'll also delve into the importance of self-love and self-compassion as the foundation for authentic and fulfilling relationships. You'll discover how prioritizing your own well-being, setting healthy boundaries, and extending kindness and understanding to yourself can create a ripple effect of positivity in your connections with others. By the end of this part, you'll have a powerful toolkit for nurturing the relationships that matter most to you and creating a life rich in love, support, and meaningful connections. So, let's dive in and explore how you can become the architect of your own relational well-being.

PART FOURTEEN
THE ART OF CONNECTION: NURTURING MEANINGFUL RELATIONSHIPS FOR A FULFILLING LIFE

In the fabric of existence, our relationships are the threads that keep us connected. The connections we forge with others, whether in our personal lives, professional spheres, or social circles, have a profound impact on our overall well-being and happiness. Nurturing positive relationships is not just a nice-to-have; it is a fundamental necessity for a fulfilling existence.

At the core of our human experience lies the need for connection and belonging. Positive relationships serve as a powerful support system, giving us the strength and resilience to navigate life's challenges. When we have people in our lives who offer a listening ear, a comforting embrace, or a word of encouragement, we are better equipped to face adversity head-on. These connections remind us we are not alone and that there are individuals who believe in us and stand by our side.

The impact of positive relationships extends far beyond having a shoulder to lean on. Research has consistently shown that the quality of our relationships directly influences our mental health and emotional well-being. When we feel genuinely connected to others, we experience a boost in self-esteem, a reduction in feelings of loneliness, and an overall sense of contentment. The love, acceptance, and validation we receive from our positive relationships act as a balm for our souls, nurturing our inner selves and letting us flourish.

Effective communication is the lifeblood of any healthy relationship. Building positive connections requires open, honest, and respectful dialogue. When we engage in meaningful conversations, we create a space for understanding, empathy, and growth. By actively listening to others, expressing our own thoughts and feelings, and working through conflicts with compassion, we strengthen the bonds that tie us together. Positive relationships thrive on the foundation of trust, vulnerability, and mutual respect.

The relationships we cultivate serve as catalysts for personal growth and development. When we surround ourselves with individuals who challenge us, inspire us, and push us to be our best selves, we expand our horizons and unlock new possibilities. Through the exchange of ideas, experiences, and perspectives, we gain valuable insights and broaden our understanding of ourselves and the world. Positive relationships become the fertile ground in which we can plant the seeds of our dreams and aspirations.

The joy and happiness that positive relationships bring into our lives cannot be overstated. Sharing laughter, creating memories, and experiencing the warmth of human connection are some of the most precious gifts life offers. When we have people to celebrate our successes with, shoulder our burdens, and share in the simple pleasures of everyday life, we experience a deep sense of fulfillment and purpose. Positive relationships remind us of the beauty and richness that exists in the world and in ourselves.

In the professional realm, nurturing positive relationships is equally important. Building strong connections with colleagues, mentors, and industry peers opens doors to opportunities, fosters collaboration, and enhances career growth. When we approach our professional interactions with authenticity, respect, and a genuine desire to contribute, we create a network of support that can propel us forward in our chosen paths.

Nurturing positive relationships requires intentional effort and commitment. It means being present, showing up for others, and investing time and energy into the connections that matter most. It involves practicing empathy, forgiveness, and gratitude, and recognizing that every relationship is a two-way street. By focusing on the cultivation of positive relationships, we create a life filled with love, support, and meaningful connections.

In a world that can often feel disconnected and isolated, the power of positive relationships serves as a beacon of hope and healing. By nurturing the connections that uplift us, inspire us, and fill our hearts with joy, we create a life rich in love, purpose, and fulfillment. So let us cherish the relationships that matter, invest in the bonds that strengthen us, and embrace the transformative power of positive connections.

EMOTIONAL INTELLIGENCE: THE KEY TO UNLOCKING MEANINGFUL CONNECTIONS

In the intricate dance of human relationships, emotional intelligence emerges as a powerful tool for nurturing positive connections and fostering deep, meaningful bonds. Beyond mere intellectual prowess, emotional intelligence encompasses the ability to recognize, understand, and manage one's own emotions while sensitively navigating the emotional landscape of others. It is through the lens of self-awareness, self-regulation, empathy, and social skills we can cultivate the rich soil in which healthy relationships take root and flourish.

At the core of emotional intelligence lies the transformative power of self-awareness. By turning our gaze inward and attuning to the subtle whispers of our own emotions, we gain a profound understanding of the forces that shape our thoughts, behaviors, and interactions. This introspective journey lets us recognize the triggers that ignite our reactions, the patterns that guide our responses, and the values that define our authentic selves. Through self-awareness, we develop the clarity and insight necessary to make conscious, deliberate choices in our relationships, making sure our actions align with our deepest truths and highest aspirations.

Yet, self-awareness alone is not enough; it must come with the skill of self-regulation. In the heat of emotional moments, when impulses threaten to override reason and reactivity clouds our judgment, the ability to manage and control our responses becomes paramount. Self-regulation is the steadying hand that guides us through the tempests of life, letting us maintain composure, adapt to changing circumstances, and channel our energies toward constructive ends. By cultivating self-regulation, we create a foundation of trust and stability in our relationships, showing to others we are reliable, consistent, and emotionally grounded.

While self-awareness and self-regulation focus on our internal world, empathy bridges the gap between ourselves and others. Empathy is the profound ability to step into the shoes of another, to feel their joys and sorrows as if they were our own. It is the art of active listening, of attuning to the unspoken messages beneath the words, and of offering genuine understanding and compassion. When we approach our relationships with empathy, we create a haven for others to share their vulnerabilities, fears, and dreams. We become the trusted confidants, the shoulders to lean on, and the beacons of hope in times of darkness. Empathy weaves the threads of connection, fostering a deep sense of belonging and emotional intimacy.

Empathy, however, is incomplete without the presence of social skills. These skills are the tools we wield to navigate the complex tapestry of human interactions, to communicate effectively, to negotiate differences, and to resolve conflicts with grace and wisdom. Social skills encompass the ability to express ourselves clearly and assertively, to listen attentively and respond thoughtfully, and to collaborate and cooperate toward shared goals. By honing our social skills, we become adept at building bridges of understanding, forging alliances of support, and creating harmonious environments where relationships can thrive.

The cultivation of emotional intelligence is a lifelong journey, a continuous process of self-discovery, growth, and refinement. It requires a willingness to embrace vulnerability, to confront our own limitations, and to learn from the wisdom of others. By committing ourselves to the development of self-awareness, self-regulation, empathy, and social skills, we become the architects of our own emotional well-being and the catalysts for positive change in the lives of those around us.

In a world that often emphasizes external measures of success, emotional intelligence reminds us that true fulfillment lies in the quality of our connections, in the depth of our relationships, and in the positive impact we have on others. By nurturing our emotional intelligence, we unlock the door to a life rich in meaning, purpose, and profound human connection.

So let us start this transformative journey, armed with the tools of self-awareness, self-regulation, empathy, and social skills. Let us approach our relationships with open hearts and curious minds, ready to learn, grow, and evolve. And let us remember that in the tapestry of life, it is the threads of emotional intelligence that weave the most beautiful and enduring patterns of love, understanding, and connection.

CULTIVATING A POSITIVE ATTITUDE: THE KEY TO NURTURING MEANINGFUL CONNECTIONS

OUR ATTITUDES ARE the threads that intertwine our relationships in the tapestry of life. The way we approach the world, the thoughts we cultivate, and the energy we emit have a profound impact on the connections we forge with others. Fostering a positive attitude is not only essential for our personal well-being but also for nurturing the meaningful relationships that enrich our lives.

The power of a positive attitude lies in its ability to transform our interactions with others. When we radiate positivity, we become a magnet for like-minded individuals drawn to our optimism and enthusiasm. Our positive energy creates a ripple effect, influencing the mood and atmosphere of those around us. By approaching life with a positive outlook, we open the doors to deeper, more authentic connections built on a foundation of trust, support, and mutual understanding.

To cultivate a positive attitude, one of the most effective practices is gratitude. Taking a moment each day to reflect on the blessings in our lives shifts our focus from what we lack to the abundance that surrounds us. By consciously acknowledging the people, experiences, and opportunities that bring joy and meaning to our lives, we train our minds to seek the good in every situation. This practice of gratitude not only elevates our own spirits but also lets us approach others with a heart filled with appreciation and kindness.

Self-reflection is another powerful tool in the pursuit of a positive mindset. By turning our gaze inward and examining our thoughts and emotions, we gain valuable insights into the patterns that shape our attitudes. Through honest introspection, we can identify negative thought loops and work on reframing them into more constructive and optimistic perspectives. By cultivating self-awareness, we empower ourselves to make conscious choices about the lens through which we view the world and the energy we bring to our interactions with others.

Mindfulness, the practice of being present in the moment, is a cornerstone of maintaining a positive attitude. When we engage in mindfulness techniques such as deep breathing, meditation, or mindful movement, we anchor ourselves in the present, releasing the grip of past regrets or future anxieties. By cultivating a state of inner calm and clarity, we become more receptive to the beauty and possibilities that surround us. This heightened awareness lets us approach our relationships with greater presence, empathy, and understanding.

The company we keep plays a significant role in shaping our attitudes and outlooks. Surrounding ourselves with positive, supportive, and uplifting individuals can have a profound impact on our own mindset. By seeking out and nurturing connections with people who inspire and encourage us, we create a network of positivity that reinforces our own optimistic perspective. Engaging in meaningful conversations, sharing dreams and aspirations, and supporting one another through life's challenges foster a sense of belonging and connection that feeds our positive attitude.

Faced with obstacles and setbacks, maintaining a positive attitude requires a solution-oriented mindset. Instead of dwelling on problems or limitations, we can choose to focus our energy on finding creative solutions and opportunities for growth. By approaching challenges with a spirit of resilience and determination, we cultivate a sense of empowerment and optimism that radiates to those around us. This proactive stance not only strengthens our own resolve but also inspires and uplifts others in our circle of influence.

Acts of kindness, no matter how small, have the power to ignite positivity and forge meaningful connections. By extending compassion, generosity, and support to others, we create ripples of goodwill that spread far beyond the initial gesture. Whether it's offering a listening ear, lending a helping hand, or simply sharing a genuine smile, these acts of kindness foster a sense of warmth and connection that nourishes both the giver and the receiver.

Celebrating our own successes and the achievements of others is another essential part of cultivating a positive attitude. By acknowledging and appreciating the milestones, breakthroughs, and victories, both big and small, we reinforce a sense of progress and accomplishment. Sharing in the joys and triumphs of others strengthens the bonds of our relationships and creates an atmosphere of mutual support and encouragement.

Cultivating a positive attitude is a daily practice, a conscious choice to seek the good, to find meaning in challenges, and to approach life with an open heart and mind. By embracing gratitude, engaging in self-reflection, practicing mindfulness, surrounding ourselves with positivity, focusing on solutions, extending kindness, and celebrating victories, we create a fertile ground for nurturing the meaningful connections that enrich our lives.

Remember, the power to shape our attitudes and, in turn, our relationships, lies within us. By consciously cultivating a positive mindset, we become the architects of our own happiness and the catalysts for positive change in the lives of those around us. So let us approach each day with a spirit of optimism, radiating the light of positivity and nurturing the connections that make life a beautiful and fulfilling journey.

~

THE POWER OF EMPATHY: CULTIVATING UNDERSTANDING AND NURTURING MEANINGFUL CONNECTIONS

IN THE TAPESTRY of human relationships, empathy emerges as a golden thread, weaving together the hearts and minds of individuals, creating a bond that transcends the boundaries of our individual experiences. Empathy, the ability to understand and share the feelings of others, is a transformative force with the power to strengthen connections, heal wounds, and foster a deep sense of understanding and compassion.

At its core, empathy is an invitation to step into the world of another, to see through their eyes, and to feel the echoes of their emotions in our own hearts. This bridge spans the gap between our unique perspectives, letting us connect on a profound level. When we practice empathy, we acknowledge the inherent humanity in others, recognizing that beneath the surface of our differences lies a shared tapestry of hopes, fears, and dreams.

Cultivating empathy begins with a journey inward, a process of self-discovery and emotional attunement. By developing a keen awareness of our own emotions, we lay the foundation for understanding the feelings of others. This self-awareness lets us recognize the subtle nuances of our own experiences, the triggers that ignite our reactions, and the values that guide our actions. Through this introspective lens, we gain the clarity and insight necessary to extend our understanding to those around us.

The practice of active listening is a cornerstone of empathy. When we listen with an open heart and a curious mind, we create a sacred space for others to share their stories, their struggles, and their triumphs. We suspend judgment and preconceived notions, allowing ourselves to be present in the moment. By listening attentively and empathetically, we communicate a powerful message: "I hear you, I see you, and I validate your experiences."

Empathy calls upon us to challenge our own biases and assumptions, to step beyond the limits of our limited perspectives and embrace the richness of diverse experiences. It requires a willingness to suspend judgment, to approach each interaction with a beginner's mind, and to seek understanding rather than making assumptions. By cultivating a non-judgmental mindset, we create an atmosphere of safety and trust, where individuals express their authentic selves without fear of criticism or rejection.

To foster empathy in our relationships, we must make a conscious choice to focus on understanding over being right. It means setting aside our own agendas and egos, and instead focusing on the needs and feelings of others. By consistently showing empathy in our interactions, we model compassion and understanding, inspiring others to reciprocate and creating a ripple effect of positive connection.

Empathy is a skill that can be developed and strengthened through practice and intentionality. It involves seeking out opportunities to listen, to understand, and to confirm the experiences of others. By engaging in acts of kindness, volunteering, or simply offering a supportive ear to a friend in need, we cultivate the muscles of empathy, expanding our capacity for compassion and understanding.

In a world that often feels divided and disconnected, empathy serves as a unifying force, reminding us of our shared humanity and the power of connection. By nurturing empathy in our relationships, we create a tapestry of understanding, where each thread represents a unique story, a valuable perspective, and a life touched by compassion.

As we navigate the complexities of human relationships, let us embrace empathy as our guiding light. Let us approach each interaction with an open heart, a curious mind, and a willingness to understand. And let us remember that through the power of empathy, we can transform our relationships, our communities, and ultimately, the world.

THE ART OF SELF-LOVE: NURTURING YOUR RELATIONSHIP WITH YOURSELF TO FOSTER MEANINGFUL CONNECTIONS

THE FOUNDATION of all our connections is the relationship we have with ourselves. It is through the lens of self-love and self-compassion that we learn to navigate the world with grace, resilience, and an open heart. By nurturing our relationship with ourselves, we cultivate a deep well of inner strength and emotional intelligence that lets us form authentic and meaningful connections with others.

At the core of self-love lies the idea of self-compassion – the act of extending the same kindness, understanding, and forgiveness to ourselves that we so readily offer to those we cherish. It is a recognition of our shared humanity, an acknowledgment that imperfection is an inherent part of the human experience. When we embrace self-compassion, we let go of the harsh inner critic and instead treat ourselves with the gentleness and care we deserve.

Practicing self-compassion is a transformative journey that begins with self-awareness. By engaging in regular self-reflection, we gain valuable insights into our thoughts, emotions, and behaviors. Through journaling, meditation, or simply taking moments of quiet introspection, we create a sacred space to explore our inner landscape. As we shed light on our fears, doubts, and insecurities, we can begin to replace self-judgment with self-acceptance, gradually nurturing a more loving and compassionate relationship with ourselves.

An essential part of self-care is setting healthy boundaries. When we learn to say no to demands that drain our energy or compromise our values, we send a powerful message to ourselves that our well-being matters. By establishing clear boundaries, we create a protective shield around our emotional and mental health, making sure we have the space and resources to nurture ourselves and our relationships with others.

Engaging in activities that bring us joy and fulfillment is another key part of self-love. When we focus on pursuits that ignite our passion and feed our soul, we cultivate a deep sense of purpose and contentment. Whether it's immersing ourselves in a beloved hobby, spending time in nature, or practicing mindfulness, these activities serve as a reminder that we are worthy of happiness and deserve to invest in our own well-being.

In moments of struggle or setback, self-compassion becomes a lifeline. Instead of berating ourselves for our perceived failures, we can extend the same understanding and support we would offer a dear friend. By speaking to ourselves with words of encouragement and kindness, we build emotional resilience and foster a more positive self-image. This inner dialogue of self-compassion becomes a soothing balm, helping us navigate life's challenges with greater ease and grace.

Cultivating a self-care routine is another essential part of nurturing our relationship with ourselves. By focusing on activities that nourish our mind, body, and soul, we create a sacred ritual of self-love. Whether it's engaging in regular exercise, preparing nourishing meals, ensuring adequate rest, or carving out time for relaxation, these practices send a powerful message we value ourselves and our well-being.

As we deepen our relationship with ourselves through self-compassion and self-care, we begin to radiate a sense of inner peace and confidence that naturally attracts positive connections with others. When we approach relationships from a place of self-love, we are better equipped to set healthy boundaries, communicate our needs with clarity, and extend empathy and understanding to those around us.

Nurturing our relationship with ourselves is a lifelong journey, one that requires patience, commitment, and a willingness to embrace our imperfections. It is a sacred practice of self-discovery, a path of learning to love ourselves unconditionally. As we cultivate self-compassion and focus on self-care, we not only enhance our own well-being but also create a ripple effect of positivity that touches the lives of those around us.

So let us start this transformative journey of self-love, armed with the tools of self-reflection, boundary setting, joyful pursuits, and self-care. Let us treat ourselves with the same tenderness and understanding we so freely give to others. And let us trust that by nurturing our relationship with ourselves, we lay the foundation for a life filled with meaningful connections, profound growth, and boundless love.

Case Study:

Meet Janice, a successful marketing executive who seemed to have it all – a thriving career, a beautiful home, and a busy social life. Despite her outward success, Janice often felt a deep sense of disconnection and loneliness. She constantly put the needs of others before her own, sacrificing her well-being in the process.

One day, a close friend recommended a workshop on the power of positive connections. Intrigued by the concept, Janice decided to attend, hoping to gain insights into building more fulfilling relationships.

At the workshop, Janice learned about the profound impact that the quality of our relationships has on our overall happiness and well-being. The facilitator explained that positive connections serve as a powerful support system, giving us the strength and resilience to navigate life's challenges. They also contribute to our mental and emotional health, boosting self-esteem and reducing feelings of loneliness.

As Janice reflected on her own relationships, she realized that many of her connections lacked the depth and authenticity she craved. She often engaged in superficial interactions, afraid to reveal her true self fearing rejection or judgment.

The workshop emphasized the importance of effective communication in building positive relationships. Janice learned about the power of active listening, expressing thoughts and feelings openly, and working through conflicts with compassion and respect. She recognized that by engaging in meaningful conversations and creating a space for vulnerability, she could foster stronger, more genuine connections.

Inspired by these insights, Janice began to apply the principles of effective communication in her interactions. She made a conscious effort to listen attentively to others, to confirm their experiences, and to express her own thoughts and feelings with honesty and clarity. As she practiced these skills, Janice noticed a shift in the quality of her connections. Her relationships began to feel more authentic and supportive, and she looked forward to spending time with others.

The workshop also highlighted the role of emotional intelligence in nurturing positive relationships. Janice learned about the importance of self-awareness, self-regulation, empathy, and social skills in navigating the complexities of human interactions. She realized that by cultivating these abilities, she could become more attuned to her own emotions and the emotions of others, allowing for deeper understanding and connection.

Janice began to focus on self-reflection and introspection, taking time each day to explore her own thoughts and feelings. She practiced self-regulation techniques, such as deep breathing and mindfulness, to manage her reactions in challenging situations. Janice also focused on developing her empathy skills, seeking to understand the perspectives and experiences of others.

As Janice continued to work on her emotional intelligence, she noticed a profound shift in her relationships. She became more adept at reading social cues, communicating effectively, and resolving conflicts with grace and understanding. Her connections began to feel more authentic and meaningful, and she found herself surrounded by a supportive network of individuals who uplifted and inspired her.

One of the most transformative parts of Janice's journey was learning the art of self-love and self-compassion. The workshop emphasized that the foundation of all positive connections is the relationship we have with ourselves. By nurturing self-love and extending compassion to ourselves, we create a well of inner strength and resilience that lets us form authentic connections with others.

Janice began to focus on self-care and self-compassion in her daily life. She engaged in activities that brought her joy and fulfillment, such as practicing yoga and spending time in nature. She learned to set healthy boundaries, saying no to demands that drained her energy and compromised her well-being. Janice also practiced self-compassion, speaking to herself with kindness and understanding, especially in moments of struggle or setback.

As Janice cultivated a more loving and compassionate relationship with herself, she noticed a ripple effect in her connections with others. She approached interactions with greater patience, empathy, and understanding. Her relationships began to feel more authentic and supportive, and she attracted individuals who valued her true self.

Looking back on her journey, Janice realized that the power of positive connections had transformed her life in profound ways. By focusing on effective communication, emotional intelligence, and self-love, she had created a tapestry of relationships that gave her a deep sense of belonging, support, and fulfillment.

Janice's story serves as a powerful reminder that the quality of our connections directly affects our happiness and well-being. By cultivating the skills and mindsets necessary for nurturing positive relationships, we can create a life rich in love, understanding, and authentic human connection.

Her journey also highlights the interconnectedness of our relationship with ourselves and our relationships with others. As we learn to extend compassion and kindness to ourselves, we develop the capacity to form more genuine and supportive connections with those around us.

Building positive relationships is an ongoing process that requires intention, effort, and vulnerability. It involves stepping out of our comfort zones, confronting our own limitations, and being open to learning and growth. But as Janice's experience shows, the rewards of this journey are immeasurable – a life filled with meaningful connections, emotional resilience, and a deep sense of belonging.

So let Janice's story be an invitation to all of us – to focus on the cultivation of positive relationships in our lives, to approach our interactions with empathy and understanding, and to extend compassion and love to ourselves and others. By doing so, we not only enrich our own lives but also contribute to a world where authentic human connection is valued and celebrated.

Remember, the power to create positive connections lies within each of us. By developing the skills of effective communication, emotional intelligence, and self-love, we become the architects of our own relational well-being. We create a tapestry of connections that support us, inspire us, and remind us of the beauty and resilience of the human spirit.

So let us embrace the journey of nurturing positive connections, knowing that each step we take brings us closer to a life of greater fulfillment, purpose, and love. Let us approach our relationships with open hearts and curious minds, ready to learn, grow, and evolve. And let us remember that in the tapestry of life, the threads of positive connection create the most beautiful and enduring patterns of happiness and well-being.

The path to nurturing positive connections is not always easy, but it is always worth it. It requires us to be vulnerable, to confront our fears, and to take responsibility for our own growth and healing. But as we navigate this journey, we discover that the challenges we face are not obstacles, but opportunities – opportunities to deepen our self-awareness, to expand our capacity for empathy and compassion, and to create a life of authentic connection and belonging.

So let us approach this journey with courage and determination, knowing that each step we take is a step toward a more fulfilling and connected existence. Let us surround ourselves with individuals who uplift and inspire us, who challenge us to grow and evolve. And let us remember that in nurturing positive connections with others, we also nurture the most important relationship of all – the one we have with ourselves.

In a world that often feels disconnected and divided, the power of positive connections serves as a beacon of hope and healing. By focusing on the cultivation of authentic, supportive relationships, we create ripples of kindness and compassion that extend far beyond our immediate circles. We become agents of change, contributing to a world where empathy, understanding, and love are the guiding principles.

So let us embrace the transformative power of positive connections, knowing that in doing so, we not only enrich our own lives but also make a positive impact on the lives of those around us. Let us approach each interaction with presence, curiosity, and an open heart. And let us remember that in the tapestry of life, the threads of positive connection create a masterpiece of love, resilience, and shared humanity.

~

PART FOURTEEN WRAP-UP:

KEY POINTS:

• Nurturing positive relationships is important for overall well-being, happiness, and a sense of belonging.

• Positive connections serve as a powerful support system, providing strength and resilience to navigate life's challenges.

• The quality of relationships directly influences mental health, emotional well-being, self-esteem, and feelings of loneliness.

• Effective communication, including open and honest dialogue, active listening, and working through conflicts with compassion, is essential for building positive connections.

• Emotional intelligence, encompassing self-awareness, self-regulation, empathy, and social skills, is key to navigating the complexities of human interactions and fostering meaningful relationships.

• Cultivating a positive attitude through gratitude, self-reflection, mindfulness, surrounding oneself with positivity, and focusing on solutions is important for nurturing positive connections.

• Resolving conflicts in relationships requires effective communication, active listening, compromise, empathy, taking time-outs when needed, and seeking support from a neutral third party if necessary.

• Empathy, the ability to understand and share the feelings of others, is a transformative force that strengthens connections, heals wounds, and fosters understanding and compassion.

• Self-love and self-compassion form the foundation of all connections, enabling individuals to form authentic and meaningful relationships with others.

Action Items:

• Practice active listening by immersing yourself in the words and emotions of others, showing a genuine desire to understand their perspective.

• Cultivate self-awareness through regular self-reflection, journaling, or meditation to gain insights into your thoughts, emotions, and behaviors.

• Develop self-regulation techniques, such as deep breathing or mindfulness, to manage reactions in challenging situations and maintain emotional balance.

• Engage in activities that bring joy and fulfillment, focusing on self-care and setting healthy boundaries to nurture your relationship with yourself.

• Practice self-compassion by treating yourself with kindness, understanding, and forgiveness, especially in moments of struggle or setback.

• Express gratitude daily by acknowledging the blessings in your life and focusing on the positive aspects of your relationships.

• Seek and nurture connections with individuals who inspire, support, and encourage personal growth and positivity.

• When faced with conflicts, approach conversations with openness, honesty, and respect, using "I" statements to express your thoughts and feelings without blame or judgment.

• Develop empathy by seeking to understand and confirm the experiences and emotions of others, suspending judgment and embracing diverse perspectives.

• Continuously work on enhancing your emotional intelligence through self-reflection, seeking feedback, and engaging in personal development activities.

• Create a supportive network of individuals who uplift and inspire you, fostering an environment of mutual support and encouragement.

• Practice forgiveness and letting go of grudges, recognizing that forgiveness is a gift you give yourself for your own well-being and the health of your relationships.

• Regularly assess and reflect on the quality of your relationships, making conscious efforts to nurture and strengthen the connections that matter most to you.

• Be open to seeking support from a neutral third party, such as a therapist or counselor, when facing persistent challenges in your relationships.

• Continuously focus on the cultivation of positive connections in your life, recognizing their transformative power in fostering happiness, resilience, and a sense of belonging.

In our next part...

... we'll start a transformative journey into the art of self-love and discover the profound impact it has on our overall well-being, resilience, and ability to form meaningful connections with others. We'll explore the idea of self-compassion and learn how to cultivate a kind, understanding, and forgiving relationship with ourselves, even in the face of imperfections and challenges. You'll gain insights into the importance of setting healthy boundaries, engaging in activities that bring you joy and fulfillment, and committing to a lifelong practice of self-care and personal growth.

As we dig into the world of affirmations, we'll uncover the science behind their transformative power and learn how to harness their potential for personal transformation. You'll discover how to craft affirmations tailored to your specific needs and goals, focusing on areas such as self-love, confidence, abundance, health, and goal setting. We'll explore practical techniques for incorporating affirmations into your daily life, from morning rituals and visual reminders to journaling and meditation practices. By the end of this part, you'll have a comprehensive toolkit for reframing your mind, conquering self-doubt, and cultivating an empowering inner dialogue that propels you toward your highest aspirations. So, let's start this journey of self-discovery and unlock the transformative power of self-love and affirmations.

PART FIFTEEN
EMBRACING SELF-LOVE AND AFFIRMATIONS: NURTURING YOUR INNER WORLD FOR PROFOUND PERSONAL GROWTH

In the intricate tapestry of human connections, the relationship we have with ourselves serves as the foundation on which all other relationships are built. It is the cornerstone of our emotional well-being, the source of our resilience, and the wellspring of our capacity to love and be loved. Nurturing a deep and compassionate relationship with ourselves is not a luxury, but a necessity – a sacred act of self-care that ripples outward, touching the lives of those around us.

At the heart of self-love lies the transformative power of self-compassion. It is the gentle art of treating ourselves with the same kindness, understanding, and forgiveness we so readily extend to others. In a world that often demands perfection and perpetuates self-criticism, self-compassion emerges as a revolutionary act. It invites us to embrace our imperfections, to acknowledge our struggles, and to treat ourselves with the tender care we deserve.

Cultivating self-compassion begins with the practice of self-reflection. By turning our gaze inward, we start a journey of self-discovery, unearthing the layers of our thoughts, emotions, and behaviors. Through the lens of curiosity and non-judgment, we learn to observe our inner landscape, recognizing the patterns that shape our experiences and the stories we tell ourselves. This process of self-reflection serves as a compass, guiding us toward a deeper understanding of our authentic selves.

As we navigate the path of self-love, the art of setting boundaries emerges as an important tool. Boundaries are the gentle guardians of our emotional and mental well-being, making sure we prioritize our own needs and values. They are the lines we draw in the sand, communicating to ourselves and others what we will accept. By learning to say "no" when necessary, we create space for the things that matter, nurturing our own growth and protecting our inner peace.

In the pursuit of self-love, we must also embrace the joy and fulfillment that comes from engaging in activities that nourish our souls. These are the moments of pure presence, where we lose ourselves in the flow of creativity, the thrill of adventure, or the serenity of nature. By focusing on the things that bring us joy, we send a powerful message to ourselves – that our happiness matters, that our passions are worthy of pursuit, and that we are deserving of a life filled with meaning and purpose.

Self-love is not a destination, but a lifelong journey – a commitment to showing up for ourselves with compassion and understanding, even in the face of challenges and setbacks. In these moments of struggle, self-compassion becomes our greatest ally. By offering ourselves words of encouragement, validation, and support, we cultivate the resilience necessary to weather life's storms. We learn to treat ourselves with the same tenderness and care we would offer a beloved friend, recognizing that our worth is not defined by our achievements or failures, but by the inherent beauty of our being.

As we nurture our relationship with ourselves, we create a ripple effect that touches the lives of those around us. By embodying self-love and self-compassion, we become beacons of light, inspiring others to embrace their own worthiness and to treat themselves with kindness and respect. We cultivate a world where empathy, understanding, and connection thrive, recognizing that the love we give to ourselves is the foundation on which all other love is built.

So let us start this transformative journey of self-love, armed with the tools of self-reflection, boundary setting, joy-seeking, and self-compassion. Let us treat ourselves with the tenderness and care we so deeply deserve, knowing that by nurturing our own hearts, we create a world where love and connection can flourish. And let us remember that in the tapestry of life, the thread of self-love weaves together the most beautiful and resilient patterns of all.

~

UNRAVELING THE SUBCONSCIOUS: THE SCIENCE BEHIND AFFIRMATIONS AND THEIR TRANSFORMATIVE POWER

IN THE REALM of personal growth and self-improvement, affirmations have long been celebrated as a powerful tool for reshaping our thoughts, beliefs, and ultimately, our lives. These simple yet potent statements, repeated with conviction and regularity, have the potential to penetrate the depths of our subconscious mind, planting the seeds of positivity and self-empowerment. But what is the science behind affirmations, and how do they wield such transformative influence over our mental landscape?

At the heart of the efficacy of affirmations lies the concept of neuroplasticity – the brain's remarkable ability to rewire itself, forging new neural pathways in response to our thoughts, behaviors, and experiences. When we engage in the practice of repeating affirmations, we are essentially starting a process of self-directed brain sculpting. Each affirmation serves as a chisel, carefully carving away the negative self-talk and limiting beliefs that have taken root in our subconscious.

As we consistently affirm our strengths, our worth, and our potential, we activate specific regions of the brain associated with self-processing and reward. This neurological engagement triggers a cascade of positive emotions and self-perceptions, elevating our self-esteem and fostering a deep sense of well-being. By consciously choosing to focus on the affirmative parts of ourselves and our lives, we gradually retrain our minds to default to a more optimistic and empowering outlook.

Affirmations also serve as a powerful counterbalance to the negativity bias – our brain's innate tendency to give more weight and attention to negative experiences and thoughts. This evolutionary adaptation, while once important for survival, can often lead to a disproportionate focus on our shortcomings and perceived failures. By intentionally redirecting our attention toward the positive through affirmations, we begin to tip the scales for self-compassion, resilience, and a more balanced perspective.

The practice of affirmations goes beyond mere wishful thinking; it is an act of self-empowerment that cultivates a profound sense of self-efficacy. When we affirm our capabilities, our strengths, and our potential for growth, we are essentially reinforcing the belief in our own ability to shape our lives and meet our goals. This enhanced self-confidence becomes a catalyst for action, propelling us forward in the face of challenges and setbacks.

The science behind affirmations also highlights the importance of consistency and repetition when rewiring our subconscious mind. Just as physical exercise strengthens our muscles over time, the regular practice of affirmations fortifies our mental resilience and positive self-perception. Each repetition acts as a gentle reminder, gradually etching the desired beliefs and attitudes into the fabric of our being.

❧

TAILORING AFFIRMATIONS FOR PERSONAL GROWTH: A COMPREHENSIVE GUIDE TO THE DIFFERENT TYPES AND THEIR APPLICATIONS

AFFIRMATIONS HAVE EMERGED as a powerful tool for personal transformation, offering a pathway to cultivate a more positive mindset, reprogram limiting beliefs, and unlock our fullest potential. By repeatedly focusing on carefully crafted statements that affirm our worth, abilities, and aspirations, we can effectively rewire our subconscious mind and align our thoughts with the reality we wish to create. However, the art of crafting effective affirmations lies in understanding the different types available and tailoring them to specific areas of personal development.

Self-love affirmations serve as a foundation for nurturing a healthy relationship with oneself. These affirmations focus on building self-esteem, self-compassion, and self-acceptance – the cornerstones of a positive self-image. Statements such as "I am worthy of love and respect," "I am enough just as I am," and "I love and accept myself unconditionally" help to counteract negative self-talk and cultivate a deep sense of self-appreciation. By regularly affirming our inherent worth, we begin to embrace our imperfections, treat ourselves with kindness, and develop a more loving and compassionate relationship with ourselves.

Confidence affirmations are designed to bolster self-assurance and belief in one's capabilities. These affirmations serve as a powerful antidote to self-doubt and fear, empowering individuals to step into their greatness and pursue their dreams with unwavering conviction. Statements like "I believe in myself and my abilities," "I have the confidence to overcome any challenge," and "I trust myself to make the right decisions" help to cultivate a mindset of self-efficacy and resilience. By consistently affirming our confidence, we begin to trust in our own judgment, take bold action toward our goals, and embrace challenges as opportunities for growth.

Abundance affirmations are geared toward shifting our focus from scarcity to abundance, helping us cultivate a mindset of gratitude and prosperity. These affirmations recognize the limitless potential that exists within and around us, inviting us to open ourselves up to the flow of abundance in all areas of life. Statements such as "I am grateful for all the abundance in my life," "Money flows to me easily and effortlessly," and "I attract positive opportunities and abundance into my life" help to rewire our relationship with wealth, success, and prosperity. By consistently affirming abundance, we begin to notice and appreciate the blessings in our lives, attract more positive experiences, and develop a deep trust in the universe's ability to provide for our needs.

Health affirmations focus on promoting physical, mental, and emotional well-being, recognizing the interconnectedness of our mind, body, and spirit. These affirmations serve as a powerful reminder to focus on self-care, make healthy choices, and cultivate a sense of inner peace and alignment. Statements such as "I am healthy and strong in mind, body, and spirit," "I nourish my body with healthy choices," and "I am at peace and aligned with my inner well-being" help to reinforce positive habits and create a supportive inner dialogue. By consistently affirming our commitment to health and well-being, we develop greater self-awareness, make more conscious choices, and cultivate a deep sense of vitality and resilience.

Goal-setting affirmations are specifically tailored to support individuals in achieving their aspirations and realizing their full potential. These affirmations serve as a powerful catalyst for action, helping to maintain focus, motivation, and perseverance in the face of challenges. Statements like "I am focused and determined to achieve my goals," "I am capable of reaching my full potential," and "I am unstoppable in pursuit of my dreams" help to create a clear mental image of success, bolster self-confidence, and inspire consistent effort toward the realization of one's goals. By regularly affirming our commitment to our goals, we develop a growth mindset, embrace challenges as opportunities for learning, and cultivate the resilience necessary to overcome obstacles and achieve our dreams.

To maximize the effectiveness of affirmations in personal development, it is essential to tailor them to our specific needs and areas of growth. This process begins with self-reflection and honest assessment of our strengths, weaknesses, and desired outcomes. By identifying the areas in which we seek to cultivate positive change, we can craft affirmations that resonate deeply with our unique experiences and aspirations. Choose affirmations that feel authentic and aligned with our values, as this helps to foster a genuine belief in their transformative power.

Consistency and repetition are key to harnessing the full potential of affirmations. By incorporating affirmations into our daily routine, ideally in the morning or before bed, we create a sacred ritual of self-nurturing and positive reinforcement. As we repeat these affirmations with conviction and emotion, we gradually rewire our subconscious mind, replacing limiting beliefs with empowering thoughts and cultivating a more positive and proactive mindset.

Affirmations offer a powerful tool for personal transformation, enabling us to reshape our inner dialogue, cultivate self-love, build confidence, attract abundance, focus on well-being, and meet our goals. By understanding the different types of affirmations available and tailoring them to our specific needs, we can harness their full potential and create lasting positive change in our lives. As we embrace the practice of affirmations with consistency, authenticity, and belief, we open ourselves up to a world of limitless possibilities, where our thoughts align with our highest aspirations and our dreams become our lived reality. So let us start this transformative journey of personal growth, armed with the power of affirmations, and trust in our inherent capacity to create the life we desire.

Tailoring Affirmations for Personal Growth: Harnessing the Power of Positive Self-Talk

Affirmations, those powerful statements of positive self-talk, can remarkably reshape our mindset, boost our confidence, and guide us toward personal growth and transformation. By consciously choosing to focus on uplifting and empowering thoughts, we can effectively reprogram our subconscious mind, aligning our beliefs and behaviors with our deepest aspirations. The beauty of affirmations lies in their versatility – they can be tailored to address specific areas of personal development, making them a potent tool for self-improvement.

When cultivating self-love, affirmations serve as gentle reminders of our inherent worth and value. By repeating statements such as "I am worthy of love and respect" or "I love and accept myself unconditionally," we begin to chip away at the layers of self-doubt and self-criticism that may have accumulated over time. These affirmations act as a soothing balm, nurturing a deep sense of self-compassion and self-acceptance. As we consistently affirm our worthiness, we gradually rewire our neural pathways, fostering a more loving and compassionate relationship with ourselves.

For those seeking to boost their self-confidence, affirmations can be a powerful ally. Statements like "I believe in myself and my abilities" or "I have the confidence to overcome any challenge" serve as a mental armor, fortifying our belief in our own capabilities. By repeatedly affirming our confidence, we train our minds to focus on our strengths and potential, rather than dwelling on perceived weaknesses or past failures. This shift in perspective can have a profound impact on our ability to tackle obstacles, pursue our goals, and embrace new opportunities with courage and self-assurance.

In the realm of abundance and prosperity, affirmations play an important role in cultivating a mindset of gratitude and openness. By affirming statements such as "I am grateful for all the abundance in my life" or "I attract positive opportunities and abundance into my life," we attune our minds to recognize and appreciate the blessings that surround us. This practice of intentional gratitude not only enhances our overall well-being but also magnetizes us to attract more abundance and positive experiences into our lives.

When it comes to nurturing our physical, mental, and emotional well-being, health affirmations serve as powerful reminders of our commitment to self-care. Statements like "I am healthy and strong in mind, body, and spirit" or "I nourish my body with healthy choices" help to reinforce positive habits and encourage a holistic approach to well-being. By consistently affirming our dedication to health and wellness, we create a mental blueprint that guides our actions and choices, supporting us in cultivating a vibrant and fulfilling life.

For those with specific goals and aspirations, goal-setting affirmations can be a catalyst for success. By repeating statements such as "I am focused and determined to achieve my goals" or "I am unstoppable in pursuit of my dreams," we ignite a fire within ourselves, fueling our motivation and drive. These affirmations help to keep us anchored in our purpose, even in the face of challenges or setbacks. By consistently affirming our commitment to our goals, we create a mental roadmap that guides us toward the realization of our deepest desires.

To maximize the impact of affirmations, it is essential to choose statements that resonate deeply with our individual needs and aspirations. By taking the time to reflect on the areas of personal growth we wish to focus on, we can craft affirmations that are both authentic and empowering. The key lies in consistency – by repeating these affirmations regularly, ideally as part of a daily ritual, we gradually ingrain them into our subconscious mind, effecting lasting change from the inside out.

∾

TECHNIQUES FOR INCORPORATING AFFIRMATIONS INTO DAILY ROUTINES AND PRACTICES TO REINFORCE POSITIVE SELF-TALK

In the journey of personal growth and transformation, affirmations serve as powerful threads that can be woven into the fabric of our daily lives. By integrating these positive statements into our routines and practices, we create a tapestry of self-empowerment, resilience, and unwavering belief in ourselves. The art of incorporating affirmations into our daily rituals is a gentle yet profound way to reinforce positive self-talk, gradually reshaping our internal narrative and aligning our thoughts with our highest aspirations.

As the first rays of morning light filter through our windows, we have the opportunity to set the tone for the day ahead. By dedicating a few moments to a morning affirmation routine, we plant the seeds of positivity and self-love in the fertile soil of our minds. Whether spoken aloud with conviction or whispered softly to ourselves, these affirmations serve as a compass, guiding our thoughts and actions toward a more empowered and purposeful path. As we repeat these uplifting statements while getting ready or savoring our morning meal, we infuse our day with a sense of clarity, focus, and unwavering self-belief.

Throughout the day, visual reminders of our affirmations can serve as gentle nudges, anchoring us in the present moment and rekindling the flame of positive self-talk. By strategically placing affirmation sticky notes in prominent locations – on our bathroom mirror, computer screen, or refrigerator door – we create a network of encouragement and support. Each glimpse of these handwritten notes acts as a loving reminder of our worth, our potential, and our commitment to personal growth. These visual cues become touchstones, helping us navigate the ebb and flow of daily life with grace and resilience.

As the day unfolds, the practice of journaling affirmations provides a sacred space for self-reflection and introspection. By dedicating a few minutes each morning or evening to writing down affirmations in a dedicated journal, we engage in a powerful act of self-discovery and self-affirmation. The process of putting pen to paper, letting the words flow freely, becomes a meditative exercise. As we articulate our positive attributes, celebrate our accomplishments, and affirm our potential, we cultivate a deeper sense of self-awareness and self-acceptance. This daily ritual of affirmative journaling becomes a compass, guiding us toward a more authentic and fulfilling life.

In the stillness of meditation, affirmations find a natural home. By weaving affirmations into our meditation practice, we create a synergistic blend of mindfulness and positive self-talk. As we settle into the quiet space within, we can silently repeat affirmations that resonate deeply with our soul. Each repetition becomes a gentle ripple, radiating outward and permeating our entire being with love, compassion, and self-acceptance. This fusion of affirmations and meditation creates a sacred container for personal growth, letting us access the wisdom and strength that live within.

As the day draws to a close and we prepare to surrender to the embrace of sleep, affirmations offer a soothing balm for the soul. By reciting affirmations before bed, we create a ritual of self-love and gratitude. Reflecting on the day's accomplishments, no matter how small, and reaffirming our self-worth through positive statements, we cultivate a sense of peace and contentment. These evening affirmations become a lullaby, gently guiding us into a restful slumber, knowing we are worthy, capable, and deserving of all the good that life offers.

Incorporating affirmations into our daily routines and practices is an act of self-care and self-empowerment. By consistently reinforcing positive self-talk through these various techniques, we gradually rewire our neural pathways, creating a mental landscape that is fertile ground for personal growth and transformation. As we weave affirmations into the tapestry of our lives, we become the architects of our own reality, shaping our thoughts, beliefs, and actions in alignment with our highest potential.

So let us embrace the art of infusing our days with the power of affirmations. Let us start each morning with a heart full of self-love, carry visual reminders of our worth throughout the day, pour our affirmations onto the pages of our journals, invite them into the sacred space of meditation, and let them lull us into a peaceful slumber each night. For in the consistent practice of affirming our truth, we open ourselves to the boundless possibilities that await us on the path of personal transformation.

REFRAMING THE MIND: HARNESSING AFFIRMATIONS TO CONQUER RESISTANCE AND SELF-DOUBT

IN THE PURSUIT of personal growth and self-actualization, we often find ourselves face to face with the formidable forces of resistance and self-doubt. These negative thinking patterns, deeply rooted in our subconscious, can cast a shadow over our dreams, limiting our potential and hindering our progress. However, within the transformative power of affirmations lies a potent tool for reframing our thoughts, dismantling the walls of self-doubt, and unleashing the full force of our inner strength.

Affirmations, when used consistently and with conviction, can remarkably rewire our neural pathways, gradually replacing negative self-talk with empowering beliefs. By consciously choosing to focus on our capabilities, resilience, and worthiness, we begin to shift the lens through which we perceive ourselves and the world. Each affirmation becomes a beam of light, illuminating the dark corners of our minds and dispelling the shadows of self-doubt.

When we affirm, "I am capable of overcoming any obstacle that comes my way," we are not merely reciting empty words; we are making a powerful declaration of our inherent strength and resourcefulness. This affirmation serves as a reminder that challenges are not insurmountable barriers, but opportunities for growth and self-discovery. By embracing this belief, we cultivate a mindset of resilience, equipping ourselves with the mental fortitude to face adversity head-on and emerge victorious.

As we repeat the affirmation, "I trust in my abilities and believe in my own power to succeed," we are tapping into the wellspring of self-confidence that lives within us. By placing unwavering faith in our own capacities, we begin to dismantle the walls of self-doubt brick by brick. This affirmation acts as a catalyst, igniting a fire within us that propels us forward, fueling our determination and drive. With each repetition, we reinforce the belief that we are the architects of our own success, capable of achieving anything we set our minds to.

The affirmation, "I release all self-doubt and embrace my worthiness," serves as a powerful declaration of self-acceptance and self-love. By consciously letting go of the negative self-talk that often plagues our minds, we create space for a more compassionate and nurturing inner dialogue. This affirmation reminds us that our worth does not depend on external validation or perfection, but rather it is an inherent part of our being. As we embrace our worthiness, we begin to show up in the world with greater confidence, authenticity, and self-assurance.

When we affirm, "I am resilient and strong, capable of facing any challenge with grace," we are acknowledging our innate capacity to adapt, persevere, and thrive in the face of adversity. This affirmation becomes a suit of armor, protecting us from the arrows of self-doubt and fear. By focusing on our resilience, we cultivate a mindset of flexibility and adaptability, enabling us to navigate life's challenges with poise and determination. Each repetition of this affirmation reinforces our belief in our own strength, empowering us to rise above the obstacles that may come our way.

The affirmation, "I choose to focus on my strengths and let go of negative self-talk," serves as a powerful reminder of our agency in shaping our inner dialogue. By consciously redirecting our attention toward our unique talents, skills, and positive attributes, we begin to reframe our self-perception. This affirmation encourages us to release the grip of negative self-talk, replacing it with a narrative of self-appreciation and self-acceptance. As we focus on our strengths, we cultivate a more balanced and empowering view of ourselves, one that celebrates our individuality and potential.

Finally, the affirmation, "I am deserving of success, and I am worthy of all the good things that come my way," serves as a potent reminder of our inherent deservingness. By affirming our worthiness of success and abundance, we begin to dismantle the limiting beliefs that may have held us back in the past. This affirmation encourages us to open ourselves up to the limitless possibilities that life offers, knowing we are worthy recipients of all the blessings and opportunities that come our way.

As we start the journey of reframing our minds through the power of affirmations, it is important to approach the practice with consistency, patience, and self-compassion. Each repetition of these empowering statements is a step toward rewiring our thought patterns, gradually replacing resistance and self-doubt with resilience and self-belief. By making affirmations a daily ritual, we create a sacred space for personal transformation, inviting positive change to take root in our lives.

So let us embrace the transformative potential of affirmations, armed knowing that our thoughts have the power to shape our reality. Let us stand tall in the face of resistance and self-doubt, affirming our strength, worthiness, and limitless potential. And let us trust in the journey of reframing our minds, knowing that with each affirmation, we are laying the foundation for a life of boundless growth, success, and self-actualization overcome resistance and self-doubt.

AFFIRMING SUCCESS: REAL-LIFE TESTIMONIALS OF TRANSFORMATION THROUGH THE POWER OF POSITIVE SELF-TALK

IN THE REALM of personal growth and self-transformation, affirmations have emerged as a powerful tool for reshaping one's mindset, overcoming limitations, and manifesting dreams into reality. The success stories of countless individuals who have harnessed the power of affirmations serve as a testament to the profound impact that positive self-talk can have on one's life. These real-life testimonials illuminate the transformative potential of affirmations, inspiring others to embrace this practice as a catalyst for personal growth and change.

One such story is that of Marisa Peer, a global speaker and best-selling author who credits affirmations with playing a pivotal role in her journey of overcoming self-doubt and building unshakable self-confidence. By dedicating herself to the daily practice of repeating empowering statements, Peer was able to rewire her subconscious mind, replacing limiting beliefs with a narrative of self-assurance and worthiness. Her success in the field of therapy and personal development stands as a shining example of the transformative power of affirmations when applied with consistency and conviction.

Another luminary in the realm of personal growth, Louise Hay, has touched the lives of millions through her teachings on the healing potential of affirmations. In her renowned book, "You Can Heal Your Life," Hay shares her own journey of self-discovery and transformation, illustrating how the practice of positive affirmations can serve as a catalyst for profound inner healing. Her message, rooted in the belief that our thoughts shape our reality, has resonated with countless individuals seeking to create positive change in their lives. Hay's own success story serves as a powerful reminder that by affirming our inherent worth and potential, we open ourselves up to a world of limitless possibilities.

In the realm of entertainment, actor and comedian Jim Carrey has openly shared how affirmations played an important role in his rise to success in Hollywood. Before achieving fame, Carrey engaged in the powerful practice of writing himself a check for $10 million, affirming his future success and visualizing his dreams coming to fruition. By repeating positive affirmations daily and maintaining an unwavering belief in his abilities, Carrey ultimately manifested his goal of becoming a highly sought-after and successful actor. His story serves as a testament to the power of aligning one's thoughts and beliefs with their deepest aspirations, and the transformative potential of affirming one's worth and potential.

Media mogul Oprah Winfrey, a beacon of inspiration for millions, has long advocated for the power of affirmations in cultivating a mindset of abundance, gratitude, and resilience. Throughout her remarkable career, Winfrey has relied on the practice of positive self-talk to navigate challenges, stay focused on her goals, and maintain a steadfast belief in her own potential. Her success story stands as a shining example of how affirmations can serve as a guiding light, illuminating the path toward personal growth and self-actualization. Winfrey's journey reminds us that by affirming our inherent strength and worthiness, we tap into a wellspring of inner resources that can propel us toward our highest aspirations.

Renowned motivational speaker and life coach Tony Robbins has long championed the practice of affirmations as a means of reprogramming the subconscious mind and aligning one's beliefs with their highest aspirations. Robbins encourages his clients to craft empowering affirmations that resonate with their unique goals and values, recognizing the transformative potential of positive self-talk in catalyzing personal growth and success. His own journey from humble beginnings to becoming a global force in the personal development industry serves as a powerful testament to the impact of affirmations on one's mindset and ability to create lasting change.

These real-life success stories and testimonials serve as powerful reminders of the transformative potential that lies within the practice of affirmations. By consistently engaging in positive self-talk, we have the power to reshape our beliefs, overcome limitations, and manifest our deepest desires into reality. These inspiring individuals, each with their own unique journey of transformation, invite us to embrace affirmations as a tool for personal growth, self-discovery, and the realization of our fullest potential.

As we navigate the path of personal development, let us draw strength and inspiration from these stories of transformation, knowing that the power to create profound change lies within us. By affirming our worth, our resilience, and our limitless potential, we open ourselves up to a world of possibilities, where our dreams can take flight and our highest aspirations can become our lived reality. So let us embrace the practice of affirmations with open hearts and minds, trusting in the transformative power of positive self-talk to guide us toward a life of purpose, fulfillment, and boundless growth.

Case Study:

Meet Jenifer, a talented artist who had always dreamed of turning her passion into a thriving career. Despite her undeniable skills and creativity, Jenifer found herself consistently held back by a deep-seated sense of self-doubt and a lack of self-love. She often questioned her abilities, comparing herself unfavorably to other artists and feeling unworthy of success.

One day, a friend recommended a workshop on the art of self-love and the power of affirmations. Intrigued by the concept, Jenifer decided to attend, hoping to gain new insights into nurturing a more positive relationship with herself.

At the workshop, Jenifer learned about the transformative impact of self-compassion and the importance of treating oneself with the same kindness and understanding that one would extend to a beloved friend. The facilitator emphasized that the foundation of all personal growth and fulfillment lies in cultivating a deep and loving relationship with oneself.

As Jenifer reflected on her own inner dialogue, she realized that she had been engaging in a pattern of negative self-talk, constantly criticizing and doubting herself. She recognized this harsh inner critic was holding her back from embracing her potential and pursuing her dreams with confidence.

The workshop introduced Jenifer to the power of affirmations as a tool for reprogramming her subconscious mind and cultivating a more self-loving and empowering inner narrative. She learned about the science behind affirmations, how they work to rewire neural pathways and gradually replace limiting beliefs with more positive and expansive ones.

Inspired by this knowledge, Jenifer began to craft her own affirmations, tailoring them to her specific needs and goals. She created statements that affirmed her creativity, her worthiness of success, and her ability to overcome challenges with resilience and grace. Jenifer committed to repeating these affirmations daily, both in the morning and before bed, as a way of consistently reinforcing a more positive self-image.

As Jenifer incorporated affirmations into her daily routine, she also learned about setting healthy boundaries and practicing self-care. She began to focus on activities that brought her joy and nourishment, such as spending time in nature, engaging in mindfulness practices, and surrounding herself with supportive and uplifting individuals.

Gradually, Jenifer noticed a shift in her mindset and overall well-being. The consistent practice of affirming her worth and potential began to chip away at the layers of self-doubt and self-criticism that had collected over the years. She started to approach her art with a greater sense of confidence and purpose, trusting in her unique vision and abilities.

As Jenifer's self-love blossomed, she found herself more open to opportunities and taking bold steps toward her goals. She began to share her work with a wider audience, participating in art shows and collaborating with other creatives. With each success and positive feedback, Jenifer's belief in herself grew stronger, reinforcing the transformative power of self-love and affirmations.

Jenifer's journey also had a ripple effect on those around her. As she embodied a more self-loving and compassionate presence, she inspired others to focus on their own self-care and to embrace their authentic selves. Jenifer became a beacon of light, showing true success and fulfillment begin with nurturing a loving relationship with oneself.

Looking back on her transformation, Jenifer realized that the art of self-love had been the missing piece in her personal and professional growth. By learning to treat herself with kindness, to affirm her worth and potential, and to set healthy boundaries, she had unlocked a wellspring of creativity, resilience, and joy.

Jenifer's story serves as a powerful reminder that the relationship we have with ourselves is the foundation on which all other parts of our lives are built. By focusing on self-love and engaging in practices like affirmations and self-care, we create a solid base from which to pursue our dreams and navigate life's challenges with grace and confidence.

Her journey also highlights the transformative potential of consistent and intentional inner work. By committing to daily practices that nurture a positive self-image, we gradually reshape our subconscious beliefs and align our thoughts with our highest aspirations. This internal shift then manifests in our external reality, attracting opportunities and experiences that reflect our growing self-love and self-belief.

Cultivating self-love is an ongoing process, one that requires patience, compassion, and a willingness to confront and release old patterns of self-doubt and criticism. But as Jenifer's experience shows, the rewards of this inner journey are immeasurable – a life filled with purpose, fulfillment, and the joyful expression of one's authentic self.

So let Jenifer's story be an invitation to focus on the art of self-love in our own lives. Let us embrace the power of affirmations, self-care, and healthy boundaries as tools for nurturing a deep and loving relationship with ourselves. And let us trust that as we fill our own cups with compassion and kindness, we become more able to show up fully and authentically in all areas of our lives.

Remember, the journey of self-love is not a destination but a daily practice, a sacred commitment to honoring and cherishing the magnificent beings that we are. By choosing to love ourselves fiercely and unapologetically, we open the door to a life of boundless potential, creativity, and joy.

So let us approach this path with open hearts and curious minds, ready to uncover the radiant truth of our inherent worthiness. Let us affirm our brilliance, our resilience, and our capacity for growth and transformation. And let us celebrate each step forward, knowing that every act of self-love is a powerful declaration of our commitment to living a life of authenticity, purpose, and unbridled self-expression.

In a world that often encourages self-doubt and comparison, the art of self-love becomes a revolutionary act – a bold reclamation of our right to thrive and to shine. By nurturing ourselves with the same devotion and care we so freely give to others, we become a force for positive change, inspiring those around us to embrace their own self-love journey.

So let us rise to the occasion, armed with the transformative tools of affirmations, self-compassion, and unwavering self-belief. Let us become the authors of our own stories, crafting narratives of resilience, joy, and boundless potential. And let us remember that in the grand tapestry of life, the thread of self-love weaves together the most beautiful and empowering patterns of all.

The path to radical self-love is not always easy, but it is always worth it. It requires us to confront our deepest fears, to release the stories that no longer serve us, and to embrace the fullness of our being – flaws, quirks, and all. But as we navigate this journey with courage and compassion, we discover a strength and beauty within ourselves that we never knew existed.

So let us approach this sacred work with reverence and devotion, knowing that each step we take toward self-love is a step toward our highest potential and most authentic expression. Let us surround ourselves with reminders of our worth, with affirmations that anchor us in truth and love. And let us trust in the transformative power of our own hearts, knowing that as we learn to love ourselves fully and unconditionally, we become a beacon of hope and healing for all those we touch.

The art of self-love is not a solitary pursuit, but a ripple effect of grace and goodness that extends far beyond ourselves. By embodying the principles of self-compassion, self-acceptance, and self-celebration, we become a living testament to the truth that love – in all its forms – is the most powerful force for change and growth.

So let us embrace this journey with open arms and grateful hearts, knowing that the love we cultivate within ourselves is the same love that will transform the world. Let us affirm our right to be here, to take up space, and to shine our light with abandon. And let us remember that in the grand orchestra of life, the melody of our self-love sets the tempo for all the beauty and magic yet to come.

~

PART FIFTEEN WRAP-UP:

• Self-love serves as the foundation for emotional well-being, resilience, and the capacity to love and be loved.

• Self-compassion involves treating oneself with kindness, understanding, and forgiveness, embracing imperfections as part of the human experience.

• Cultivating self-compassion begins with self-reflection, observing one's inner landscape without judgment.

• Setting boundaries is important for emotional and mental well-being, focusing on one's needs and values.

• Engaging in activities that bring joy and fulfillment nourishes the soul and reinforces the message that happiness and self-care matter.

• Self-love is a lifelong journey that requires commitment to showing up for oneself with compassion and understanding.

• Affirmations have the power to rewire neural pathways and replace negative self-talk with empowering beliefs when used consistently and with conviction.

• Different types of affirmations, such as self-love, confidence, abundance, health, and goal-setting affirmations, can be tailored to specific areas of personal development.

• Incorporating affirmations into daily routines, such as morning rituals, visual reminders, journaling, meditation, and bedtime practices, reinforces positive self-talk.

• Affirmations can help reframe the mind, conquer resistance and self-doubt, and cultivate resilience, self-confidence, and a growth mindset.

• Real-life success stories and testimonials from various individuals show the transformative potential of affirmations in personal growth and self-actualization.

Action Items:

• Practice self-reflection through journaling or meditation to gain insights into your inner landscape and thought patterns.

• Identify areas of your life where you need to set healthy boundaries and communicate them assertively to others.

• Engage in activities that bring you joy and fulfillment, making time for self-care and pursuits that nourish your soul.

• Develop a self-compassion practice, such as speaking to yourself with kindness and understanding, especially in moments of difficulty or setback.

• Create a list of affirmations that resonate with your specific needs and goals, focusing on areas like self-love, confidence, abundance, health, and goal setting.

• Incorporate affirmations into your daily routines, such as reciting them during your morning ritual, placing visual reminders in your environment, or journaling them regularly.

• Practice self-forgiveness and letting go of self-judgment, embracing your imperfections as opportunities for growth and learning.

• Identify and challenge limiting beliefs and negative self-talk, reframing them with empowering affirmations and a growth mindset.

• Seek success stories and testimonials of individuals who have transformed their lives through the power of affirmations, drawing inspiration and motivation from their experiences.

• Cultivate a support system of individuals who uplift and encourage your journey of self-love and personal growth.

• Regularly assess your progress and celebrate your successes, acknowledging the positive changes you've made in your relationship with yourself.

• Practice consistency and patience in your affirmation practice, trusting in the gradual process of rewiring your thought patterns and cultivating a more loving and empowering inner dialogue.

• Embrace vulnerability and authenticity in your self-love journey, acknowledging that growth and transformation require courage and a willingness to confront discomfort.

• Extend compassion and understanding to others, recognizing that everyone is on their own unique path of self-discovery and personal development.

• Continuously educate yourself on the science and application of affirmations, seeking resources and guidance to deepen your understanding and enhance your practice.

∽

CONCLUSION: SOARING TO NEW HEIGHTS

As we come to the end of this transformative journey, I want to congratulate you on your commitment to personal growth and self-empowerment. By diving deep into the art of goal setting, visualization, and cultivating a positive mindset, you've equipped yourself with the tools and strategies needed to overcome limiting beliefs, break through barriers, and achieve the extraordinary.

Throughout these pages, you've discovered the immense power of your attitude in shaping your reality and determining the altitude of your success. You've learned to set clear, compelling goals that align with your values and passions, and to break these goals down into manageable steps and actionable plans. You've harnessed the transformative power of visualization and positive affirmations to reprogram your subconscious mind for success and build unshakable self-confidence.

But perhaps most importantly, you've embarked on a journey of self-discovery and personal transformation. By learning to embrace your unique strengths, talents, and experiences, you've cultivated a deep sense of self-awareness, self-acceptance, and self-love. You've discovered how to reframe setbacks and failures as opportunities for growth and learning, and how to use your experiences to fuel your determination and resilience.

As you move forward from here, remember that the journey of personal growth and self-empowerment is a lifelong pursuit. The tools and strategies you've learned in this book are not meant to be one-time fixes, but rather ongoing practices you can integrate into your daily life. By consistently setting goals, visualizing success, and cultivating a positive mindset, you'll continue to unlock new levels of potential and achieve ever greater heights of success and fulfillment.

But the impact of your transformation extends far beyond your own life. By embracing a mindset of positivity, possibility, and unwavering self-belief, you become a beacon of hope and inspiration for those around you. Your story and your success have the power to touch the lives of countless others, inspiring them to embrace their own limitless potential and pursue their dreams with passion and purpose.

As you continue on your journey, remember to surround yourself with positive influences and to seek mentors, coaches, and like-minded individuals who can support and guide you along the way. Embrace the power of community and connection, and never hesitate to reach out for help and support when you need it.

Above all, remember that your attitude is the key to your altitude. By maintaining a mindset of positivity, resilience, and unwavering self-belief, you have the power to overcome any obstacle, achieve any goal, and soar to new heights of success and fulfillment. So, keep pushing yourself beyond your comfort zone, keep embracing the discomfort and uncertainty that comes with growth and progress, and keep believing in your own limitless potential.

The sky is not the limit, it's the beginning. With the right attitude and the tools and strategies you've learned in this book, there's no limit to what you can achieve. So go out there and make your mark on the world, knowing you have the power to create a life of passion, purpose, and boundless potential.

Thank you for joining me on this transformative journey. I am honored to have been a part of your growth and development, and I can't wait to see the incredible impact you'll make in the world.

With gratitude, love, and unwavering belief in you,

Rae A. Stonehouse

~

ABOUT THE AUTHOR

Rae A. Stonehouse is an author, speaker, and self-publishing consultant dedicated to helping others embrace constant improvement and overcome challenges. With over 40 years of experience as a Registered Nurse in psychiatry and mental health, Rae brings a wealth of knowledge and passion for self-development to his writing and presentations.

As a 30+ year member of Toastmasters International, Rae has systematically built his communication abilities and self-confidence to share his insights as an author and speaker. His self-help books and personal development presentations aim to have conversational one-on-one connections with readers and audiences.

Rae is known for his wry sense of humor and sage advice delivered in a relatable coaching style. After four decades as a nurse, Rae has *rewired* rather than retired, actively writing and pursuing public speaking. He strives to share lessons learned to help others achieve personal and professional growth.

To learn more about Rae and his approach to constant improvement, visit his website at https://raestonehouse.com or to learn more about his publications visit https://liveforexcellence.store

ALSO BY RAE A. STONEHOUSE

VISIT HTTPS://LIVEFOREXCELLENCE.STORE/ for a selection of personal/professional self-development books by Rae A. Stonehouse.

If you have found this book to be helpful, please leave us a warm review wherever you purchased it.